# POWER RESTRUCTURING

# IN CHINA AND RUSSIA

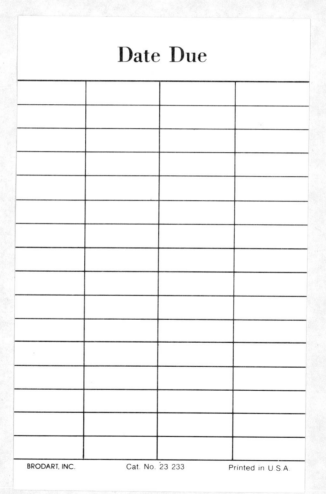

## Date Due

| | | | |
|---|---|---|---|
| | | | |
| | | | |
| | | | |
| | | | |
| | | | |
| | | | |
| | | | |
| | | | |
| | | | |
| | | | |
| | | | |
| | | | |
| | | | |
| | | | |
| | | | |
| | | | |

BRODART, INC.          Cat. No. 23 233          Printed in U.S.A.

## Social Change in Global Perspective

Mark Selden, *Series Editor*

Exploring the relationship between social change and social structures, this series considers the theory, praxis, promise, and pitfalls of movements in global and comparative perspective. The historical and contemporary social movements considered here challenge patterns of hierarchy and inequality of race, gender, nationality, ethnicity, class, and culture. The series will emphasize textbooks and broadly interpretive synthetic works.

*Power Restructuring in China and Russia,* Mark Lupher

*The Transformation of Communist Systems: Economic Reform Since the 1950s,*
Bernard Chavance

*The Challenge of Local Feminisms: Women's Movements in Global Perspective,*
edited by Amrita Basu, with the assistance of C. Elizabeth McGrory

FORTHCOMING

*African Women: A Modern History,* Catherine Coquery-Vidrovitch

*Japanese Labor and Labor Movements,* Kumazawa Makoto

# Power Restructuring in China and Russia

*Mark Lupher*

WestviewPress

*A Division of* HarperCollins*Publishers*

*Social Change in Global Perspective*

Copyright © 1996 by Westview Press, Inc., A Division of HarperCollins Publishers, Inc.

Published in 1996 in the United States of America by Westview Press, Inc., 5500 Central Avenue,
Boulder, Colorado 80301-2877, and in the United Kingdom by Westview Press, 12 Hid's Copse Road,
Cumnor Hill, Oxford OX2 9JJ

A CIP catalog record for this book is available from the Library of Congress.

ISBN 0-8133-2546-3; 0-8133-2545-5 (pb)

The paper used in this publication meets the requirements of the American National Standard for
Permanence of Paper for Printed Library Materials Z39.48-1984.

10    9    8    7    6    5    4    3    2    1

To those who study it as an isolated phenomenon the French Revolution can but seem a dark and sinister enigma; only when we view it in light of the events preceding it can we grasp its true significance. And, similarly, without a clear idea of the old regime, its laws, its vices, its prejudices, its shortcomings, and its greatness, it is impossible to comprehend the history of the sixty years following its fall.

❧

Alexis de Tocqueville
*The Old Regime and the French Revolution*

# Contents

# Acknowledgments

The extended gestation of this book occurred in stages. *Power Restructuring in China and Russia* in a very real sense represents the culmination of events set in motion some three decades ago when I arrived in Peking, where I would live for four years. Unaware of the significance of my experience at the time, I learned Chinese, attended Peking University Middle School, and witnessed the first two years of the Cultural Revolution. These were formative events without which this book would never have been written.

Motivated by my experience, when I returned to the United States I was drawn to the scholarly study of China and an academic career. As a graduate student at Berkeley, I worked on Soviet history and politics, developed a comparative and historical view of issues and processes I had previously known only in the contemporary Chinese context, and launched the research that forms the groundwork of this book. It is a pleasure to acknowledge the contributions of my teachers: Harold L. Wilensky, whose comparative expertise and systematic perspective greatly improved my work; Victoria E. Bonnell, who first introduced me to comparative-historical analysis and the fascinating complexities of Soviet history, society, and politics; and Frederic Wakeman Jr., whose work on conflict and control in late imperial China shaped my view of power dynamics in Chinese and Russian history. I also wish to acknowledge the special influence of Franz Schurmann, whose masterful macrosociology of Communist China was and remains an inspiration.

The actual writing of *Power Restructuring* in the late 1980s and early 1990s was exciting and challenging, given the momentous events occurring in China and the Soviet Union during this time. All the key events of these years—the origins, aftermath, and significance of the June 4 crackdown in China; perestroika and systemic collapse in the Soviet Union; and the transition from socialism unfolding in China and Russia in the 1990s—had to be addressed in full. Three readers were especially helpful in preparing the manuscript for publication. John Israel, my senior colleague at the University of Virginia, gave my China chapters a tough and insightful read and made criticisms that resulted in substantial improvements. I am grateful to Marc Raeff, whose critique of Chapters 3 and 4 forced me to rethink important issues and to recast the discussion. Even though Professor Raeff will no doubt disapprove of my macrosociological analyses and comparisons, his sharp criticisms helped improve my work. But it is Mark Selden to whom I owe a special debt of gratitude and appreciation. It was a privilege and a pleasure to work with Professor Selden; throughout the final writing and revision of the present volume, I learned constantly from his knowledge of all things Chinese and was inspired by his penetrating analysis and criticism of my work. Needless to say, the remaining defects of *Power Restructuring in China and Russia* are my responsibility alone.

For the successful completion of this project, I am grateful for the various forms of research support provided by the University of Virginia during the writing of the book. But my deepest debt is to my family for its love and encouragement.

*Mark Lupher*

# Abbreviations

CCP     Chinese Communist Party
CCRG   Central Cultural Revolution Group
CPSU   Communist Party of the Soviet Union

FFYP   First Five-Year Plan

GDP    gross domestic product

KGB    State Security Committee
KMT    Kuomintang

MTS    Machine Tractor Station

NEP    New Economic Policy
NKVD   People's Commissariat for Internal Affairs

PAP    People's Armed Police

# 1

# Power in Macrosociological Perspective

As waves of economic reform, political upheaval, and revolutionary change swept China and the Soviet Union in the final decades of the twentieth century, one of the great dramas of our time unfolded. Yet the origins of this drama are murky and its outcome unclear. Were we witnessing the death throes of an archaic, inefficient, and discredited authoritarian order and its gradual or inexorable displacement by more pluralistic political and economic arrangements? Or did these tumultuous events mark the latest playing out of recurrent patterns and processes in Chinese and Russian history, in which cycles of power concentration and power deconcentration oscillate and central power ebbs and flows? Did the massive changes of the post-Mao period and the period of perestroika signify a definitive break with the past, or did these events underscore essential continuities in the political history of China and Russia? How have political, economic, and social formations now emerging in China and the former Soviet Union been shaped by the legacies of the past? To what extent are these formations the result of new political, economic, and social forces? How are we to understand the interplay of past and present in China and Russia historically and today?

I address these questions with a discussion of power restructuring in China and Russia. Rather than speak of "reform" in China and Russia, which too often is understood as political and economic liberalization along Western lines, my discussion is focused on power restructuring—struggles for power and resources among central rulers, political and economic elites, and nonprivileged groups. In this book, power restructuring patterns and processes in China and Russia in imperial times, under communism, and today are identified, assessed, and compared. The discussion encompasses late imperial, Republican, and revolutionary China; Muscovite, imperial, and revolutionary Russia; the Soviet 1920s and the rise and consolidation of Stalinism; power restructuring under Nikita Khrushchev and its defeat; Chinese communism in the 1950s and the origins of the Cultural Revolution; the Cultural Revolution and the origins of post-Mao reform; post-Mao reform and power dynamics in contemporary China; and power restructuring in the period of perestroika. I take a comparative and historical view of power relations and political process in China and Russia and seek to uncover and discuss systematically the political conflicts and power contests that drive the restructuring of power historically and presently. This is an enterprise dedicated to what Elizabeth J. Perry has called "the pressing goal of connecting both past and present to their future," "the important task of integrating contemporary and historical lines of inquiry," and the establishing of "genuine historical continuity."[1] While pursuing these goals, my central purpose is to show how power restructuring has shaped and reshaped China and Russia in modern times. The bulk of the discussion is therefore centered on the two great communist systems of the twentieth century, the Soviet Union and Communist China. The argument advanced in these pages is focused on three recurrent and interrelated power restructuring patterns.

The first pattern is continuity. My discussion identifies and compares vertical continuities, "continuities through time within a single space," and horizontal continuities, "parallels which span large areas to form continuities," in China and Russia.[2] I assert that the Chinese and Russian imperial systems; the Russian and Chinese Revolutions; the Soviet and Chinese Communist systems; the power restructuring initiatives of Khrushchev, Mao Zedong, and Mikhail Gorbachev; and the transition from socialism now unfolding in China and the former Soviet Union are linked by precisely such continuities.[3] On the one hand, continuity in power relations and political process is manifested in the recurrent concentration of power in the imperial and communist state apparatus and the attendant effort to use this power to control and reshape the human and material world. On the other hand, these processes of concentration and control are problematic and contested. Throughout the discussion, I focus attention on the concentration and deconcentration of political power, the ebb and flow of central power, and the power contests that both trigger and stem from these events.

The second pattern is interaction. I view power restructuring as the recurrent manifestation of struggles among central rulers, various elite configurations, and nonprivileged groups. In contrast to the Marxian image of unremitting material struggles between owners and nonowners regularly resulting in revolutionary reconstitutions of society, my discussion of the elemental struggle over power and resources is inspired by Max Weber. Weber located contests to control, appropriate, and redistribute power and resources at the center of his political macrosociology. He understood these processes as ongoing "three-way" struggles among ruler, staff, and subjects occurring in myriad sociopolitical settings—revolutionary and traditional, historical and contemporary.[4] More recently, Charles Tilly encompassed European state formation in all its variation within a common framework of "coercion and capital," wherein monarchs playing the same "game of war and competition for territory" had to interact with their subjects and "bargain for its wherewithal."[5]

In the present discussion, three-way power contests are viewed as the key internal dynamic of change in China and Russia in imperial times, under communism, and today. Although the interaction between state power and social forces is a universal phenomenon, this book examines the manifestations and consequences of such interactions during key episodes in Chinese and Russian political history. I view the ebb and flow of central power, its concentration and deconcentration, and the control, appropriation, and redistribution of resources in light of three-way political interactions and power contests. Accordingly, my analysis is focused simultaneously on the political processes, institutional arrangements, and power-restructuring methods that build central power and the political conflicts and power-restructuring initiatives that undercut central power. The rise and consolidation of autocratic power in late imperial China and czarist Russia are interpreted in this light, as are the decline and destruction of the imperial order and the rise of revolution and communism in the late nineteenth and twentieth centuries. But the main thrust of my discussion is centered on the political interactions and power contests that occurred in the Soviet Union in the 1920s and 1930s, over the course of the Khrushchev period and the Cultural Revolution decade, and in the period of post-Mao reform and perestroika.

The third pattern is synthesis. I pair my exploration of processes of historical continuity with a corresponding assessment of the sources of historical change and argue that internal political interaction and interactions with the outside world have repeatedly resulted in political, institutional, and cultural syntheses. Three important instances of synthesis are identified and compared in these pages. First, I view the power structures of the consolidated imperial autocracies of late imperial China and Muscovite and imperial Russia as syntheses wherein elements of Inner Asian nomadic political practice became fused with Chinese and Russian imperial culture. Second, I see the mature Soviet and Chinese Communist systems as syntheses of traditional imperial autocracy, Marxist-Leninist ideology and organization, and social revolution. Third, I depict the political, economic, and cultural formations that emerged in China and the Soviet Union in the 1980s and 1990s as the most recent manifestations of synthesis. The primary consequence of Maoist power restructuring and post-Mao reform in China and the reforms and upheavals of the period of perestroika in the Soviet Union was the setting in motion of a historic transition from socialism. In China and the former Soviet Union today, the transition from socialism is a synthesis of old patterns and new realities combining political and economic decentralization, privatization and marketization, cultural liberalization and an opening up to the outside world, and authoritarianism and nationalism.

My analysis of power restructuring in China and Russia differs from recent comparative-historical analyses of China and Russia in four important respects. First, whereas Theda Skocpol and Jack A. Goldstone insisted that structural, ecological, and demographic forces drove processes of revolution, rebellion, and political breakdown in early modern China and Russia, my discussion focuses attention on the actions of individual and collective political actors and their struggles to control, appropriate, and redistribute power and resources.[6] Key events discussed in this book, such as the Stalin revolution, the Cultural Revolution, and power restructuring under Gorbachev, were set in motion by political decisions at the top and driven by the actions of political actors.[7] Second, whereas Skocpol and Goldstone were primarily interested in processes of revolution, rebellion, and state breakdown, I assert that processes of power building and processes of power breakdown are closely interrelated. My discussion of late imperial China, for example, simultaneously focuses attention on the logic and mechanisms of the early Ming and Qing autocracies and processes of breakdown, decentralization, and deconcentration in late Ming and late Qing China. Third, whereas Skocpol and Goldstone made no sustained attempt to apply their analyses to events in the contemporary world, my discussion explicitly connects power restructuring in China and Russia in imperial times, under communism, and today.[8] Fourth, whereas Skocpol and Goldstone compared societies and events separated by great gaps in time, history, and culture, this book compares in chronological sequence two civilizations that have experienced similar forms of imperial rule, old regime crisis, communist revolution, communist state building, and power-decentralizing and power-deconcentrating processes.

## Images of Power and Politics in China and Russia

The comparative and historical view of power restructuring in China and Russia put forward in these pages differs markedly from prevailing images of power and politics in China and Russia. Important recent analyses have depicted the rise of communism in the twentieth century as a phenomenon disconnected from history. In the triumphant *The Grand Failure: The Birth and Death of Communism in the Twentieth Century,* Zbigniew Brzezinski spoke of the "terminal crisis" of communism and proclaimed that "the idea of communism is essentially dead."[9] Understood in this light, the historical significance of communism was psychological in essence. The Marxist-Leninist view of a future communist utopia therefore appealed to the semiliterate masses and the more intellectually inclined alike; as such, communism amounted to no more than "a passion masquerading as scientific reason."[10] Similarly, Martin Malia claimed that "Sovietism" was "unique," "something radically different from anything that preceded it, whether in Russia or in the West," and he spoke of "seventy years of an abnormal society."[11] In a sweeping account of the evolution of communism, Adam Westoby stated, "I have circumscribed 'communism,' in all its variety, by its common ancestry in Lenin's Bolshevik party and the early Comintern," an analysis that encompassed all communist parties, including the Soviet, Chinese, Eastern European, Indian, Cuban, Indochinese, and even "Eurocommunist" variants.[12]

These ideas are squarely contradicted in my discussion. As Richard Pipes noted, "Even someone entirely ignorant of Russia should find it inconceivable that on a single day, October 25, 1917, in consequence of an armed putsch, the course of a thousand-year-old history of a vast and populous country could undergo complete transformation. The same people, inhabiting the same territory, speaking the same language, heirs to a common past, could hardly have been fashioned into different creatures by a sudden change of government."[13] The Soviet and the Chinese Communist systems replicated in more intense, far-reaching, and institutionalized fashion the power-building, resource mobilization, and social control functions of their imperial predecessors. Even as the Soviet and Chinese Communist systems were shaken by power-restructuring processes and a transition from socialism set in motion, extensive continuities with the socialist past remained in place.[14] Thus, I cannot speak of an initial "birth" or a final "death" of communism in the twentieth century. Similarly, I do not view Soviet and Chinese socialism as generic phenomena revolving around Leninist doctrine. Instead, I understand the Russian and Chinese Revolutions and the formation of the Soviet and Chinese Communist systems in light of recurrent power-restructuring patterns and processes in Chinese and Russian history. There can consequently be no question of placing the indigenous Soviet and Chinese Communist systems in the same conceptual category as the imposed communist systems of Eastern Europe or the communist parties of Western Europe.

Some Russian and Chinese commentators also viewed communism as historically aberrant or backward and sought to disconnect the rise and consolidation of Soviet and Chinese communism from history. Long before the advent of Gorbachev, Alexander Solzhenitsyn maintained that Soviet communism was a culturally alien system forcibly imposed on the Russian people, a violation of the fundamental spiritual essence of Russia.[15] In the period of perestroika, this view was widely aired in the Soviet Union. According to Russophile intellectual Vladimir Krupin, Russia was coerced by the communist "red wheel" into a "government system of militant godlessness," where "the culture that is doing the forcing is nothing, it possesses no national identity, it is mechanistic, dead, and faceless."[16] In the post-Mao period, some Chinese intellectuals advanced a different, yet equally bleak view of the connection between communism and history. Rather than disconnect communism from history, the narrators of the documentary *Heshang* (River Elegy) accented the interrelation of the backwardness and "rural idiocy" of China's earthbound peasantry, the communist revolution and the communist system, and China's myriad contemporary ills.[17]

In the present discussion, Chinese history and Russian history are neither glorified nor bemoaned; Soviet communism and Chinese communism are not viewed as historically aberrant or seen as solely perpetuating the backwardness of the past. Instead, I assert that both histories in imperial times, under communism, and today are linked by power-restructuring patterns and processes. On the one hand, these recurrent patterns and processes represent historical continuity; on the other hand, the restructuring of power in China and Russia drives processes of reform, revitalization, and revolutionary change.

## Totalitarian Theory and Interest Group Theory

The classic image of power in the Soviet Union and Communist China was that of totalitarianism and the absolute subordination of social forces and politics to the all-powerful leader and all-encompassing state. Yet the totalitarian notion that political life had been extinguished in the Soviet Union was conclusively invalidated by the tumultuous events of the Khrushchev era. Moreover, there is good reason to question the general conceptual utility of totalitarianism; certainly any theory that speaks of "the unquestioned leadership of the dictator" and the "spineless attitude of subjection of party members towards the man at the top" sheds little light on the recurrent political interactions and power contests that are the central concern of this book.[18] In my discussion of the Stalin revolution and the Stalin system, totalitarian notions of all-encompassing social control and the extinction of political life cannot explain Soviet power dynamics even at the height of the Great Purges of 1937–1938.

But the totalitarian image of power dynamics in communist systems cannot be discarded entirely. The Bolsheviks and the Chinese Communists who attacked and attempted to destroy the Russian and the Chinese ancien régime were Leninists. Just as the Russian and Chinese imperial systems monopolized political power and maximized state control of society, Leninism was a power-concentrating ideology that systematically sought to eliminate competing centers of power and maximize the political domination of the vanguard party. Because totalitarian theory stressed political domination and social control and was focused on "the regime's efforts to remold and transform the human beings under its control in the image of its ideology," the model did capture crucial dimensions of power dynamics under communism.[19] My discussion shows that the all-encompassing control that totalitarian theory took to be the reality in the Soviet Union and China was often limited and sometimes wholly illusory. Yet as the late Kendall E. Bailes observed, the claim of the vanguard party and its leaders to intervene in and attempt the structural and ideological transformation of society was crucial; even if this claim was only partially or even entirely unrealizable in practice, the consequences were nonetheless momentous.[20]

By delineating the ubiquity of group political action in communist systems, interest group theorists in the late 1960s and 1970s demolished the totalitarian image of uncontested and depoliticized state domination of political life and social forces. In the Soviet case, interest group theorists demonstrated the means by which "loose associations" of "like-minded or like-interested" party apparatchiks, industrial managers, military officers, security officials, and elite intellectuals successfully exerted influence on decisionmaking processes at "key points of authority."[21] Similarly, a "pluralistic decision-making process" was described in Communist China, wherein Maoist policies during the height of the Cultural Revolution were resisted, modified, and circumvented by a "multiplicity of political participants," ranging from other top leaders, to central ministerial bureaucrats, to party officials at the regional, provincial, and district levels.[22]

Although interest group theory corrected the totalitarian view of communism, its conceptual utility was limited by two major defects. First, because interest group theory was "society centered," it gave inadequate conceptual weight to such crucial features of Soviet and Chinese communism as concentrated political power, vanguard party institutional hegemony, personal rulership, and the all-important claim of party and state to intervene in and attempt the transformation of society. Second, interest group theory was not grounded in history and culture. As Alexander Yanov put it, the attempt of Western social scientists "to apply to the analysis of a medieval system the methodologies currently in use in political science and derived from the experiences of modern Western polities (factional conflict theory or theories of bureaucratization, oligarchy, coalition-building, and political participation) succeeded only in giving the Russian empire an unrealistic modern, and in some cases, even Western cast."[23] Yet an attempt to use Western conceptual and methodological tools to analyze political process in the Soviet Union was key in the work of U.S. sovietologist Jerry F. Hough. In 1977, Hough stressed the "similarities between the Soviet political system and the pluralist model of American political science" and argued, "We see a very wide range of inputs in the Soviet Union and the United States; we see people in both countries striving to push through their pet policy alternatives; we see policy decisions and outcomes that inevitably correspond to some societal input."[24] Positing a model of Soviet "institutional pluralism," Hough suggested that "thus far the regime has been moving towards a diffusion of real political power."[25]

Always controversial, the Soviet "institutional pluralism" thesis became obviously untenable with the advent of Gorbachev in March 1985. As the general secretary himself asserted, the "period of stagnation" marked the "excessive governmentalization of public life" in the Soviet Union, when the "functions of economic management became increasingly concentrated in the hands of the Party-political leadership and the role of the executive apparatus at the same time increased out of all proportion."[26] Moreover, when political controls were lifted in the period of perestroika and Soviet society erupted in unprecedented tumult, it was plainly evident that no significant diffusion of political power had occurred in the Brezhnev era. Instead, the chaotic outburst of political activity and the vehement venting of social and economic grievances in the late 1980s underscored both the reality of political repression under Leonid Brezhnev and the novelty of political pluralism in Soviet society.

Even though totalitarian imagery overstated the extent of state control in communist society and interest group imagery erred in the opposite direction, both approaches captured important dimensions of power relations and political process in the Soviet Union and China. A satisfactory conceptualization of power dynamics under communism must incorporate both the reality of concentrated state power and the ubiquity of bargaining and conflict. But it is not enough to simply identify these competing dimensions; the interaction between concentrated state power and political bargaining and conflict must be also highlighted. Moreover, an adequate conceptualization of power dynamics in the Soviet Union and China must be grounded in history and culture. Recent intellectual developments in sociology and political science now facilitate this task. On the one hand, the related concepts of neotraditionalism, clientelism, and patrimonialism have been articulated and refined by Western scholars studying the Soviet Union and China in particular.[27] On the other hand, comparative-historical theorists have developed large-scale macroanalytic constructs focusing attention on the interaction between state power and social forces.[28] Appropriately synthesized, the insights of the area specialists and the comparative-historical macroanalysts are essential ingredients in a conceptualization of power relations and political process in China and Russia.

## Area Specialist and Macroanalytic Perspectives

The area specialist approach is exemplified in the work of Andrew G. Walder, Barrett L. McCormick, and Jean C. Oi. Specialists in the politics and society of contemporary China, all three focused their analyses on the interaction between state and society, the interplay between the central government and its "agents" at the local level, and the relationship between official "patrons" and their "clients."[29]

Even though Walder's discussion was centered on power relations in the Chinese Communist factory, he claimed "explicitly comparative" aims and argued that the Chinese and Russian Revolutions gave rise to "a distinctive kind of party-state" and "a novel set of political relationships."[30] These "modern," yet "neo-traditional" patterns of authority were manifested in a system of industrial organization that maximized worker dependence on the enterprise, fostered strong vertical ties between party and management and a minority of politically loyal workers, and facilitated a rich subculture of patron-client interactions.[31] Although patron-client interactions were ubiquitous, however, communist officials exercised a historically unprecedented degree of control over the workforce by means of their monopolistic control over resources.

In contrast to Walder's imagery of comprehensive state control, McCormick presented a more ambiguous view and argued that in China, and in communist systems generally, a synthesis exists of Leninist and patrimonial rulership. Hence, whereas "Leninist states are relatively autonomous of society" and thereby dominate the polity, economy, and society, "the strength of formal organization in Leninist states makes extensive patrimonialism inevitable."[32] Because state officials so thoroughly control resources and avenues of mobility, corruption, the building of patron-client networks, and the pursuit of special interests are key systemic features. Unlike Walder, McCormick viewed particularistic arrangements as essentially dysfunctional, spoke of a state that is "poorly rooted in society," and asserted, "A nation wrapped in this form of organization is condemned to inefficiency, poverty, and weakness."[33]

While echoing Walder on the ubiquity of patron-client networks, Oi presented a more complex picture of patron-client relations in the Chinese countryside and emphasized constant mutual adjustment rather than one-sided official domination. From my perspective, Oi's discussion of the three-way interaction among the central authorities, local officials, and villagers in the course of "dividing the harvest" and "struggl[ing] to control the surplus" is especially useful.[34] By charting the ebb and flow of state grain procurement policy over several decades, Oi was able to examine the tactics by which state authorities and Chinese peasants sought to maximize their respective interests. Unlike McCormick, Oi did not view official behavior as "purely exploitative and coercive" and showed how local cadre "patrons" helped their "clients" evade the full thrust of state grain procurement efforts in the period of collectivization; these symbiotic patron-client relationships continued to flourish in the decollectivized post-Mao rural environment.[35]

These findings are essential in the conceptualization of power relations and political process in China and Russia advanced in this book. Yet the area specialists presented a largely static view of power dynamics in Chinese Communist society. Because Walder stressed pervasive state control in the factory and McCormick equated Leninist-patrimonial state domination with systemic stagnation, neither was able to adequately explain the rapid and far-reaching transformations that occurred in post-Mao China. Even Oi, who located the three-way contest for resources at the center of her analysis, provided no explanation for the processes of decollectivization and marketization that swept the Chinese countryside in the late 1970s and the 1980s.[36] Moreover, the work of the area specialists lacked a sustained comparative and historical thrust. Despite Walder's discussion of generic communist patterns of authority, McCormick's insistence on the prevalence of patrimonial rulership in communist systems, and Oi's expectation that clientelism plays a similarly important role in other communist nations, none of these analysts systematically related his or her findings to the experience of other communist countries.

The work of comparative-historical macroanalysts Theda Skocpol, Roberto Mangabiera Unger, and Michael Mann featured strengths and weaknesses of an entirely different order. All three took the long historical view and, in the words of Karl A. Wittfogel, used "big structured concepts" to identify and compare "big patterns of societal structure and change."[37]

In a discussion of the dynamics of the French, Russian, and Chinese "social revolutions," Skocpol discerned a common pattern: old regime crisis and breakdown stemming from a combination of external challenges from more technologically and militarily advanced competitors and internal challenges in the form of peasant insurrections. But the crux of the matter was the always competitive and increasingly contradictory relationship between central rulers and nominally subordinate elites. In old regime France, Russia, and China, the imperial states and landed classes were both "partners in exploitation" and "competitors in controlling the manpower of the peasantry and in appropriating surpluses from the agrarian-commercial economies."[38] Yet because "landed upper classes were primarily interested in either preventing increased state appropriations or in using state offices to siphon off revenues in ways that would reinforce the domestic status quo," they had "the interest and the capacity to curb state initiatives."[39]

For Unger, it was the rapacious appropriation of power and resources by "magnates of the realm" that repeatedly resulted in "cycles of reversion" in many premodern agrarian-bureaucratic empires.[40] In a discussion of recurrent "cycles of commercial vitality and decommercialization, of governmental unity and fragmentation" in imperial China, Rome, and Byzantium, Unger identified processes whereby "the state disintegrated, withdrew, or fell entirely into the hands of military, ecclesiastical, and landholding grandees"; towns and commercial activity shrank; and the "peasantry were driven in ever larger numbers into servile, nonmonetary labor for large landholders."[41] Hence, "the effort to avoid the reversion cycles ranked as the most persistent concern of the most lucid rulers and reformers in all the societies that remained vulnerable to these recurrent crises."[42]

Similarly, Mann located the struggle to control power and resources at the center of his "history of power." Drawing directly from Weber, Mann spoke of the "continuous struggle" and "mutual interdependence" of "a socially useful, despotic, universal state" versus "a decentralized, particularistic aristocracy in actual possession of much of the power infrastructure of society."[43] In Mann's view, such interactions constituted an overall "dialectic of development," whereby universalistic "empires of domination" unintentionally generated "more diffuse power reactions within their own interstices."[44]

These analyses are equally essential in my conceptualization of power relations and political process in China and Russia. My discussion relies on big structured concepts to identify big patterns of societal structure and change and focuses special attention on power contests among central rulers, various elite configurations, and nonprivileged groups. But the work of macroanalysts was also lacking in crucial respects. Whereas the area specialists presented empirically detailed analyses of specific aspects of contemporary politics and society, the macroanalysts developed general arguments about broad patterns in history and never attempted to relate their findings to events in the world today. The power-restructuring argument advanced in this book is inspired and guided by a compelling and still vital synthesis of empirical detail and macroanalytic conceptualization, Max Weber's model of patrimonial domination.

## Patrimonial Society and Patrimonial Politics

Weber's political sociology is the formidable intellectual standard against which contemporary comparative-historical analyses must still be measured. In *Economy and Society,* Weber set forth in world-historical depth and breadth the interactive view of patrimonial power dynamics variously emphasized by the area specialists and the macroanalysts alike. In the classic Weberian formulation, the strengths of both approaches are combined—a view of patrimonial society and the sources of stability and continuity is paired with a view of patrimonial politics and the sources of instability and change. Stable patron-client relations, particularism, and ongoing processes of appropriation at the local level are linked in Weber's discussion with political conflict, attempts to combat processes of appropriation, and structural reconfiguration at the level of the state.

The predominant feature of patrimonial society is the weak or entirely absent separation of "private" from "public," of "personal" from "official." Rooted historically in the "master's authority over his household," patrimonial power relations hinge in the first instance on the personal discretion of the patriarchal ruler.[45] At all levels of patrimonial society, therefore, patron-client networks become the single most important determinant of individual fate—prince and aristocrat, official and commoner, landlord and peasant, central rulers and the masses, all are bound by relations of patronage and interdependence. In Weber's words, "Practically everything depends explicitly on personal considerations: upon the attitude toward the concrete applicant and his concrete request and upon purely personal connections, favors, promises, and privileges."[46] Personal rulership of this type is not a solely premodern phenomenon. As Guenther Roth noted, "Even the total victory of a totalitarian minority merely leads to a highly centralized variant of personal governance in which the ruler has maximum discretion."[47] Unlike feudal systems, where the rights and obligations of central rulers and local elites are more closely defined, patrimonial power relations are characterized by looseness, ambiguity, and constant flux. Given the extensive sway of personal rulership, the rule of law is either weakly developed or absent altogether.

Much the same logic prevails in the economic realm; since all property ultimately belongs to the ruler or state, there can be no strict separation of public from private. Hence, "the ruler's favor or disfavor, grants and confiscations, continuously create new wealth and destroy it again."[48] Yet patrimonial power relations are not inimical to extensive trade, economic development, and capitalism of a certain type. Indeed, as Weber stressed, "patrimonialism is compatible with household and market economy, petty-bourgeois and manorial agriculture, absence and presence of capitalist economy."[49] In the "politically oriented capitalism" of patrimonialism, however, "the source of the accumulation of wealth is not acquisition by exchange, but the exploitation of the tax capacities of the subjects and the latter's need to buy all official actions of the ruler and the officials, given the wide latitude for granting favors and for arbitrariness."[50]

We have already seen how patrimonial concepts have been deployed by area specialists and macroanalysts. Other contemporary commentators have seen the "ruler's unchecked and unlimited domination" as the defining attribute of patrimonial rule. Hence, Vatro Murvar depicted patrimonialism as a form of "societal monism, which refers to the unity/identity of the entire power structure of society."[51] Under such conditions, "the ruler successfully claims all spheres of power as his own absolute domain"; in systems of modern patrimonialism the "unlimited exercise" of the ruler's personal power is used to fashion "instruments of total domination."[52] Similarly, while identifying the many continuities linking Soviet communism with czarist patrimonialism, Pipes claimed that both systems "owned the people" and were able to demand "unlimited services from their subjects," thereby effecting the "virtual absence of private property."[53] In fact, patrimonial power relations in traditional and modern times are more complex, ambiguous, and dynamic than these one-sided conceptualizations suggest.

It is precisely because of the putatively absolute power of ruler and state over lives, careers, and fortunes that elite groups at all levels of the system constantly seek to modify and attenuate unconstrained patrimonial power. Systemic relations of patronage and interdependence go hand in hand, therefore, with systemic processes of conflict and contestation. Weber described the modification and attenuation of unconstrained patrimonial power as a process of "appropriation." Some contemporary analysts have spoken of "manifest" versus "latent" appropriation, the former connoting an "individual's political and bureaucratic power resulting in personal appropriation of public authority," the latter connoting "various forms of struggle within organizations which are designed to appropriate organizational authority and resources."[54]

Manifest and latent processes of appropriation regularly result in the gradual transformation of official benefices and privileges into the personal property and rights of nominally subordinated political and economic elites. Offices, privileges, and possessions originally made contingent on service and submission to central power are slowly, yet inexorably transmuted into the personal property of the officeholder and his family, ultimately becoming heritable and alienable.[55] Processes of appropriation are further accelerated by the weak or nonexistent separation of public from private in patrimonial society. Out of this "decentralized appropriation of offices that eventually results in the formation of estates and feudalization" arise autonomous patron-client networks at the local level.[56] In Weber's view, these local power structures are rigid, unadaptable to new tasks, and unamenable to reform, rationalization, and regulation.[57]

Yet the apparently inexorable process of appropriation does not go unchallenged in patrimonial society, and central rulers periodically contest the decentralized appropriation of power and resources. Historically, central rulers have attempted to combat processes of appropriation in two ways: from the top down, with assertive personal rulership and the creation of centrally controlled power structures; and from the bottom up, with appeals to the masses and alliances with nonprivileged social strata.

Central rulers have regularly relied on top-down methods to build new and more compliant elites at the expense of established or hereditary elites. In Weber's words, "A universal means of assuring loyalty was the use of officials who did not come from socially privileged strata, or even foreigners, and who therefore did not possess any social power or honor of their own but were entirely dependent for these on the lord."[58] Strategies of this type are encountered throughout the history of seventeenth- and eighteenth-century absolutist rule, in France under Louis XIV and XV, in Prussia under the great Hohenzollern rulers, in Russia under Peter I, and in China under the Kangxi emperor.[59] My discussion of power concentration in late imperial China and Muscovite and imperial Russia shows that central rulers also attempted to combat decentralized processes of power and resource appropriation by energetically practicing personal rulership, regularly conducting tours of inspection, tending to myriad administrative details with their own hands, and implementing far-reaching institutional changes.

But central rulers combating processes of appropriation have not relied solely on the top-down creation of competing elites and the practice of personal rulership and autocracy. In the Weberian formulation of power and politics in patrimonial society, the struggle to control power and resources is conceived as a three-way power contest among central rulers; political, economic, and military elites; and the masses. In the struggle against processes of power and resource appropriation, central rulers attempt to ally with and win over nonprivileged groups, to affirm and extend the patriarchal bond between the ruler and the common people, and to direct the animosity of the masses against the privileged orders. Hence, "against the dangerous aspirations of the privileged status groups patriarchalism plays out the masses who everywhere have been its natural following," thereby "legitimating itself as guardian of the subjects' welfare in its own and their eyes."[60]

In this book, the historically recurrent effort of central rulers to combat decentralized processes of appropriation by combining top-down and bottom-up methods is termed a *top and bottom versus the middle* power-restructuring strategy.[61] This kind of interaction is repeatedly in evidence in late imperial China and czarist Russia and is especially central in the history of the Soviet Union and Communist China. Throughout the twentieth century, the struggle against decentralized processes of power and resource appropriation was broadened, energized, and made more tumultuous by new methods of mass mobilization, the Marxian belief in the dynamic historical role of the common people, and the unprecedented engagement of the Russian and Chinese masses in power-restructuring processes.

The Weberian view of patrimonial society and patrimonial politics is interactive. Just as the sources of stability and continuity are understood in light of relations of patronage and interdependence, processes of conflict, instability, and change are understood in light of three-way contests to control, appropriate, and redistribute power and resources. The source of political change in patrimonial society is thus the ever-present tension and recurrent oscillation between processes of centralization and concentrated control and decentralized processes of power and resource appropriation. In my discussion, Weber's view of patrimonial society and patrimonial politics is used to illuminate a broad range of political, institutional, social, and economic phenomena.

## Logic and Purpose of the Book

The logic of this book is straightforward. The discussion is focused on power restructuring in China and Russia in imperial times, under communism, and today. An interactive view of patrimonial society and patrimonial politics is advanced.

Several recurrent and interrelated power-restructuring phenomena are identified, assessed, and compared.

Chapters 2 and 3 present a general view of power relations and political process in late imperial China and Muscovite and imperial Russia. The discussion encompasses the rise and consolidation of patrimonial autocracy in China and Russia, the structure and methods of autocratic rule, power contests between central rulers and various elite configurations, processes of decentralized power and resource appropriation, old regime crisis and systemic breakdown in the nineteenth century, and the rise of revolutionary power restructuring in the twentieth century.

Chapters 4 and 5 examine power relations and political process in the Soviet Union in the 1920s and 1930s and during the Khrushchev period. The discussion in Chapter 4 encompasses state-society power dynamics and political interactions in the 1920s; contending developmental and organizational strategies; collectivization, industrialization, and social engineering in the late 1920s and 1930s; the political, social, and economic dynamics of the Stalin system; and political conflict and the origins of the Great Purges of 1937–1938. The principal themes of Chapter 5 include the crisis of the mature Stalin system, the revitalization of party power in the 1950s, Khrushchev's power-restructuring initiatives in the late 1950s and early 1960s and their defeat, and power and politics under Brezhnev.

Chapters 6, 7, and 8 examine power relations and political process in China in the 1950s and early 1960s, during the Cultural Revolution decade, and in the ensuing post-Mao period. In these core chapters, I illuminate my general view of power restructuring in China and Russia with a detailed examination of a specific historical case, the Cultural Revolution, and the years 1966–1967 in particular. At the same time, I use my overall power-restructuring argument to shed new new light on the events of this fateful episode in the history of Chinese communism. Chapter 6 examines contending developmental and organizational strategies in the 1950s, the Hundred Flowers Movement and the Great Leap Forward, the rise of moderation and political conflict in the early 1960s, the origins of the Cultural Revolution, and Maoist power restructuring in 1966. Chapter 7 assesses the consequences of the Cultural Revolution and examines power contests, political conflicts, and policy disputes in the late 1960s and early 1970s; the extent of Maoist dictatorship; the role of the People's Liberation Army (PLA); the "theory and program" of veteran officialdom; and the last stand of Cultural Revolution radicalism. I complete my analysis of the Cultural Revolution in Chapter 8 by reassessing the origins and consequences of post-Mao reform and focusing on the changing relation between center and locality in the 1980s, official power and privilege in post-Mao China, and conflict and control in contemporary Chinese society. Chapter 8 concludes with a discussion of the significance of the June 4, 1989, crackdown and an outline of the transition from socialism in China in the 1990s.

I end this book with an analysis of power restructuring in the period of perestroika. In Chapter 9, the comparative-historical view of power relations and political process developed in this book is brought to bear on the momentous events in the Soviet Union in the late 1980s and early 1990s. The discussion encompasses a wide array of familiar power-restructuring phenomena, including the deconcentration of political power, three-way power contests and political conflicts, decentralized power and resource appropriation, and top and bottom versus the middle interactions. A new perspective on recent Soviet power restructuring is put forward, and the origins, dynamics, and consequences of power restructuring in the period of perestroika are compared to power restructuring during the Cultural Revolution and the post-Mao period. I conclude with an outline of the transition from socialism in the former Soviet Union and contrast it to the Chinese transitional experience.

These aims are ambitious and necessarily so. At a time of rapid change and mounting ferment in China and the former Soviet Union, the need for conceptual and interpretive tools has never been greater. By advancing a general view of power relations and political process in China and Russia, this book establishes an analytic framework encompassing recurrent power-restructuring patterns and processes. By establishing linkages between late imperial China and Muscovite and imperial Russia, the Soviet Union and Communist China, and contemporary China and Russia, my discussion sheds new light on key episodes in Chinese and Russian political history. At the same time, I hope that the interrelation of past and present undertaken in these pages will facilitate assessment of the future trajectory of power restructuring in China and Russia.

## Notes

1. Elizabeth J. Perry, "State and Society in Contemporary China," *World Politics* 41, 4 (July 1989):590.

2. R. Bin Wong, "China and World History," *Late Imperial China* 6, 2 (December 1985):6. Wong discussed Joseph Fletcher Jr.'s exploration of the "common links among Eurasian empires" whereby "nomadic conventions" were "transplanted to agrarian bureaucratic empires" (6). Continuities, interactions, and reconfigurations of this type are recurrent in Chinese and Russian political history.

3. Franz Schurmann, "Neo-Communism Could Come to the Soviet Union," *Pacific News Service*, December 24–28, 1990, 1.

4. Guenther Roth introduced Weber's sociology of domination by noting, "At the core of his approach to rulership is the three-way struggle between ruler, staff, and subjects" ("Introduction," in Max Weber, *Economy and Society* [Berkeley and Los Angeles: University of California Press, 1978], vol. 1, xciii).

5. Charles Tilly, *Coercion, Capital, and the European States, AD 990–1990* (Cambridge, Mass.: Basil Blackwell, 1990), 188. Hence, "bargaining ranged from co-optation with privilege to massive armed repression, but it left behind compacts between sovereign and subjects. Although rulers of states such as France and Prussia managed to circumvent most of the old representative institutions for several centuries, those representative institutions or their successors eventually acquired more power vis-à-vis the crown as regular taxation, credit, and payment of national debt became essential to the continued production of armed force" (188).

6. Theda Skocpol unequivocally embraced a "nonvoluntarist, structural perspective" on the causes and processes of social revolution (*States and Social Revolutions* [Cambridge: Cambridge University Press, 1979], 14). Jack A. Goldstone emphasized "material changes as the cause of state breakdown," yet argued that outcomes "depend chiefly on particular cultural frameworks and the development of elite ideologies" (*Revolution and Rebellion in the Early Modern World* [Berkeley and Los Angeles: University of California Press, 1991], 27).

7. Goldstone suggested that "underlying pressures" such as state fiscal distress, elite alienation and competition, and rising mass mobilization were key in the breakdown of communism in Eastern Europe and the Soviet Union. Yet he also noted that these pressures were "triggered by Soviet leader Mikhail Gorbachev's criticism and efforts at reform of the Soviet state" (*Revolution and Rebellion in the Early Modern World,* 482). In Chapter 9, we see that the revolutionary events of the period of perestroika were set in motion by political decisions and political actions, with one man at the top often playing the key role.

8. Goldstone concluded his discussion of early modern Europe, China, and the Middle East by drawing some parallels with the contemporary United States, yet he also noted that industrialization and administrative modernization mean that "population growth lost its ability to trigger the processes that earlier led to state breakdown," thereby effectively conceding the irrelevance of his theory for the twentieth century (*Revolution and Rebellion in the Early Modern World,* 461).

9. Zbigniew Brzezinski, *The Grand Failure: The Birth and Death of Communism in the Twentieth Century* (New York: Collier, 1989), xi.

10. Ibid., 6.

11. Martin Malia, *The Soviet Tragedy* (New York: Free Press, 1994), 14.

12. Adam Westoby, *The Evolution of Communism* (New York: Free Press, 1989), 14.

13. Richard Pipes, *Russia Under the Bolshevik Regime* (New York: Knopf, 1994), 503.

14. In 1994, Malia spoke of the "totality" of the Soviet collapse and claimed that "Soviet history may now at last be written entirely in the past tense" (*The Soviet Tragedy,* 521). Just as it is unacceptable to disconnect the Soviet system from its imperial predecessor, however, we see that the post-Soviet Russian state displays extensive political, institutional, and cultural linkages to its Soviet predecessor.

15. Alexander Solzhenitsyn, *The Gulag Archipelago* (New York: Harper and Row, 1973), 26–27.

16. Vladimir Krupin, "The Strange Soul of Russia," *Soviet Life* (October 1990):8–10. For a discussion of Russophile thought in the Soviet Union in the 1970s and 1980s, see Vladimir Shlapentokh, *Soviet Intellectuals and Political Power: The Post-Stalin Era* (Princeton: Princeton University Press, 1990).

17. *Heshang* (River Elegy), Xian Film Studios, 1988.

18. Carl J. Friedrich and Zbigniew Brzezinski, *Totalitarian Dictatorship and Autocracy* (Cambridge, Mass.: Harvard University Press, 1965), 58.

19. Ibid., 16.

20. Bailes articulated this crucial distinction in his graduate seminar "Soviet Society: History and Interpretations," University of California, Berkeley, Fall 1985.

21. H. Gordon Skilling, "Groups in Soviet Politics: Some Hypotheses," in H. Gordon Skilling and Franklyn Griffiths, eds., *Interest Groups in Soviet Politics* (Princeton: Princeton University Press, 1971), 29, 40.

22. Parris H. Chang, *Power and Policy in China,* 2d, enl. ed. (University Park: Pennsylvania State University Press, 1981), 176–179.

23. Alexander Yanov, *The Drama of the Soviet 1960s* (Berkeley: Institute of International Studies, University of California at Berkeley, 1984), xiii.

24. Jerry F. Hough, *The Soviet Union and Social Science Theory* (Cambridge, Mass.: Harvard University Press, 1977), 8–9.

25. Ibid., 10. An insistence that Soviet political process in the Brezhnev era had taken on an increasingly "pluralist" cast permeated Hough's revised version of Merle Fainsod's *How Russia Is Ruled*, which Hough retitled *How the Soviet Union Is Governed* (Cambridge, Mass.: Harvard University Press, 1979); see esp. chap. 14.

26. Mikhail Gorbachev, "Report by the General Secretary of the CPSU Central Committee to the 19th All-Union Party Conference," June 28, 1988, *Novosti Press Agency,* in *Reprints from the Soviet Press* 47, 1 (July 15, 1988):37.

27. For the concept of neotraditionalism see Ken Jowitt, "Soviet Neotraditionalism: The Political Corruption of a Leninist Regime," *Soviet Studies* 35, 3 (July 1983):275–297. For neotraditionalism in Communist China, see Andrew G. Walder, *Communist Neo-Traditionalism* (Berkeley and Los Angeles: University of California Press, 1986). For clientelism in China, see Jean C. Oi, *State and Peasant in Contemporary China* (Berkeley and Los Angeles: University of California Press, 1989). For patrimonial rulership in China, see Barrett L. McCormick, *Political Reform in Post-Mao China* (Berkeley and Los Angeles: University of California Press, 1990).

28. See Michael Mann, *The Sources of Social Power* (Cambridge: Cambridge University Press, 1986); Theda Skocpol, *States and Social Revolutions*; Roberto Mangabeira Unger, *Plasticity into Power* (Cambridge: Cambridge University Press, 1987); Goldstone, *Revolution and Rebellion in the Early Modern World*.

29. Oi, *State and Peasant in Contemporary China,* 3.

30. Walder, *Communist Neo-Traditionalism,* 1.

31. Ibid., xiii–xv, 10.

32. McCormick, *Political Reform in Post-Mao China,* 6–7, 21.

33. Ibid., 199–200, 196.

34. Oi, *State and Peasant in Contemporary China,* chaps. 2, 3.

35. Ibid., 221–222, 124–125.

36. Hence, "the return to household farming signaled the state's decision to change the terms of the struggle over the harvest" (ibid., 155).

37. Karl A. Wittfogel, *Oriental Despotism* (New Haven: Yale University Press, 1957), iii. His is a badly biased but nonetheless masterful example of comparative-historical macroanalysis.

38. Skocpol, *States and Social Revolutions,* 49.

39. Ibid., 49–50.

40. Unger, *Plasticity into Power,* 5–10.

41. Ibid., 4.

42. Ibid., 21.

43. Mann, *The Sources of Social Power,* 171.

44. Ibid., 172, 537.

45. Weber, *Economy and Society,* vol. 2, 1006.

46. Ibid., 1041.

47. Guenther Roth, "Personal Rulership, Patrimonialism, and Empire-Building in the New States," *World Politics* 20, 2 (January 1968):196.

48. Weber, *Economy and Society,* vol. 2, 1099.

49. Ibid., 1091.

50. Ibid., 1091, 1094.

51. Vatro Murvar, "Patrimonialism, Modern and Traditionalist: A Paradigm for Inter-disciplinary Research on Rulership and Legitimacy," in Vatro Murvar, ed., *Theory of Liberty, Legitimacy, and Power* (London: Routledge and Kegan Paul, 1985), 46.

52. Ibid., 84, 48.

53. Pipes, *Russia Under the Bolshevik Regime,* 503–504.

54. Lloyd I. Rudolph and Susanne Hoeber Rudolph, "Authority and Power in Bureaucratic and Patrimonial Administration: A Revisionist Interpretation of Weber on Bureaucracy," *World Politics* 31, 2 (January 1979):215–216.

55. Weber, *Economy and Society,* vol. 2, 1028–1033.

56. Jeffrey C. Alexander, *Theoretical Logic in Sociology,* vol. 3, *The Classical Attempt at Theoretical Synthesis: Max Weber* (Berkeley and Los Angeles: University of California Press, 1983), 91.

57. Weber, *Economy and Society,* vol. 2, 1040. In an important book, Alexander J. Motyl described the "built-in weaknesses" of "highly centralized political-economic systems like the USSR," which generate a "cyclical pattern" in which periods of "systemic recentralization" oscillate with "systematic decentralization," when local autonomy increases and local forces are able "to utilize their *own resources* for their *own ends*" (*Sovietology, Rationality, Nationality* [New York: Columbia University Press, 1990], 88–93).

58. Weber, *Economy and Society,* vol. 2, 1043.

59. For France, see Roland E. Mousnier, *The Institutions of France Under the Absolute Monarchy, 1598–1789,* vol. 2, *The Organs of State and Society* (Chicago and London: University of Chicago Press, 1984). For Prussia, see Hans Rosenberg, *Bureaucracy, Aristocracy, and Autocracy* (Cambridge, Mass.: Harvard University Press, 1958). For Petrine Russia, see Marc Raeff, *The Origins of the Russian Intelligentsia* (New York: Harcourt Brace Jovanovich, 1966). For Qing China, see Jonathan D. Spence, *Ts'ao Yin and the K'ang-hsi Emperor* (New Haven: Yale University Press, 1966).

60. Weber, *Economy and Society,* vol. 2, 1106–1107.

61. The significance of top and bottom versus the middle processes in Soviet and Chinese Communist history is recognized by some Western analysts. Motyl noted that Gorbachev's strategy of undermining "his opponents by means of assaults from above and below . . . , perhaps not incidentally, bears an uncanny resemblance to that pursued by Stalin in the late 1930s and by Mao Zedong during the Cultural Revolution" (*Sovietology, Rationality, Nationality,* 177).

# 2

# Power Restructuring
# in Late Imperial, Republican,
# and Revolutionary China

I begin with an analysis of power relations and political process in Ming China (1368–1644), Qing China (1644–1911), and Republican China (1911–1949). My discussion encompasses the rise and consolidation of the Ming and Qing autocracies, the recurrent challenges posed to Ming and Qing rulers by decentralized processes of power and resource appropriation, and the mounting processes of systemic breakdown and crisis of the mid- and late nineteenth century. I extend this view of power dynamics in late imperial China with an analysis of the unsuccessful Nationalist attempt to reestablish central power, the rise of Chinese communism, and the revolutionary restructuring of power set in motion by the victory of the Chinese Communist Party (CCP) in 1949. Processes of power concentration versus power devolution drove power restructuring in late imperial China, Republican China, and revolutionary China. In this chapter, and throughout this book, these processes are understood as three-way struggles among central rulers, various elite configurations, and nonprivileged groups to control, appropriate, and redistribute power and resources.

## Power Relations in Late Imperial China

Power dynamics in traditional China have been conceptualized in three basic ways. Some analyses have emphasized the long-term political and ideological domination of the state structure by Confucian scholar-officialdom, whereas others have stressed the authoritarian domination of Chinese sociopolitical elites by an overtowering imperial autocracy.[1] Another view has focused on the ebb and flow of central power vis-à-vis the power of the scholar-official and landholding elite. This interactive understanding of power dynamics is increasingly stressed in contemporary Western analyses and finds support in traditional Chinese political philosophy and historiography.

Viewed from an interactive perspective, Chinese elites were both politically allied with the imperial state and a perennial source of political competition; whether power relations were primarily cooperative or competitive depended on constantly changing circumstances and conditions. As Albert Feuerwerker put it, "Political power was never rightfully the exclusive possession of either the monarch or his officials. The substance of traditional Chinese politics was that they shared political power but continuously contested with one another over its allocation."[2] In traditional Chinese political philosophy, this interplay was manifested in the constant tension between Confucian ideals of self-regulation and the reality of Legalist methods in political and administrative practice.[3] Yuan historiographer Ma Duanlin (1254–1324) periodized Chinese history in terms of the transition from a "feudal" *(fengjian)* system of local power to a "prefectural" *(junxian)* system of central power.[4] Yet as Yang Lien-sheng observed, the two systems "need not be viewed as two completely contradictory modes of government. In reviewing the history of political institutions, it seems more meaningful to treat the two traditionally accepted models as two polarities with a wide spectrum of shades of colors between them."[5] In these pages, I rely on and develop an interactive view of power relations and political process in late imperial China.

If power dynamics in late imperial China were always fluid and complex, there nevertheless were periods of vigorous central power and periods of relative decline and breakdown. The power arrangements of the early Ming dynasty concentrated unprecedented powers in the hands of the emperor and maximized central control of the elite and mass population alike. While incorporating classic attributes of the Chinese imperial tradition, the early Ming autocracy was characterized by major changes in power organization and institutional structure. Where did these changes originate? I suggest that a discussion of power restructuring in late imperial China most appropriately begins with an assessment of a chronologically brief, yet politically fateful phase in Chinese history—the Mongol invasions and establishment of the non-Han Yuan dynasty (1280–1368) in the thirteenth century.

## The Mongols and Chinese Political Culture

The Mongol impact is not easily summed up. For William Theodore de Bary, the era of Mongol domination was "in many ways the least typical period" in Chinese history. During this period, China was "totally subdued," "shaken to its institutional foundations," and "exposed to foreign ideas and influences" by "an alien conqueror far removed in his nomadic ways and tribal customs from the conventional picture of the stately Chinese dynasty."[6] Jacques Gernet concurred and noted that at the time of the Mongol invasions China, "the richest and most advanced country in the world," was "dealt a profound blow" and "suffered a drastic break in its history as a result of that event."[7] Yet important changes were precipitated by the Mongol invasion. In the view of Joseph F. Fletcher Jr., the political and institutional significance of the Mongol period was considerable, for it was at this time that methods of rule patterned on "Inner Asian models" were extended and implemented throughout China. These methods included the strengthening of the central ruler's position vis-à-vis officialdom and the elimination of bureaucratic checks on autocratic power, the tightening of government controls over scholar-officials and merchants, the creation of a stronger military garrison system, and the registration and classification of the population into ethnic and professional categories.[8] In contrast to the preceding Southern Song (1127–1279) period, when the emperor was often the "plaything of the conflicts and rivalries that arose within the very core of the upper class" and a rich and powerful merchant class flourished, central power was reinforced under the Mongols.[9]

This view, which accented the extensive political and institutional significance of Mongol rule, has been countered by an apparently different perspective. According to John D. Langlois Jr., "Identifying areas of enduring Mongol impact on Chinese civilization is extremely difficult. . . . It is hard to demonstrate the existence of causal links between Mongol rule and specific cultural responses."[10] Indeed, the Mongols deliberately set themselves apart from the canons and conventions of Chinese civilization. Chinese scholar-officials were systematically discriminated against and their privileges restricted, while non-Han tax-farmers and officials were systematically employed; despite the urgings of Chinese officials, Mongol rulers consistently resisted the introduction of a legal code of the normal dynastic type.[11] In matters of food, drink, and clothing, the invaders stubbornly clung to their nomadic traditions of boiled mutton, koumiss (fermented mare's milk), and unwashed leather and fur garments, much to the disgust and disdain of the Chinese recording these alien and "barbaric" practices.[12]

In fact, these apparently contradictory images accurately depict different aspects of the period of Mongol domination. The Mongols were empire builders, territorial unifiers, and political centralizers on a massive and possibly unprecedented scale. Driven by what Morris Rossabi termed "seemingly insatiable revenue requirements," the Mongols were masters of resource mobilization, tirelessly and ruthlessly imposing new fiscal controls, concocting sweeping state monopolies, and conducting exhaustive population censuses.[13] In China, the Mongols were keenly aware of the potential threat to their power posed by Confucian scholar-officialdom; the Mongol tendency to appoint officials rather than revive the examination system, to rely on foreigners and nonprivileged strata to staff the bureaucracy, and to resist codification and institutionalization are ample testimony to such fears.

But the Mongol state was not effectively centralized, and central policies were implemented neither comprehensively nor consistently. In David M. Farquhar's view, the engagement of the Yuan imperial government in "empire-wide administration was at best transitory or limited to very restricted activities."[14] Comprising central potentates, autonomous princelings, Muslim tax-farmers, an array of special bureaus and personal appointees, and a vast, unstructured stratum of government clerks at the local level, the structure of power in Yuan China was arbitrary and chaotic, virtually uninstitutionalized, and rife with corruption. At the top, Mongol aristocrats incessantly engaged in bloody power contests, and political succession routinely entailed assassination and civil war.[15] In the middle, rapacious tax-farming was the norm; geared primarily toward maximizing the amount of revenue raised for the court, Yuan fiscal and taxation practices were harsh and onerous.[16] At the local level, weak or nonexistent institutionalization, as well as Mongol laxness and inability to police local officialdom, meant that the bureaucracy was "largely ungovernable." As Langlois observed, "Illicit practices by bureaucratic personnel, the un-ranked clerks, in fact became the chief complaint that Ming Taizu lodged against Yuan rule."[17] While attributing the Yuan collapse to the corruption and malfeasance of the bureaucracy, however, the Ming founder traced this state of affairs to the "laxity" of the imperial house and the later Yuan rulers' neglect of their duties.[18]

## The Early Ming Autocracy

The early phases of the Ming dynasty witnessed a comprehensive restructuring and forcible reordering of the badly disrupted late Yuan political and social order. During the reign of the Ming founder, Ming Taizu (r. 1368–1399), concentration and control processes were set in motion that would shape power relations and political process in China for centuries to come. In the political and institutional features of the early Ming autocracy, we can discern the interplay of Mongol methods of rule, the Chinese response to the difficult and harsh conditions of the time, and the personality of the brilliant, brutal, and tireless Ming founder himself.[19]

During Taizu's reign, real and potential centers of competing power were fiercely attacked, and the state structure was rocked by a succession of bloody purges and massive personnel shake-ups. In 1376, ten thousand civil officials were punished on charges of administrative laxity; in 1380, thirty thousand people were executed and the office of chief councillor abolished in the wake of an apparent coup attempt; in 1385, ten thousand officials were executed in a tax and grain racketeering scandal; in 1393, the military was purged and fifteen thousand officers executed.[20] This physical attack on centers of competing power was paralleled by far-reaching political and institutional changes. When Taizu banned in perpetuity the office of chief councillor, he deliberately and formally concentrated power in the hands of the emperor. In the early Ming period, power was effectively concentrated; Taizu held court three times daily and was personally involved in all phases of civil and military administration.[21] The strengthening of the emperor's position vis-à-vis Confucian scholar-officialdom was reinforced by new methods of bureaucratic recruitment, the use of organizational alternatives, and the imposition of more direct forms of central economic control.

Taizu bypassed conventional patterns of bureaucratic recruitment in favor of more flexible and egalitarian methods. Thus, "from the very beginning the Ming founder repeatedly issued orders that men of merit be recommended by central and provincial officials for government service, with almost no consideration to be given to the social status of the recommended."[22] In this Ming version of a top and bottom versus the middle power-restructuring strategy, Taizu sought to revitalize scholar-officialdom and to vitiate the power of entrenched elites by means of massive social engineering and direct appeals to nonprivileged social strata. This effort was sustained, vigorously enforced, and generally successful. Although Taizu's reign "was probably the high point of the greatest vertical social mobility in China's history," the emperor "made a point of letting his distrust of official-dom be known to the people at large . . . and intended local officials to be hemmed in between pressures and controls issuing from all levels."[23]

Power concentration in the early Ming autocracy was reinforced by the creation and utilization of organizational alternatives to established channels of scholar-official power. Although Taizu himself warned of the dangers, eunuchs played an important and increasingly pervasive role in the power arrangements of the Ming dynasty from the start.[24] As irregular channels through which the emperor could exercise his power, eunuchs functioned as an informal, yet systematic check on the power of orthodox scholar-officialdom. At the same time, the early Ming rulers relied extensively on the "Embroidered Uniform Guard," a private army and secret police that had tens of thousands of operators, maintained its own system of jails and torture chambers, and focused the bulk of its surveillance and terror activities on the scholar-official establishment.[25]

Finally, elite groups were subjected to more direct economic controls under the early Ming autocracy. In the first decades of the Ming period, a substantial proportion of land was state owned, much of it confiscated from local notables in the Jiangnan region, China's wealthiest and most culturally advanced area at this time. Potentially formidable political opponents were thereby deprived of their economic base, and many Jiangnan scholar-official families were subsequently forced to reside in Nanking, the initial Ming capital. By 1502, one-seventh of all registered land in China was state owned, as were the richest revenue sources in the Jiangnan region.[26] Even though the power drives of the early Ming state were most directly focused on the degree-holding and landholding elite, ambitious efforts to control and restructure the economy and society at the mass level were undertaken as well. With the aid of Yuan census data, the Ming state divided the population in the countryside into three occupational categories—ordinary civilians, soldiers, and artisans—and "the form of each household's obligatory service to the state was determined by its permanent census category."[27] New forms of local government designed to enhance the capacity of the state to extract tax revenues and service obligations were introduced. The local population was organized into tithings of 110 families, with the 10 wealthiest families responsible for supervising the others in corvée operations; by the same token, local notables were made "grain captains" responsible for the collection and delivery of the land tax.[28] Yet Taizu was wary of excessive taxation and attempted in various ways to promote economic stability and development in the countryside. In the early Ming period, land was widely distributed to small farmers, while people bringing wasteland under cultivation were allowed to claim it as their property and were taxed at a reduced rate.[29] As in the political realm, the Ming founder sought to restructure and revitalize the economy and society at the local level through processes of concentration and control, while also attempting to build popular support and draw on local energies.

## Decentralized Power and Resource Appropriation in Ming China

The concentration and control capacities of the early Ming autocracy were impressive and apparently all encompassing, and throughout the Ming dynasty the emperor always commanded extensive formal powers. Charles O. Hucker described the "despotism," "the servile and subservient position of officialdom," and "the absence of formal checks on imperial authority" that characterized the Ming system.[30] Although accurate enough, this imagery fails to account for the many countervailing forces that became increasingly prevalent and assertive over the course of the dynasty and, in the end, played the decisive role in the Ming demise. I understand these countervailing forces as decentralized processes of power and resource appropriation. As early as the middle of the fifteenth century, processes of appropriation were reshaping the power arrangements of the early Ming autocracy and affecting the fiscal policies and financial condition of the Ming state.

The overriding political goal of the early Ming system was to subordinate the interests of degree-holding and landholding elites to those of the autocrat and the state. According to John W. Dardess, from the turmoil and breakdown of the late Yuan "Taizu drew the lesson that when a dynasty fails to maintain strict controls over its ruling apparatus, it will eventually attack its own population base of 'good people,' force them to turn outlaw, and in the end perish from its self-inflicted wounds."[31] Despite many institutional obstacles and a formally subservient position, however, the scholar-official establishment at the court steadily expanded its power and authority in the fifteenth and sixteenth centuries. The dynamics of this process are familiar; quite simply, a political and institutional arrangement erected on premises of autocracy and personal rulership succumbed over time to processes of bureaucratic routinization.

The early Ming emperors, Taizu and his equally vigorous and formidable son, the Yongle emperor (r. 1403–1425), were veritable supermen who personally shouldered incredible workloads and practiced true personal rulership.[32] Subsequent emperors, softer and no doubt less driven, did not maintain such a frenetic pace and tended to leave all but the most pressing or unusual administrative matters in the hands of palace officials.[33] But this tendency was not solely a reflection of the personal failings of later Ming emperors, for "once the Ming Dynasty had become settled, the mainstay of the government was the bureaucracy, not the monarchy."[34] As the civil service became increasingly able to select its own members through the examination system and to discipline and promote them according to established procedures, and as "grand secretaries" arose as influential spokesmen and coordinators of the bureaucracy, it was the scholar-official establishment that wielded de facto power, despite the ultimate authority of the emperor. Cabinet secretaries whose power was purely advisory in theory were able to appropriate the power of the emperor, to control the flow of documents to and from the throne, to suppress material with which they disagreed, and to draft edicts for the emperor to sign.[35] Inexorably and inevitably, power arrangements premised on dynamic personal rulership were displaced by processes of normalization and routinization.[36]

The long-term dominance by the scholar-official establishment was ideologically and organizationally reinforced by the supremacy of Confucianism as official state doctrine. Even though the emperor occupied first place in the Confucian sociopolitical hierarchy, Ming rulers were themselves increasingly subject to the Confucian worldview. Thus, "before enthronement as emperor, the heir apparent was tutored by the literary-educational branch of the bureaucracy to be familiar with the principles of self-restraint and mutual deference," a process Ray Huang described as "compulsorily institutionalizing benevolent despotism."[37] Over the long course of the fifteenth and sixteenth centuries, Confucian doctrine and ritual constrained the authority of Ming rulers in pervasive and irresistible ways.

Although Taizu used unconventional methods to recruit and promote officials in the early Ming period, the examination system soon regained its place as the dominant mode of bureaucratic training, selection, and appointment.[38] The examination system exemplified Confucian dualism and functioned simultaneously as an institution of central power and as a self-serving vehicle for Confucian scholar-officialdom. While strengthening state control of elites by controlling all significant avenues of upward mobility, the examination system was premised on the mastery of skills and knowledge that were overwhelmingly the exclusive preserve of the degree-holding elite.[39] The dominance of the examination system over alternative modes of official recruitment reinforced the ability of scholar-officialdom to dictate the terms on which it would serve, terms that scholar-officials, as masters of the Confucian canon, interpreted.

As Confucian doctrine became entrenched in Ming China, Confucian ritual grew all encompassing. A classic account of the Wanli emperor (r. 1572–1620) depicts a ruler whose every action was circumscribed by a comprehensive web of accumulated Confucian ritual and precedent; whose actions were constantly contested, albeit in servile terms, by a host of remonstrating scholar-officials; and whose freedom of movement was so limited that he was able to undertake brief journeys to the Peking suburbs only after protracted negotiations with the palace officials in charge of ritual.[40] Although Wanli possessed sufficient power to defy his officials, and to refuse to conduct official business, he was unable to alter a system of ritual and precedent whose authority exceeded his own. The resulting standoff between the emperor and the scholar-official establishment badly impaired central administrative functions. By the middle of the sixteenth century, Ming rulers had long since lost the capacity to direct the political and institutional life of the court and state; "much of the ordinary business of government had come to be managed by the outer court at a distance from the emperor and without constant recourse to him for guidance."[41] At the same time, decentralized processes of resource appropriation were undercutting the fiscal vitality of the Ming state.

Whereas modern states are able to draw on many revenue sources, the finances of the Ming state depended overwhelmingly on the land tax. Yet the large rural population and proportionately minute number of civil officials meant that local elites necessarily performed vital coordinating functions in the tax collection process. As was true of power relations generally, this arrangement combined cooperative and competitive elements. In Feuerwerker's view, land tax revenues in late imperial China tended to be split fifty-fifty between the central authorities and local officials and local elites, which took their cut in the form of "customary exactions."[42] Customary exactions were only one component in the complex and constantly evolving mix of privileges, exemptions, evasions, and outright extortions that local officials and influential local families routinely claimed and practiced to maximize their wealth, while shifting the tax burden onto the nonprivileged rural population. Some of these practices were officially condoned since tax collection at the local level was impossible or impractical without the cooperation of local privileged orders. By the middle of the fifteenth century, however, local landholders were brazenly evading and resisting land tax quotas.[43] Decentralized processes of power and resource appropriation accelerated throughout the sixteenth century and into the late Ming period, ultimately producing a flight of the poor from the land and a virtual breakdown of the state tax-collecting machinery.[44]

Taizu had erected institutions to combat decentralized resource appropriation. The grain captain system was designed to enlist local leaders in the tax collection process while guaranteeing fixed revenue levels. Yet this system fell victim to tax evasion within decades of Taizu's death. Faced with false registration by the manipulation of land registers, on the one hand, and the responsibility for meeting tax quotas regardless of the accuracy of these registers, on the other, grain captains soon found themselves caught in a hopeless bind and were unable to function.[45] This system was then eliminated and various reforms undertaken, an effort that culminated in the "Single Whip" reform of 1581. The early successes and ultimate failure of this reform highlight basic trends in power relations and political process in the late Ming period.

The Single Whip reform was an attempt to centralize and rationalize the tax collection process. A new land survey and land registration were undertaken, a complex variety of payments in kind were commuted to two installments in silver, the authority of local government officials was expanded, and the privileged orders at the local level were subjected to increased scrutiny and pressure from the court.[46] The reform achieved impressive initial results: A substantial amount of tax evasion was curtailed; the performance of officialdom at the local, regional, and central levels was made more efficient; and the flow of revenue into central coffers was significantly increased. These power-restructuring achievements gave the Ming dynasty a new lease on life but came at a high price. In the course of maximizing state revenues and central power, the Single Whip reform necessarily attacked the power and resource appropriations of degree-holding and landholding elites at all levels.[47] The enmity and resistance that ensued were then manifested with devastating consequences in the violent and destabilizing political conflicts that preceded the Ming demise.

## Political Conflict and the Ming Demise

Frederic Wakeman Jr. showed that internal challenges to the authority of the Ming state grew increasingly powerful in the late sixteenth and early seventeenth centuries. Contending centers of power in the form of well-organized and articulate "gentry clubs" and party movements proliferated during the late Ming, while at the mass level local notables led social movements in the urban centers of Jiangnan and defied imperial police and tax collectors.[48] Political conflict at the local and regional levels was mirrored in factional conflict at the top, in which "righteous" Confucian activists and government officials belonging to the Donglin Academy attacked the corruption and nepotism of the "eunuch dictator," Wei Zhongxian and were in turn bloodily suppressed. The Donglin–Wei Zhongxian clash highlighted the rise of competing centers of power and the intensification of processes of power and resource appropriation in the late Ming period.

The roots of this conflict can be traced back to grand secretary Zhang Juzheng's (1525–1582) attempt to reconcentrate the power of the Ming state between 1572 and 1582. In Zhang's view, the dynasty had passed through three stages of decline: first, a deterioration of "excellent customs" and a loosening of authority; second, a growth in the power of the princes and a disregard for law; and third, a rise of unequal taxation, whereby the people lost their employment and became victims of "monopolies."[49] In the spirit of the early Ming autocracy, Zhang attacked these problems by attempting to reconcentrate power, putting pressure on officialdom, and more rigorously enforcing laws and combating processes of appropriation. Despite considerable initial successes, however, this revitalization effort failed. In the years following the grand secretary's death in 1582, the scholar-official establishment became mired in factional strife as "group struggled against group to prevent the emergence of a new leader like Zhang," while the emperor "lost patience with his officials, ignored the bureaucracy as much as possible, and relied more and more on trusted eunuchs to get essential business done."[50] When the Wanli emperor finally passed from the scene in 1620, the Ming state was virtually crippled by "bureaucratic factionalism that made effective government action impossible" and "eunuch intrusions into government that quickly led to the ruth-less dictatorship of Wei Zhongxian."[51] The last Ming ruler, the Chongzhen em-peror (r. 1628–1644), attempted to combat the destabilizing and debilitating proliferation of political factionalism and power fragmentation with familiar methods of autocratic rule. Under Chongzhen, senior civil and military officials were subjected to increased central pressure, the jails filled with political prison-ers, and personnel turnover was accelerated.[52]

Although the actual collapse of the dynasty came from a combination of peas-ant insurrection and foreign invasion, processes of institutional deterioration and decentralized power and resource appropriation underlay the Ming inability to successfully combat these menaces. When, for example, the financially strapped court attempted to increase military expenditures by cutting back on the govern-ment-financed postal system, destitute ex-couriers in the impoverished provinces of Shanxi and Shenxi rose in rebellion.[53] With bureaucratic factionalism occupy-ing center stage at court and rampant tax evasion and related abuses reducing state revenue and inflaming the countryside, Chongzhen faced an out-of-control situation. Unable to pay the troops facing the looming Manchu menace, the em-peror sought to reclassify some Jiangnan gentry land as state property; this pro-posal elicited indignant outbursts about the sanctity of private wealth and the role of the rich as protectors of the poor.[54] Politically and institutionally enfeebled from top to bottom, the Ming dynasty finally succumbed in 1644 to massive inter-nal upheaval and a formidable external challenge.[55]

## Power Relations, Political Process, and the Manchus

The deterioration and collapse of the Ming state posed fundamental questions about the Chinese political order. In the years spanning the final collapse of the Ming, the rise of the Manchus, and the formation of the Qing state system, two competing political philosophies came to the fore. State-society relations and the role of central power were conceptualized in different ways in these contending perspectives.

A school of thought emerged that linked the political, fiscal, and social prob-lems of the day to the "despotic character" of the Yuan and Ming systems.[56] Ac-cording to *fengjian* theorists Huang Zongxi (1610–1695) and Gu Yanwu (1613–1682), imperial exclusion of Confucian scholar-officials from the real exercise of power was the root cause of such ills as excessive eunuch influence at court, petty official corruption in the countryside, a weakened civil service, oppressive taxa-tion, and popular discontent. In this view, a comprehensive loosening of power was needed, along with a deconcentration of authority into the hands of qualified people. By virtue of superior moral cultivation and close ties with the common people, Confucian scholar-officials were the only ones who could be counted on to rule fairly and effectively.[57]

If the many contemporary ills decried by Huang and Gu were real enough, their power deconcentration argument was marred by a basic defect, for it was precisely the educated and privileged orders that colluded with corrupt local officials, used their influence to secure exemptions for themselves and their relatives, shifted the tax burden onto those least able to bear it, and in myriad ways appropriated power and resources and enriched themselves at the expense of the common people and the state. Moreover, we have seen how the "despotic" powers of Ming rulers became increasingly circumscribed over time and in the end succumbed to pervasive processes of power and resource appropriation. Self-serving *fengjian* rhetoric notwithstanding, this was the enduring political reality of the late Ming period. China's new rulers understood this reality, and it was no coincidence that *fengjian* notions found no place in the power arrangements of the early Qing dynasty, which instead replicated, reinforced, and refined the power-concentrating mechanisms of the early Ming autocracy.

The Manchus, a militaristic and nomadic people, differed from the Mongols in one particularly notable respect—they were familiar with and ready to make selective use of the political and institutional achievements of traditional Chinese statecraft. The paramount importance of cooperative state-elite relations was recognized by the new rulers, and Dorgon's first action on occupying Peking was to solicit the support of the Chinese scholar-official establishment by assuring it that loyalty to the new dynasty meant the retention of rank and privileges.[58] While reaffirming the partnership between the imperial state and the privileged orders, however, the early Qing rulers took care to ensure that they were the dominant partners in the relationship. Like the Ming founder, the new Manchu rulers sought especially to curb and eliminate competing centers of power. In addition to confronting the perennial challenge posed by Chinese degree-holding and landholding groups, the early Qing emperors also had to contend with the aspirations of their own Manchu aristocracy. It was the achievement of the emperors Shunzhi (r. 1644–1661), Kangxi (r. 1662–1722), and Yongzheng (r. 1722–1735) to develop and then institutionalize power arrangements that combined, contained, and elicited the cooperation of Chinese and Manchu elites while simultaneously maximizing central prerogatives. This system of power, the Qing autocracy, gradually emerged in the course of processes of political conflict, institutional reconfiguration, and cultural synthesis.

## The Qing Autocracy

Wakeman characterized power arrangements under the first Qing emperor as a blend of "Manchu tribal personalism and Chinese imperial patrimonialism."[59]

While attempting to curb the power of Manchu nobles by relying on Chinese officials, Shunzhi sought to undercut patronage networks and factional groupings among palace officials by means of active personal rulership.[60] Since "political factionalism at the capital was a manifestation of the literati's social organization in the provinces, which in turn protected the gentry's economic interests at the local level," the emperor also attempted to constrain the privileges of landholding elites at the local level.[61] In the succeeding Kangxi and Yongzheng periods, this attempt to concentrate power and maximize state control was extended and made more systematic.

The coterie of Manchu aristocrats who came to power after Shunzhi's death also sought to minimize Chinese political influence by means of concentration and control mechanisms; at the same time they introduced important innovations in the exercise of central power. Whereas Ming rulers, and Shunzhi also, had relied on eunuchs to bypass the scholar-official establishment, the Oboi regents utilized Chinese bond servants and bannermen to perform a range of extrabureaucratic administrative, control, and surveillance functions.[62] Personal servants were also used to staff the Imperial Household, a secret institution that controlled major revenue sources for the private use of the emperor. While retaining orthodox examination and official appointment procedures, the regents shook the system up: Regular paths of promotion were deemphasized in favor of performance-based evaluations, the content of official examinations was changed and simplified, degree quotas were reduced, and personnel turnover was accelerated.[63] This attempt to decrease the size and increase the efficiency of officialdom was accompanied by a fierce attack on Chinese landholding elites at the local level. On assuming power in 1661, the regents determined to deal conclusively with tax arrears and tax evasion in the affluent and always recalcitrant Jiangnan region. When provincial and local administrators were pressured to meet their full tax quotas and encountered the usual resistance, an unprecedented crackdown ensued: Thousands of local notables were arrested, interrogated, imprisoned, and humiliated.[64] The Oboi crackdown was overtly coercive and punitive, and there was no effort to enlist the cooperation or secure the compliance of elites in Jiangnan.

In contrast, the power arrangements subsequently established under Kangxi and Yongzheng simultaneously subjected Chinese and Manchu elites to high levels of central control and elicited their cooperation. The first decades of Kangxi's reign were taken up with the destruction of the primary threat to the new Qing state: regionally based warlord power. At the same time, this period witnessed the further refinement of a powerful set of concentration and control mechanisms. In the evolving Qing autocracy, we can discern the interplay of the emperor's personal style of political leadership, Manchu methods of rule, and the still powerful political and institutional legacy of the Ming.

Kangxi was a true personal ruler. He individually interviewed thousands of officials; regularly held audiences for thousands more; personally supervised the examination, appointment, and promotion of all top officials; maintained close contact with and watched over deputies and officials throughout the empire by means of a confidential communication and control system; conducted numerous tours of inspection in the southern Chinese heartland; and led several important military expeditions.[65] In the manner of the early Ming emperors, Kangxi was thus a dynamic practitioner of autocratic personal rulership. Furthermore, the emperor retained and refined organizational changes introduced under Shunzhi and the Oboi regents. While cultivating a style of "Manchu tribal personalism," the emperor continued to rely on Chinese bond servants instead of eunuchs and developed the Imperial Household into a separate, centrally controlled bureaucracy. Unlike the Oboi regents, whose sinophobia undercut their political effectiveness, Kangxi appointed a mix of Chinese bannermen, Manchus, and Chinese as officials, thereby giving all these key groups a stake in the system while preventing any single group from accumulating significant powers.[66] Finally, the power arrangements of the early Qing autocracy drew on the Ming legacy. Under Kangxi, the concentration of power in the hands of the emperor was reinforced and made more effective; whereas the temporary dispatch of central plenipotentiaries into the provinces was a Ming device, this practice was extended and formalized in the Qing system.[67]

Kangxi's concentration and control devices were refined and institutionalized by one of his sons, the Yongzheng emperor. Under Yongzheng, three existing power-restructuring patterns were accelerated: The efficiency and autonomy of central decisionmaking and policy implementation were further strengthened; administrative structures and fiscal practices at the central, regional, and local levels were reformed and made more systematic; and real or potential centers of competing political and military power were either destroyed or conclusively subjected to central bureaucratic controls.

Beatrice S. Bartlett showed how Yongzheng "intensified the role of the monarch as administrator" by transforming the Grand Council into a powerful mechanism of personal rulership, wherein the emperor was able to "rule autocratically, coordinating high policy in his own hands with the assistance of a select handful of inner-court advisers."[68] Autocratic power was further enhanced by refinements in communications. Kangxi's confidential communication and control system was expanded massively under Yongzheng and came to function as a source of detailed information, a tool for organizational reform and policy implementation, and a far-reaching mode of imperial surveillance.[69] According to Bartlett, the number of documents in the secret palace memorial system increased tenfold from the last thirteen years of the Kangxi reign to the thirteen-year Yongzheng period "from approximately 2,500 to 25,000, statistics that indicate a change of substantial magnitude."[70] This bypassing of orthodox official decisionmaking channels represented a familiar pattern; Yongzheng simply reinforced and extended "the consistent tendency in the later imperial period for Chinese rulers to replace bureaucratically routinized offices with new ad hoc secretariats."[71]

Yongzheng mounted an especially vigorous and effective effort to reform administrative procedures in the critical arena of fiscal control and tax collection. As previously discussed, although a certain level of "squeeze" was necessary to cover "management fees" in late imperial China, the propensity of officialdom to collude with local elites in avoiding taxes, appropriating revenue, and mercilessly milking the rural population constantly threatened to disrupt the balance between "state finances" and the "people's livelihood."[72] As Madeleine Zelin noted, the early Manchu rulers were aware that official misconduct at the local level undercut dynastic legitimacy along with state revenues and were thus moved to action by the "belief that the corruption of Han officials was the main threat to an almost sacred bond between the dynasty and the people."[73] Yongzheng sought to curb resource appropriation at the local level by formalizing the informal system of "customary exactions," by reforming tax collection procedures, and by restricting the privileges of local notables. Customary fees and gratuities were legalized and reduced, official salaries were supplemented by stipends entitled "silver for the cultivation of incorruptibility" (*yang lian yin*), and a variety of service obligations and taxes were merged into a single tax.[74] By rationalizing a capricious informal system, these reforms sought to "relieve the local population of the burden of indiscriminate surcharges previously levied on the pretext of supporting local administration."[75] Yongzheng also imposed limits on the petitionary rights and tax exemptions of the privileged orders, which he warned to abstain from their time-honored practices of proxy tax remittance and influence peddling.[76]

Finally, Yongzheng presided over the elimination of the last serious challenge to the centralized power of the Qing state—the "feudal" autonomy of the Manchu aristocracy. Even Kangxi was periodically forced to contend with the ambitions of powerful Manchu nobles, who still commanded semi-independent military formations and were capable of mounting formidable political challenges. These competing centers of power were finally reined in with the same concentration and control mechanisms that Yongzheng successfully imposed on other important political actors.[77]

The Qing system achieved its greatest successes in the eighteenth century, a remarkable period of external security, internal stability, economic and fiscal vitality, and population growth.[78] These accomplishments must be understood in light of the restructuring of power realized under Kangxi and Yongzheng.[79] As Susan Naquin and Evelyn S. Rawski noted, "The eighteenth century was a period of surplus revenues for the Qing state: bulging treasuries and a fat Privy Purse, the product not only of peace and prosperity but also of the successful tightening of control over tax remittances from the provinces under Yongzheng."[80] It was the signal accomplishment of the early Qing rulers to erect a system of power that simultaneously maximized state control of elites and elicited their active cooperation. We have seen that the power- and resource-appropriating propensities of the privileged orders were a perennial source of conflict and instability; yet these elites performed vital administrative and control functions. The early Qing rulers successfully sought to hold predatory elite impulses in check while eliciting and rewarding cooperative behavior.

The Qing system achieved this complex policy goal with an adroit mix of formal and informal power. Formal power was the exclusive preserve of the center, and the power of the emperor was absolute in theory. In practice, of course, central power was limited. The small size of the civil service, the even smaller size of the Manchu ruling group, and the huge size of the mass population, which grew much larger in the eighteenth century, meant that local landholding and degree-holding groups necessarily shouldered major administrative responsibilities and wielded considerable authority. But the extensive de facto powers of local elites were never formalized.[81] The mature Qing autocracy concentrated formal decisionmaking power in the hands of the emperor and his inner circle and thereby inhibited the formation of real or potential centers of competing power. Yet by granting subordinate elites extensive informal powers and setting these groups apart from the masses through formal privileges and exemptions, the system elicited elite political loyalty and vital services.

The power arrangements of the Qing rested on principles of concentration and control. By means of systematic power restructuring, central rulers in eighteenth-century China were able to realize impressive political, administrative, fiscal, and economic accomplishments. In the nineteenth century, this system of power began to erode and decline. As internal processes of power and resource appropriation accelerated and external military and technological pressures intensified, the Qing system broke down and finally collapsed.

## Decentralized Power and Resource Appropriation

The institutional deterioration of the Chinese state began before the close of the eighteenth century and did not end with the fall of the Qing dynasty in 1911. Processes of power devolution set in motion in the late Qing period continued to accelerate throughout the Republican era and were reversed only with the emergence and consolidation of the Chinese Communist state. As with the fall of the Ming, attention must first be focused on the internal origins of the Qing deterioration and collapse.

The foreign incursions of the nineteenth century were preceded by increasingly pervasive processes of decentralized power and resource appropriation, and the resulting erosion of central political and economic power undercut the ability of the Qing state to more effectively respond to outside threats. The devolution and erosion of central power were first manifested in the areas of military organization and fiscal control and became evident during the major White Lotus Rebellion of 1796–1803.[82] Over the course of this rebellion, processes of local militarization burst forth that would soon undercut and finally destroy the power arrangements of the Qing system. Local militia—irregular military formations raised, financed, and led by local elites—were officially sanctioned and played the decisive part in defeating the White Lotus rebels.[83] Yet official toleration of potential centers of competing power was a sharp break with established Qing practice; organized military operations had heretofore always been the exclusive preserve of the state. How did the power-concentrating principles and practices of the Qing autocracy become altered in the late eighteenth and the nineteenth centuries?

By 1800, the political vitality and power-restructuring spirit of the Kangxi and Yongzheng periods were a distant memory. From the top to the bottom, in the institutions of the state and at the village level, circumstances had slowly changed for the worse by the end of the remarkably long and generally prosperous and stable reign of the Qianlong emperor (r. 1736–1795). At court, the dynamic mechanisms of personal rulership had long since succumbed to familiar processes of bureaucratic routinization and power appropriation. Bartlett noted the "transformation from the autocracy of earlier reigns to the monarchical-conciliar form of government" and observed that "the new secret inner-court communications system, which has been viewed as having been an important prop for eighteenth century autocrats, in fact had chiefly enhanced the power of only the Kangxi and Yongzheng emperors, after which time it came as much to enhance the influence of its managers, the Grand Council."[84] The closing years of the Qianlong period witnessed the rise to power of a scandalously corrupt court favorite, the young Manchu guards officer Heshen (1750–1799), and the rot that soon permeated the imperial apparatus contributed in no small measure to the incapacity of regular Qing troops during the White Lotus Rebellion.[85]

But the decline of the Qing system did not stem solely from waning vitality at the top, for the system was also a victim of its own successes. China in the eighteenth century experienced a massive population boom, the by-product of a century of internal peace and prosperity following the imposition of the Qing political and social order. By 1800, the penalty for success was being felt in the form of intensified population pressure on the land, weakened administrative and control capacities in the countryside, and widespread popular revolts and rebellions.[86] Indeed, the limits of Qing power restructuring became increasingly evident over the course of the eighteenth century, as "the Qing system soon became so vast and complex that it was hard to carry out any policy at a distance."[87]

Political incapacity at the top and the erosion of local control steadily undercut the cooperative relationship between the Qing state and Chinese elites. Although official toleration of irregular local militia was a radical departure from orthodox Qing practices, the state retained essential control of these organizations during the White Lotus Rebellion.[88] Yet the very existence of local militia was tangible evidence of the deterioration of central power capacities. These weaknesses were fully exposed during the Taiping Rebellion (1850–1864), a devastating cataclysm that almost destroyed the Qing dynasty outright and from which the system never recovered. When imperial armies were unable to stem the rebel tide, the government was again forced to rely on irregular local and regional military formations; at the same time, local populations militarized to fend off government troops, bandits, or rebels.[89] As before, indigenous military forces proved especially effective because of their familiarity with the local terrain and social structure and their superior leadership and esprit de corps; such forces achieved major successes against the Taipings and provided the winning edge on the imperial side.[90] But these victories came only at the price of further damage to the political authority and fiscal integrity of the Qing system.

In the desperate struggle against rebellion, the Qing state officially endorsed all loyalist military formations and granted them extensive military, judicial, and fiscal powers. Most important, these rapidly proliferating regionally based armies and local militias were empowered to levy taxes to fund their operations; in many areas the situation was so chaotic that local militia bureaus took over the tax collection process.[91] Once victory was realized, however, local and regional power holders did not readily relinquish their newly acquired authority. Instead, these now-formalized political, judicial, fiscal, and military powers were used to more vigorously enforce the interests and privileges of local elites in the villages.[92] By the closing decades of the nineteenth century, the social forces that the concentration and control mechanisms of the Ming and Qing autocracies had been designed to contain were loose. Once in motion, this centrifugal devolution of power accelerated, a process that came to an end only when the traditional political and social order was destroyed by revolution and Chinese communism in the twentieth century.

Internal crisis was accentuated by the aggressive advent of industrialized foreign predators. Whether the Qing system at the height of its vigor could have fended off the imperialist challenge is open to question; in any case increasing external pressures coincided with and exacerbated the already declining capacity of the Chinese state to tap local and regional resources for national purposes. Yet as Philip A. Kuhn remarked, "The modernizing nation requires . . . the promotion of economic growth and national power. . . . Local energies have to be enlisted in a new way: one which will call forth the required amount of willing involvement, and at the same time weld local energies into national programs."[93] As in the seventeenth century, the inability of the Qing state to maintain internal order and combat external threats raised basic questions about the Chinese political order, and in the closing decades of the imperial era two responses emerged. On the one hand, the Qing state reluctantly and not very capably undertook a series of organizational, economic, and educational reforms.[94] These ranged from the "Self-Strengthening" movement of the 1860s, through which Qing officials sought to copy, master, and themselves deploy the advanced industrial and military technology of the West, to a complex of sweeping institutional reforms in the 1900s. But these efforts, problematic in any case, were undercut by accelerating processes of decentralized power and resource appropriation.

On the other hand, critics of the Qing found the answer to China's ills in more decentralization and power devolution. Explicitly drawing on the *fengjian* thinkers of the Ming-Qing transition, "statecraft" advocate Feng Guifen (1809–1874) argued that the solution to problems of internal disorder, economic and technological backwardness, and declining systemic vitality lay in increased gentry self-government. Feng advanced a familiar argument: Because imperial officials were too far removed from local concerns and conditions, national revitalization depended on a new coalition of committed and knowledgeable urban and rural leaders capable of eliciting and directing local energies and enthusiasm.[95] Almost a century later, this "new coalition" would come in the form of a radical restructuring and reconsolidation of central power by revolution and communism; yet a string of disasters around the turn of the century appeared to lend credence to Feng's statecraft argument.

While China suffered successive defeats at the hands of foreign predators, the Japanese victory in the Russo-Japanese War of 1904–1905 demonstrated that an Asian nation could stand up to a Western imperial power. In the view of many educated Chinese, Japan's innovative adaptation of certain parliamentary institutions contrasted with the absence of such bodies in China, and the idea took hold that a more representative political system was the key to China's national revitalization. In the 1900s, demands for a constitution and provincial assemblies mounted; this movement, which Joseph W. Esherick termed "the institutional expression of the political power of the urban reformist elite," set the stage for the final destruction of the Qing system.[96]

The creation of a constitution and the establishment of provincial assemblies had the unintended effect of completing the estrangement between the Qing state and Chinese regional and local elites. As Wakeman put it, "From the dynasty's point of view, the bureaus and assemblies were ultimately intended to build national unity without surrendering imperial sovereignty. To the provincial gentry, on the other hand, they seemed designed to facilitate the transfer of considerable local and national power into their own hands."[97] While institutional changes deepened the chasm between state and society, ambitious and expensive reform programs only intensified popular political and social discontent. As the government attempted to introduce a new educational system, modernize the army, and create new industries and infrastructure, the closing years of the dynasty were marked by the proliferation of new and more onerous taxes. In the Revolution of 1911, popular outrage fused with Chinese nationalism and the increasingly assertive demands of provincial elites and swept aside Manchu rule, the Qing system, and the Chinese imperial order.[98]

## Power Devolution and the Nationalist
## Default of Authority

If the Revolution of 1911 represented the victory of regional and local Chinese elites over the Qing state, this restructuring of power would in four tumultuous decades culminate in the total destruction of the victors themselves. The predatory regimes that emerged in the warlord period of the 1910s and 1920s were tragic testimony to the dangers that arise when elite groups at local and regional levels are freed from central controls and constraints.[99] As warlord armies built and defended territorial power bases through incessant low-level warfare, their "exploitative tax systems" and "unscrupulous currency policies" "conspired to disrupt beyond repair the social fabric and economic equilibrium of traditional agrarian China."[100] In the villages, "local bullies and evil gentry" formed alliances with regional power holders and engaged in an unchecked orgy of revenue appropriation, rent and fee extortion, and tax evasion.[101] Prasenjit Duara termed this process one of "state involution," whereby "the formal structures of the state grow simultaneously with informal structures," the state is then unable to control these informal structures, and "informal groups become an uncontrollable power in local society."[102] Understood in light of the argument advanced in these pages, the early decades of the twentieth century witnessed the further extension and apogee of processes of decentralized power and resource appropriation.

The fiscal and political crises of the Qing system and their social and economic consequences were only fully manifested in the early decades of the twentieth century. Whereas processes of local militarization funded by revenue levied by increasingly autonomous local elites undercut the Qing system in the nineteenth century, these processes accelerated in the warlord period and created a fiscal, political, and social crisis of catastrophic proportions. Militarist regimes taxed unmercifully, plundered imperial famine relief granaries, and seized grain that peasants had saved for seed or emergencies, while in the villages the population was beset by what Ralph Thaxton termed "immoral landlordism," as rural elites abandoned all pretense of Confucian paternalism and relied on armed coercion to enforce their prerogatives and demands.[103] As Thaxton detailed, these fiscal and political pressures combined with natural disasters in the 1920s to produce a staggering social crisis. Through large swaths of rural China, peasants by the hundreds of thousands migrated, fled, or were uprooted by famine, war, and intensified exploitation; while tens of thousands died of starvation, other peasants turned en masse to banditry, theft, the sale of children, and prostitution.[104] In a detailed investigation of processes of social and economic change in North China during this time, Philip C.C. Huang clearly linked the "pervasive semiproletarianization" of the peasantry to the increased fiscal burdens imposed by county governments of "questionable legitimacy" and "powerful absentee landlords."[105] Along with the usual proliferation of banditry, this period witnessed extensive processes of local militarization and self-defense mobilization at the village level.

Why was the Nationalist regime unable to reverse accelerating processes of decentralized power and resource appropriation? Of course, Kuomintang (KMT) leaders were fully aware that national unification and the reestablishment of central authority were imperative. In the course of the Northern Expedition of 1926–1927, the Nationalists vigorously attacked the military and political power of regionally based warlords and forced many to recognize KMT central authority; in the 1930s the central government attempted to erect administrative structures in the countryside and effect political and fiscal "penetration" at the village level.[106] As the extreme fiscal weakness of the Chinese state during the "Nanking decade" of 1927–1937 attested, however, these efforts were essentially unsuccessful and ended in failure. The KMT regime throughout the Nanking period depended on a few narrow revenue sources, with customs duties, the salt tax, and excise taxes applied to the products of Chinese-owned modern industry making up the vast bulk of state receipts.[107] Unable to collect the land tax or to expand the tax base, the Nationalist government regularly ran large budget deficits, which it financed in increasingly costly, reckless, and destabilizing ways.

The fiscal weakness of the central state stemmed from the feeble power arrangements of the KMT regime. In the Nanking decade, no genuine destruction of competing centers of political power occurred at the regional or local level. Seeking to attain "power by compromise," and ever fearful of the processes of social revolution being fanned by the Chinese communists, Chiang Kai-shek cut deals with the more powerful warlords, most of whom "were simply taken into the Kuomintang at the top level," and set out to destroy the communist threat.[108] Although KMT forces did attack this competing center of revolutionary power with considerable success, the regime's failure or inability to control traditional power holders in the villages and provinces fueled the decentralized processes of power and resource appropriation that spelled its doom in the end.[109]

KMT power attainment by compromise, whereby the central government did not challenge regional power blocs or interfere in the affairs of rural elites in exchange for formal pledges of loyalty and the maintenance of the political status quo in the villages, constituted the core of what Suzanne Pepper termed the regime's "default of authority."[110] Whereas the Qing state had relied on local degree-holding and landholding elites to enforce order in the villages, so, too, had powerful concentration and control mechanisms harnessed these forces with considerable initial success. In contrast, the Nationalist government allied with traditional elites at the regional and local levels without ever imposing a comparable degree of political or institutional control, an arrangement that immediately placed the regime in an insoluble bind. Even though decentralized processes of power and resource appropriation siphoned off vital tax revenues at the district *(xian)* level and below, the central authorities were unable and unwilling to forcefully attack these activities since the appropriators supported the regime politically and maintained "order" in the villages.[111] Unable to maintain fiscal control at the local level, the Nationalist government was forced to rely on a variety of predatory and destabilizing financial practices.[112] When the Japanese invaded China proper and drove the KMT out of its political and financial base in the Yangtze Delta, these practices spiraled out of control, and government finances became almost totally dependent on the printing press. As a result, "the average level of prices rose two thousand times between 1937 and August, 1945" and during the civil war period (1946–1949) ballooned to levels unprecedented before or since in China or anywhere else in the world.[113]

By compromising and allying with regional power blocs and local bullies and evil gentry, the Nationalists left unchecked the corrosive social and political forces that the Ming and Qing autocracies had been designed to contain and control. If the undercutting of central rule by assertive local and regional elites was a familiar phenomenon, this process was compounded by the Nationalist regime's inability or unwillingness to forcefully combat resource appropriation by the officials of the party and state itself. Even at the height of the KMT's power in 1935, when the communists had been driven from their bases in south-central China and before the Japanese invasion of China proper, the Nationalist government was rotten with corruption from top to bottom. As state banks issued government paper at up to 40 percent interest to bondholders who were high state officials and often related to Chiang as well, China's "central" rulers themselves profited from and contributed to the fiscal bind. Under the guise of state control of the economy, "various government-controlled sectors of the economy became the private domain of certain members of the Kuomintang, who built vast personal fortunes from government monopolies and the management of public funds."[114]

Of course, rampant corruption at the top bred similarly rapacious behavior throughout KMT officialdom. When Nationalist officials reoccupied Shanghai after the defeat of Japan in 1945, they engaged in a gigantic bout of profiteering, extortion, and outright theft, all on the pretext of rounding up traitors and recovering state property. Their depredations were so extreme that Chiang himself heard of it and personally ordered a stop; but, as Pepper noted, "no concerted actions were taken either by central or local authorities to enforce Chiang's wishes."[115] With Nationalist rule already undercut by predatory local elites in the countryside, the blatant corruption and increasingly predatory behavior of KMT officials in the cities quickly and irrevocably vitiated that rule in the years following World War II.

## Concentration, Control, and the Rise of Chinese Communism

It was the historic accomplishment of the CCP to reverse the decentralized power and resource appropriation processes of the late Qing and Republican periods by rebuilding state power at the local level. Amid the corruption, misery, and breakdown of the Republican period, the Chinese Communists developed and erected an institutional alternative to the crumbled imperial order. This revolutionary reconfiguration of power rebuilt the political constraints, infrastructural foundations, and social controls of the mature Qing system, while at the same time addressing in a new and revolutionary way the political, social, and economic problems that had destroyed the imperial order. These achievements were a direct function of the capacity of the CCP to concentrate political power and to control social forces. Unlike the KMT, the Chinese Communists consistently combated and sought to destroy competing centers of power, both in the villages under their control and in the party and state system they were constructing. In contrast to the imperial concentration and control system, communist officials interacted with the peasantry in the course of establishing the new system of state power. Indeed, it was the interplay and mutual reinforcement of CCP power-building processes and the aspirations of China's rural masses that underlay the spectacular communist victory in 1949. This fusion of Marxist-Leninist ideology and organization with popular energies gave rise to a state system that governed and restructured power in a manner both historically unprecedented and fully reminiscent of vigorous Ming and Qing rule.

That the Chinese Revolution represented a synthesis of popular upheaval and Marxism-Leninism is abundantly clear. But how did this synthesis work? In seeking a systematic explanation for communist revolution, Western social scientists first focused on the centralized leadership, mobilizational capacity, and political vision of Leninist parties. These qualities enabled communists to form themselves into an organizational weapon, to institutionalize destabilized social forces, and to make revolutionary transformations by breaking through the political, social, and cultural obstacles of existing systems.[116] Barrington Moore Jr. challenged this voluntarist image of communist revolution in his *Social Origins of Dictatorship and Democracy*. Focusing on the causal importance of rural social structure in revolutionary upheavals, especially the relationship between landed elites and the peasantry, Moore argued that revolutionary activities were historically circumscribed by existing political, economic, and social structures.[117]

Building on Moore's argument, Skocpol in *States and Social Revolutions* unequivocally rejected the idea that social revolutions are "made" by revolutionary parties and attempted to articulate a "structural perspective" on the French, Russian, and Chinese Revolutions.[118] In her view:

> The extent to which peasants have had such internal leverage (i.e., insurrectionary potential), particularly during historical political crises of agrarian states, is explained by structural and situational conditions which affect: 1) the degrees and kinds of solidarity in peasant communities; 2) the degrees of peasant autonomy from direct day to day supervision and control by landlords and their agents; and 3) the relaxation of state coercive sanctions against peasant revolts.[119]

Thus, societies most likely to experience "widespread and irreversible peasant revolts against landlords" are characterized by high levels of community solidarity and autonomy and landlords who depend on state power to control popular unrest.[120] These were precisely the conditions that did *not* prevail in late Qing and Republican China.

Skocpol's insistence on the secondary significance of communist political organization was echoed by a scholar far more familiar than she was with the complex history of revolutionary China. Thaxton's richly textured *China Turned Rightside Up* documented an important historical fact: The CCP rise to power was an interactive process, over the course of which communist methods and goals were powerfully influenced by peasant aspirations and values.[121] After making this point, Thaxton then presented an overblown and romanticized picture of peasant insurrection in the Republican period. In his discussion of the Red Spear movement in north-central China in the 1920s, Thaxton spoke of "the peasants' attempt to pull back from all outside authority and to define their own liberation without outside moral domination by militarists and parties."[122] To win peasant support, CCP cadres in the 1930s therefore had to identify themselves "with the promise of world without the state" and to develop a political work style "in harmony with peasant conceptions of a nonhierarchical order."[123]

The historical realities of the Red Spear movement confirm neither Skocpol's notions of peasant autonomy and landlord dependence on the state nor Thaxton's belief in the primacy of nonhierarchical peasant values and aspirations. The movement was indeed a powerful insurrection; in addition to forcefully resisting *unjust* taxes and conscription, the Red Spears developed their own system of law and taxation.[124] But this armed peasant secret society fit the pattern of gentry-dominated local militarization characteristic of the late Qing and Republican periods and was controlled by local landed elites that sought no more than the restoration and stabilization of the traditional order.[125] Hence, "one finds no trace of opposition to the land rent, which in Henan (the center of the movement) could approach seventy percent of the harvest, at least not before political parties began to propagandize."[126] CCP leader Li Dazhao feared Red Spear conservatism and warned that the major obstacle to peasant revolution was the existence of village, local, and provincial loyalties that could be manipulated by warlords and gentry in the absence of communist leadership.[127] In Weber's terms, the Red Spear movement represented an instance of "traditionalist revolution," wherein opposition is directed not against the system but against a master who has failed to observe the traditional limits of his power.[128]

If the peasant insurrections of the 1920s were neither autonomous nor revolutionary, they were expressions of potentially explosive levels of popular discontent. In the 1930s and the 1940s, the energies and aspirations of China's rural masses were fused with CCP-sponsored concentration and control processes and channeled in revolutionary directions.

Despite the breakdown and increasingly precarious conditions of the late Qing and Republican periods, the grip of traditional elites remained firm. With their historic leadership and high culture roles reinforced by newly acquired political and military clout, local elites were able to deal with the restive but incoherent masses from positions of unassailable ideological and organizational strength. It was only when the Chinese Communists forcefully deployed top and bottom versus the middle power-restructuring methods in the villages that the ideological and organizational hegemony of the traditional order was undercut and finally destroyed. When the Red Army occupied an area for any length of time, a "revolutionary committee" was established under its armed protection; this "Soviet" protostate then organized a broad range of "mass organizations."[129] Under CCP leadership and control, these organizations engaged in a complex of power-restructuring activities that built communist power, subjected the traditional order to political and physical attack, and institutionalized mass energies and social upheaval.[130] The linchpin was agrarian revolution, a process that simultaneously undercut the economic base of the old order and vitiated its political and cultural hegemony, addressed the economic and social grievances of the impoverished majority and enlisted it on the side of the CCP, and built a resource and labor power base to support the war effort of the emerging communist state.[131] As Chinese commentators observed at the time, land reform enabled the communists "to put down roots in the villages and to grow strong."[132] While rebuilding state power at the local level, power restructuring in the villages destroyed at the source the social forces that had most tenaciously capitalized on the power devolution processes of the late Qing and Republican periods. In Chen Yung-fa's words, "The formation of peasant associations enabled the Party's peasant followers to enforce CCP economic programs at the expense of the old rural elite" and thereby "fundamentally changed rural power relations."[133]

At the same time, CCP-sponsored power restructuring in the villages created new forms of political power and social control. While actively allying with the masses to control and displace traditional elites, the Chinese Communists were able to transcend the limited horizons of the peasants and channel mass energies in revolutionary directions. Unlike some Western analysts, the communists had no illusions concerning the independent revolutionary potential of the peasantry and themselves quite openly termed the process of mass mobilization *fadong qunzhong*, "activating the masses."[134] As set forth in a CCP Central Committee "Resolution on Methods of Leadership" in 1943, "activation" of this type "means taking the views of the masses (unintegrated, unsystematized views) and subjecting them to concentration (they are transformed through research into concentrated systematized views), then going to the masses with propaganda and explanation in order to transform the views of the masses, and seeing these views are maintained by the masses and carried over into their activities."[135] Far from going along with peasant initiatives, the Chinese Communists consistently linked particularistic peasant concerns with their broader objectives of power building and social and economic transformation. This strategy was tremendously effective in World War II, when by combining programs of agrarian reform and patriotic resistance to Japan, the CCP was able to massively expand the territory and population under its control. In the succeeding civil war period, CCP work teams, according to Steven I. Levine, orchestrated the land revolution and pushed the attack on the traditional rural elite; when communist cadres were not in place, no significant mass upheavals occurred.[136]

If CCP-sponsored concentration and control processes were critical in destroying the old political, social, and institutional order and in structuring the eruption of mass energies, these mechanisms performed equally vital functions within the communist movement itself. As we see in Chapters 6, 7, and 8, the sociopolitical deportment of Chinese Communist officials would in time resemble that of their imperial and Nationalist predecessors. In the decade preceding the communist victory in 1949, however, the CCP evinced an impressive capacity for organizational control, bureaucratic discipline, and state building.

In 1941–1942, a fierce Japanese offensive and "scorched earth" policy drastically reduced the area under communist control while cutting the size of the Eight Route Army from four hundred thousand to three hundred thousand.[137] The CCP leadership reacted to these defeats with a major power-restructuring effort, the Rectification Campaign of 1942–1944. This campaign, which sometimes foreshadowed important aspects of the Cultural Revolution in the 1960s, sought to revitalize the party by strengthening central control, combating internal factional fragmentation, and reinforcing the relationship between party officials and the masses.

In the speech that launched the campaign, "Rectifying the Party's Workstyle," Mao argued that the CCP's shortcomings were both internal and external. Internally, "intra-party sectarianism" and "particularism" threatened a "centralized, unified party, pure and clean from top to bottom, with no factional struggles on questions of principle."[138] It was therefore imperative that all party officials, military and civil, new and old, upper and lower, transcend the "particular work under their own management" and recognize the party's system of "democratic centralism"; in this system, the minority obeyed the majority, the lower levels obeyed the higher levels, the particular obeyed the universal, and the entire party obeyed the Central Committee.[139] In a speech a few days later, "Oppose the Party Eight-Legged Essay," Mao argued that the external defects of the party stemmed from extreme formalism. Whereas detached bureaucratism and dogmatic Marxist-Leninist rhetoric were no better than Confucian formalism and rhetoric, the political effectiveness of the party and its ability to win popular support still depended on a fresh and lively leadership style, knowledge of practical social and political conditions, and avoidance of empty jargon and dictatorial attitudes.[140]

Mao's speeches linked the very survival of the communist movement to the improved control of officialdom. In the 1930s and the 1940s, Chinese Communist leaders consistently sought to combat the emergence of competing centers of power within the new party and state structures and argued that processes of bureaucratization and routinization would weaken the revolution and the popular support on which it depended. If the Chinese Communists were the ultimate beneficiaries of the decentralized processes of power and resource appropriation that had fatally undercut the Qing system and the Nationalist regime, CCP leaders were determined to avoid a similar fate. In the "crack troops and simple administration" and "to the villages" movements of 1942–1944, the Chinese Communists success-fully deployed a political strategy that strengthened central control of party and state officials, cut the size and "top-heaviness" of the bureaucracy, and mobilized mass energies by sending officials into the villages.[144] In the forthcoming discus-sion of the Great Leap Forward and the events of the Cultural Revolution espe-cially, we encounter several variants of this power-restructuring strategy, which seeks to promote organizational dynamism and vitality by exerting political pres-sure from the top and encouraging social movements at the mass level. We will see that attempts to apply the experience of the Yenan period in the 1950s and 1960s were problematic and even catastrophic. But it was the fusion of CCP-sponsored concentration and control processes with mass energies and aspirations that pro-pelled the communists to victory in 1949.[142]

## Notes

1. For an analysis of the uninterrupted domination of officials as a class, see Etienne Balazs, *Chinese Civilization and Bureaucracy* (New Haven: Yale University Press, 1965), 6–10. For totalitarian state domination in traditional China, see Karl A. Wittfogel, *Oriental Despotism* (New Haven: Yale University Press, 1957).

2. Albert Feuerwerker, *State and Society in Eighteenth-Century China: The Ch'ing Em-pire in Its Glory* (Ann Arbor: Center for Chinese Studies, University of Michigan, 1976), 76.

3. See Frederic Wakeman Jr., *The Fall of Imperial China* (New York: Free Press, 1975), 30.

4. Hok-lam Chan, "'Comprehensiveness' (*T'ung*) and 'Change' (*Pien*) in Ma Tuan-lin's Historical Thought," in Hok-lam Chan and William Theodore de Bary, eds., *Yuan Thought: Chinese Thought and Religion Under the Mongols* (New York: Columbia Univer-sity Press, 1982), 56–57.

5. Yang Lien-sheng, "Ming Local Administration," in Charles Hucker, ed., *Chinese Government in Ming Times: Seven Studies* (New York: Columbia University Press, 1969), 1. John E. Schrecker placed the *fengjian-junxian* dichotomy at the center of the argument in *The Chinese Revolution in Historical Perspective* (New York: Praeger, 1991). In contrast to the interactive view of Yang and myself, Schrecker saw the two modes as antithetical and focused his attention on linear transitions from one mode to the other.

6. William Theodore de Bary, "Introduction," in Chan and de Bary, eds., *Yuan Thought*, 1.

7. Jacques Gernet, *Daily Life in China on the Eve of the Mongol Invasion, 1250–1276* (Stanford: Stanford University Press, 1962), 16.

8. Joseph F. Fletcher Jr. argued that these methods of rule were not a Chinese creation. Rather, "these were the basic features of the later Chinese empire, and it was the Mongols who, in conquering the Chin (Jin) empire and adapting its institutional framework to their own requirements, extended these features to the whole of the Chinese subcontinent" ("Bloody Tanistry: Authority and Succession in the Ottoman, Indian Muslim, and Later Chinese Empires," unpublished conference paper; cited in R. Bin Wong, "China and World History," *Late Imperial China* 6, 2 [December 1985]:6).

9. Gernet, *Daily Life in China on the Eve of the Mongol Invasion*, 75, 76–91.

10. John D. Langlois Jr., "Introduction," in John D. Langlois Jr., ed., *China Under Mongol Rule* (Princeton: Princeton University Press, 1981), 12.

11. See Karl A. Wittfogel, "The Hereditary Privilege vs. Merit," in Johanna M. Menzel, ed., *The Chinese Civil Service* (Boston: Heath, 1963), 39–40, for a discussion of the Mongol effort to limit the number of high Chinese officials and restrict their hereditary privileges. See John D. Langlois Jr., "Yuan Political Thought," in Chan and de Bary, eds., *Yuan Thought*, 92–102, for an account of Chinese efforts to introduce a general code and Mongol resistance. As Langlois noted, "The Yuan abolition of the *lu* and the failure to introduce a replacement for it struck a blow at the traditional authority of the scholar-official" (102).

12. Frederick W. Mote, "Yuan and Ming," in K. C. Chang, ed., *Food in Chinese Culture: Anthropological and Historical Perspectives* (New Haven: Yale University Press, 1977), 205–207.

13. Morris Rossabi, "The Muslims in the Early Yuan Dynasty," in Langlois, ed., *China Under Mongol Rule,* 281. See Thomas T. Allsen, *Mongol Imperialism* (Berkeley and Los Angeles: University of California Press, 1987), for a discussion of population registration and taxation as vehicles for Mongol resource mobilization in China, Russia, and the Islamic lands.

14. David M. Farquhar, "Structure and Function in the Yuan Imperial Government," in Langlois, ed., *China Under Mongol Rule,* 50–51.

15. See John Dardess, *Conquerors and Confucians: Aspects of Political Change in Late Yuan China* (New York: Columbia University Press, 1973), chaps. 6, 7, for an account of the increasingly chaotic and destructive processes of factionalism, regionalism, and violent political strife that characterized the late Yuan period.

16. Rossabi, "The Muslims in the Early Yuan Dynasty," in Langlois, ed., *China Under Mongol Rule,* 279.

17. Langlois, "Introduction," 16.

18. Hence, "the Mongol and *se-mu* (Central Asian) conquerors, stated T'ai-tsu, had never fully understood the 'Way of the Former Kings'; they instead acted for selfish ends, running the bureaucracy as though it were a private preserve for the benefit of their own kind. . . . They lacked the 'impartial mind of empire,' and were thus easily deceived or bribed by corrupt lower officials" (John W. Dardess, *Confucianism and Autocracy: Professional Elites in the Founding of the Ming Dynasty* [Berkeley and Los Angeles: University of California Press, 1983], 186).

19. Edward L. Dreyer identified five general areas in which early Ming practices "correspond to Yuan attitudes and practices" and "contradict Confucian prescriptions that had become established by the end of the Song (960–1276), the last native dynasty." Early Ming rulers (1) actively engaged in military conquest, (2) promoted foreign trade, (3) promoted the preponderance of military over civil officials, (4) made many official appointments based on heredity, and (5) resisted the revival of the civil service examination system (*Early Ming China: A Political History, 1355–1435* [Stanford: Stanford University Press, 1982], 2–4). At the same time, John W. Dardess showed that Confucian thinkers, alarmed at the chaos and breakdown of the late Yuan period, provided much of the theoretical rationale for the establishment of the Ming autocracy, which Ming Taizu then extended ruthlessly and harshened horribly (*Confucianism and Autocracy,* esp. 105–118).

20. Charles O. Hucker, *The Ming Dynasty: Its Origins and Evolving Institutions* (Ann Arbor: Center for Chinese Studies, University of Michigan, 1976), 68.

21. Albert Chan, *The Glory and Fall of the Ming Dynasty* (Norman: University of Oklahoma Press, 1982), 22. According to court records, Ming Taizu read and ruled on 1,660 documents dealing with 3,391 different matters in one eight-day period (Dreyer, *Early Ming China,* 132).

22. Ho Ping-ti, *The Ladder of Success in Imperial China* (New York: Columbia University Press, 1962), 216.

23. Hucker, *The Ming Dynasty,* 67; John R. Watt, *The District Magistrate in Late Imperial China* (New York: Columbia University Press, 1972), 117.

24. Ray Huang, *1587, a Year of No Significance* (New Haven: Yale University Press, 1981), 19–21.

25. Hucker, *The Ming Dynasty,* 68. The systematic use of terror to control officialdom is another example of Inner Asian nomadic influence. Taizu continued the Mongol practice of "court beating," in which officials were publicly beaten with wooden clubs, often to death and always with crippling effects. This torture, which the entire court observed, was introduced in the "Sino-barbarian" Sui dynasty (518–618). See Chan, *The Glory and Fall of the Ming Dynasty,* 14–15, for a graphic account.

26. Chan, *The Glory and Fall of the Ming Dynasty,* 134.

27. Romeyn Taylor, "Yuan Origins of the Wei-so System," in Hucker, ed., *Chinese Government in Ming Times,* 36–37.

28. Chan, *The Glory and Fall of the Ming Dynasty,* 138.

29. Ibid., 75.

30. Charles O. Hucker, *The Traditional Chinese State in Ming Times (1368–1644)* (Tucson: University of Arizona Press, 1961), 40–43.

31. Dardess, *Confucianism and Autocracy,* 192–193.

32. Taizu especially took a personal interest in all aspects of administration and was quick to address perceived problems. As Ray Huang noted, "Of the twelve ministers of revenue who served him only three are known to have left office gracefully. The rest were jailed, dismissed, banished, or executed" ("Fiscal Administration During the Ming Dynasty," in Hucker, ed., *Chinese Government in Ming Times,* 78).

33. Charles O. Hucker, "The Tung-lin Movement of the Late Ming Period," in John K. Fairbank, ed., *Chinese Thought and Institutions* (Chicago: University of Chicago Press, 1957), 138–139.

34. Ray Huang, *China: A Macro History* (Armonk, N.Y.: M. E. Sharpe, 1988), 168.

35. Wakeman, *The Fall of Imperial China,* 99.

36. In Max Weber's classic formulation, "It is the fate of charisma to recede before the powers of tradition . . . after it has entered the permanent structures of social action. This waning of charisma generally indicates the diminishing importance of individual action" (*Economy and Society* [Berkeley and Los Angeles: University of California Press, 1978], vol. 2, 1148–1149).

37. Huang, *China,* 168.

38. Hucker, *The Traditional Chinese State in Ming Times,* 68.

39. The interrelation of wealth, education, success in the examination system, and official appointment is a complex question I cannot consider in any detail in these pages. Although wealth was not the ultimate source of power in late imperial China, and bureaucrats wielded de jure power, wealth could be used to purchase official appointments, to purchase high-quality tutoring, to fund private academies, or simply to finance years of study. Once office was attained, moreover, there was always the opportunity and expecta-

tion of massive personal and familial enrichment. Yet large fortunes were vulnerable to imperial confiscation. See Ho, *The Ladder of Success in Imperial China,* 43–48.

40. Huang, *1587, a Year of No Significance;* chaps. 1–4 detail the growing frustration of the Wanli emperor at the hands of court officialdom, which culminated in his withdrawal from state functions altogether.

41. Beatrice S. Bartlett, *Monarchs and Ministers: The Grand Council in Mid-Ch'ing China, 1723–1820* (Berkeley and Los Angeles: University of California Press, 1991), 28.

42. Feuerwerker, *State and Society in Eighteenth-Century China,* 19.

43. Despite Taizu's attempt to undercut their power, landholders in the Jiangnan region hung onto their properties and mounted a determined tax resistance effort, which by 1430 had produced massive tax arrears. As Huang noted, "The basic cause for tax delinquency was that 'affluent households refused to pay the surcharges, which had to be collected exclusively from the poor'" ("Fiscal Administration During the Ming Dynasty," 107–108).

44. Watt, *The District Magistrate in Late Imperial China,* 151–152.

45. Jerry Dennerline, "Fiscal Reform and Local Control: The Entry-Bureaucratic Alliance Survives the Conquest," in Frederic Wakeman Jr. and Carolyn Grant, eds., *Conflict and Control in Late Imperial China* (Berkeley and Los Angeles: University of California Press, 1975), 93.

46. Ibid., 194. The Single Whip reform marked the apex of the Zhang Juzheng period (1572–1582). This dictatorial and efficiency-minded grand secretary attempted to reinvigorate the Ming state by putting pressure on officialdom and demanding better performance. In Charles O. Hucker's words, Zhang succeeded in "cowing both the emperor and officialdom into a state of well-disciplined alertness that had been lacking in government for more than a century" (*The Censorial System of Ming China* [Stanford: Stanford University Press, 1966], 153).

47. In Huang's view, "When Zhang Juzheng insisted that all districts make their tax payments in full, he actually put undue pressure on the Civil Service at the operational level . . . and abandoned indirect rule through the local gentry" (*1587, a Year of No Significance,* 63).

48. Frederic Wakeman Jr., *The Great Enterprise: The Manchu Reconstruction of Imperial Order in Seventeenth-Century China* (Berkeley and Los Angeles: University of California Press, 1985), vol. 1, 105–108. See Yuan Tsing, "Urban Riots and Disturbances," in Jonathan D. Spence and John E. Wills, eds., *From Ming to Ch'ing* (New Haven: Yale University Press, 1979), for an account of lower-level degree holders allying with workers to oppose, in most cases, eunuch tax commissioners.

49. Robert Crawford, "Zhang Juzheng's Confucian Legalism," in William Theodore de Bary, ed., *Self and Society in Ming Thought* (New York: Columbia University Press, 1970), 373.

50. Hucker, *The Censorial System of Ming China,* pp. 153–154; see chap. 5 for a detailed account of the interplay of the Zhang Juzheng reforms, Donglin factionalism and partisanship, and the Wei Zhongxian blood purge.

51. Ibid.

52. Wakeman, *The Great Enterprise,* vol. 1, 88–89.

53. Significantly, Li Zicheng, leader of the mass insurrection that toppled the Ming, was a former postal courier from Shanxi province; see Chan, *The Glory and Fall of the Ming Dynasty,* 338, 354.

54.  Dennerline, "Fiscal Reform and Local Control," 101–103.

55.  Political fragmentation and rampant factionalism continued to undercut the effectiveness of the Ming state even after the Manchus occupied Peking. See Lynn Struve, *The Southern Ming, 1644–1662* (New Haven: Yale University Press, 1984), 27–31, for an account of the sorry performance of the Ming resistance.

56.  Schrecker, *The Chinese Revolution in Historical Perspective*, 55. This author stressed the oppositional and quasi-revolutionary elements in *fengjian* thought and tried to develop a connection between its emphasis on decentralization and potential opposition to autocratic rule and the Chinese Revolution. This interpretation is questionable; the Chinese Revolution revitalized and reinforced structures of concentrated power and sociopolitical control.

57.  William Theodore de Bary, "Chinese Despotism and the Confucian Ideal: A Seventeenth-Century View," in Fairbank, ed., *Chinese Thought and Institutions*, 163–203. Like Schrecker, de Bary stressed the quasi-democratic, constitutional, and liberal potential in Huang Zongxi's thought.

58.  Frederic Wakeman Jr., "The Shun Interregnum of 1644," in Spence and Wills, eds., *From Ming to Ch'ing*, 74–76.

59.  Wakeman, *The Great Enterprise*, vol. 2, 1013.

60.  Ibid., 969–971, 1006–1009.

61.  Ibid., 1064.

62.  Robert B. Oxnam, *Ruling from Horseback: Manchu Politics in the Oboi Regency, 1661–1669* (Chicago: University of Chicago Press, 1975), 53. See Jonathan D. Spence, *Ts'ao Yin and the K'ang-hsi Emperor* (New Haven: Yale University Press, 1966), 7–11, for a classic discussion of the origins and role of Chinese bond servants and bannermen under the Manchus.

63.  Oxman, *Ruling from Horseback*, 83–88.

64.  Dennerline, "Fiscal Reform and Local Control," 110–112.

65.  Jonathan D. Spence, *Emperor of China* (New York: Vintage, 1975), chap. 2. Kangxi's personal touch was felt at court, in the provinces, at all levels of military and civil officialdom, and even in the adjudication of common criminal cases. See Silas H.L. Wu, *Communication and Imperial Control in China* (Cambridge, Mass.: Harvard University Press, 1970), for the definitive account of the confidential palace memorial system.

66.  Wakeman, *The Fall of Imperial China*, 98–99.

67.  Feuerwerker, *State and Society in Eighteenth-Century China*, 73.

68.  Bartlett, *Monarchs and Ministers*, 64–65.

69.  Wu, *Communication and Imperial Control in China*, chap. 7.

70.  Bartlett, *Monarchs and Ministers*, 50.

71.  Wakeman, *The Fall of Imperial China*, 98–99.

72.  Madeleine Zelin, *The Magistrate's Tael* (Berkeley and Los Angeles: University of California Press, 1984), 202.

73.  Ibid., 115. We see here a manifestation of the patriarchal bond between the ruler and the masses emphasized by Weber.

74.  Huang Pei, *Autocracy at Work: A Study of the Yongzheng Period, 1723–1735* (Bloomington: Indiana University Press, 1974), 246–258.

75.  Zelin, *The Magistrate's Tael*, 173.

76.  Huang, *Autocracy at Work*, 233. See Wang Yeh-chien, *Land Taxation in Imperial China, 1750–1911* (Cambridge, Mass.: Harvard University Press, 1973), 45–46, for a discussion of proxy remittance.

77. Huang, *Autocracy at Work,* 162.

78. The state-run system of public granaries, famine relief facilities, and economic stabilization mechanisms reached its peak of efficiency in the Yongzheng period. As Pierre-
Etienne Will showed, "The essential decisions were made in time after sufficient analysis of
the situation, and purchases and allocations of grain were made soon enough to avoid
waiting periods. . . . Here the bureaucracy managed to keep on top of the crisis" (*Bureaucracy and Famine in China* [Stanford: Stanford University Press, 1990], 86).

79. The Yongzheng tax reform, for example, was so successful that numerous tax officials in the mid-eighteenth century reported surplus revenue in addition to fulfillment of
normal tax quotas. By curbing irregular land tax surcharges, this reform both invigorated
central finances and reduced financial pressures on the general population (Wang, *Land
Taxation in Imperial China,* 68–69).

80. Susan Naquin and Evelyn S. Rawski, *Chinese Society in the Eighteenth Century* (New
Haven: Yale University Press, 1987), 219.

81. Ch'u T'ung-tsu, *Local Government in China Under the Ch'ing* (Cambridge, Mass.:
Harvard University Press, 1962), 198–199.

82. This rebellion was the most widespread and successful of a wave of popular rebellions propelled by millenarian White Lotus ideology; these upheavals began as early as
1768 and culminated in the Eight Trigram uprising of 1813. See Susan Naquin, *Millenarian
Rebellion in China* (New Haven: Yale University Press, 1976), 63–66.

83. Philip A. Kuhn, *Rebellion and Its Enemies in Late Imperial China* (Cambridge, Mass.:
Harvard University Press, 1980), chap. 2.

84. Bartlett, *Monarchs and Ministers,* 199, 278.

85. Jonathan D. Spence, *The Search for Modern China* (New York: Norton, 1990), 114–
115.

86. According to official figures, in 1749 there was on average one district magistrate
per 100,000 people, whereas by 1819 the average was one per 250,000. See Hsiao Kung-
chuan, *Rural China: Imperial Control in the Nineteenth Century* (Seattle: University of
Washington Press, 1960), 5. For a discussion of increasing population pressure in the land
in the eighteenth and early nineteenth centuries, see 380–382.

87. Naquin and Rawski, *Chinese Society in the Eighteenth Century,* 10. They further
noted that "the streamlining of the documentary flows to the emperor should not be taken
(as it frequently has) as proof that the rulers had achieved despotic control over the bureaucracy. The continuing bureaucratization resulted in the would-be despot being engulfed in a sea of paperwork and procedural consultation" (10).

88. Kuhn, *Rebellion and Its Enemies in Late Imperial China,* 62–63.

89. Processes of local militarization are delineated in Elizabeth Perry's account of the
Nien Rebellion (1851–1863), in which bandits and local populations came together in a
"common antagonism toward the state" (*Rebels and Revolutionaries in North China,
1845–1945* [Stanford: Stanford University Press, 1980], 96).

90. Kuhn, *Rebellion and Its Enemies in Late Imperial China,* 138–142.

91. James Polacheck, "Gentry Hegemony: Soochow in the T'ung-chih Restoration," in
Wakeman and Grant, eds., *Conflict and Control in Late Imperial China,* 228.

92. Kuhn, *Rebellion and Its Enemies in Late Imperial China,* 209–210. Edward A. Mc-
Cord presented a different view and showed how a prominent local family in Guizhou dissolved its militia forces when order was restored but revived them again when conditions
deteriorated in the late nineteenth and early twentieth centuries. Throughout these years,
however, "family military power" was used to guarantee and expand the economic and

political position of the lineage ("Local Military Power and Elite Formation: The Liu Family of Xingyi County, Guizhou," in Joseph W. Esherick and Mary Backus Rankin, eds., *Chinese Local Elites and Patterns of Dominance* [Berkeley and Los Angeles: University of California Press, 1990], 162–188).

93. Philip A. Kuhn, "Local Self-Government Under the Republic: Problems of Control, Autonomy, and Mobilization," in Wakeman and Grant, eds., *Conflict and Control in Late Imperial China*, 269.

94. The reforming efforts of the Qing state were complicated by the fragmentation and factionalization of the imperial power structure; the most vigorous proponent of official organizational and economic reform, Li Hongzhang, profited politically and financially from the devolution of power. See Kenneth Folsom, *Friends, Guests, and Colleagues* (Berkeley and Los Angeles: University of California Press, 1968), chap. 7.

95. Kuhn, "Local Self-Government Under the Republic, 266–267.

96. Joseph W. Esherick, *Reform and Revolution in China: The 1911 Revolution in Hunan and Hubei* (Berkeley and Los Angeles: University of California Press, 1976), 91.

97. Wakeman, *The Fall of Imperial China*, 236.

98. Winston Hsieh, "Triads, Salt Smugglers, and Local Uprisings: Observations on the Social and Economic Background of the Waichow Revolution of 1911," in Jean Chesneaux, ed., *Popular Movements and Secret Societies in China, 1840–1950* (Stanford: Stanford University Press, 1976), 171.

99. Esherick, *Reform and Revolution in China.*

100. Ch'i Hsi-cheng, *Warlord Politics in China, 1916–1928* (Stanford: Stanford University Press, 1976), 171.

101. See Robert A. Kapp, "Chungking as a Center of Warlord Power," in Mark Elvin and G. William Skinner, eds., *The Chinese City Between Two Worlds* (Stanford: Stanford University Press, 1974), 164–166, for an account of relations between the Sichuan warlord government and local "militia lords." Such local military formations, which numbered several thousand per county and five hundred thousand to six hundred thousand in Sichuan Province, "knew every move of the local people, set up their own customs barriers, forced peasants to plant opium, and executed victims without consulting any other authority" (165), as well as routinely defying the power of the warlord regime itself!

102. Prasenjit Duara, *Culture, Power, and the State—Rural North China, 1900–1942* (Stanford: Stanford University Press, 1988), 74.

103. Ralph Thaxton, *China Turned Rightside Up* (New Haven: Yale University Press, 1983), 29–47.

104. Ibid., 64–66, 80–81.

105. Philip C.C. Huang, *The Peasant Economy and Social Change in North China* (Stanford: Stanford University Press, 1985), 280–284.

106. Duara, *Culture, Power, and the State,* 113–115. Duara also showed that when KMT administrative structures were established in the villages, their thrust was purely extractive, and no effort was undertaken to win over the local people or to foster regime legitimacy (248–249).

107. Thomas G. Rawski, *Economic Growth in Prewar China* (Berkeley and Los Angeles: University of California Press, 1989), 12–14, 26. Rawski also discussed the fiscal weakness of provincial and local governments, concluded that "the extent and impact of Chinese taxation remained modest throughout the prewar decades," and therefore suggested that other analysts had erred in emphasizing the burdens of "crushing," "extortionate," and "oppressive" taxation (26).

Viewed in light of my discussion, Rawski is wide of the mark. The inability of the Chinese government at all levels to strengthen its tax base underscored the broad extent of decentralized processes of power and resource appropriation in the Republican period, whereby crushing, extortionate, and oppressive impositions were levied on the population by local landholders, landlord militia *(mintuan)*, and assorted local bullies and evil gentry. The result was socioeconomic distress at the village level and fiscal weakness at the state level.

108. Lucien Bianco, *Origins of the Chinese Revolution, 1915–1949* (Stanford: Stanford University Press, 1971), 123.

109. For a detailed account of the means by which local elites were able to survive the Nationalist political takeover and successfully compete for power and prestige with official government counterparts, see Lenore Barkin, "Patterns of Power: Forty Years of Elite Politics in a Chinese County," in Esherick and Rankin, eds., *Chinese Local Elites and Patterns of Dominance*, 191–215.

110. Suzanne Pepper, *Civil War in China: The Political Struggle, 1945–1949* (Berkeley and Los Angeles: University of California Press, 1978), 6.

111. Kuhn, "Local Self-Government Under the Republic," 295.

112. The Nationalists were not entirely unable to impose controls over centers of elite power. As Parks M. Coble Jr. documented, while pursuing a policy of deficit financing, the Nanking regime derived huge cash infusions from Shanghai banks by selling government notes at substantial discounts. When KMT finances became increasingly chaotic in the mid-1930s and the bankers resisted government demands for more funding, the regime simply expropriated the banks (*The Shanghai Capitalists and the Nationalist Government, 1927–1937* [Cambridge, Mass.: Harvard University Press, 1980], 66–72, 172–183). But dealing with landed elites in the countryside was a different and more thorny matter.

113. Pepper, *Civil War in China*, 95.

114. Bianco, *Origins of the Chinese Revolution*, 114–115. My forthcoming discussion of power dynamics in post-Mao China echoes Coble's description of the situation under the KMT: In the 1930s, "political factors frequently dictated the appointment of business personnel; often relatives of high officials or their proteges with no practical business experience were given top-management positions.... Because government-connected enterprise was assured of profits through subsidies, monopoly privileges, and access to banking resources, the firms were rarely forced to implement rigorous cost-accounting techniques" (*The Shanghai Capitalists and the Nationalist Government*, 258).

115. Pepper, *Civil War in China*, 20.

116. For the organizational weapon, see Philip Selznick, *The Organizational Weapon* (New York: McGraw-Hill, 1952). For institutionalization, see Samuel P. Huntington, *Political Order in Changing Societies* (New Haven: Yale University Press, 1968). For breaking through, see Kenneth Jowitt, *Revolutionary Breakthroughs and National Development* (Berkeley and Los Angeles: University of California Press, 1971).

117. Barrington Moore Jr., *Social Origins of Dictatorship and Democracy* (Boston: Beacon Press, 1966), 477.

118. Theda Skocpol, *States and Social Revolutions* (Cambridge: Cambridge University Press, 1979), 17.

119. Ibid., 115.

120. Ibid., 117.

121. Thaxton, *China Turned Rightside Up*, 229.

122. Ibid., 89.

123. Ibid., 100, 130.

124. Ramon H. Myers, *The Chinese Peasant Economy: Agricultural Development in Hopei and Shantung, 1890–1949* (Cambridge, Mass.: Harvard University Press, 1970), 260–263.

125. See Perry, *Rebels and Revolutionaries in North China,* 216–223, for an account of the counterrevolutionary activities of the Red Spears and CCP efforts to wrest control of the movement from local bullies and evil gentry.

126. Roman Slawinski, "The Red Spears in the Late 1920s," in Chesneaux, ed., *Popular Movements and Secret Societies in China,* 203.

127. Maurice Meisner, *Li Dazhao and the Origins of Chinese Marxism* (Cambridge, Mass.: Harvard University Press, 1967), 251. A CCP cadre instruction manual noted the limitations of the Red Spears by stating, "The strongest force in these groups is a kind of superstition, and as a result their conservatism is particularly intense" (cited in Chalmers Johnson, *Peasant Nationalism and Communist Power* [Stanford: Stanford University Press, 1962], 89).

128. Weber, *Economy and Society,* vol. 1, 227.

129. Ilpyong J. Kim, *The Politics of Chinese Communism: Kiangsi Under the Soviets* (Berkeley and Los Angeles: University of California Press, 1973), 34–40.

130. Power restructuring in the villages was generally a violent process. As a 1933 CCP document stated, "A village in the Pai-k'eng township was originally difficult to penetrate, because there were two notorious 'big tigers' who were lording it over there. In view of such a situation, the comrades adopted a different method by first arresting those two bad eggs and putting them on trial before the local circuit court. With the warm support of the masses, the two men were shot on the spot. Since then, the mass struggle has been afire like a fierce conflagration" (Mao Zedong, "Preliminary Conclusions Drawn from the Land Investigation Drive"; cited in Hsiao Tso-Liang, *The Land Revolution in China* [Seattle: University of Washington Press, 1969], 240).

131. In an account of the agrarian revolution in Manchuria, Steven I. Levine spoke of the CCP "instituting an exchange relationship with the peasantry" whereby "taxation, military and labor service, provisioning and other obligations" were exchanged for "land, a portion of the wealth confiscated from the old elite, and the right to participate in the new institutions established in the countryside to exercise power" (*Anvil of Victory: The Communist Revolution in Manchuria* [New York: Columbia University Press, 1987], 230, 234).

132. Pepper, *Civil War in China,* 268.

133. Chen Yung-fa, *Making Revolution—the Communist Movement in Eastern and Central China, 1937–1945* (Berkeley and Los Angeles: University of California Press, 1986), 221. This work is notable in placing calculated CCP power building at the grassroots level at the forefront of the discussion. Thus, the author focuses attention on the "techniques of controlled polarization with which the Party sought to create a new rural order" and to "minimize enemies and maximize friends" (11–12).

134. Pepper, *Civil War in China,* 268.

135. Cited in Boyd Compton, *Mao's China: Party Reform Documents, 1942–1944* (Seattle: University of Washington Press, 1952), 179.

136. Levine, *Anvil of Victory,* 205.

137. Johnson, *Peasant Nationalism and Communist Power,* 58–59.

138. Mao Zedong, "Rectifying the Party's Workstyle," in Compton, *Mao's China: Party Reform Documents,* 23–24.

139. Mao Zedong, "Zhengdun dang de zuofeng" (Rectifying the Party's Workstyle), in Chi Wen-shun, ed., *Readings in Chinese Communist Ideology* (Berkeley and Los Angeles: University of California Press, 1968), 78.

140. Mao Zedong, "Fandui dang bagu" (Oppose the Party Eight-Legged Essay), in ibid., 85–86.

141. Mark Selden, *The Yenan Way in Revolutionary China* (Cambridge, Mass.: Harvard University Press, 1971), 212–225.

142. Chen described the "revolution built by the Chinese Communists during the war" as comprising "two concomitant processes": "the peasants' seizure of power at the grass-roots level and the CCP's state-building at all levels"—in my terms, a top and bottom versus the middle power-restructuring process (*Making Revolution,* 499).

# 3

# Power Restructuring
# in Muscovite, Imperial,
# and Revolutionary Russia

I turn now to power relations and political process in Muscovite Russia (1345–1598) and imperial Russia (1613–1917). Following the logic of Chapter 2, the discussion encompasses the rise and consolidation of the Muscovite and Romanov autocracies; the recurrent involvement of central rulers, various elite configurations, and nonprivileged groups in struggles to control power and resources; and systemwide processes of crisis, reform, and breakdown in the mid-nineteenth century. I conclude with an assessment of the tumultuous sociopolitical ferment of the Russian masses in the late nineteenth and early twentieth centuries, a process that culminated in the Russian Revolutions of 1905 and 1917 and the revolutionary restructuring of power under Bolshevism. Many differences in size, complexity, and level of institutional and military development separate Muscovite and imperial Russia from late imperial China. My discussion is centered on power restructuring. As in late imperial and revolutionary China, I focus attention on political interactions, power contests, and the recurrent interplay between autocratic power concentration and processes of decentralized power and resource appropriation.

## Power Relations in Muscovite
## and Imperial Russia

Although analysts of virtually every ideological persuasion stress the steady reinforcement of central power in the history of Muscovy and imperial Russia, some commentators have depicted this development as an essentially one-sided process. As Pipes described it, "The Russian state grew and took shape without having to contend with entrenched landed interests—an absolutely fundamental factor in its historical evolution."[1] This view was echoed by Marc Raeff, who spoke of the "virtually unchallenged power of the Tsar over all his subjects and all facets of national life" and the "virtual absence of corporations and political or social estates, and thus the extreme insecurity and limited rights which characterized even the so-called privileged classes."[2] In a similar vein, other analysts focused on the common heritage of "oriental despotism" and "total" state domination that supposedly links the traditional (and modern) Russian and Chinese political systems.[3] These "despotist" interpretations of Russian history are squarely contradicted by the interactive view of power dynamics I advance throughout this book.[4] An interactive view of power relations and political process in Muscovite and imperial Russia is, moreover, articulated in the work of Nancy Shields Kollmann, Robert O. Crummey, Brenda Meehan-Waters, and Richard Hellie.

Shields Kollmann started with the premise that "the growth of Muscovite autocracy is the story not just of the sovereign's power, but of his interaction with his boyars and of the boyars with one another."[5] While rejecting "comparisons with the development of Western European political systems," she emphasized "the uniqueness of the Muscovite political system." The Muscovite political order was a form of "patrimonial rule," where personal relationships, respect for tradition, loyalty to family, and the obligations of honor and of dependency took precedence over "constitutional institutions, enfranchised political classes, and corporate privileges."[6] The Muscovite political order was characterized by stability and dynamism; even though networks of personal relations held it together, the system was tolerant of dynamic change and permitted the entrance of new elite groups. In contrast to the image of one-sided state domination, Shields Kollmann suggested that her interpretation "implies the need for a new conceptual vocabulary for Muscovite politics, one that recognizes the mutual dependence and complex interaction of the men in power."[7]

Crummey and Meehan-Waters also put forward an interactive view of power dynamics in their studies of Muscovite and Petrine elites. As underscored by the title of a study of the boyar elite in seventeenth-century Russia, *Aristocrats and Servitors*, the interplay between central rulers and elites was essential in Crummey's analysis. He showed how insecure central rulers in the Time of Troubles and throughout the early Romanov period tried to win the support and allegiance of prominent aristocrats and provincial nobles by grants of large tracts of crown or confiscated private land. These landholdings were politically important and figured pivotally in the subsequent rise of various elite groups to high official rank and positions of political power.[8] As Meehan-Waters documented, moreover, traditional aristocratic groups successfully held onto their share of power even in the wake of Peter I's revolutionary restructuring of power, so that by 1730 the officials serving in the top four civil and military ranks still "came predominantly from families at the top of the Muscovite social structure."[9] Yet the apparently undiminished position of traditional elite groups in 1730 must be understood in light of the interaction between central rulers and the privileged orders. The Petrine political order maximized central control of elites by extending and reinforcing their privileges.

Nor were power contests confined to the narrow circle of state servants at the top. In an analysis of the rise and consolidation of serfdom in the sixteenth and seventeenth centuries, Richard Hellie showed that the enserfment of the Russian peasantry was an interactive process in which the political, military, and fiscal interests of the state, the often-conflicting financial interests of various elite groups, and mass resistance all played a part. Whereas Russian rulers imposed mobility restrictions on the masses to bolster armies, revenue sources, and political support, and the financially strapped middle service elite pushed for more comprehensive rights and controls, the peasant population resisted with flight and outright rebellion and was only gradually subdued.[10]

Russian landholding, military, and administrative elites in the Muscovite and imperial periods were simultaneously allies of central rulers and a perennial source of competition. Rulers and elites had a shared interest in dominating the peasant masses and appropriating their produce and labor, but the control and distribution of power and resources were regularly contested. As in late imperial China, whether power relations were primarily cooperative or competitive depended on changing political circumstances and power balances. Even though this interactive relationship was a constant, periods of stability and active cooperation between central rulers and elites were periodically punctuated by periods of more or less open conflict, competition, and power and resource appropriation. I begin this examination of the Muscovite political order, "an absolute monarchy, tempered by an aristocratic administrative personnel,"[11] with a discussion of processes of institutional and cultural synthesis set in motion over the course of the Mongol invasions.

## The Mongols and the Emergence of the Muscovite Autocracy

The significance of the Mongol invasions is debated in Russian historiography. In the landmark work *The Mongols and Russia*, George Vernadsky highlighted the close historical relationship between the "Tsardom of Muscovy and the Golden Horde" and showed how Mongol political practices and institutional arrangements permeated the emerging Muscovite state system.[12] Yet Nicholas V. Riasanovsky unequivocally rejected Vernadsky's "Eurasian" view of the Russian historical process, argued that the Mongol legacy was overwhelmingly one of turmoil and destruction, and pointed to the Mongols' failure to "contribute a superior statecraft" and to the "unstable and short-lived" nature of the Mongol states as evidence of the political, institutional, and cultural irrelevance of the Mongol invasions.[13] But we have seen that the inability of the Mongol invaders to construct an enduring political order in China did not prevent subsequent Chinese rulers from adapting Inner Asian political practices to their own power-building agendas. This is essentially what happened in Russia as well. Compared to late imperial China, moreover, the early Muscovite state was considerably less physically, politically, and institutionally developed, and the Mongol impact was therefore propor-tionately greater.[14]

I follow Vernadsky and assert that the Mongol contribution was vital to the im-mediate political and military survival of the emerging Muscovite autocracy and to its long-term institutional development as well. It was Mongol power-building and resource mobilization techniques that first enabled the grand princes of Moscow to concentrate political power in their own hands and to expand the power of the principality of Moscow. When the Mongols conquered large swaths of Russia in the thirteenth century, they initially attempted to administer the ter-ritory themselves. By the early fourteenth century, however, leading Russian princes holding office at the pleasure of the Golden Horde had been granted the right of collecting taxes and delivering tribute. A cooperative relationship was thereby established in which Russian princes, Tatar overlords, and mixed Russian-Tatar military detachments worked together to collect taxes, enforce order, quell rebellions, and smash popular opposition to Mongol rule.[15]

In addition to bolstering the political authority, military power, and financial strength of the Muscovite grand princes, the Mongols also reinforced the power of Moscow vis-à-vis competing Russian principalities and foreign powers. The Mon-gols at first pursued a policy of playing one Russian prince off against the other, but by the early fourteenth century the grand princes of Moscow had emerged as the primary beneficiaries of Golden Horde military support and political patron-age for two main reasons. First, "the khan, the real ruler of north-east Russia, threw his support to the princes of Moscow, seeing them as the Horde's most reli-able agents in the Russian lands."[16] Second, the princes of Moscow were used to buffer and obstruct the rising power of Lithuania in the west. As John Fennell noted, "Ivan I was allowed to conduct his own business unhindered by local rivals and to gain certain benefits for Moscow at the expense of his neighbors so that he might provide a safeguard against excessive Lithuanian growth. Playing off Tver' or Suzdal' against Moscow might have been sound policy in the past; but now it had become evident that only a strong Moscow could satisfactorily combat a strong Lithuania."[17]

If the Mongol contribution was vital to the early rise of Moscow and the power-concentrating capacities of the grand princes, it was Mongol institutions that reinforced these processes when Moscow gradually freed itself from the direct military and political control of the Golden Horde. As in all conquered lands in the Mongol empire, the Mongols immediately established in the Russian princi-palities a comprehensive, simple, and rigorously enforced system of universal tax-ation and military conscription. As early as 1245, the Mongols conducted detailed censuses to determine the total of taxpayers, to ascertain the population's capacity to pay, and to establish the number of recruits to be drafted.[18] Whatever the suf-ferings of the common people under the "Tatar yoke," this resource mobilization system in time was turned to the political and fiscal advantage of the emerging Muscovite autocracy.

When Russian princes were granted the right to collect taxes and deliver tribute, they soon learned to reap handsome profits by means of institutional mechanisms already established on a population cowed into submission by decades of
direct Mongol control.[19] As the power of the Golden Horde waned, the grand
princes gradually appropriated Mongol power and resources, and by the middle
of the fifteenth century "the rulers of Moscow had long since stopped regular payments of tribute, preferring to keep the revenue in their own treasury."[20] Similarly,
the Mongol system of universal conscription was used to build up the military capacities of Moscow and in the end turned against the Tatar invaders themselves.[21]
Finally, the Mongol principle of universal state service, whereby common people
paid taxes and supplied labor and elites performed military service for the state on
demand, was incorporated into the ideological ethos and organizational arrangements of the emerging Muscovite autocracy.[22]

The swift rise of the principality of Moscow in the fifteenth and sixteenth centuries was propelled by the extension and intensification of concentration and control processes set in motion during the period of Mongol domination.[23] Externally,
the rise of Moscow was driven by territorial expansion and the subjugation and incorporation of competing Russian principalities and city-states, a process encompassing the annexation of Novgorod in 1478–1479 and the liquidation of the grand
princedom of Tver' thirteen years later.[24] Internally, this "gathering" of Russian
lands reinforced the power of Muscovite rulers. Power-concentrating processes
gained particular momentum in the course of the long reign of Ivan III (r. 1462–
1505), who confiscated 3 million acres of populated agricultural land during and
after the annexation of Novgorod and distributed the property to two thousand
carefully chosen men on condition of service to the Muscovite state. As Crummey
stressed, "While conditional land tenure was not unknown in earlier times in Russia, the creation of *pomeste* (conditional tenure) estates on a massive scale in the
Novgorodian lands was an innovation of momentous consequences."[25] While using
conquered land to bind Russian elites more closely to the state, Muscovite rulers
also sought to formalize autocratic power. The will of Ivan III reserved numerous
previously fragmented judicial, fiscal, and administrative rights for the throne exclusively; bequeathing to his eldest son the great bulk of Moscow's territory, Ivan
left his four younger sons only a small number of unimportant holdings.[26]

Yet autocratic power concentration did not go unchallenged in fifteenth- and
sixteenth-century Moscow. Landholding notables throughout this period exercised independent administrative and judicial rights on their hereditary estates
and only recognized the authority of Muscovite rulers elsewhere. At court, hereditary aristocratic prerogatives were clearly manifested in the cumbersome *mestnichestvo* (precedence-ranking) arrangement, a system of honor, precedence, and
ranking that stipulated military and administrative officials need not occupy positions lower in prestige than those held by their ancestors. Some analysts have asserted that this system facilitated autocratic domination by promoting rivalry and
feuding within the aristocracy. But V. O. Kliuchevsky argued that the *mestnichestvo*

system expressed a certain elite corporate autonomy since the arrangement's complex rules "made the political status of the individual or the family independent alike of the personal favor of the tsar and the personal service or achievements of the servitors themselves."[27]

This view is supported by Shields Kollmann, who spoke of the "boyars' exercise of real power behind the facade of the sovereign's autocracy" in the Muscovite political order.[28] At the top of the power structure, in a fluid context of mutual dependence for political legitimation and military support, hereditary elites and the grand princes forged personal bonds, intermarried, and maneuvered for influence and power. Although important aristocratic families routinely used proximity to the czar as a means of self-aggrandizement and power building, they sometimes became "overmighty," incurring the enmity of the sovereign and competing elite families and thereby suffering disgrace or arrest.[29] In the emerging Muscovite autocracy, Shields Kollmann suggested, autocratic power concentration coexisted with and was circumscribed by a deeply entrenched aristocratic ethos and formidable networks of elite families. In the middle of the sixteenth century, this patrimonial order, which pivoted on the close personal bonds and cooperative interaction between autocrat and aristocracy, experienced an unprecedented sociopolitical battering and upheaval. For these violent and tumultuous power-restructuring processes, Ivan IV (r. 1533–1584) is known to history as Ivan the Terrible.

## Political Conflict and the *Oprichnina*

Ivan IV is a controversial figure in Russian historiography and has long been depicted as everything from a great patriot and state builder to a blood-stained madman whose senseless policies resulted only in chaos, destruction, and retrogression.[30] Yet these sharply contradictory images are not mutually exclusive. Although individual pathology probably played a role, the events of the era are best understood in light of a power-restructuring perspective. Beginning with the ambitious reform of local administration in the 1550s and the political collisions that ensued, power restructuring under Ivan the Terrible was driven by struggles between the central ruler and various elite groups and by their competing efforts to secure and expand the material and human resources under their control. As these struggles mounted in intensity, so, too, did accompanying waves of violence, brutality, destruction, and madness.

Power contests were recurrent throughout the reign of Ivan IV. Enthroned as a child of three in 1533, the young grand prince for more than a decade was a helpless pawn in the political rivalries of competing aristocratic factions.[31] S. F. Platonov suggested that the bloody violence of Ivan's subsequent policies was conditioned by these experiences.[32] But the collision between autocrat and aristocracy was not solely the consequence of the ruler's personal animosity or the harsh politicial milieu in which he grew up. In a complex of reforms in the early and mid-1550s, Ivan's government sought to further restrict *mestnichestvo* privileges, formalize elite service obligations, expand conditional land tenure, and establish more central adminstrative and fiscal control at the local and provincial levels.[33] Hellie insisted that these reforms were "not part of a grand design to undermine the power of the boyars in order to strengthen the monarchy," but he also showed how the customary *kormlenie* (feeding) system, wherein local magnates appropriated and "fed" off the resources of the area under their purview, was replaced in 1555–1556 with a "Moscow-directed provincial self-administration dominated by the middle service class."[34] Other commentators have focused attention on the restrictions imposed by the Muscovite state on the landholding prerogatives of the princely aristocracy in this period.[35] This attempt to expand central authority at the expense of established elite privileges was resented and resisted, and political tensions between autocrat and aristocracy mounted accordingly.[36]

In 1565, Ivan IV created the *oprichnina* (thing apart), wherein large chunks of territory and bodies of troops were separated from the national administration and placed under his personal control, and forced the boyar establishment to increase his autocratic powers and authority to punish traitors.[37] The *oprichnina* organization was then violently and haphazardly deployed against real and potential enemies of the czar, with elements of the old Muscovite aristocracy attacked with particular ferocity. Members of prominent princely families were deported from their ancestral estates, and hereditary landholdings and property were seized and confiscated on a large scale; in the reign of terror and political intimidation that ensued, a large segment of the old aristocracy was physically destroyed.

The rationale and function of the *oprichnina* are much debated. Kliuchevsky and Riasanovsky both stressed the irrational and chaotic nature of *oprichnina* activities, which, they argued, involved no more than looting, terror, and aimless slaughter, all propelled by the czar's pathological hatred of real and imagined enemies.[38] Proponents of the "pathological" interpretation argue that the *oprichnina* was a "madman's debauch" that engulfed members of the rising service elite and *oprichniki* along with members of the old aristocracy, some of whom themselves participated in the *oprichnina*.[39] In contrast, following Platonov, Jerome Blum suggested that Ivan IV was in fact pursuing a purposeful, though chaotic, power-building strategy. Hence, the confiscatory and terroristic activities of the *oprichnina* tended to be focused on territories held by hereditary proprietors, with deportees and survivors given conditional tenure holdings in frontier areas "far from their old homes and from the people over whom they had any hereditary or traditional influence."[40] Ruslan G. Skrynnikov argued that the initial targets of the *oprichnina* were the ancient princely families of Suzdal', Yaroslavl, and Rostov, "younger brothers of the Muscovite rulers, filled with envy of the ruling dynasty," who claimed many privileges, owned large amounts of land in their former duchies, wielded considerable power at court, and still cherished political ambitions.[41] While acknowledging the inconsistent and chaotic aspects of *oprichnina* activities, Crummey pointed to the essential continuity of political process over the course of Ivan IV's reign. Hence, "Muscovite autocracy rested on the cooptation of the aristocratic clans of east Russia into the imperial political and social system, the creation of numerous lesser nobility as military servitors and dependents of the monarchy, and the creation of a rudimentary but crudely effective bureaucracy. All three of these processes began long before Ivan IV's reign and went on throughout the years of reform and *oprichnina*."[42]

Viewed in comparative and historical perspective, the rationale and function of the *oprichnina* are familiar. Like assertive central rulers before and since, Ivan IV attacked competing power centers by developing organizational alternatives to established channels of power, using terror to smash or intimidate real and potential political opposition, and subjecting powerful and wealthy clans, social groups, and territories to direct economic control or expropriation.[43] Equally familiar was Ivan's reliance on top and bottom versus the middle power-restructuring methods. When the *oprichnina* was declared in 1565, Ivan IV coupled his denunciation of boyar power appropriation and treachery with a public appeal to the merchants and commoners of Moscow. As Vernadsky observed, this attempt to enlist the masses against the upper classes worked, for "the threat of the commoners' uprising, abetted by the tsar, was real. The ruling institution capitulated."[44] Even more telling, the "class background" of potential *oprichnina* members was closely scrutinized, and the organization was deliberately made up of lowborn Russian gentry and foreigners.[45]

If many dimensions of the *oprichnina* paralleled power-concentrating processes we encounter thoughout this book, Ivan IV was unable to effect systematic political and institutional change. As Weber noted, the ruler seeking to contain elite challenges "must have an administrative organization of his own which can replace them with approximately the same authority over the local population."[46] Although Ivan sought to create an alternative administration in the *oprichnina,* he still remained organizationally dependent on the hereditary and service elites and "did not succeed in crushing boyardom as a political institution."[47] The composition of the political elite was changed and enlarged, but old aristocratic families continued to wield influence, to shape decisionmaking at court, and to dominate the Boyar Council.[48] In the closing years of Ivan IV's reign, the battered old aristocracy was able to stage a political comeback, while the rising service elite, threatened with economic ruin by peasant flight from the land, increased its demands for more rights and privileges. Faced with the mounting depopulation of the center of the Muscovite state and the political imperative of winning the support of elite servitors, Russian rulers in the final decades of the sixteenth century responded by intensifying controls at the mass level and setting the stage for a full-scale enserfment of the peasantry.[49]

## The Time of Troubles and the Romanov Power Reconfiguration

Scarcely a decade after Ivan's death, the accumulated social and political tensions of his reign erupted in widespread civil strife, followed by economic collapse and foreign invasion. The ensuing Time of Troubles (1598–1613) is best understood as a period of internal political disarray and social crisis, on which foreign powers attempted to capitalize. Internal disarray and crisis were the manifestations of unresolved political conflicts, social tensions, and fierce three-way struggles to control power and resources. Over the course of these struggles, a restructuring of power relations occurred in which both old and new elite groups emerged victorious, while the peasant masses lost further ground.

By disrupting the power arrangements of Muscovite society, the ravages of the *oprichnina* resulted in economic dislocation and crisis, famine and plague, and massive peasant flight. In this profoundly disordered setting, leaders of the old aristocracy took advantage of the death of Ivan IV's only surviving son, Fedor (r. 1584–1598), and the questionable legitimacy of his successor, Boris Godunov (r. 1598–1605), to more forcefully challenge the claims and impositions of the autocracy. A capable and assertive personal ruler in the Muscovite mode, Boris Godunov attempted to grapple with the political, social, and economic fallout of Ivan IV's reign. From our perspective, his efforts to restrict the political power of the great aristocratic families and curb their authority over peasant tenants are notable.[50] Opposed by potent boyar forces from the start, Boris Godunov's "political line of basing the tsar's authority on the support of the middle classes of Russian society, the gentry and the burghers" precipitated intense political conflict.[51]

Abetted by the Poles, the leaders of the old aristocracy probably had a hand in sponsoring False Dmitrii, a pretender to the throne whose appearance in 1600–1601 undercut Boris Godunov's attempts to wield autocratic power. The czar, in turn, assumed aristocratic complicity and violently attacked several old noble families. When False Dmitrii was enthroned, however, aristocratic forces then engineered his downfall and raised a leading member of the boyar elite, Prince Vasilii Shuisky, as czar. As the promises and guarantees made during his accession made clear, Shuisky's main agenda was to curb unconstrained autocratic power and reaffirm aristocratic privileges and immunities.[52] During his brief reign (r. 1606–1610), however, the perennial power contest between Russian central rulers and their elite servitors was eclipsed by a more pressing conflict, that of popular rebellion.

Slave revolts, peasant flight, and mass upheavals were widespread during the Time of Troubles. Kliuchevsky spoke of the telling change that occurred in the attitude of the masses at this time as long-suffering tolerance gave way to resistance and rebellion.[53] Along with mass resistance to mounting enserfment, this shift was the consequence of the unstable political conditions of the time. Thus, "the circumstances of the reigns of Ivan IV and Boris Godunov also permitted landowners to ignore the traditional rent structure, and some opened economic warfare against the peasantry. The agriculturalists responded to the provocations by resort to flight and violence."[54] So dire was the threat to the privileged orders that some aristocratic forces committed a fatal error and enlisted Swedish and Polish forces in the effort to smash the mass upheaval. The subsequent repulsion of foreign invasion and the formation of the new Romanov dynasty in 1613 are often viewed in Russian historiography as a miraculous national rally, a spontaneous coming together of the Russian people in the face of dire adversity. Without discounting national, religious, and cultural factors, I suggest that reconstitution of the Russian state under the Romanovs pivoted on a restructuring of power relations among central rulers, the old aristocracy, and the rising service elite.

The early Romanov rulers had to simultaneously win the support of key elite groups and rebuild the social controls at the mass level on which the Muscovite system depended. The new rulers attempted to achieve these goals by expanding the rights of the old aristocracy and the service elite and by reinforcing the power of these groups over the peasant population. The leading positions of the reconstituted Russian state were dominated by members of old aristocratic families. Just as the enthronement of Vasilii Shuisky had been marked by promises and concessions to boyardom, Mikhail Romanov guaranteed elite privileges and immunities and agreed to limitations on autocratic power during his accession.[55] Mikhail's reign (r. 1613–1645) was thus a period of restoration, when the "government's central concern was to bring back the good old ways and encourage the good old families."[56]

At the same time, the early Romanov rulers sought to win over and build up the emerging service elite. A crucial aspect of this process was the transformation of land tenure relations. By the mid-seventeenth century, land that Ivan IV had granted contingent on state service was effectively the hereditary property of the service elite.[57] This process gained momentum during the Time of Troubles, when weak rulers sought to enlist elite support by means of large-scale land grants, and was accelerated by the early Romanovs for the same reasons. In the seventeenth century, processes of resource appropriation became sanctified by custom and the passage of time. Hereditary tenure, which at the end of the sixteenth century was an issue of intense political contestation, had become by the end of the seventeenth century the dominant form of elite land tenure.[58] Natural processes of decentralized power and resource appropriation were then reinforced by state policy. Despite periodic bans, Romanov rulers in the seventeenth century distributed huge grants of land and peasants to relatives, favorites, and supporters, practices that became the "order of the day in the 1670s and 1680s."[59]

But the clearest manifestation of elite gains in the decades following the Time of Troubles was the final consolidation of serfdom, a process crowned by the promulgation of the Ulozhenie, the law code of 1649. The Ulozhenie was a mutually advantageous compromise between Russian central rulers and the hereditary and service elites effected in a setting of intense political conflict and popular restiveness.[60] Nevertheless, the code reinforced the political and economic power of the autocracy; as a personification of the state, "the tsar as sovereign was the holder of the supreme rights on all state property."[61] But the real centerpiece of the code was a meticulous listing and exhaustive codification of the prerogatives of the various elite strata, with political immunities, property rights, and status distinctions addressed in particular detail.[62] The principle of equality in the administration of justice to all men of rank was proclaimed, trials before a boyar court were guaranteed, and it was stipulated that the land and possessions of privileged groups were not to be confiscated by the state but turned over to kin, widow, and children. This formalization of the land rights of the aristocracy and service elite was key. For the boyars, the ownership and hereditary rights of their patrimonial estates and of land grants made during the Time of Troubles was confirmed; for the service elite, conditional land tenure was essentially abolished and hereditary landholding and land exchange rights affirmed.[63] Finally, while affirming the rights of the privileged orders vis-à-vis one another and the state, the code confirmed the servile status of the mass population. The Ulozhenie bound the peasant forever to the estate on which he was a tenant, thereby codifying the long-sought goal of Russian aristocratic and service elites.[64]

By midcentury, central rulers occupied a powerful position, with their autocratic prerogatives sanctioned by law and not subject to political challenge. As Crummey described, Russian elites had little reason to oppose the autocracy: "Their power derived, above all, from their position as leaders of an increasingly centralized system of administration and social and economic rewards. Power and wealth derived not from resistance to royal power but from exploiting the power of the tsar's office for individual and clan profit."[65] But we have seen that elite gains were realized only over the course of sustained political struggle. The shift from conditional to hereditary tenure, royal grants of land and peasants, and the final consolidation of serfdom itself were concessions that Russian elites were able to extract from Russian rulers in exchange for the fulfillment of vital political and military support functions.[66] Even though power contests between central rulers and the privileged orders continued throughout the seventeenth century, the balance had shifted to the manifest advantage of the latter.[67]

## The Petrine Autocracy

Under Peter I (r. 1682–1725), power relations among Russian central rulers, various elites, and nonprivileged groups underwent important changes. In Raeff's view, Peter the Great set out to effect a radical transformation of Russia's government and political institutions on the basis of Western European models of "cameralism" and the "well-ordered police state."[68] Yet William C. Fuller showed that autocracy and serfdom were the essential ingredients in Peter's power-building program and the principal foundations on which his historic military successes rested.[69] I suggest that political process and power dynamics in the Petrine era are best understood in light of the power-restructuring argument advanced in these pages. Peter I was a dynamic personal ruler who assertively formulated and enforced far-reaching political and institutional reforms, changes that pivoted on reinforced state controls on the elite as well as the mass population. Yet the Petrine state offensive was followed by a sustained effort on the part of the privileged orders to reverse the verdict. The political counterattack of Russian elites got under way in the immediate aftermath of the reforming sovereign's death and achieved its greatest successes during the reign of Catherine II (r. 1762–1796), with consequences that endured until the collapse of the imperial order a century and a half later.

Power restructuring under Peter I was both an extension of political patterns already under way in the Muscovite period and an ad hoc response to incessant military pressure and the attendant imperatives of technological and organizational modernization. In the Petrine era, concentration and control methods were used to extract and mobilize the human and material resources on which central policies depended, and both the elite and mass populations were subjected to extremely harsh and often unprecedented political and economic pressures. Although this attempt to autocratically command the loyalty and performance of elite servitors was not new, Peter I made state service more systematic by enforcing a "general mobilization of the provincial nobility."[70] An extensive and generally successful effort to categorize and register the elite population was undertaken, and members of all privileged groups were assigned to permanent, lifelong service positions in newly created military and administrative arms of the state apparatus. In contrast to earlier attempts to enforce service obligations, Peter I's program was more sustained, compulsory, and systematic. Default was punished with public condemnation, loss of privileges, and confiscation of estates; would-be evaders were tenaciously hunted down and assigned to the toughest posts.[71] Elite servitors in the Petrine era faced the real prospect of spending their entire adult lives in a series of demanding, often dangerous, and usually low-paying service assignments.

Yet the new impositions of the Petrine autocracy were difficult to enforce, as attested by the constant stream of threatening decrees, the prosecution of numerous individuals, and "regular manhunts, confiscation of property, taking of family members as hostages, and heavy fines and imprisonment for repeated violations."[72] But punitive measures were only one means of securing elite compliance, and concessions to elite interests were routine. The Petrine era witnessed extensive grants of land and serfs to Russian aristocratic and service elites and the further expansion of their authority over the peasant population. Because Peter I pursued a policy of using confiscated estates for imperial land grants, the elite "was not just the victim of confiscations but the agent and recipient of confiscated estates."[73] While attempting to enforce service obligations, the state rewarded loyal and effective performance extravagantly. As Meehan-Waters detailed, the Petrine ruling elite benefited from "favorable contracts for agricultural and manufacturing enterprises, loans at low interest rates, and indulgence of tax arrears," along with high salaries and royal grants of estates.[74] By combining sanctions and incentives, Peter attempted to enforce the linkage between service and privilege that Russian central rulers had long sought to establish; in an equally familiar pattern, this linkage was contested and modified when less able and determined rulers succeeded him.

Peter I also subjected the mass population to new and extremely onerous service obligations in two areas especially. For the first time since the period of Mongol domination, Russian peasants were subjected to a regular system of military conscription, and all rural communities were ordered to supply and outfit a given number of recruits for lifelong military service.[75] So insistent were state requirements for military manpower that in 1700 Peter decreed that all freed slaves and serfs were to report to army recruiting officers, thereby abolishing the right of the emancipated serf to live as a free man.[76] Even more onerous was imposition of a new system of taxation. Whereas Russian peasants had previously been assessed on a household basis, the "soul tax" was introduced by Peter I. A census was conducted, and new taxes were assessed on the basis of the individual male "soul," thereby eliminating the possibility of grown sons living in their father's household and escaping taxation.[77]

The Petrine effort to intensify resource extraction was resisted by the peasants themselves and by the landholders who were responsible for collecting and delivering tax revenues. Peasant flight occurred on a massive scale. But an examination of the 1719 census revealed that 27 percent of eligible taxpayers, some 1.5 million male souls, had been omitted from the registers by their masters.[78] Yet the imposition of new burdens was so successful that state revenues were more than tripled during Peter's reign.[79] In the face of widespread elite and mass noncompliance, the achievements of the Petrine effort to categorize and control all segments of the Russian nation are striking. How was Peter the Great able to accomplish this feat? Viewed historically and comparatively, the power dynamics of the Petrine autocracy resembled and often paralleled those of the early Ming and Qing autocracies and prefigured the power-concentrating and resource-mobilizing drives of the communist dictatorships of the twentieth century.

Peter I's reign was characterized by high levels of organizational change, personnel turnover, and vertical mobility. Expansion in the military and administrative apparatus increased the size and prestige of the service establishment and improved career and promotion opportunities. Yet advancement in this emerging hierarchy depended primarily on merit, talent, and achievement in state service.[80] Like the Chinese imperial examination system, the Petrine system focused the aspirations and energies of the wellborn, the talented, and the ambitious on state-controlled avenues of mobility.[81] Although hereditary aristocrats resisted competing on equal terms with the commoners Peter recruited into the service establishment, the momentum and allure of the rapidly expanding system were too powerful to resist. Finally, the Petrine autocracy combined positive incentives with coercion and terror. The headquarters of Peter's favorite military unit, the Preobrazhensky Regiment, functioned as an independent tribunal and control mechanism, and over the course of his reign the Preobrazhensky Prikaz (Office of State Investigations) tried and punished thousands of political "crimes" with executions, dismemberment, torture, flogging, and banishment.[82]

In addition to controlling avenues of mobility, the Petrine system sought to combine disparate elite groups and organizational principles by integrating the aristocracy and its principle of heredity with the imperial bureaucracy and its principle of expertise. Peter I was able to manipulate these key groups by bureaucratizing the aristocracy and promoting according to talent and achievement while aristocratizing the bureaucracy by granting noble rank and hereditary privilege.[83] In this partially bureaucratized patrimonial system, both groups competed for favors the personal ruler alone could grant.[84] This intraelite rivalry, which weakened and destabilized the imperial system in the nineteenth century, enhanced the power of the Petrine autocracy by pitting various elite groups against one another. Potential competing centers of power were further vitiated with policies directly paralleling those of late imperial China. Peter regularly distributed massive land grants, but these properties were widely dispersed throughout the empire, and nobles typically owned properties in many different locales.[85] Like the Chinese "rule of avoidance," which prohibited officials from serving in their native region, the dispersion of elite landholdings in Petrine Russia was an effective means of inhibiting the formation of territorially based power centers. Within the state structure, the formation of interest groups and competing policies was constrained by frequent personnel turnovers and assignment shifts, as elite servitors were constantly shifted back and forth between military and civilian posts.[86]

The Petrine autocracy secured mass compliance with state policy by relentlessly reinforcing social controls. As Kliuchevsky observed, the demands of Peter I's tax collectors were even harsher than those of the Tartar khans centuries before.[87] Even though these impositions were levied by a Russian ruler defending and strengthening the motherland, the Russian masses nonetheless bore the fiscal brunt and suffered the human cost of Peter's military and administrative restructuring. However glorious the image of Peter the Great was in Russian history and thought, he was widely viewed by his people as a veritable Antichrist, whose blasphemous and alien rule brought suffering and dislocation.[88]

Although Peter I successfully overcame or held in check elite and popular resistance over the course of his reign, the exertions of the period subjected the entire fabric of Russian society to immense strains. Many members of the aristocratic and service elites suffered impoverishment, as estates were neglected and wealth consumed while service obligations and military duties took precedence. At the mass level, social ferment was intensified by Peter's relentless policies of resource extraction and the increased levels of mobility set in motion by his military and construction projects as well.[89] The political, social, and economic conflicts that ensued shaped the remainder of the eighteenth century and resulted in a partial modification of the Petrine system of concentration and control.

## Power and Resource Appropriation in Catherinian Russia

The years 1725–1762 have been termed the "epoch of palace revolutions," when "women and boys ruled Russia."[90] Understood in light of my argument, the political instability of this period was the manifestation of successful efforts by Russian elites to loosen the controls imposed on them by Peter. As early as the government crisis of 1730, various proposals to curb autocratic power were aired; although no formal limits to autocracy resulted, elite demands for protection and guarantees, for limitations on the years of obligatory state service, for orderly pay and promotion, and for a return to traditional inheritance laws did not fall on deaf ears.[91] As Richard S. Wortman noted, "Elizabeth and Catherine were elevated to the throne by guards officers and officials seeking amenable rulers who would not abuse their power. In the treacherous politics of the Russian court, female rulers seemed more reliable and dependent, less subject to uncontrolled despotic whims. They represented benevolence and stability on the throne, a taming of autocratic authority."[92] Royal benevolence and stability went hand in hand with far-reaching political concessions to Russian elites and the acceleration of processes of power and resource appropriation.

The loosening of state controls over Russian elites in the mid- and late eighteenth century was paralleled by the intensification of serfdom. Even though the term of obligatory state service was shortened and elites were given the right to enter military service as officers, the years 1730–1760 witnessed legislation giving landholders a monopoly on serf ownership, the right to sell serfs apart from land, easier recovery of runaway serfs, and greatly increased police and disciplinary powers.[93] The culminating "emancipation" and "demobilization" of the privileged orders occurred in 1762, when compulsory service was abolished and Russian elites were allowed to decide whether to serve, travel abroad, and seek employment with foreign rulers. Post-Petrine politics mirrored this shift in power relations, as the state structure increasingly became an arena for "political clans vying for supremacy in the name of unconditional support for autocratic rule," while autocratic decisionmaking was supplanted by "nongovernmental" councils comprising representatives of the leading families of the realm.[94]

The dual processes of increased elite privilege and tightened mass controls came together in the reign of Catherine II to form a restructured and reinforced state-elite alliance. Whereas Peter I was able to control Russian elites with a forceful and often onerous combination of incentives and sanctions, Catherine elicited the cooperation of elite groups by means of concessions, payoffs, and royal indulgences. Catherinian policy sought to contain the social and political tensions engendered by the Petrine autocracy by accommodating and allying with the privileged orders and thereby enlisting their services as agents of local control. Spurred by the requirements of war and the political and economic demands of the elite, the Catherinian era witnessed the high tide of Russian serfdom and the imposition of new forms of resource extraction and social control. Catherine II is depicted in some scholarly interpretations as a liberalizer and a reformer. Isabel de Madariaga spoke of Catherine's efforts to "mobilize local initiative and promote voluntary social activity and enterprise" and attributed her failure to "intervene decisively in the vexed field of serfdom" to "the conviction . . . that the time was not yet ripe to tackle a problem so closely linked with public order, finance, and military strength."[95] In contrast, John P. LeDonne depicted the reforms of 1775–1785 as a process of "aristocratic reaction" whereby the state apparatus at the central and local levels was taken over and appropriated by the great families and lesser nobility.[96] The latter interpretation is both closer to the mark and fully consistent with the thrust of my interpretation of power and politics in imperial Russia.

In Arcadius Kahan's words, "The nobility during the eighteenth century was the most vocal group in Russian society in demanding a larger share of national income or national wealth."[97] The demands of the elite were extensive, encompassing the granting of legal guarantees and economic monopolies, more group immunities and privileges, and the distribution of more land and serfs. Throughout Catherine's reign, she dispensed huge amounts of state-owned land and serfs to court favorites, generals, and government officials.[98] Indeed, extensive land and serf grants were intrinsic to the pattern of accommodation and alliance with the privileged orders that formed the basis of Catherinian social and political arrangements.

The proclamation in 1767 of the "Great Instruction," a compendium of principles on which good government and orderly society should be based, and the simultaneous convening of the Legislative Commission, a consultative assembly of privileged orders, are conventionally cited as examples of reform and "national dialogue" under Catherine II. As de Madariaga herself documented, however, the reformist language of the Great Instruction and the passages proposing reform of serfdom in particular were heavily edited by Catherine's aristocratic councillors.[99] And the Legislative Commission itself was riven by sharp social tensions, as gentry representatives quarreled with merchant representatives over the right to own serfs and to engage in industry and trade and peasant representatives complained of unbearable financial pressures and demanded lower taxes.[100] Before any concrete recommendations were agreed on, Catherine dismissed the commission in 1768.

It was the Pugachev Rebellion of 1773, rather than liberal or reformist ideals, that most profoundly shaped the reforms of 1775–1785. This explosive popular outburst, which for a time threatened Moscow itself, challenged the legitimacy of the Catherinian order and rapidly assumed the dimensions of an all-out social war. Significantly, Emelian Pugachev himself deployed top and bottom versus the middle appeals and methods. Hence, the rebel leader declared himself to be Czar Peter III. As "tsar deliverer," he promised liberation from "recruiting levies, poll taxes, and other money taxes . . . and all oppressions which the gentry-malefactors and urban bribe-taking judges impose on the peasant and on the entire people," and by his personal *ukaz* (decree), Pugachev rewarded loyal followers with "possession of lands, forests, hay-mowing meadows and fishing places, and salt lakes, without leases and without money dues."[101] Pugachev's assault on the privileged groups was merciless, and so was the official counterattack that ensued. Terrified and infuriated by the thousands of casualties inflicted on the elite by the rebels, government punitive expeditions conducted a systematic reign of terror in rebellious areas and "pacified" the population with mass hangings, dismemberments, floggings, and banishments.[102]

Catherine II's government attributed the successes of the rebellion to the weakness of local administration and the ineffectiveness of local military leadership. After the revolt was smashed, a far-reaching decentralization of power into the hands of local landholders and serf owners was implemented. Whereas local elites had previously wielded absolute authority only on their own estates, they now exercised local administrative, police, and judicial functions formerly under the jurisdiction of central representatives.[103] Unlike Chinese landholding elites in the nineteenth century, Russian elites did not take the lead in defeating popular rebellion; like their Chinese counterparts, Russian landholders and serf owners were quick to use their newly acquired powers to more vigorously enforce their interests and privileges at the local level. As LeDonne put it, "The conduct of investigations, the settlement of a large number of civil disputes, above all those involving boundaries, and to a large extent the collection of taxes passed under the control of local landowners, whose influence in the *gubernia* (provincial) capital was strong enough to checkmate state peasants seeking protection against them."[104]

The political aspirations of Russian elites were realized in Catherine II's Charter to the Nobility of 1785, which formally recognized landholding and service elites as autonomous corporate bodies entitled to a variety of rights. Especially important was the right to act as a legitimate interest group before the throne, a privilege denied virtually every other segment of Russian society. This was a crucial and highly paradoxical development—in strengthening the system of local control by expanding elite privilege, the state itself created favorable conditions for the formation of future centers of opposition.[105] (I have already examined this pattern in nineteenth- and early-twentieth-century China, wherein local elites secured a hold on fiscal and military powers formerly monopolized by the state.) Even more fateful was the intensification of serfdom, which as a system of social control and resource extraction was becoming ever more unstable and economically backward. Whereas Peter I had attempted to subject the entire society to autocratic power, power decentralization in Catherinian Russia entailed new powers for the privileged orders and the imposition of more controls at the mass level.

With the decentralization of power in late-eighteenth-century Russia occurred a decentralization of elite social life and culture. Raeff noted the positive aspects of this process, whereby Russian elites, freed from the constraints of obligatory service, were able to involve themselves in local affairs, develop a certain civic consciousness, and expand their educational and cultural horizons.[106] Other commentators were less enthusiastic. As Baron Haxthausen reported in his 1843 travel memoir, corporate rights for local elites put the "election of the estates' officers in the hands of the unrefined, uneducated and, for the most part, corrupt nobles. . . . As a result, the worst subjects are frequently, or perhaps generally, chosen for positions in the estates and entrusted with the local administration of the police and justice."[107] The predominantly low level of elite civic consciousness was well illustrated by prevailing attitudes toward estate management. Few proprietors were interested in technological or organizational improvements; instead, most were content to extract the maximum from the enserfed population by traditional means.[108] As for expanding cultural horizons, elite preferences primarily took the form of importing Western luxuries and imitating Western lifestyles, at the cost of ruinous indebtedness. So desirous were Russian rulers of securing the loyalty of their servitors that state loans to landed elites in 1800 exceeded expenditures for all other purposes.[109]

Predatory local officials, poor estate management, and an extravagant, state-funded elite lifestyle were not the only adverse consequences of Catherinian political and social policy, for the entire order hinged on the intensification of serfdom.[110] Yet by the turn of the century it was increasingly evident to Russian policymakers that serfdom was both an economically backward institution and a perennial source of peasant ferment and rebellion and had to be reformed. With the accession of Paul I (r. 1796–1801), Russian rulers began their hesitant quest to effect systemic reform.

## Autocratic Reform and Aristocratic Resistance

Paul I has been portrayed as a repressive and capricious tyrant whose "peculiar behavior left officials and ministers afraid for themselves and their careers" and whose determination to recall nobles to active state service jeopardized the ability of the elite to "create a cultivated and carefree life in the country."[111] In fact, Paul forcefully and arbitrarily tried to revive the Petrine mode of personal rulership, attempted to reverse Catherinian power decentralization, introduced the idea of reforming serfdom, and sought to weaken the influence of the leading families "by imposing rules to limit their freedom of action."[112] During his brief reign, the universal service requirement was reimposed, the administrative and police powers of local elites were weakened, corporal punishment for nobles was restored, and a new tax on the aristocracy was enforced.[113] In the manner of reforming autocrats in imperial times and under communism, Paul sharply accelerated personnel turnover. As David L. Ransel noted, Paul "discharged more civil and military servitors in a shorter time than any tsar before or since," dismissing three thousand officers in three years in the military alone.[114] At the same time, the emperor tried to build up political support by continuing Catherine II's policies of massive land and serf grants and state-supplied financial subsidies. But Paul was assassinated by a band of officers in 1801, and his attempt to "cram his program down the throats of his unwilling subjects" failed.[115] Wisely enough, his son Alexander I (r. 1801–1825) expeditiously restored the privileges that Paul had attempted to take away.

Yet the reign of Alexander I began with a flurry of reform activity. For almost a decade, the young czar attempted to implement ambitious administrative, legal, educational, and social reforms, not least the creation of separate supreme judicial and legislative organs in the central government, the restructuring of provincial government, the introduction of educational requirements for nobles serving in the civil service, and provisions for the voluntary emancipation of serfs.[116] With the exception of limited social legislation, however, Alexander's institutional reforms were stymied by tenacious aristocratic and official opposition and in the end came to naught. The ability of the privileged orders to effectively contest autocratic power was in part a consequence of the Catherinian political legacy, for Alexander I in his manifesto of succession had promised to rule in the spirit of his grandmother. From the start, therefore, Alexander had to contend with the great families that dominated the Senate and much of the government apparatus and distrusted the "tyrannical, arbitrary, and rationalistic designs of the emperor's youthful advisers."[117]

This collision was the opening act of the conflict that would occupy center stage in the coming decades, in which the reforming autocrat and imperial bureaucracy were opposed by the great families that controlled the Senate and ruled in the localities. Yet Alexander I was not always able to get imperial officials to do his bidding. In an account of the czar's interaction with his minister of justice, Gavrill Derzhavin, Wortman described frustrations closely paralleling those Chinese autocrats experienced at the hands of remonstrating Confucian scholar-officials. Hence, to Derzhavin's constant admonitions that the czar remain true to Catherine's principles, Alexander apparently retorted, "You always wish to instruct me. . . . I am the autocratic sovereign and I so wish"; when the czar sought to decree conditions providing for the voluntary emancipation of serfs, Derzhavin "told Alexander that 'it was dangerous to rule about freedom before our uneducated rabble' . . . and tried every stratagem to block it."[118]

But an even greater impediment to the reform or abolition of serfdom was its apparent success as a source of power. Whereas Catherine II presided over a massive expansion of the territory and population of the Russian empire, serfdom, according to Fuller, "made possible the command system of long-service conscription that produced the enormous infantry armies of the age" and thereby provided the backbone of Russian military success.[119] When Napoleon invaded Russia, moreover, "the serfdom and autocracy of Russia . . . proved equal to overthrowing one of the greatest generals and the largest army ever assembled in the history of Europe."[120] Like the Soviet victory in World War II, the Russian military triumph in 1812 legitimated and reinforced the crude and inefficient institutions on which it rested.

When Nicholas I (r. 1825–1855) came to power, the sociopolitical arrangements of the imperial order were experiencing internal and external strain. Internally, symptoms of elite discontent were manifested in the abortive December uprising of 1825, rural disturbances broke out during Nicholas's accession, and peasant unrest remained endemic throughout his reign.[121] Externally, revolutionary ferment throughout Europe culminated in the shattering revolutions of 1848. As the defender of the old order and suppressor of disorder and rebellion, Nicholas I presided over intensified central control efforts and fierce political repression. At the same time, Nicholas assumed the role of reforming autocrat and attempted a difficult balancing act, seeking on the one hand to strengthen state authority and maintain order, while on the other to prepare the ground for a reform of serfdom.

Autocratic rule in Nicolaevan Russia operated in familiar ways, and Nicholas tried to implement reforms by means of centrally controlled channels of power. Over the course of his reign, the authority of an expanded and increasingly professionalized imperial bureaucracy was sharply increased.[122] Like earlier Russian rulers, the czar sought to create a new elite that derived its power and privileges from state service instead of landownership. In Wortman's words, "Nicholas addressed the nobility without the old supplicant, pleading tone. . . . His appeal was directed at the lower and middle nobility, and represented an attempt to break free from the alliance with the noble elite."[123] Significantly, Nicholas I also recognized that serfdom posed a mounting threat and that change was inevitable. A series of secret committees met throughout his reign to study agrarian problems and propose solutions, and a few limited reforms, notably an improvement in the condition of peasants owned by the crown, were implemented.

Yet no general reform of serfdom occurred. Although Nicholas acknowledged that the system "is an evil, palpable and evident to everyone," his horror of disorder and mass violence prevailed in the end.[124] Fearing that a reduction in the power of the serf owners would both undercut rural social control and precipitate outright elite opposition and demands for a constitution, the reforming autocrat failed to act.[125] Instead, state funding for landholding and serf-owning groups expanded during his reign, even at the price of depriving the emerging industrial and commercial sectors of badly needed resources.[126] Yet by embarking on a critical discussion of serfdom, Nicholas I set the stage for the momentous power-restructuring experiment the autocracy soon felt itself compelled to undertake.

## Crisis, Reform, and the Decline of the Imperial System

Nicholas I's attempt to hold together an antiquated system was exploded by Russia's defeat in the Crimean War. It was the fate of his successor, Alexander II (r. 1855–1881), to initiate reforms that transformed the imperial system by undercutting the sociopolitical control mechanisms that constituted its core. Like the late Qing reforms, Alexander's "Great Reforms" were intended to revitalize a faltering system; as in late-nineteenth- and early-twentieth-century China, their unintended effect was to intensify three-way power contests and set in motion the social, economic, and political forces that finally tore imperial Russia apart.

The Crimean debacle exposed to high officialdom and educated society the glaring weaknesses of the traditional system, and real change seemed especially urgent in the areas of local government and serfdom. Students of nineteenth-century Russia have noted that, even though centralization and bureaucratic professionalism were the goals of Nicholas I, "undergoverned" provinces and localities remained the reality. With authority concentrated in St. Petersburg, local officials lacked power, education, and resources; local elites, though barred from decisionmaking in the capital, were responsible for an essentially uncoordinated array of fiscal, police, judicial, and welfare functions. As a result, local government was smothered in "bureaucratic formalism," yet remained thoroughly chaotic, corrupt, and inefficient.[127]

At the same time, serfdom appeared even more backward and dangerous in the wake of the Crimean defeat. The war "provided additional evidence of the dangers and deficiencies of serfdom which found reflection in both the poor physical condition and listlessness of the recruits and the general economic and technological backwardness of the country."[128] Even more alarming was the revelation that serfdom was incompatible with the requirements of modern warfare. As Alfred J. Rieber observed, unlike in other European states, serfdom prevented Russia from maintaining a large, trained, strategic reserve since "this simple expedient was fraught with dangerous consequences. Reducing the term of service would have greatly increased the number of annual recruits, freed serfs at a greater rate, and dumped a mass of landless proletarians who were trained in the use of firearms and military tactics on a society which could not absorb them."[129] Indeed, the war caused unrest among the serfs, and the "state of fermentation in the villages" was acknowledged by the czar himself in March 1856 when he announced before gentry representatives that reform was necessary because of "the hostile feelings between the peasants and their owners" and because "it is, therefore, much better for it to happen from above rather than from below."[130]

An upwelling of support for reform occurred in the years 1856–1862, as educated Russian society came together in the belief that the defects of local government could be remedied by the creation of "new centers of authority in Russia's undergoverned provinces."[131] The reform of local government took two basic forms, which S. Frederick Starr described as "the politics of decentralization" and "the politics of self-government."[132] The idea of administrative decentralization was familiar: The central government would make local government more effective by increasing the power of local officials and providing them with "greater means of getting at local needs."[133] But "the diminution of the governors' powers resulting from the reform proved unsatisfactory to the tsarist government," and by the late 1860s and 1870s the supreme authority of governors-general in administrative, judicial, and security matters had been reinforced.[134] But a genuine expansion of local self-government did occur in this period and was manifested in the zemstvo (land assembly) legislation of January 1864, which formally vested local and regional gentry-led "land assemblies" with limited welfare and taxation functions. To be sure, central policymakers from the start viewed these institutions as "purely local organs, which cannot and must not in any way touch upon matters of state, neither the national treasury or the court, nor of the executive police, that prime organ of central institutions."[135] Yet gentry-led land assemblies would in a few decades emerge as centers of opposition to central authorities, articulate independent views, and feed the flames of social and political conflict.[136]

It was in dealing with serfdom, however, that the government's attempt to maintain control while implementing reform was most problematic. We have seen that the elite's role as the all-powerful agent of local control was an essential ingredient in the imperial order. Yet the emancipation legislation abolished at one stroke and forever "the squires' unlimited and arbitrary power over their serfs," "the very core of serfdom."[137] The government attempted to contain the potentially explosive effects of this fundamental structural change in two ways. On the one hand, the autocracy sought to retain the elite's political loyalty by weighting emancipation legislation in the interests of the serf owners. Thus, purchase or redemption of land could not be initiated against the will of landlords but could be initiated against the will of peasants, while the valuation of land allotments was in the hands of gentry-dominated committees.[138] This arrangement allowed landlords in the fertile black-earth region to sharply reduce peasant land allotments, while in the agriculturally disadvantaged non-black-earth regions peasants "obtained the land, but at a price nearly 100 percent over and above the current market prices."[139] Thus, "the peasantry released from serfdom received insufficient allotments, for which it had to pay a disproportionately high purchase price."[140] Furthermore, as Daniel Field argued, "from the peasant perspective, the requirement that they pay dues or redemption payments for *their* land was a greater outrage to justice than serfdom itself."[141]

On the other hand, government policymakers attempted to retain political and fiscal control of the peasantry by reinforcing the traditional peasant land commune and thereby binding the "newly unbound peasant" to it.[142] An essential feature of the land commune was joint responsibility for taxes, which the emancipation legislation extended to include collective responsibility for land redemption payments.[143] To prevent flight, the legislation mandated that individuals seeking temporary employment elsewhere or moving permanently had to secure the permission of the commune, which was rarely granted since individual departures increased the financial burden on those who remained. Yet Boris Mironov demonstrated that the land commune strengthened peasant solidarity and collective consciousness by enforcing periodic land redistributions, worked as a buffer against outside economic intrusions, and helped preserve traditional modes of life.[144] Like the zemstvo, peasant land communes in the coming decades would also emerge as centers of opposition to the central authorities and would actively engage in social and political conflict.

## Peasants, Gentry, and the State at Loggerheads

While the attempt to maintain control and implement reform was foundering, social, economic, and political tensions were steadily escalating; these were the processes that finally erupted in the Russian Revolutions of 1905 and 1917. Modern analysts of the Great Reforms have faulted the government for failing to implement more far-reaching political change and limit autocracy.[145] But official conservatism and preoccupation with control were not misplaced, for the crisis of the imperial order stemmed precisely from the inability of the Russian state to maintain social and political control in a period of rapid internal change and intensifying external pressure. This control crisis was manifested in a series of destabilizing conflicts in which peasant economic interests were pitted against those of the gentry and the policy objectives of the central authorities collided with the interests of elite and nonprivileged groups.

As noted, the terms of emancipation legislation were highly detrimental to the rural masses. Russian peasants had to "squeeze their living out of fewer resources"; huge financial obligations "sucked from the countryside money which could have been invested in new tools, livestock, and fertilizer"; and the reinforced land commune perpetuated backward agricultural practices and made it difficult for peasants to escape poverty by moving to the cities.[146] Demographic changes and government policy in the postemancipation decades exacerbated this already oppressive situation. First, rural Russia experienced a population explosion, as the population ballooned from 73 million in 1861, to 125 million in 1897, and to almost 170 million in 1917.[147] Even though population growth was a manifestation of rational peasant attempts to expand production by increasing the supply of labor, the effect was to add to already intense pressure on the land. Second, the peasantry was again subjected to harsh government resource extraction policies. Already taxed at ten times per unit of land compared to the landed gentry, peasants in the 1880s bore the brunt of official modernization policies that attempted to cheaply and rapidly force Russian grain onto the world market by increasing consumption taxes and intensifying the collection of tax arrears.[148] Government revenues and grain exports did experience a sharp rise, but the overburdened rural economy was reduced to desperate straits, which finally resulted in a catastrophic, nationwide famine in 1891–1892.

Although state policy collided harshly with peasant welfare, it was the landed gentry that first felt the pressure of escalating mass land hunger and economic distress. We have seen that the abolition of serfdom "overturned the entire basis of the rural economy as previously practiced on the estates of the Russian gentry."[149] Having lost more than half its land and the free labor to which it had grown accustomed, the gentry in the postemancipation period faced the dual challenge of coping with the steady reduction of state funding and supporting itself economically. Many members of the old landed elite were unequal to the challenge; lacking the inclination or ability to farm on their own, these proprietors sold their holdings and attempted to maintain an aristocratic lifestyle on the dwindling proceeds. Thus, "by 1905 approximately 40 percent of the land held by the gentry at the time of emancipation had passed into other hands—most of it to peasants through collective purchase."[150] These land sales partially assuaged mass land hunger, but the more entrepreneurial response of other gentry proprietors worsened the postemancipation crisis of social and political control.

As Roberta Thompson Manning showed, the turn of the century witnessed a "turn of the gentry to the land and localities."[151] A vigorous minority of gentry proprietors attempted at this time to reverse the economic decline of the old landed elite and to retake the political initiative. Although some gentry families sold their holdings, others moved to the country, took an active role in the management of their estates, learned how to turn a profit, introduced new organizational and technological forms, and actively upgraded and expanded their property. While hardly widespread or successful enough to reduce the overall pattern of gentry economic decline, the attempt of some landed elites to adapt to changed circumstances precipitated outright conflict with the rural masses. In Manning's view, the gentry's turn to the land, the advanced agricultural techniques, and the increasing commercialization of gentry agriculture both reduced the amount of land available to local peasants and shattered the customary paternalism by which Russian landed elites and peasants had historically mediated their economic and social conflicts.[152]

At the same time, gentry involvement in local and regional politics increased. Gentry activism was both the political manifestation of the foregoing economic counteroffensive and a symptom of the deepening cleavage between the government and its traditional political infrastructure. Thomas Fallows noted that the zemstvo was from the start "dualistic" in its relationship to St. Petersburg, simultaneously functioning as a welfare agency and agent of control in localities and as a potential source of political opposition.[153] From the 1890s until the Revolution of 1905, the oppositional stance of the zemstvo became increasingly pronounced, a trend that finally culminated in demands for limited representative institutions and a constitution. This process was fueled by two related developments.

As peasants suffered the full force of state-imposed extractive practices, local elites were also pressured by official policies that favored industry over agriculture. Thus, "when, in the 1890s, the government committed itself to a policy of extreme protectionism for industry, many of the landlords protested that the tariffs and the whole fiscal system were designed to burden agriculturalists inordinately for the benefit of the owners of mines and factories."[154] As the financial demands of an expensive national modernization effort ran increasingly counter to local interests, exacerbated mass discontent, and magnified state-elite tensions, a collision occurred that closely paralleled processes I have already examined in late Qing China.

State-elite tensions also stemmed from the increasing bureaucratization and professionalization of Russian government. Well before the 1860s, Russian officialdom was increasingly split into two distinct groups—educated and professionally trained officials versus landowning officials of the traditional type.[155] With the postemancipation economic decline of the gentry, an equally dramatic political retreat took place as landowning and aristocratic representation at the higher levels of imperial officialdom declined precipitously. Whether from patrician disdain for the "plodding and pedantic" professional bureaucrat, or from a desire to tend to holdings in the countryside, landed elites disengaged in large numbers from state service over the course of the nineteenth century.[156] As the influence of the local elites in the state structure waned, they took up an oppositional stance, began to define themselves as "provincial gentry" and "local activists," and became increasingly hostile to the policies of the government and its professional officials.[157]

The decline of the imperial system in the postemancipation period was manifested in a proliferation of competing social, economic, and political forces. As peasant distress mounted and the alliance between Russian rulers and Russian elite groups continued to erode, the autocracy was beset by political fragmentation and intensifying social conflict. These tensions finally erupted with full force in the Revolution of 1905.

## The Revolution of 1905, Reform, and Reaction

While noting that "military prowess was crucial to the Russian state," Teodor Shanin suggested that Russian policymakers in 1904 launched "a plan for a little successful war designed to re-establish social cohesion and order," with "Japan chosen as the whipping boy."[158] But the "stupefying disaster" of the Russo-Japanese War exacerbated existing tensions as peasant economic distress escalated into outright rebellion and many segments of educated Russian society were moved into open political opposition. The year 1905 also witnessed the portentous advent of yet another sociopolitical challenge to the imperial order—the urban industrial proletariat. Russian industry expanded rapidly in the postemancipation period, and the brutal conditions of working-class life provided fertile ground for mass ferment. Before 1905, worker unrest had been contained by means of a sophisticated state-sponsored "cooptive strategy" that permitted "workers to organize for mutual benefit and self-improvement under the watchful eyes of the authorities" and attempted "to deflect workers' energies into peaceful, politically loyal channels."[159] Despite the emergence of an articulate and radical "worker intelligentsia" at the turn of the century, however, working-class protest remained "traditionalist" and overwhelmingly faithful to "the benevolent paternalism of the Tsar."[160]

Traditionalist protest was shattered on Bloody Sunday, January 9, 1905, when a procession of St. Petersburg workers carrying icons and portraits of the royal family attempted to present a petition to Nicholas II and was bloodily assaulted by imperial troops.[161] As Victoria E. Bonnell explained, this break with paternalism "was critical because it led workers to focus instead on their own collective efforts to win improvements in their lives."[162] As a nationwide wave of strikes and demonstrations erupted, working-class "collective behavior" was increasingly characterized by what Bonnell called an "eagerness for organization."[163] Class-based and nationality-based popular associations proliferated in summer and fall 1905: Mass demonstrations under red banners and armed clashes with the army and police took place in the Polish, Baltic, and Caucasian peripheries of the Russian empire; a nationwide general strike occurred in October; and Councils of Factory and Workshop Representatives, or soviets, were established in Moscow and St. Petersburg.[164] Initially stunned and cowed into concessions, the imperial government fought back with a ferocious campaign of repression and terror. Beginning with the suppression of the Moscow soviet in December 1905, when regular troops used artillery to level large areas of the Presnya district where the mass insurrection was centered, government "punitive expeditions" ranged far and wide, shooting and hanging hundreds of workers, flogging and arresting thousands, and systematically intimidating the population.[165]

Ferment in the cities was paralleled by the even more fateful eruption of mass land hunger in the countryside. Peasants in many regions attacked gentry landholdings, looted and burned down estates, and drove away or assaulted the proprietors themselves. The worst violence occurred where the terms of the emancipation settlement had been most detrimental, and the fertile black-earth provinces, where peasants had been apportioned the most "beggarly allotments," were "the hotbeds of peasant unrest throughout the 1905–1907 period."[166] In seeking to more favorably resolve the redistribution of resources initiated by the emancipation settlement, the peasants directed their fire against the landed elite in general and the new class of gentry entrepreneurs in particular. The political consequences of this collision were momentous. Zemstvo activists and much of the provincial nobility in summer and fall 1905 had seen the peasants as allies in the effort to wrest concessions from the autocracy. As the uncompromising thrust of mass land hunger became evident, however, the gentry moved en masse to the side of repression and reaction. In mounting a determined defense of property and privileges, the "reformist" gentry in the end subverted sophisticated official efforts to defuse peasant land hunger and militant collective action.

Even though government forces put down the upheaval in the countryside with the usual ferocity, an awareness nonetheless developed at the highest levels of imperial officialdom that peasant land hunger had to somehow be assuaged. The Kutler land reform plan of 1905 called for the expropriation, with due compensation, of all gentry land currently rented to peasants, along with the abolition of the peasant land commune. In attempting to simultaneously relieve land hunger and foster respect for private property, this proposal sought to "undermine the cohesiveness of the agrarian movement by enhancing the social and economic differentiation among the peasantry."[167] Similarly, fundamental changes in the condition of the peasantry were at the heart of Prime Minister Pyotr Stolypin's program of "pacification and social and economic reform."[168] Even as he presided over a bloody crackdown, Stolypin vigorously pushed the idea of peasant landownership and the transformation of the rural population "into citizens by giving them a stake in society, by making them realize that order and discipline were in their own interest."[169] But these farseeing proposals were vociferously opposed by the mouthpiece of the landed elite, the reactionary aristocratic organization the United Nobility, which in alliance with other right-wing parties successfully obstructed land reform and monopolized political power in the last years of the imperial era. Gentry reaction was formalized in the new national election law of June 3, 1907, "which gave the Russian squires incredible parliamentary powers—the Duma deputies representing 30,000 of them were now more than twice as numerous as those representing nearly 20 million peasant households."[170] Conservative, nationalist, and monarchist, "squiredom's political will was mostly limited to its own welfare and advancement."[171] Alarmed by and unable to comprehend the mass upheaval, the landed elite rejected the proposition that rural reform represented "the best protection of property and order" and tenaciously defended the traditional order and its own preeminent position in that order.[172]

Skocpol argued that a prerequisite for "widespread and irreversible peasant revolts against landlords" is a weak and dependent landed elite. We have already seen that this condition did not prevail in revolutionary China. In Skocpol's view, the Russian state until 1905, and from 1906 on, "retained the power and initiative to squeeze and significantly remake Russian society, even to the further detriment of the nobility."[173] In fact, state efforts in the post-1905 period to stabilize the situation in the countryside through land reform were derailed by the increasingly assertive and well-organized opposition of Russian landed elites. Even after the system of electoral representation had been revised in favor of the gentry, it opposed any diminution of its power at the local level and thereby doomed the government's attempt to build new bases of support with rich peasants.[174] This elite counterrevolution, centered on gentry resistance to peasant land hunger, captured state power in the wake of the Revolution of 1905, overturned the tenuous reform efforts of the imperial bureaucracy, and thereby sealed the fate of the imperial system.

## Revolution and the End of
## the Imperial Order

This is not the place to undertake a detailed account of the February and October Revolutions; the momentous and complex events of 1917 are the subject of a vast specialist literature.[175] It is evident, moreover, that the upheavals of 1917 should be understood as the culmination of power-restructuring processes long since in motion. As LeDonne concluded in this regard, "It was no surprise that the dynasty collapsed in February 1917 without even a revolution—without a political base, ruler and ruling elite had become superfluous, and its ruling class had disintegrated."[176] Although 1917 marked the final playing out of processes of imperial decline and breakdown, it also witnessed the onset of processes of revolutionary power restructuring that would gain momentum throughout the 1920s and finally come together in the formation of the Stalin system.

When imperial authority was undercut by economic crisis and military defeat in 1917, the urban and rural mass energies suppressed in 1905–1907 erupted with renewed force. In the cities, working-class attitudes and collective action became increasingly radicalized and polarized. Workers turned en masse against their employers and capitalist property relations in general, engaged in strikes and attacks on factories, and turned to violence in resolving disputes.[177] In the countryside, Russian peasants spontaneously renewed the attack on gentry estates, this time with conclusive results. Finally, 1917 witnessed the emergence of competing centers of political power and the systematic deployment of top and bottom versus the middle power-restructuring methods by the Bolsheviks. Capitalizing on mass radicalism and popular hopes that "for the first time in history ordinary people would be able to run their own affairs,"[178] Bolshevik propaganda relentlessly denigrated the authority of the Provisional Government, the bourgeoisie, and even the intelligentsia, while glorifying working-class organization.

As in revolutionary China, it was the interaction of popular aspirations and energies with communist power-building processes that undergirded the Bolshevik victory in October 1917. While allying with the masses to destroy the old order, the Bolsheviks also began the construction of a new and more far-reaching political, economic, and social order. When fanning the flames of "mass maximalism," the Bolsheviks insistently preached a program of elite leadership and vanguard party organization and "proclaimed 'discipline' not merely the basic requirement of proletarian organization but also the basic virtue of proletarian psychology."[179] The result was a historic synthesis of traditional patrimonial political culture, Marxist-Leninist ideology and organization, and social revolution. As Tim McDaniel argued, "The tsarist regime had taught workers a general lesson about the state, that its duty was to protect them." When the autocracy and the Provisional Government violated these assumptions, Russian workers did not reject the paternalist ideal; instead, in the Bolsheviks' "dictatorship of the proletariat" they embraced "a strong state that would represent only their interests and do so in a way that would achieve immediate results."[180] In Chapter 4, I discuss processes of revolutionary power restructuring and the rise of a system of power that would rule and reshape Russia in a manner both historically unprecedented and fully reminiscent of the traditional autocratic order.

### Notes

1. Richard Pipes, *Russia Under the Old Regime* (New York: Scribner's, 1974), 172.

2. Marc Raeff, *Plans for Political Reform in Imperial Russia, 1730–1905* (Englewood Cliffs, N.J.: Prentice-Hall, 1966), 3. Raeff argued elsewhere that Peter I's imposition of universal service requirements was the culminating act in creating a system of overwhelming state domination. As late as 1785, therefore, "in almost all respects the nobleman was as much subject to the arbitrariness of the sovereign and his agents as the lowliest serf was to that of his master" (*Origins of the Russian Intelligentsia* [New York: Harcourt Brace Jovanovich, 1966], 102).

3. Karl A. Wittfogel, *Oriental Despotism* (New Haven: Yale University Press, 1957), is the classic statement of this argument. See also Tibor Szamuely, *The Russian Tradition* (New York: McGraw-Hill, 1974). Szamuely spoke of a "Russian social structure" in which "all became compliant and powerless dependents of the State" and "a State stronger than the society over which it was raised" (36).

4. In *The Origins of Autocracy* (Berkeley and Los Angeles: University of California Press, 1981), 96–119, Alexander Yanov attacked the despotist interpretations of Pipes, Wittfogel, Szamuely, and Arnold Toynbee and attempted to put forward a new view of Russian political history focused on the distorting effects of the reign of Ivan IV.

5. Nancy Shields Kollmann, *Kinship and Politics: The Making of the Muscovite Political System, 1345–1547* (Stanford: Stanford University Press, 1987), 2.

6. Ibid., 3–5. Even though Shields Kollmann correctly rejected comparisons with Western Europe, the Muscovite system was not unique. Both it and the traditional Chinese political order were fully consistent with Weber's general model of patrimonial domination.

7. Ibid., 4.

8. Robert O. Crummey, *Aristocrats and Servitors: The Boyar Elite in Russia, 1613–1689* (Princeton: Princeton University Press, 1983), 110–111. Crummey also emphasized the uniqueness of the Muscovite high nobility and explicitly rejected comparisons with China since "its bureaucratic elite chosen by competitive examinations bears little resemblance to the Russian high nobles" (168). In fact, China's examination system was not a purely meritocratic instrument of bureaucratic recruitment and was riddled with particularistic features. It was, in any case, only one aspect of the late imperial political order, many features of which are closely paralleled in the Russian experience.

9. Brenda Meehan-Waters, *Autocracy and Aristocracy: The Russian Service Elite of 1730* (New Brunswick, N.J.: Rutgers University Press, 1982), 2.

10. Richard Hellie, *Enserfment and Military Change in Muscovy* (Chicago: University of Chicago Press, 1971), part 2. Thus, "the Bolotnikov rebellion, the first large-scale uprising in Muscovite history, evoked a clarification of the law on the peasant serf. . . . It may well be that the uprising, because of the fear and desire for revenge it instilled among the ruling elite, injected added life into serfdom" (109).

11. V. O. Kliuchevsky, *A History of Russia* (New York: Russell and Russell, 1955), vol. 1, 83. Recent Western analyses are not the first to view Russian political process in interactive terms.

12. George Vernadsky, *The Mongols and Russia* (New Haven: Yale University Press, 1953), 387. As Vernadsky noted elsewhere, "From the geopolitical point of view, the Russian tsardom was based on the Russians' rebuilding the political unity of the area of the Mongol empire. That historical process started from a different center of gravity—Moscow instead of Karakorum in Mongolia. In Prince N. S. Trubetskoy's words, the Russian Empire can be called Chingis-Khan's legacy *(Nasledie Chingis-Khana)*" (*The Tsardom of Moscow, 1547–1682* [New Haven: Yale University Press, 1969], Part 1, 4–5).

13. Nicholas V. Riasanovsky, *A History of Russia* (New York: Oxford University Press, 1963), 80–84.

14. Shields Kollmann described fourteenth-century Moscow as a tiny principality, "virtually a rural settlement," with a population well under twenty thousand. Prior to the reign of Dimitrii Donskoi, the Kremlin fortifications "consisted of earthen ramparts topped by a wooden stockade." Its small political system was "based on personal, comradely associa-

tion" (*Kinship and Politics*, 32–33). The contrast with imperial China could not have been greater; yet such humble beginnings formed the future basis of a great Eurasian empire.

15. John Fennell, *The Emergence of Moscow, 1304–1359* (Berkeley and Los Angeles: University of California Press, 1968), 41. As Vernadsky noted in this regard, "The Mongol invasion was a crushing blow to the urban democratic institutions which had flourished in the Kievan period all over Russia (and continued to flourish in Novgorod and Pskov in the Mongol period). . . . Because of this, the Mongols were determined to crush the opposition of the cities and eliminate the *veche* as a political institution. For this task, they engaged the cooperation of the Russian princes, who were themselves afraid of the revolutionary tendencies of the *veche*" (*The Mongols and Russia*, 345).

16. Robert O. Crummey, *The Formation of Muscovy, 1304–1613* (London: Longman, 1987), 39. When a revolt broke out in Tver', a combined Tatar-Muscovite punitive force sacked the city, ultimately putting an end to the aspirations of this longtime political and territorial rival.

17. Fennell, *The Emergence of Moscow*, 146.

18. Vernadsky, *The Mongols and Russia*, 215.

19. Shields Kollmann, *Kinship and Politics*, 29.

20. Crummey, *The Formation of Muscovy*, 99. In Max Weber's words, we see here the "natural process of decentralization and appropriation" under conditions of patrimonial rule (*Economy and Society* [Berkeley and Los Angeles: University of California Press, 1978], vol. 2, 1040).

21. See Vernadsky, *The Mongols and Russia*, 365. "It was on the basis of the Mongol system that Dimitri Donskoy succeeded in mobilizing the army with which he defeated Mamay at Kulikovo Pole. His son Vasili I used general conscription once more when he prepared to meet Tamerlane's invasion. In the 16th century conscription was used on several occasions" (365).

22. Ibid., 105, 372.

23. In Crummey's view, the period of significant Mongol overlordship ended in 1458 when Vasili II designated Ivan III as heir without first securing the approval of the Golden Horde (*The Formation of Muscovy*, 76).

24. In attempting to substantiate the argument that Russian political culture changed fundamentally over the course of Ivan IV's reign, Yanov contrasted the annexation of Novgorod by Ivan III, "an essentially European king," with Ivan IV's destructive assault almost a century later. "Both reprisals against Novgorod were cruel; both were accompanied by executions, persecution, and confiscations. . . . But in the first case, the reprisal was dictated by political necessity; in the second, it was an act of mass terror to facilitate the plundering of an already frightened people" (*The Origins of Autocracy*, 132–138). However, this interpretation is untenable; rather, the latter phases of Ivan IV's reign witnessed the intensification of power-restructuring processes already in motion under conditions of political conflict and terror.

25. Crummey, *The Formation of Muscovy*, 90.

26. Kliuchevsky, *A History of Russia*, vol. 1, 29–30.

27. Ibid., vol. 2, 54.

28. Shields Kollmann, *Kinship and Politics*, 44–45.

29. Shields Kollmann explained the rise to power and disgrace of the Patrikeev family in this light (ibid., 73–75).

30. In the 1930s especially, Soviet historians depicted Ivan IV in a positive light and sought to delineate the historically progressive nature of his centralizing policies. Yet Kliuchevsky and Riasanovsky, among others, emphasized the irrationality of Ivan IV's political behavior, and Yanov traced the origins of autocracy and virtually everything objectionable in Russian political culture to Ivan IV.

31. In 1551, Ivan IV condemned the boyars for failing to offer good counsel, "usurping independent power," and "seizing the opportunity for themselves" during his minority (Shields Kollmann, *Kinship and Politics,* 150).

32. S. F. Platonov, *Ivan the Terrible* (Gulf Breeze, Fla.: Academic International Press, 1974). Thus, "we have dwelt with these disturbances among the boyars in some detail, in order to demonstrate what Ivan witnessed during his childhood. Not an ideological struggle, not great political clashes, but petty hostility and spite, mean intrigues and acts of violence, pillage and caprice—all this he had to observe and tolerate day in and day out. Against this background Ivan's first perceptions were formed and his spirit developed" (33).

33. Robert O. Crummey, "Reform Under Ivan IV: Gradualism and Terror," in Robert O. Crummey, ed., *Reform in Russia and the U.S.S.R.* (Urbana: University of Illinois Press, 1989), 16–18.

34. Hellie, *Enserfment and Military Change in Muscovy,* 34–35. See Platonov, *Ivan the Terrible,* 50–56, for a discussion of the *kormlenie* system and Ivan's effort to secure control of local revenues previously appropriated by local power holders.

35. See Ruslan G. Skrynnikov's discussion of the land law of January 15, 1562, which forbade princes to sell or alienate their ancestral estates; established treasury control over escheated property, which had formerly gone to monasteries; required the czar's consent for nephews and brothers to inherit the estates of deceased princes; and empowered the treasury to confiscate, with or without compensation, ancestral estates princes had transferred to others (*Ivan the Terrible,* 61).

36. Instances of mounting political tension included boyar opposition to the reform of local administration in 1552; boyar refusal to swear allegiance to Ivan IV's son when he appeared about to die in 1553; Ivan's suspicion of top advisers in the death of Czarina Anastasia in 1560; the exile, expropriation, and execution of leading aristocrats in 1562–1563; and sharp foreign policy disagreements in 1563–1564. See George Vernadsky, *A History of Russia: The Tsardom of Moscow, 1547–1682,* 60, 61–63, 100–102, 103–104, 106–107.

37. Ibid., 107–109.

38. Kliuchevsky, *A History of Russia,* vol. 2, 86; Riasanovsky, *A History of Russia,* 170.

39. Richard Hellie, "In Search of Ivan the Terrible," in Platonov, *Ivan the Terrible,* xxi–xxiii.

40. Jerome Blum, *Lord and Peasant in Russia* (Princeton: Princeton University Press, 1961), 145.

41. Skrynnikov, *Ivan the Terrible,* 94. He also noted, "The tsar needed his own army because he planned widespread confiscations of princely estates. The authorities understood that seizing patrimonial estates, which always was considered illegal, without hearings at which landowners might offer a defense, was bound to produce intense dissatisfaction, and they were prepared to crush the nobility's opposition by force" (92).

42. Crummey, "Reform Under Ivan IV," 24.

43. Financial considerations were key in the sacking of Novgorod and Pskov. As Skrynnikov noted, "The needs of the state treasury were mainly responsible for the attacks on the

church, rich merchants and artisans of Novgorod. . . . Financial pressure caused the authorities to cast covetous eyes on the church, which was extremely wealthy, but the clergy had no intention of giving up its property" (*Ivan the Terrible*, 128–129).

44. Vernadsky, *The Tsardom of Moscow*, 108.

45. Thus, "the *oprichnina* council, headed by Basmanov, questioned each man closely about his origins, his wife's antecedents, and his friends. Low born gentry with no ties to the boyars were enrolled in the *oprichnina*" (Skrynnikov, *Ivan the Terrible*, 87).

46. Weber, *Economy and Society*, vol. 2, 1055.

47. Vernadsky, *The Tsardom of Moscow*, 174.

48. Shields Kollmann, *Kinship and Politics*, 183.

49. Among the many factors precipitating peasant flight from old Muscovy in the mid- and late sixteenth century, Hellie noted the internal disorders of the *oprichnina*, the Livonian War, high taxes, Tatar invasions, famines and plagues, and a "rise in the level of exploitation of the peasantry by their lords" (*Enserfment and Military Change in Muscovy*, 93).

50. Vernadsky, *The Tsardom of Moscow*, 219.

51. Ibid., 230.

52. Robert O. Crummey, "Constitutional Reform During the Time of Troubles," in Crummey, ed., *Reform in Russia and the U.S.S.R.*, 30–31.

53. V. O. Kliuchevsky, "Kliuchevsky's Analysis," in Warren Walsh, ed., *Readings in Russian History* (Syracuse: Syracuse University Press, 1963), 131.

54. Hellie, *Enserfment and Military Change in Muscovy*, 103.

55. Whether Mikhail Romanov signed formal pledges limiting his authority is unclear; among the many conditions he probably agreed to were promises not to avenge those responsible for abuses against his father, to rule by law, not to create new laws or abolish old laws on his authority, and not to wage war or conclude peace, by his own will. See Vernadsky, *The Tsardom of Moscow*, 278–280. But Marc Raeff noted that none of this is documented and may have been fabricated by Tatishchev and his circle in the 1730s (personal communication).

56. Crummey, *Aristocrats and Servitors*, 27. Crummey further noted, "Indeed, the extent to which Tsar Mikhail's council was aristocratic in composition, and the care with which genealogical seniority was recognized, suggest that the new regime was consciously trying to rebuild the shattered sixteenth century elite" (27).

57. Edward L. Keenan, *The Kurbskii-Groznyi Apocrypha* (Cambridge, Mass.: Harvard University Press, 1971), 83.

58. Blum, *Lord and Peasant in Russia*, 187–188.

59. Crummey, *Aristocrats and Servitors*, 111.

60. See Hellie, *Enserfment and Military Change in Muscovy*, 135–137, for a discussion of the sociopolitical setting, which included political demands on the state from the service elite, protests from townspeople, and the Moscow riot of June 1648, when members of the ruling elite were killed in mob violence, the houses of the wealthy were looted, and some twenty-four thousand structures were burned.

61. Vernadsky, *The Tsardom of Moscow*, 403. We see the patrimonial ideal in full flower here; hence, "that principle was applied in its clearest form to Siberia. The whole land fund of Siberia belonged to the sovereign. No private ownership of land existed in Siberia" (403).

62. See Richard Hellie, ed. and trans., *The Muscovite Law Code (Ulozhenie) of 1649* (Irvine, Calif.: Charles Schlacks Jr., 1988).

63. Vernadsky, *The Tsardom of Moscow*, 405–407.

64. Ibid., 408.

65. Crummey, "Constitutional Reform During the Time of Troubles," 39.

66. This process is voluminously documented in Hellie, *Enserfment and Military Change in Muscovy*.

67. Central rulers continued their efforts to develop alternative channels of power during this time. Czar Alexis (r. 1645–1676) used the "Secret Chancery" as an "alternative power base" and a "nerve center of the Tsar's interests." As Hans J. Torke concluded, however, the activities of the Secret Chancery were "unsystematic and accidental" ("Crime and Punishment in the Pre-Petrine Civil Service: The Problem of Control," in Ezra Mendelsohn and Marshall S. Shatz, eds., *Imperial Russia, 1700–1917: State, Society, Opposition* [DeKalb: Northern Illinois University Press, 1988], 12–13).

68. Marc Raeff, *Understanding Imperial Russia* (New York: Columbia University Press, 1984), 24–33. Raeff further asserted that "Moscow in the late seventeenth century was ready to accept and to copy the new cameralist political culture that came to it from Western and Central Europe" (33).

69. William C. Fuller, *Power and Strategy in Russia, 1600–1914* (New York: Free Press, 1992). Autocracy and serfdom were thus the foundations on which eighteenth-century Russian military power and success were built, as "the former institution mobilized military resources, while the latter supplied them" (455). Hellie long ago noted the Muscovite antecedents of the Petrine system; thus, "Peter the Great inherited three well-developed strands of the autocratic system, which he was to perfect even further. Ivan IV had a reliable police force, while the seventeeth century witnessed the formation of an army and a bureaucracy almost totally subservient to the will of the monarch" (*Enserfment and Military Change in Muscovy*, 258).

70. John P. LeDonne, *Absolutism and Ruling Class: The Formation of the Russian Political Order, 1700–1825* (New York: Oxford University Press, 1991), 25.

71. Kliuchevsky, *A History of Russia*, vol. 5, 74–75.

72. Raeff, *Origins of the Russian Intelligentsia*, 42.

73. Meehan-Waters, *Autocracy and Aristocracy*, 93.

74. Ibid., 92. As in all patrimonial systems, however, political considerations remained paramount. In Meehan-Waters's words, "Nevertheless, in the nature of an autocratic system, the power and wealth of any given official within the elite was tenuous, ultimately resting, as it did, on imperial favor" (92). Russian elites were able to guarantee and regularize their privileges in the post-Petrine era.

75. The Petrine military recruitment system mandated that every twenty households provide a fully supplied recruit and a replacement if necessary. See Fuller, *Power and Strategy in Russia*, 45.

76. Blum, *Lord and Peasant in Russia*, 415.

77. Ibid., 463.

78. Kliuchevsky, *A History of Russia*, vol. 5, 74–75.

79. "Towards the end of his reign, Peter's budgets came to three and a half times those of his elder brother. In the money of 1900, the budget of 1680 came to twenty million roubles, and that of 1724 to seventy million roubles" (V. O. Kliuchevsky, *Peter the Great* [New York: St. Martin's Press, 1958], 177).

80. Raeff, *Origins of the Russian Intelligentsia*, 46–47. See LeDonne, *Absolutism and Ruling Class*, 9–15, for an illuminating discussion of upward mobility and cooptation into the

elite in the Petrine era and in eighteenth-century Russia generally. In contrast to late imperial China, a virtually constant state of war and the need to replenish elite ranks were the driving forces.

81. This similarity was noted by Weber, who said of czarist patrimonialism, "However, political power and social prestige were—wholly in accordance with the Chinese pattern—dependent solely upon office-holding or directly upon court connections; this was especially true of all opportunities for economic advancement deriving here as everywhere from the exercise of political power" (*Economy and Society*, vol. 2, 1065).

82. James Cracraft, "Opposition to Peter the Great," in Mendelsohn and Shatz, eds., *Imperial Russia*, 24–25. This institution was an especially effective control device since "fear was nourished also by the realization that birth, family connection, social position, and rank in service were insufficient to shield anyone from the secret police" (Arcadius Kahan, *The Plow, the Hammer, and the Knout: An Economic History of Eighteenth-Century Russia* [Chicago: University of Chicago Press, 1985], 361).

83. Kliuchevsky, *A History of Russia*, vol. 5, 199.

84. In contrast to scholars like Raeff who stressed processes of institutional regularization under Peter I, Meehan-Waters emphasized personal rulership: "Imperial favor was a grace that descended down a ladder of patron-client relations, diminishing in efficacy at the lowest level of the bureaucracy, but seriously challenging the regularity of promotions and autonomy of institutions" (*Autocracy and Aristocracy*, 67).

85. We have already seen how Muscovite rulers sought to break up hereditary landholdings; Petrine policy was thus an extension of a long-standing effort to assert autocratic versus aristocratic prerogatives.

86. Raeff, *Origins of the Russian Intelligentsia*, 45–46.

87. Kliuchevsky, *A History of Russia*, vol. 5, 235.

88. Nicholas V. Riasanovsky, *The Image of Peter the Great in Russian History and Thought* (New York: Oxford University Press, 1985), 74–85.

89. Raeff, *Understanding Imperial Russia*, 69–73.

90. Kliuchevsky, *A History of Russia*, vol. 5, 267.

91. David L. Ransel, "The Government Crisis of 1730," in Crummey, ed., *Reform in Russia and the U.S.S.R.*, 62.

92. Richard S. Wortman, "Images of Rule and Problems of Gender in the Upbringing of Paul I and Alexander I," in Mendelsohn and Shatz, eds., *Imperial Russia*, 59.

93. Kliuchevsky, *A History of Russia*, vol. 5, 337–338.

94. LeDonne, *Absolutism and Ruling Class*, 88, 85. For an illuminating analysis of the centrality of intraelite battles for power and resources in Catherinian Russia, see David L. Ransel, *The Politics of Catherinian Russia* (New Haven: Yale University Press, 1975), chap. 4.

95. Isabel de Madariaga, *Russia in the Age of Catherine the Great* (New Haven: Yale University Press, 1981), 581–583.

96. John P. LeDonne, *Ruling Russia: Politics and Administration in the Age of Absolutism* (Princeton: Princeton University Press, 1984), 61–62.

97. Kahan, *The Plow, the Hammer, and the Knout*, 63.

98. Ibid., 64. According to Kahan's calculations, the male population of estates granted by Catherine II over the course of her reign exceeded four hundred thousand; by the 1790s, the estimated loss of revenue to the state exceeded four hundred thousand rubles per annum. Even though these estates were not previously state owned or were located in conquered

territory, the appropriation of state-owned property under Catherine was nonetheless extensive.

99. In Catherine's words, she "summoned several persons of different ways of thinking . . . to hear the Instruction. Every part of it evoked division. I let them erase what they pleased and they struck out more than half of what I had written" (cited in de Madariaga, *Russia in the Age of Catherine the Great*, 158). What a contrast to the Petrine mode of personal rulership!

100. Riasanovsky, *A History of Russia*, 287.

101. The text of this Pugachev manifesto is contained in John T. Alexander, *Autocratic Politics in a National Crisis* (Bloomington: Indiana University Press, 1969), 151. As Alexander discussed, "Mutinies and other forms of 'disobedience' by the peasantry marked every year of Catherine's long reign, the apogee of serfdom in Russia." Because of the "patent illegality of Catherine's accession," imposters and pretenders were a recurrent manifestation of popular discontent, and "submerged elements of society projected their aspirations for liberty and land" onto the image of a benevolent, legitimate czar (36–39).

102. Ibid., 186. The Pugachev uprising left a haunting impression on the collective psyche of Russian elites; fear of mass rebellion was a recurrent theme in the thinking of the aristocracy and officialdom well into the nineteenth century. See Richard S. Wortman, *The Development of a Russian Legal Consciousness* (Chicago: University of Chicago Press), 130, 144.

103. De Madariaga, *Russia in the Age of Catherine the Great*, 279–282.

104. LeDonne, *Ruling Russia*, 81.

105. Raeff, *Understanding Imperial Russia*, 99.

106. Ibid., 100–101.

107. August von Haxthausen, *Studies on the Interior of Russia* (Chicago: University of Chicago Press, 1972), 242.

108. Blum, *Lord and Peasant in Russia*, 390. As LeDonne remarked in this regard, "The aspirations of the nobility in the third quarter of the eighteenth century were not directed toward constitutional change. They aimed at securing control over land and serfs as sources of wealth, and the reforms gave them the mechanism to do so" (*Ruling Russia*, 80–81).

109. Blum, *Lord and Peasant in Russia*, 383. The primary function of banks in mid- and late-eighteenth-century Russia was to make loans to the nobility; the state supplied the capital and guaranteed deposits, rates were generous, rules were lax, and rollovers were frequent. As Kahan noted, "Officially the nobility mortgaged their serfs, but in fact the 'loans' turned into revolving accounts and were rarely repaid during the century" (*The Plow, the Hammer, and the Knout*, 311).

110. According to Kahan, "The increase of the tax burden on the taxpaying population toward the end of the eighteenth century, in comparison with the first years of the century, was on the order of a maximum of 80 percent. Adjusting for rent payments, the burden increase would be reduced to less than 50 percent." Peasant communities were also responsible for supplying and outfitting army draftees (or financing a replacement), a burden that increased drastically under Catherine II (*The Plow, the Hammer, and the Knout*, 345).

111. Raeff, *Understanding Imperial Russia*, 113–114.

112. LeDonne, *Absolutism and Ruling Class*, 51. Thus, "the accession of Paul in November 1796 represented a military coup by the head of the Romanov house against an oligarchic government of ruling families. The tsar, an adult male for the first time in the 71 years since the death of Peter in 1725, asserted his authority as commander in chief, pro-

ceeded to secure a political base in the army," and initiated "the militarization of the imperial government" (99).

113. Blum, *Lord and Peasant in Russia,* 354.

114. Ransel, *The Politics of Catherinian Russia,* 287.

115. Ibid.

116. Wortman, *The Development of a Russian Legal Consciousness,* 35–39, 116–117.

117. Raeff, *Understanding Imperial Russia,* 125.

118. Wortman, *The Development of a Russian Legal Consciousness,* 117.

119. Fuller, *Power and Strategy in Russia,* 455.

120. Ibid., 218.

121. Blum, *Lord and Peasant in Russia,* 354.

122. Walter M. Pintner showed that the expansion and increasing professionalization of the imperial bureaucracy represented both continuity and change. On the one hand, Russian officialdom had been undergoing an increase in absolute size and technical sophistication since the middle of the eighteenth century. On the other hand, under Nicholas I the split between professional bureaucrats and traditional landed elites was accelerated ("The Evolution of Civil Officialdom, 1755–1855," and "Civil Officialdom and the Nobility in the 1850s," in Walter M. Pintner and Don K. Rowney, eds., *Russian Officialdom: The Bureaucratization of Russian Society from the Seventeenth to the Twentieth Century* [London: Macmillan and the University of North Carolina Press, 1980], 192–193, 242).

123. Wortman, *The Development of a Russian Legal Consciousness,* 46. Nicholas successfully imposed more direct forms of state control on the nobility; young aristocrats, for example, had to meet university educational standards before appointment in the civil service (48–49).

124. Blum, *Lord and Peasant in Russia,* 547–548.

125. The waspish and sharply insightful Marquis de Custine had this to say about Nicholas's predicament: "It is true that the courtiers of the Czar have no acknowledged or assured rights; but they are still strong against their masters, by virtue of the perpetuated, traditional customs of the country. . . . This double struggle of the sovereign with his infuriated slaves on the one hand, and his imperious courtiers on the other, is a fine spectacle" (*Empire of the Czar: A Journey Through Eternal Russia* [New York: Doubleday, 1989], 312–313).

126. Walter M. Pintner, *Russian Economic Policy Under Nicholas I* (Ithaca: Cornell University Press, 1967), 35–44.

127. S. Frederick Starr, *Decentralization and Self-Government in Russia, 1830–1870* (Princeton: Princeton University Press, 1972), chap. 1.

128. Riasanovsky, *A History of Russia,* 411. This observation is substantiated in Steven L. Hoch's social history of a serf village. Russian serf owners did not invest capital in their property and were uninterested in technological improvements; rather, they focused all efforts on social control and labor discipline. Along with coercion and the cooptation of family elders, an important way of controlling young peasant men was the threat of being sent away as an army recruit. Although the universal horror of conscription worked as an effective control device, it also ensured that recruiting levies were full of social rejects, criminals, and cripples (*Serfdom and Social Control in Russia* [Chicago: University of Chicago Press, 1986], 9, 152).

129. Alfred J. Rieber, *The Politics of Autocracy: Letters of Alexander II to Prince A. I. Bariatinskii, 1857–1864* (Paris: Mouton, 1966), 28.

130. Cited in Alexander Gerschenkron, "Russia: Agrarian Policies and Industrialization," in *Continuity in History and Other Essays* (Cambridge, Mass.: Harvard University Press, 1968), 144.

131. Starr, *Decentralization and Self-Government in Russia,* 50.

132. Ibid.

133. Ibid., 120.

134. Richard G. Robbins Jr., "His Excellency the Governor: The Style of Russian Provincial Governance at the Beginning of the Twentieth Century," in Mendelsohn and Shatz, eds., *Imperial Russia 1700–1917,* 77.

135. N. A. Miliutin, cited in Starr, *Decentralization and Self-Government in Russia,* 250.

136. Even the conservative "counterreforms" of the late 1880s and early 1890s were unable to reverse the processes of power devolution set in motion by the reforms of the 1860s. As Robbins noted, "Central officials understood that these and other measures could never restore the powers of the prereform governorship. Authority at the local level was now thoroughly fragmented among institutions of self-government, the *gubernia* agencies of the several ministries, and the administrative apparatus subject to the governors" ("His Excellency the Governor," 78).

137. Daniel Field, "The Year of Jubilee," in Ben Eklof, John Bushnell, and Larissa Zakharova, eds., *Russia's Great Reforms, 1855–1881* (Bloomington: Indiana University Press, 1994), 41.

138. Gerschenkron, "Russia," 174–176.

139. Ibid., 178–179.

140. Ibid., 182.

141. Field, "The Year of Jubilee," 48–49.

142. Dorothy Atkinson, *The End of the Russian Land Commune* (Stanford: Stanford University Press, 1983), 23.

143. Gerschenkron, "Russia," 187.

144. Boris Mironov, "The Peasant Commune After the Reforms of the 1860s," in Ben Eklof and Stephen P. Frank, eds., *The World of the Russian Peasant: Post-Emancipation Culture and Society* (Boston: Unwin Hyman, 1990), 30–33.

145. John Bushnell attributed the "failure" of military reforms to the absence of "fundamental change in the political system." Hence, "inept command grew out of the practice of autocracy. Fundamental political, intellectual, and social characteristics of Imperial Russia produced faulty military performance" ("Miliutin and the Balkan War," in Eklof et al., *Russia's Great Reforms,* 155–156).

146. Richard G. Robbins Jr., *Famine in Russia, 1891–1892* (New York: Columbia University Press, 1975), 5–6.

147. Riasanovsky, *A History of Russia,* 479.

148. Robbins, *Famine in Russia,* 6–8.

149. Roberta Thompson Manning, *The Crisis of the Old Order in Russia* (Princeton: Princeton University Press, 1982), 4.

150. Atkinson, *The End of the Russian Land Commune,* 32. This unwillingness to engage in market-oriented economic activity is consistent with the cultural orientation of patrimonial elites. We have seen that Russian elites gained land and serfs through political action and royal favor; by the same token, serf owners took little interest in economic or technological improvements to their estates. In keeping with their military and administrative

training, they were oriented toward controlling and extracting resources from a subject population.

151. Manning, *The Crisis of the Old Order in Russia*, 43.

152. Ibid., 163. Thus, the new breed of gentry farmers no longer allowed peasants the customary free access to forests and pastures and no longer felt obliged to offer aid in times of economic distress, crop failures, or famine.

153. Thomas Fallows, "The Zemstvo and the Bureaucracy, 1890–1904," in Terence Emmons and Wayne S. Vucinich, eds., *The Zemstvo in Russia: An Experiment in Self-Government* (Cambridge: Cambridge University Press, 1982), 182.

. 154. Gerold T. Robinson, *Rural Russia Under the Old Regime* (New York: Macmillan, 1949), 146.

155. Pinter, "Civil Officialdom and the Nobility in the 1850s," 242–243.

156. Manning, *The Crisis of the Old Order in Russia*, 28–29.

157. Ibid., 39.

158. Teodor Shanin, *Russia, 1905–1907: Revolution as a Moment of Truth* (New Haven: Yale University Press, 1986), 28.

159. Victoria E. Bonnell, *Roots of Rebellion: Workers' Politics and Organization in St. Petersburg and Moscow, 1900–1914* (Berkeley and Los Angeles: University of California Press, 1983), 87.

160. Ibid., 93. Daniel Field argued that "the most obvious problem of the (paternalist) myth is that the tsar was not the benefactor of the *narod* (common people). . . . The tsar delivered millions of peasants and their families into serfdom and upheld and enhanced serfholders' authority with all the resources of the state" (*Rebels in the Name of the Tsar* [Boston: Unwin Hyman, 1989], 17). Yet the paternalist ideal was not without substance; in the nineteenth century it was the state that sought, ineffectively to be sure, to reform serfdom.

161. For a definitive account, see Walter Sablinsky, *The Road to Bloody Sunday: Father Gapon and the St. Petersburg Massacre of 1905* (Princeton: Princeton University Press, 1976).

162. Bonnell, *Roots of Rebellion*, 190.

163. Ibid., 149.

164. Shanin, *Russia*, 34–41.

165. For a detailed account, see Abraham Ascher, *The Revolution of 1905: Russia in Disarray* (Stanford: Stanford University Press, 1988), chap. 11.

166. Manning, *The Crisis of the Old Order in Russia*, 158.

167. Ibid., 223.

168. Abraham Ascher, *The Revolution of 1905: Authority Restored* (Stanford: Stanford University Press, 1992), 268–269. For an account of state repression and terror under Stolypin, see Ascher's discussion of the "fields courts-martial," whereby martial law was declared throughout the empire and arrested individuals were to be tried and convicted behind closed doors and their sentences carried out within four days. "When the law on the fields court was allowed to lapse on April 19, 1907, they had taken a terrible toll: 1,144 men had been executed, and 329 people had been sentenced to hard labor, 443 to prison terms of varying periods, and seven to exile. Only 71 of the accused were acquitted" (247–248).

169. Ibid., 269.

170. Shanin, *Russia*, 204.

171. Ibid.

172. Francis William Wcislo, *Reforming Rural Russia: State, Local Society, and National Politics, 1855–1914* (Princeton: Princeton University Press, 1990), 269–270.

173. Theda Skocpol, *States and Social Revolutions* (Cambridge: Cambridge University Press, 1979), 90.

174. Manning, *The Crisis of the Old Order in Russia,* 336–346.

175. See Roy Medvedev, *The October Revolution* (New York: Columbia University Press, 1979), for Bolshevik policy and organization in 1917; Rex A. Wade, *Red Guards and Workers' Militias in the Russian Revolution* (Stanford: Stanford University Press, 1984), for the "self-organized" workers' militias that emerged in the February Revolution; John L.H. Keep, *The Russian Revolution: A Study in Mass Mobilization* (New York: Norton, 1976), for the spontaneous mass upheavals of 1917 and Bolshevik containment efforts; Allan K. Wildman, *The End of the Russian Imperial Army* (Princeton: Princeton University Press, 1980), for the military collapse that sealed the fate of the autocracy.

176. LeDonne, *Absolutism and Ruling Class,* 309.

177. Tim McDaniel, *Autocracy, Capitalism, and Revolution in Russia* (Berkeley and Los Angeles: University of California Press, 1988), 312–317.

178. Keep, *The Russian Revolution,* 114. See also McDaniel, *Autocracy, Capitalism, and Revolution in Russia,* 390–391.

179. Theodore Dan, *The Origins of Bolshevism* (New York: Harper and Row, 1964), 254.

180. McDaniel, *Autocracy, Capitalism, and Revolution in Russia,* 351–352.

# 4

# The Rise and Consolidation
# of Stalinism

In this chapter, I take a more closely focused look at power relations and political process during the first two decades of Soviet rule and delineate the sociopolitical dynamics of the Stalin revolution in the late 1920s and 1930s. My discussion is focused on state-society interactions, three-way power contests, and top and bottom versus the middle power-restructuring phenomena during these years. I explore the manifestation of these processes over the course of the Stalin revolution and in the Stalin system that was consolidated in its wake.

In the Russian civil war and throughout the 1920s, the Bolsheviks built increasingly formidable military and administrative structures; yet these processes of concentration and control occurred in a setting of mounting societal flux and conflict. As an inchoate constellation of social forces contested the imposition of the new order and a nationwide struggle to control power and resources broke out, Soviet rulers sought to consolidate their still-tenuous grip in the 1920s by allying with and attempting to bring into existence supportive social forces. This pattern of expanded mass involvement in power-restructuring processes, first manifested in the revolutionary upheavals of 1917, accelerated during the 1920s and figured pivotally in the cataclysmic sociopolitical collisions of the 1930s. The genesis and dynamics of the Stalin revolution and the Stalin system must be understood in the context of these societal conflicts, three-way power contests, and sociopolitical collisions. Viewed in this light, Stalinism was neither a horrible aberration nor an unfathomable mystery. Without minimizing the violence and trauma of the power-restructuring events of the 1920s and 1930s, my discussion shows how familiar aspects of czarist autocracy were fused with essential features of Marxist-Leninist ideology and organization in the system that arose out of the turmoil and dislocation of the 1920s. But Stalinism was not simply a preordained scheme imposed on Russian society from on high; Stalinist power restructuring was a manifestation of the societal tensions, structural upheavals, and new demands of the day.

## Conceptualizing Stalinism

There is no scholarly consensus on the historical origins of the Stalin system or its connection with Leninist ideology and organization. In the conventional totalitarian terminology of Carl J. Friedrich and Zbigniew Brzezinski, "The first to formulate and set in motion the operational principles of the totalitarian party was Lenin," who thereby laid the ideological and organizational foundations of Stalinism.[1] In the wake of the Soviet collapse, this argument was put forward with renewed force by conservative analysts such as Martin Malia and Richard Pipes.[2] Yet in the 1970s, revisionist historian Stephen F. Cohen persuasively attacked the notion that Leninism foreshadowed Stalinism and argued that a deep divide separated important "liberal" and "pluralistic" strains in Bolshevism from the horrors of the Stalinist collectivization and terror campaigns.[3] In Cohen's view, the gradualist, market-oriented policies of the defeated Nikolay Bukharin were more consonant with Vladimir I. Lenin's developmental vision than with the coercive Stalin program that was implemented in the late 1920s and 1930s.[4] This positive assessment of Leninism was repeatedly aired in the Soviet Union in the period of perestroika, and Gorbachev always framed his liberalizing reform program in terms of reviving Leninist principles and restoring the Leninist vision of democratic centralism.[5]

But other revisionist analysts in the West were reluctant to so completely disconnect the events of the late 1920s and 1930s from the early history of the Soviet state. Sheila Fitzpatrick saw the Russian Revolution as a continuous process extending from 1917 to 1932 and therefore linked Stalinist collectivization and industrialization with the earlier formation of the Soviet state.[6] In this chapter, I draw on numerous revisionist studies of the Soviet 1920s and 1930s. Most of these studies take a less apocalyptic view of this period and focus instead on the building of a new Soviet economy and society in what is often viewed as an optimistic and dynamic period. Revisionist analyses emphasize the close ties between the Soviet state and urban workers in the late 1920s and early 1930s and the importance of social forces and of input from "below." With one or two exceptions, however, these studies do not attempt to establish linkages with subsequent developments in the 1930s.[7] For Fitzpatrick, who ended her account of the Russian Revolution in 1932, the Great Purges of 1937–1938 remain "a monstrous and still baffling episode," a "monstrous postscript added under the stress of impending war."[8]

None of the preceding arguments is fully tenable. To ignore or downplay the influence of Marxism, Leninism, and Bolshevism on the Stalin system is as mistaken as disconnecting the events of the New Economic Policy (NEP) and the First Five-Year Plan (FFYP) from related processes in the mid- and late 1930s. My discussion shows how processes of coercion and terror went hand in hand with the mass movements, economic development, and upward mobility that revisionist historians stress. But I do not embrace a clear-cut Lenin-Stalin linear continuity thesis. With concentration and control efforts contested from the outset, the actions of the new Soviet state were shaped and constrained by the social, economic, and cultural setting in which it operated. While drawing on essential aspects of Marxist-

Leninist ideology and organization, the Stalin system arrived at its ultimate form only in the course of protracted interaction with contending sociopolitical forces, both outside of and within the state apparatus itself.

An interactive view of Soviet politics and society in the 1920s and 1930s has been advanced by some Western scholars. In an account of strategies of political-economic organization in Soviet history, Moshe Lewin focused on the recurrent interplay of competing organizational models, especially those of NEP versus War Communism.[9] Attention to the ongoing interaction between state power and social forces is a prominent feature in all of Lewin's writing.[10] Similarly, Kendall E. Bailes suggested a view of Soviet society and of communist systems generally centered on "the interaction between the forces that tend to hold groups together for cohesive action and the forces of social conflict that tend toward their dissolution or transformation."[11]

State-society interactions and three-way power contests occupy center stage in my interpretation of power relations and political process in the first two decades of Soviet rule. My discussion of the 1920s and the period of the FFYP focuses particular attention on the interactions between the Soviet party-state and three key social forces—the peasantry, the urban working class, and the Russian technical intelligentsia, known at this time as "bourgeois specialists." As central rulers sought to redefine power relations with these groups, a series of conflicts and upheavals ensued that permanently restructured the economy and society of Soviet Russia. By the early 1930s, collectivization in the countryside, industrialization in the cities, and cultural revolution in government and higher education were marking the completion of the first phase of the Stalin revolution.

Yet this new social, economic, and bureaucratic order, so recently created and apparently firmly implanted, underwent in the mid-1930s a political upheaval as far-reaching as the social and economic transformation of the FFYP. This political cataclysm, which pivoted on renewed three-way power contests, culminated in the Great Purges of 1937–1938. Unlike the first phase of the Stalin revolution, when power relations between the Soviet party-state and the social forces of old Russia were recast, the second phase occurred within the structure of political power itself. Whereas the social forces of old Russia were brought to heel from 1928 to 1933, the years 1934–1938 witnessed the subjugation of the Bolshevik party and communist officialdom to the concentrated power of the Stalinist state. I begin my discussion of the rise of the Stalin system with an examination of state-society interactions and contending organizational and developmental approaches during the first decade of Soviet power.


## State and Society Under War Communism

During the Russian civil war, 1918–1920, the Bolsheviks sought to mobilize resources by imposing stringent controls on the economy, polity, and society through the policies of War Communism. While successfully resolving pressing organizational and military difficulties, War Communism aggravated the already profoundly disrupted economic situation and soon precipitated sociopolitical conflicts that threatened to overturn the new regime. In March 1921, the Bolsheviks reversed course and introduced NEP, a set of liberal policies hinging on loosened economic and social controls. Like War Communism, however, NEP resolved some difficulties while aggravating others. A series of political-economic debates was conducted throughout the 1920s, in which Russia's new rulers attempted to formulate organizational and developmental responses to the social and economic challenges of the day. This debate was finally resolved with the advent of the Stalin revolution, an extreme, yet entirely recognizable, version of War Communism.

War Communism was driven by pragmatic and ideological concerns. On the one hand, the Bolsheviks were preoccupied with sheer physical survival in a desperate situation during the civil war. All efforts were focused on rapidly mobilizing every available human and material resource, by force if necessary. In this sense, War Communism was the ad hoc by-product of extraordinary wartime circumstances; as Lewin noted, the massive wave of centralization, nationalization, and coercive mobilization that characterized War Communism did not get under way until June 1918, when civil war broke out.[12]

On the other hand, some Bolshevik theoreticians viewed War Communism as a necessary stage in the revolutionary transformation that Russian society was undergoing. Nationalization of industry, concentration of decisionmaking, distribution via rationing instead of the market, and "militarization" of labor were justified in terms of the Marxian canon and depicted as logical developments in the transition to socialism. In *The Economics of the Transition Period*, Bukharin argued, "Proletarian coercion in all of its forms, beginning with shooting and ending with labor conscription, is . . . a method of creating communist mankind out of the human materials of the capitalist epoch."[13] Even though the Bolsheviks in 1918–1920 were never able to decide whether such policies were short-term expedients or a long-term strategy, the War Communism experience was nonetheless portentous. It was at this time that the economic, social, and political tensions that erupted with full force in the upheavals and collisions of the Stalin revolution were first manifested.

The Bolsheviks were acutely conscious of their minority position and ever fearful of being overwhelmed by "the chaotic, elemental petty bourgeois forces of this backward country."[14] As the system of transportation and economic distribution collapsed and the urban population struggled to survive during the civil war, these fears were confirmed and reinforced. The contest between the new rulers and the social forces of old Russia was first played out in the primal arena of food supply. In May and June 1918, a system of compulsory grain deliveries was set in motion; these methods were ostensibly directed against rich peasants (kulaks), who were perceived to be profiteers withholding surplus grain from the cities.[15] As grain supplies in the villages were either purchased with worthless currency or confiscated outright, however, grain requisitioning became overtly coercive, and the already intense anti-urbanism of the peasantry was exacerbated.[16] At the same time, the urban population was forced into a desperate dependence on the food supplies still trickling in from the countryside, a situation on which the predominantly peasant private traders of the "second economy" were quick to capitalize.[17] As Daniel R. Brower concluded, "The impact on the towns of War Communism was thus to strengthen, not weaken, the operations of a petty capitalist economy."[18] These tensions, which pitted city and village against each other, mounted throughout the 1920s and finally exploded with full force in the opening phases of the Stalin revolution.

Grain requisitioning was emblematic of the overall effort to forcefully bring various sections of the population in line with the policies of the revolutionary party-state. Especially fateful was the Bolshevik affirmation of the principle of forced labor, methods that were initially deployed "on a class basis as a means of suppressing the resistance of the expropriated classes and forcing their cooperation with the proletarian state."[19] While targeting the old czarist privileged classes, however, Russia's new rulers still needed the technical and managerial skills of old regime elites and professionals. Large numbers of bourgeois specialists and former czarist officers and functionaries were employed in the government, the military, and industry during the civil war and War Communism, and czarist institutions, practices, and personnel were woven into the Bolshevik state-building process.[20] How, Daniel T. Orlovsky has asked, "was it possible in such a short time for the young Soviet state to have produced hundreds of institutions with tens of thousands of functionaries?" In fact, "revolutionary state-building was a dynamic social and cultural process with roots in the institutions of tsarist Russia and especially in the social revolution of the lower middle strata that reached its crescendo in 1917. . . . These groups grafted themselves onto the workers' and peasants' revolution and indeed managed to infiltrate a wide range of revolutionary class institutions."[21] Although Lenin defended the employment of bourgeois specialists as essential, the practice immediately aroused the suspicion and resentment of party rank and filers and much of the leadership.[22] The uneasy relationship between communist power and old regime professional and technical groups worsened throughout the 1920s; these tensions then erupted in the Stalin revolution.

Nor were old regime elites the only object of mass suspicion and resentment in 1918–1920; this period also witnessed the first rifts between the revolutionary party-state and its putative bulwark, the urban working class. The Bolsheviks had garnered popular support in 1917 by championing "workers' control of industry," but such notions were soon superseded by the realities of state power and social control. By the end of 1918, "collegial," or collective-consultative, management had been rejected in favor of "one-man management." At the Second All-Russian Congress of Trade Unions in January 1919, unions were absorbed into the state apparatus on the grounds that their work and that of the People's Commissariat of Labor were one and the same.[23] These control patterns intensified throughout the civil war period, culminating finally in the "militarization of labor," which Leon Trotsky in 1920 termed "the inevitable and basic method of organizing our labor force, and bringing about its compulsory grouping in accordance with the requirements of socialism during the period of transition from the reign of capitalism to the communist state."[24] Inevitably, workers resented the promotion of repressive measures by a party and state that supposedly represented their interests. Tensions were further heightened by the concurrent rise of a system of "commissar privilege," whereby a new stratum of factory administrators and government functionaries enjoyed privileged access to scarce resources at a time of terrible mass privation.[25] These sociopolitical grievances resurfaced and were fanned with devastating effect in the Stalin revolution.

An ominous surge of peasant resistance to official grain procurement efforts and the Kronstadt sailors' rebellion in March 1921 prompted the final abandonment of War Communism. Although these state-society conflicts were decisive in forcing the Bolsheviks to change course, the attempt to concentrate power under War Communism engendered tensions with the state structure as well. The civil war period witnessed what Richard Stites termed a "virtual orgy of separatism," as dozens of "republics" and "communes" sprang up and localities and even enterprises sought to govern themselves.[26] Bolshevik efforts to centralize economic power gave rise to organizational tensions that directly foreshadowed key political conflicts in subsequent phases of Soviet history. In the realm of macroeconomic administration, central authorities in Moscow in 1919 were already contesting local and regional soviets for control of industry. As "regional economic councils" (sovnarkhozy) pushed for a system of horizontal administrative controls dominated by the provinces, and the central authorities insisted on direct vertical control, elements of the center versus regions conflict that would be played out under Joseph Stalin and then Khrushchev were already visible.[27]

## State and Society Under NEP

The economic cornerstone of NEP was the replacement of grain requisitioning with a fixed tax in kind, on payment of which peasants were free to dispose of all extra production on the open market. In the Soviet 1920s, the impact of NEP was immediate and wide-ranging. By 1922, a full-scale agricultural recovery was under way, and by 1925 the sown area and grain harvest were close to prewar levels.[28] While facilitating recovery in the countryside, however, economic liberalization and social accommodation under NEP actually sharpened sociopolitical tensions.

With the legalization of private trade, small-scale private manufacturing, and the free sale of goods produced by such operations in August 1921, the Soviet Union was rapidly enveloped in a flurry of what Lenin termed "ordinary buying and selling."[29] In the first years of NEP, free markets, private trading stores, restaurants, and cafés proliferated in the cities, while village bazaars and local fairs regained their customary vitality in the countryside. Driving this market-oriented upsurge were the "nepmen," private entrepreneurs and middlemen who supplied much of the grain and food on which the cities depended and controlled at least 40 percent of all retail trade by the mid-1920s.[30] The revolutionary party-state, scaling back its authoritative aspirations under War Communism, now "cooperated" with private traders and the peasant majority on the basis of free trade and material incentives. Although the leadership sought to justify these measures by speaking of the "link between workers and peasants" *(smychka)*, such rhetoric never mitigated the "strong feelings of revulsion that private trade aroused among many party members."[31]

Yet economic liberalization meant a more accommodating official stance vis-à-vis "alien" social forces generally. As Alan M. Ball detailed, the toleration for "expensive amusements and public displays of wealth" during NEP extended from opulent food stores, hotels, and restaurants to race tracks, casinos, nightclubs, gambling parlors, brothels, and a flourishing bootleg liquor trade.[32] In January 1922, Theodore Dan observed that in Moscow "foodstuffs of all kinds were available at prices only the new rich could afford; 'speculators' were everywhere in evidence; the word *'barin'* [baron] was once more in common use by waiters, cab-drivers, etc.; and prostitutes had reappeared on the Tverskaya."[33] Nor were entrepreneurs, "speculators," and middlemen the only beneficiaries of NEP. Despite a general antipathy to the new regime, old regime specialists occupied most managerial and technical positions in industry, while in a time of acute hardship for urban workers, this small group enjoyed handsome salaries and numerous privileges.[34]

The partial economic recovery notwithstanding, many urban workers and party members increasingly viewed NEP in an unfavorable light, seeing it as a system that rewarded their "class enemies" and penalized the very people who had fought and won the revolution.[35] Politically, it seemed intolerable that the proletarian party-state no longer set the agenda and placed the interests of the working class foremost. Mounting frustration among urban workers and party members was further sharpened by stagnation and unemployment in industry. Although Soviet industry had recovered to prewar levels by mid-decade, resource constraints obstructed further expansion. Ironically, it was the newly won independence and prosperity of the peasantry that most directly constrained investment and expansion in industry.

The czarist state had relied on two sources of investment capital to fund its industrialization drive in the late nineteenth century: foreign loans and a merciless policy of internal resource extraction (discussed in Chapter 3). In the 1920s, neither source was readily available. Although the Soviet state sought to raise funds abroad, the Bolshevik cancellation of the czarist foreign debt in 1917 effectively foreclosed this avenue. But the collapse of the old system of economic organization and social control in the countryside was more fundamental. With land redistribution and the shift to small-scale, subsistence production in the villages, Russian peasants lived better and sold less to the towns and state. But lower grain marketings both created food supply problems in the cities and significantly reduced grain exports, the main element in the czarist system of internal resource extraction.[36] As William J. Chase discussed, "Economic officials hoped that, by purchasing peasant produce at prices low relative to those of manufactured goods, the peasantry would help to pay for the costs of recovery."[37] Yet "although illiterate, peasants were not dumb. Those who could afford to do so realized that, by withholding their produce (or selling it to a private trader who paid more for it), they could force up the price."[38] In the 1920s, a vicious circle set in. As the weakness of Russian industry and the high cost of its products undercut the quest for investment capital, peasants reacted to unfavorable terms of trade by withdrawing from the national economy and reverting still further to subsistence production. In Moshe Lewin's assessment:

> This breakdown virtually assumed the proportions of a total disruption of the country's economic existence. In addition to the shortage of industrial products facing the peasants, the towns and agricultural regions which were not grain producers were faced with a shortage of grain. This was the prelude to the "procurement crisis" which overtook the country at the beginning of 1928, and to a food crisis which was to last for several years; it also foreshadowed the dreaded *razmychka,* the break with the peasantry.[39]

## Power Concentration and Its Limits in the 1920s

Economic liberalization and social accommodation under NEP were paralleled by a concentration of political power in the state apparatus and a reinforcing of controls within the party. These efforts were manifested on two levels in particular: The political hold of the party on the economic and administrative organs of the state was tightened; and the power of the central apparatus over local and regional party organizations was broadened. At the same time, a significant increase occurred in the size of the party; at the primary level total party membership increased from 472,000 in 1924 to 1,304,471 in 1928. It was the mission of these newly enrolled party members, many of working-class origin, to staff the rapidly expanding state structure. By 1927, it was claimed that three-quarters of the staffs of boards of management of state trusts and four-fifths of all directors and assistant directors of state enterprises were party members.[40] In the 1920s, the Bolshevik party was transformed from a small, predominantly intellectual, revolutionary organization into a large, bureaucratized ruling body.

As has been well documented, processes of bureaucratized concentration and control were set in motion during the Tenth Party Congress in March 1921, when open discussion and debate within the party were restricted, the formation of internal "factions" banned, and all opposition parties suppressed.[41] More than three decades ago, Robert V. Daniels argued that with "the elaboration and perfection of the institutions of party organization and control . . . and the accretion of power to the people who directed them, the Communist Party was speedily transformed into a bureaucratic monolith running far beyond Lenin's demands for a central-ized movement."[42] Especially consequential was the concentration of organiza-tional power in the hands of an emerging "Stalinist" center in the 1920s. As com-missar of the Workers' and Peasants' Inspectorate (Rabkrin) in 1919, Stalin was charged with internal party organization and control. With his appointment as general secretary of the Central Committee in April 1922, whose purview in-cluded setting the agenda for Politburo sessions, the transmission of central direc-tives, and party appointments, promotions, and demotions at the regional level and above, Stalin and his allies in the central control apparatus came to dominate the internal affairs of the party.[43]

Despite these concentration and control processes, Soviet power remained far from monolithic in the 1920s. This was especially true in the villages, where the autonomy of peasant communities posed a formidable challenge to central au-thority. The party was numerically weak in the countryside, and traditional social organization under the leadership of well-to-do peasant elders remained vigorous and intact. As a result, the peasant land commune continued to play the predom-inant role in village affairs and readily obstructed the introduction of new forms of Soviet power.[44] Central authority was additionally undercut by the corruption of local party operations. As E. H. Carr observed, "The official policy of indul-gence to the well-to-do peasant adopted in 1925, and the recruitment of rural party members from the upper strata of the peasantry, had bred a certain identity of interest and status between the well-to-do peasants and party members and of-ficials in the countryside."[45] For most of the 1920s, then, the interests and power of local village society constantly and considerably constrained the interests and power of the revolutionary party-state.

Despite ongoing efforts to staff responsible positions with party members, a sim-ilar situation prevailed in industry. Because most communist functionaries lacked technical training and expertise, "the overwhelming majority of experts—from plant engineers and chief accountants to consultants and senior officials in govern-ment commissariats—were non-Communist and, in Soviet terminology, 'bour-geois.'"[46] Although most Soviet leaders understood the vital economic role played by bourgeois specialists, doubts about their political loyalty continued to evoke fa-miliar fears of alien social forces and class enemies; throughout the 1920s, more-over, relations between specialists and workers remained tense and hostile.[47] These fears and tensions were crystallized in the Shakhty affair in 1928 when a group of mining engineers was accused of engaging in sabotage and attempting the over-throw of Soviet power. Whatever the truth of the charges, official doubts regarding the political reliability of the specialists were not unfounded. Bailes spoke of a "technocratic trend of thought" prior to 1930, which held that technical specialists should not merely execute policies formulated by others but should themselves be politically active and take important policy positions.[48] As in the countryside,

Soviet power in industry coexisted uneasily with the reality of alien social forces that continued to wield considerable technical and managerial leverage.

Although relations between the new rulers and the social forces of old Russia remained unsettled, the state structure was itself the locus of power contests in the 1920s. With power constrained in the villages and factories, Soviet rulers also confronted the familiar phenomena of bureaucratic proliferation and encrustation at the national, regional, and local levels. Of course, Bolshevik fears of being overwhelmed by bureaucracy were of long standing.[49] Even more alarming than being smothered by former czarist functionaries was the prospect of the communist party being inundated by "careerists." During the civil war period and throughout the 1920s, party leaders repeatedly sought to combat bureaucratic encrustation by weeding out unsuitable persons who had recently become party members.

As J. Arch Getty detailed, efforts to cleanse and "purge" party ranks included a party registration in 1919, a party purge in 1921, a purge of nonproductive party cells in 1924, a verification of village party cells in 1925, selective screenings of various party organizations in 1928, and a major purge in 1929.[50] In November 1926, the Central Committee instructed the Central Control Commission and the Workers' and Peasants' Inspectorate to spare no effort in eradicating bureaucratic manifestations in the party and state structures—inflated staffs and salaries, red tape or the "flood of paper," out-of-control expenditures, and so on. Yet this campaign, conducted by fully empowered central organs, made little headway. Two years later, Sergo Ordzhonikidze, a member of the emerging Stalinist leadership, complained, "The fundamental defect in our apparatus is either a devilish delay in the execution of our decisions or a complete ignoring of these decisions or a distortion of their class content."[51] The revolutionary party-state in the 1920s, faced with real limits on its power in the countryside and industry, was beset with internal political and organizational conflicts. In patterns paralleling power-restructuring processes in late imperial China and Muscovite and imperial Russia, these conflicts pitted central rulers against the new representatives of Soviet power in the 1930s.

## Contending Strategies in the 1920s

The social, economic, and political tensions of the 1920s were aired in a momentous debate, over the course of which two very different visions of state-society relations and the most effective means of developing the economy and building socialism collided. I call these contending strategies, which were inspired by the contrasting experiences of War Communism and NEP, authority–social mobilization versus market–material incentive organizational and developmental approaches.[52] As a left faction of party leaders embraced the former, and a right faction the latter, issues of momentous and recurrent significance in the subsequent history of the Soviet Union and Communist China were fiercely debated for the first time.

For Bukharin, the foremost proponent of the market–material incentive approach in the 1920s, NEP was a long-term strategy: Agricultural production was to be increased by material incentives and more available consumer goods and the state-dominated industrial sector built up gradually, a mixed economy arrangement that would remain in place for some time.[53] Adopting a conciliatory view of alien social forces, Bukharin suggested that the violent class struggles of the past were now superseded by reform, economic gradualism, and the alliance of workers and peasants. Thus, increased mass consumption and the development of the internal market were the means by which industrial expansion should be financed; such a policy, to be sure, meant adapting industry to the needs and desires of the peasantry.[54] Politically, Bukharin asserted that the Bolsheviks were no longer "the party of civil war, but the party of civil peace," and now that the violent phase of the revolution was past, official activity should be focused on civil harmony and economic collaboration.[55]

Bukharin's strategy was sharply contested by the leading proponents of authority–social mobilization tactics in the 1920s, Trotsky and E. A. Preobrazhensky. Indeed, "the conciliatory attitude toward the village rich could not but arouse most deeply the Left Wing of the Party, which had considered the compromise with the individualist peasant a bitter, if temporarily unavoidable, sacrifice and which was pushing toward resumption of the offensive against propertied classes both on the domestic and international scene."[56] As early as the Twelfth Party Congress in 1923, Trotsky stated that NEP was never intended to last indefinitely, that a "new" socialist economic policy was in the offing, and that "ultimately, we shall extend the planning principle to the entire market, and by doing so we shall absorb and eliminate it."[57]

This stance was most cogently articulated by Preobrazhensky, who spelled out a program of internally financed investment, forced savings, and economic centralization and planning in his theory of "primitive socialist accumulation." Bluntly stating that the state and private sectors of the national economy were in conflict, Preobrazhensky argued that reinforced state controls were needed to ensure the growth of the emerging and still relatively weak socialist sector vis-à-vis the capitalist forces that continued to predominate. Thus, even though "the conditions under which the Russian proletariat must undertake the task of economically subordinating the peasant economy to state industry" were extremely difficult,

> our task as far as trade with the countryside is concerned consists in the gradual elimination of private middlemen; in the elimination of private merchant capital from the relations between large-scale industry and the peasantry; in reliance on cooperatives; and in the creation of a state monopoly not only over trade in products of large-scale industry but also in the sense of controlling the bulk of agricultural products that are poured onto the big market.[58]

In hindsight, it is evident that this statement contained the conceptual foundations of the future Stalin system of resource extraction and forced savings; yet Preobrazhensky's argument was put forward in 1922, when the fate of the new Bolshevik state was uncertain and the competition for power and resources still unresolved.

Both sides in the momentous economic debates of the 1920s claimed that their programs were consistent with Lenin's legacy. This was and continued to be an important question—where did the master stand on the issues of organizational and developmental strategy, the peasantry and private trade, the role of state planning, and bureaucratic encrustation? Just as the party itself was divided, Lenin's legacy was profoundly, though not entirely, ambiguous. On the one hand, it was Lenin who abandoned the methods and philosophy of War Communism and endorsed the worker-peasant alliance in 1921, thereby sanctioning the apparent long-term coexistence and cooperation of the public and private economic sectors. On the other hand, in his final speeches and articles of 1922–1923 Lenin argued that the transition to socialism was no longer a distant prospect and suggested that the entire population within "one or two decades" could be incorporated into "a fully socialist system" via state-sponsored cooperatives.[59] Moreover, Lenin's final forebodings about the ascendancy of the bureaucracy are contradicted by the state-directed processes of bureaucratized concentration and control set in motion during the civil war and accelerated in the 1920s. As Lewin noted, by substituting party leadership for worker control, the Bolsheviks "initiated managerial rule in the factories and the country as a whole," thereby laying the foundation for a massive new stratum of officials.[60]

In the all-important arena of power and leadership, however, Lenin's legacy was clear. In fact, the concept of the vanguard party as a core of professional leaders, organizers, and fighters whose primary function was to actively guide potentially revolutionary social forces in the direction of socialism was "the most original aspect of Leninism."[61] As an organizational tool, Lenin's vanguard party concept had repeatedly proven vital to Bolshevik survival and success. Proponents of party and state activism could claim ideological legitimacy and point to impressive accomplishments as well: the triumph in October 1917, the victorious buildup of central military and administrative capacities during the civil war, and the powerful state-building processes of the 1920s. In his political style, moreover, Lenin was an energetic personal ruler of the type we repeatedly encounter throughout this book. As Andrei Sinyavsky put it, "Lenin was an unusual tsar, a tsar who wanted nothing for himself and worked sixteen hour days, tending to every detail of the enormous State organism he had set in motion. . . . Nothing happened without Lenin's personal say-so in Soviet Russia."[62] When Lenin died in January 1924, his personal aura was symbolically linked to the power and legitimacy of the Soviet state; just as the Orthodox Church had legitimated the power of the autocracy, the Lenin cult sanctified the power of the revolutionary party-state in the 1920s.[63]

In contrast, the market–material incentive program represented compromises forced on the Bolsheviks in conditions of desperation and weakness. Indeed, Bukharin was defending policies that accorded poorly with Leninist activism and were proving increasingly disadvantageous to urban workers who in January 1928 made up the bulk of party membership.[64] By the mid-1920s, the Leninist penchant for power concentration and social engineering was being buttressed by

these potent social forces. The rising tensions of NEP set this combination of political and social forces in motion, triggering an interaction that propelled the first
phase of the Stalin revolution.

## The Stalin Revolution: Phase One

The first phase of the Stalin revolution marked the confluence of revolutionary
ideology and organization with familiar power-restructuring patterns and processes. Just as Muscovite and Romanov rulers sought to mobilize resources by
maximizing political control of Russian elites and harnessing the masses to the
economic objectives of the state, these aims were central in the emerging Stalin
system. Yet these objectives were attained by means of massive social and economic upheaval and historically unprecedented popular involvement in a revolutionary restructuring of power. The Stalin system was a modern and more dynamic manifestation of the concentration and control mechanisms characteristic
of traditional autocratic rule; the new system also mirrored the changes that Russian society had experienced.

How did this modern and more dynamic concentration and control system
work? By the late 1920s, the Russian political and social order had been only partially rebuilt; indeed, social fragmentation, or in Cohen's words, "social pluralism,"
was the hallmark of NEP.[65] But the notion of social pluralism in the Soviet 1920s
is inappropriate, for it implies levels of toleration, relaxation, and conciliation
wholly inconsistent with the tensions I have discussed. In fact, two competing and
increasingly incompatible social orders existed during the first decade of Soviet
power: a new communist state that commanded political and military power, yet
was unable to control the economy, and the far more numerous representatives of
peasant Russia, who possessed no political power but continued to dominate economic life. This competition was "resolved" in the first phase of the Stalin revolution, which destroyed peasant centers of economic and social power and set in
motion comprehensive, state-directed, resource mobilization drives. While pivoting on the wholesale application of coercion and control, the Stalin revolution
combined sanctions with incentives in a compelling and enduring mix.

## Coercion and Control in the Countryside

The forcible collectivization of the peasantry in 1928–1933 is often discussed
under such headings as "Suddenly and Without Warning" and "The Great
Change."[66] Yet the brutal and traumatic uprooting of the rural population was neither a sudden occurrence nor a fundamental departure from Bolshevik philosophy
and the methods of traditional Russian statecraft. The collectivization of agriculture was sanctioned by Marxist-Leninist doctrine and rooted in the experience of
War Communism; despite disastrous long-term consequences, collectivization,

like serfdom, reinforced the power of the Soviet state and provided vital resources for the emerging Stalin system.[67]

Although the proceedings of the Fifteenth Party Congress in December 1927 were largely devoted to the political liquidation of the left by the right, it was at this time that party leaders began to more assertively articulate ideas that finally demolished NEP. In a speech to the congress, Aleksey Rykov, a leading spokesman for the right, "accepted the principle of priority for industry and industrialization in the choice of main objectives in the country's economic policy" and acknowledged that the resources of the peasantry inevitably had to be used, within certain limitations, for the benefit of industry.[68] The proclamations of the rising Stalin leadership were more ominous. With Vyacheslav M. Molotov attributing the "basic weakness of the rural economy" to capitalist elements "getting the upper hand" in the villages, and the congress resolution proclaiming, "At the present time the task of uniting and transforming the small individual peasant holdings into large collectives must become the principal task of the party in the villages," the stage was set for the wholesale application of authority–social mobilization methods.[69] Although hedged with the qualification that persuasion had to be used, antikulak and antinepman slogans that called for the "liquidation," as opposed to the "limitation," of these groups permeated the Fifteenth Party Congress.[70]

The grain procurement crisis that resurfaced in the first months of 1928 reinforced this sharpening of political attitudes. Confronted with an apparently steep decline in state grain purchases from the levels of the preceding year, the Politburo ordered "emergency measures" and revived the familiar War Communism policies of grain requisitioning. Robert Conquest argued that the procurement crisis of 1928 could have been avoided by the "intelligent use of market and fiscal measures; and a certain amount of forethought."[71] But we have seen that market–material incentive policies were unacceptable ideologically and viewed as inimical by the urban workers who constituted the party's social base. In any case, the reversion to emergency measures irrevocably undercut the always tenuous NEP arrangement and set the Soviet state on a collision course with a peasant community determined to defend its basic interests and hold onto its recent gains.

The resumption of forcible requisitioning in early 1928 exacerbated grain procurement difficulties, as Russian peasants reacted to coercive state policies with widespread acts of active and passive resistance. Even though rioting, looting, and "kulak terrorism" were reported in the provinces, it was the passive resistance of the rural population as a whole that proved most damaging. As under War Communism, peasants cut back on sowing and buried grain in hiding places; they also "sold it to poor peasants at low prices, or to illegal private traders who smuggled it in parcels, on rafts, in carts at night. . . . When they could not hide or sell their grain, they turned the crop into hay, burnt it, or threw it in rivers."[72] As the grain supply situation continued to deteriorate in late 1928 and 1929, the authority–social mobilization tactics set in motion at the Fifteenth Party Congress hardened into a comprehensive concentration and control strategy. In Lewin's view, it was at this juncture that Stalin became convinced that the only way out was a "general of-fensive" to create state-controlled "strategic positions" in the countryside.[73] When a delegate from the Donbass miners complained about food shortages in May 1929, Stalin spelled out the strategy in full: "We have to accelerate collectivization and the construction of state farms, arm the collective and state farms with trac-tors and agricultural machines, teach collective farmers modern methods of agri-culture and ways to raise the yield, and then there will be plenty of grain, plenty of meat, and plenty of butter."[74]

But the thrust of Stalinist power restructuring in the countryside extended far beyond the provision of food supplies for workers and the cities. By 1930, "emer-gency measures," the "elimination of the kulaks as a class," and agricultural collec-tivization had been linked with a national program of crash industrialization. By channeling resources into the cities and industry and deflecting the grievances of urban workers onto the countryside, agricultural collectivization both provided the cornerstone for the industrial revolution of the 1930s and ameliorated the so-ciopolitical crisis of NEP. The peasantry and agriculture paid the price, which proved incalculably high.

Collectivization was violent, wasteful, and chaotic. In many areas, collectiviza-tion assumed the proportions of all-out civil war, and this time, unlike 1918–1922, the rural population faced a much stronger and more determined Soviet state. When peasants rose in revolt and "armed themselves with pitchforks, axes, staves, shotguns and hunting rifles," army, police, and militia units equipped with machine guns, artillery, armor, and aircraft were forcefully deployed; tens of thou-sands of peasants were executed and shot; and hundreds of thousands were ar-rested and deported.[75] Faced with the expropriation of their property, the peas-ants conducted a "great Luddite-like rebellion" and "slaughtered their cattle, smashed implements, and burned crops"; by 1933 more than 50 percent of the horses, 45 percent of the cattle, and 66 percent of the sheep and goats in precollec-tivization Russia had been destroyed.[76] While attempting to radically restructure rural life, central authorities and urban cadres were constantly stymied by peasant resistance, the hostility of rural officialdom, and the sheer magnitude and com-plexities of the vast countryside. As Lynne Viola documented, "The dense network of controls designed for the countryside during collectivization were erected in a bed of sand and were quite often simply impossible to enforce. The center was both all-powerful and completely helpless."[77]

Yet the collectivization of agriculture supplied the crucial material and human inputs for the first phase of the Stalin revolution. Peasant resistance, the wholesale slaughter of livestock, and reduced crop yields notwithstanding, state grain pro-curements and Soviet grain exports rose dramatically in the early 1930s.[78] By 1935, the direct and indirect contributions of grain procurement organizations accounted for one-third of total state revenues.[79] The peasantry also provided most of the raw labor power that fueled the industrialization drive. Even though millions of displaced peasants flooded into the cities and were incorporated into the expanding factory system, deported kulaks made up the bulk of the massive system of forced labor that had come into existence by 1930. In the lumber industry, which provided the major items of Soviet export at this time, only a small fraction of the labor force of 1.3 million were free men; most were exiled peasants, prisoners, or peasants recruited forcibly.[80]

In the late 1920s and early 1930s, the power of the Soviet state was used to harness the Russian peasantry to national power-building objectives. As the peasants themselves recognized, this arrangement closely paralleled serfdom; as in pre-emancipation Russia, the collectivized peasantry constituted an inferior economic, social, and legal class. Unlike czarist serfdom, however, the Soviet variant penetrated rural society more deeply and disrupted peasant life more profoundly. Indeed, collectivization reinforced the estrangement of the peasant community from the urbanized and modernizing sectors of society and made permanent a situation with "the state perceiving the peasant as dangerous to the foundations of the regime, and the peasant viewing the state as a menace to the survival of his family."[81] Collectivization did bring to heel an economic threat to Soviet power, but the long-term cost of the victory over the peasantry was a persistently under-achieving agricultural sector plagued by pervasive absenteeism, waste, hopelessness, stagnation, and backwardness.

## Coercion and Control in Industry

Power restructuring in the countryside was paralleled by massively accelerated concentration and control processes in economic administration and industrial organization. Fueled by inputs extracted from the collectivized agricultural sector, a system of centralized economic planning and resource allocation was erected over the course of the FFYP. These mechanisms of economic decisionmaking and resource control were entirely in the hands of central ministries in Moscow, whose "domination of plants through control of inputs was so strong that autonomy for the local producing units was virtually ruled out."[82] Thus equipped, Soviet rulers were able to prioritize the economy and funnel resources into key sectors, such as heavy industry, military production, and the cities. In the period of the FFYP, huge gains occurred in a wide array of basic developmental indicators, including steel, oil, cement, hydroelectrical power, and machine tool output. Overly optimistic growth projections and statistical inflation notwithstanding, the economic achievements were truly stupendous. In Alec Nove's words, "Though the claims in their totality are dubious, there is no doubt at all that a mighty engineering industry was in the making, and output of machine tools, turbines, tractors, metallurgical equipment, etc., rose by genuinely impressive percentages."[83] In fact, it was over the course of the FFYP that the foundations of the vast military-industrial complex that enabled the Soviet Union to survive and prevail in World War II were laid.

Yet these economic achievements were attained in a setting of unremitting crisis, chaos, and conflict. By summer 1930, production in many key industrial sectors was actually dropping and even grinding to a halt as overly ambitious expansion and pressure to fulfill plan targets led to transportation bottlenecks and shortages of material resources and skilled labor.[84] Macroeconomic confusion was then exacerbated by the influx of raw peasant labor into industry. Soviet industry during the FFYP was plagued by "phenomenally high labor turnover," and in the coal industry the average worker left employment three times in 1930.[85] While creating pervasive problems of labor discipline and training, the precipitous expansion of the workforce also engendered new social tensions in the factories. Older, skilled workers of established "proletarian" pedigree tended to view the new peasant-workers with contempt and resentment, seeing them as "uncultured, unskilled, and politically illiterate elements who knew little about the history and discipline of the factories."[86] Finally, all workers, old and new, suffered persistent economic distress during the FFYP as inflationary pressures and resource shortages resulted in sharp declines in real wages and living conditions.

Soviet rulers responded to these industrial conditions in two basic ways: by intensifying processes of coercion and control and by launching a vigorous sociopolitical campaign. Whereas the power of the factory manager had been partially constrained by the party cell and the local trade union chapter prior to the FFYP, this "triangle" was broken in 1929. In March 1929, a government decree drastically reinforced the principle of one-man management by excluding the party and union organizations from the managerial realm and by giving factory managers the authority to unilaterally impose penalties on violators of labor discipline.[87] In the early 1930s, these already extensive powers were further strengthened. As Lewin observed, "The 1932 decree on discipline now authorized not just the dismissal of the transgressor but depriving him and his family, on the spot, of their ration cards and evicting them from their lodging. Giving the director's power over the workers' food, lodging, and other supplies in times of hardship and famine was a very awesome tool indeed for disciplining and motivating."[88] Conversely, trade unions were ordered to turn their "face to production" and concentrate on improving productivity and discipline; instead of functioning as advocates of worker interests, union leaders now "spent their time instead persuading workers to stay."[89]

In an atmosphere where violations of labor discipline were treated as acts of counterrevolution, the police establishment played a pervasive role in economic life. "Special departments" of state security operatives charged with personnel surveillance and dossier compilation were installed in every factory and institution. Although police activity during the FFYP was largely limited to "silent, unobserved control," these units a few years later played a decisive part in determining the fate of millions of people in factories and institutions throughout the Soviet Union.[90] Most important, it was the police establishment that presided over the colossal expansion of the system of slave labor camps in the early 1930s. This singular system, a synthesis of the coercive labor practices of the traditional Russian state, modern police state methods, and communist developmental goals, differed fundamentally from the Nazi concentration camp system with which it is sometimes compared. Unlike the Nazi camps, whose primary mission was the physical destruction of entire groups of "inferior" racial and ethnic types and social and political undesirables, the Soviet slave labor system was geared in the first instance toward resource extraction.[91] The vastly expanded slave labor system of the 1930s was thus an extension of the collectivization and industrialization process; along with the property of kulaks, their labor was expropriated and channeled into state-directed economic expansion.[92] As observers have noted, the essence of the Soviet slave labor system was the fact that prisoner labor could be deployed with little investment of capital and that with minimal expenditures major projects in remote areas could be undertaken and substantial profits realized.[93] The system was also a formidable mechanism of social and political control, and it was in the slave labor camp system that the coercive processes propelling the industrial revolution of the 1930s were manifested in the starkest and most damning light.

## "Pushing Up": The Sociopolitical Dynamics of the Stalin Revolution

Coercion and control processes were but one prong of the Stalin authority–social mobilization offensive of the late 1920s and 1930s. Throughout this period, the Soviet state made energetic sociopolitical appeals to key segments of Soviet society and successfully enlisted allies at the mass level. These "authentically social dimensions" undergirded the Stalin revolution and provided much of the momentum of the system that arose in the course of collectivization and industrialization.[94] As revisionist studies of the period documented, the dynamic sociopolitical interactions of the late 1920s and 1930s "involved a response on the part of the leadership to pressures within the Communist movement and the society as a whole."[95]

The late 1920s and the 1930s were years of upward mobility and economic opportunity for many groups in Soviet society. Hundreds of thousands of young, rank-and-file party members and workers were incorporated into the state apparatus and enrolled in advanced training programs; these people constituted the nucleus of an emerging Stalinist elite. At the mass level, technical skills were more broadly diffused, and millions of illiterates were exposed for the first time to basic education.[96] On the one hand, this process was the natural by-product of the rapidly increasing need for skilled workers, foremen, and technicians in industry. Accelerated industrialization quickly solved the problem of mass unemployment, "which during NEP amounted to well over 10 percent of the employed population of the country."[97] So, too, was the expansion of the educational system dictated in part by the demands of industry. On the other hand, economic expansion was not the only force driving the upward mobility and economic opportunity experienced by key segments of Soviet society in the late 1920s and 1930s. These processes were propelled by explicitly political motives as the Soviet state sought to build its power by systematic social engineering and the creation of a new elite.

Beginning in the late 1920s and throughout the 1930s, Soviet rulers, especially Stalin, attempted to enlist young, rank-and-file, and lower-class people in the party and factories in the state-sponsored power-restructuring drive. Political appeals were directed toward these social strata, processes of mass mobilization were intensified, and people drawn from these groups were rapidly promoted and systematically placed in positions of importance and authority. In the official and popular parlance of the times, such people were often called *vydvizhentsy,* "pushed-up people."[98] Appeals to these groups and pushing-up policies were mutually reinforcing, and the interaction of these dynamic sociopolitical processes drove the first phase of the Stalin revolution.

A combination of communist ideology and organization and customary elements of traditional Russian statecraft, pushing up was a striking instance of the patterns of interaction and synthesis described throughout this book. In the ideology, rhetoric, and sociopolitical appeals of the late 1920s and early 1930s, the Marxist faith in the unleashing of progressive, new forces in the course of violent struggle with the class enemy was fused with the Leninist emphasis on organization building and vanguard party leadership.[99] Politically, pushing up and the appeal to young, rank-and-file, and lower-class groups were Soviet variants of the familiar attempt of central rulers to combat power challenges by creating new elites to supersede or bypass existing ones. As we have seen in Chapters 2 and 3, this pattern is recurrent in the history of late imperial China and Muscovite and imperial Russia; in the Soviet Union in the late 1920s and the 1930s high levels of mass involvement infused top and bottom versus the middle power-restructuring processes with unprecedented intensity and scope. At the same time, pushing up and attacks on class enemies were the means by which the Soviet state sought to alleviate and deflect the explosive economic, social, and political tensions that its mass constituency was experiencing.

With the deepening economic and social crisis in the countryside as a backdrop, spring and early summer 1928 witnessed a sharpening of political tensions and an onset of three years of "cultural revolution" and "class war."[100] When Stalinist authority–social mobilization advocates became embroiled in fierce policy disputes with moderates in the Politburo, who were then supported by professionals in the economic and planning ministries, a violent shift in policy occurred.[101] With the arrest and trial of the Shakhty engineers and technicians on charges of conspiracy and sabotage, a ferocious, officially sponsored national campaign against the bourgeois intelligentsia was unleashed—old regime professionals were accused of attempting to subvert Soviet power for their own ends, large numbers of bourgeois specialists were arrested and imprisoned on charges of "wrecking," purges occurred at all levels of the state administrative apparatus, and in 1930 forty-eight leading officials of the food industry were shot without trial on charges of sabotage and mismanagement.[102]

In the Industrial Party and Menshevik trials of 1930 and 1931, engineers, technical specialists, economists, and professors occupying senior positions in such major Soviet institutions as Gosplan, the Air Force Academy, and the State Bank were tried on charges of conspiracy and wrecking. But these preposterous charges were only a pretext, and it is evident that the defendants' real crime was their attempt to contest as "experts" the Stalinist leadership's formulation of economic policy during the FFYP. When, for example, Stalin called for sizable increases in already ambitious production targets in 1930, he encountered "the rational warnings of specialists against the adventurism and unrealistic schemes of some Party leaders"; Stalin would dismiss these views at the Sixteenth Party Congress as "hopelessly bureaucratic."[103] It has been argued, therefore, that Stalinist "class war" was guided by a coherent sociopolitical rationale—the accused in the Shakhty trial and those that followed and old regime professionals generally "were essentially on trial not as individuals, but as representatives of a class."[104]

In the late 1920s and early 1930s, Soviet rulers were confronted with a familiar phenomenon—their crash industrialization policies were being criticized and opposed by articulate and well-connected professional and technical elites. Like the peasantry, moreover, these still-autonomous centers of opposition and competition were socially alien and politically unreliable. Just as the Soviet state in the course of collectivization destroyed competing centers of economic and social power in the countryside and put in their place centrally controlled "strategic positions," Soviet rulers in 1928–1931 launched a sociopolitical attack on old regime professional and technical groups and began to systematically train and promote a more loyal and reliable Soviet technical and managerial elite.

We have seen that NEP was a time of hardship and disappointment for many urban workers, many of whom openly resented the privileged lifestyles and highhanded ways of the old regime specialists and Soviet managers who ran the factories. In the mid-1920s, party leaders attempted to alleviate worker discontent and improve economic performance by convening "production meetings," forums for workers to discuss ways of improving productivity and management. By the late 1920s, however, workers were using production meetings to "vent their hostility toward and grievances with factory administrators and technical specialists *(spetsy)*."[105] As Chase documented, moreover, rising worker hostility was legitimated by the "mounting public campaign by the party, unions, and state agencies to expose and reduce managerial abuses and inefficiency."[106] With the onset of the Shakhty affair and in the course of class war and cultural revolution, the Stalinist leadership encouraged and drew on this powerful upwelling of popular anger and energy and then directed it with devastating effect against real and potential opponents.

In addition to undercutting and dislodging existing elites, the upheaval from below was the means by which the Soviet state was able to enlist new supporters and build a new elite. Beginning in 1929, a mass campaign of "socialist competition" was set in motion, in which model workers organized into "shock brigades" took the lead in pushing for greater production and productivity, cost reduction, and labor discipline. In an account of "the emergence of new proletarian forces" during the FFYP, Hiroaki Kuromiya showed that "shock workers" *(udarniki)* were predominantly young, male party or Komsomol members who were "impatient with the given rate of industrialization." Materially disadvantaged and discriminated against during NEP, these young men sought to improve their situation by participating in the shock movement, aspirations that "were encouraged by and coincided with the political leadership's interests in the mobilization of available and hidden resources."[107] Shock workers simultaneously put pressure on management, older workers, and peasant laggards and provided the most avid and dependable source of pushed-up people. In July 1928, a Central Committee plenum decreed that 65 percent of people placed in higher programs of industrial education were to be of working-class origin; the quota was raised to 70 percent in November 1929.[108] By the end of the FFYP, some 150,000 Komsomol and working-class adults had been pushed up into institutes of advanced technical education, while perhaps as many as 1.5 million manual workers had been moved into white-collar and administrative positions or full-time study.[109] This state-sponsored group, many of whom completed their studies only in 1935–1937, played a decisive part in the second phase of the Stalin revolution.

Top and bottom versus the middle processes constituted the second major prong of Stalinist power restructuring during the FFYP. While class war and the assault on old regime professionals and managers directed rising sociopolitical tensions and hostility at the mass level onto socially alien and politically suspect elite groups, the Soviet state enlisted large numbers of new and committed supporters with its policies of personnel turnover, pushing up, and increased access to state-sponsored training and educational programs. The young workers, Komsomol, rank-and-file party members, and communist intellectuals at the forefront of the class war and shock campaigns of 1928–1931 were the nucleus of the new Soviet elite, the coming Stalin generation. Yet this new elite did not take its place for almost a decade and then only in the course of a violent political upheaval. Understood in this light, pushing up during the FFYP and cultural revolution of 1928–1931 was the first phase of power-restructuring processes that culminated in the Great Purges of 1937–1938.

## The Stalin Revolution: Phase Two

The foregoing interpretation differs markedly from that of the foremost revisionist commentator on the cultural revolution period, Sheila Fitzpatrick. The termination of officially sponsored class war radicalism in June 1931, Fitzpatrick argued, marked "the end of the revolutionary era." As social discrimination in school admissions was ended, labor discipline in the factories was tightened, and the old intelligentsia was returned en masse to positions of authority and privilege, "class war and the revolutionary spirit of 'storming the fortresses' fell out of favor." This "abandonment of revolutionary methods" and an attendant rise of an ethos of "consolidation and institutionalization" were the result, Fitzpatrick suggested, of successful industrialization and the ensuing desire of Stalinist leaders for "a restoration of order and discipline in the factories."[110] By 1932, therefore, "the institutional and social structure and cultural values that were to last throughout the Stalin period" had been established, and "Russia's new regime [had] settled into its mould."[111]

In contrast, Malia argued that the Great Terror of 1936–1939 marked the completion of Stalin's "work of system-building," as "the Soviet system at last would come to realize its maximum totalitarian potential," the essentials of which "would remain in place until the grand collapse of 1989–1991."[112] The Stalin revolution was indeed completed only in the course of the Great Purges of 1937–1938, when power-restructuring processes that had reshaped the economic and social fabric of Soviet life during the FFYP were extended into the political realm and the power structure itself was reshaped. But this was not a "totalitarian" process worked on, as Malia would have it, an atomized population, a "pallid shadow society," or "a mass of isolated individuals afraid to associate among themselves and constrained even from thinking of doing so by the new culture of socialism triumphant."[113] In a setting already charged by the tensions and upheavals of the 1920s and the FFYP, the second phase of the Stalin revolution witnessed a violent sociopolitical collision among central rulers, competing elites, and social forces at the mass level. The Great Purges were a top and bottom versus the middle power-restructuring event, which pitted a communist autocrat and his allies in the police establishment and at the mass level against communist elites that had grown mighty in the course of industrialization and collectivization.[114]

Interpretation of the Great Purges of 1937–1938 varies widely. Some Western accounts have long emphasized the direct historical connection between the power-concentrating drives of the Bolshevik party that came to power in 1917 and Stalinist terror generally, whereas others have viewed Stalinist policies during the FFYP as "a radical departure from Bolshevik programmatic thinking" and concluded that "from that first great discontinuity others would follow."[115] Prior to the period of perestroika, both official and unofficial Soviet commentary focused blame on Stalin as an individual. In the "Secret Speech," Khrushchev argued that "arbitrary behavior by one person encouraged and permitted arbitrariness in others"; Roy A. Medvedev, despite an exhaustive analysis of the political, social, and historical preconditions of Stalinism, found a final explanation in Stalin's "measureless ambition" and desire for "absolute power and unlimited submission to his will."[116] Some Western commentators also stressed Stalin's individual culpability and monstrosity. While exploring the historical and sociopolitical roots of the purges, Robert C. Tucker emphasized Stalin's "murderous conspiring" and "dramatizing mind" and asserted, "Further history of Soviet Russia, and of Europe and the whole world would have changed in many ways, for the better, if Tomsky had shot his visitor [Stalin] instead of or along with himself."[117] Other analysts have frankly been mystified by the purges. Hence, "among the stupendous and baffling traits of the Stalinist period were the mass schooling of the population coupled with the murderous destruction of the educated cadres and the imposition of so many sacrifices for defense together with the annihilation of the best officers."[118]

Although commentators sometimes note the sociopolitical dimensions of the Great Purges, no systematic discussion has been advanced. In a survey of contending interpretations of the "Stalin Phenomenon," Giuseppe Boffa endorsed the attempt to "locate the social underpinnings of Stalinism in the great social mobility made possible first by the revolution and then by the 'revolution from above'"; he also noted, "Personally, I am convinced that this is where we should dig."[119] But most analysts have tended to depict upheaval from below as motivated primarily by the petty resentments and crude ambitions of subordinates and as set in motion and manipulated by the top from start to finish.[120] Similarly, the "history-bred passivity" of the Soviet people has been invoked to explain Stalin's ability to "work his terrorist will on a nation of 165 million."[121] As Dimitri Volkogonov put it, "However artificial the means employed to achieve it, Stalin's popularity was genuine among the masses, whose opinion of him and the nation's affairs was based on appearances, usually because they had neither the opportunity nor the inclination to delve deeper into what was going on."[122]

Having charted the sociopolitical dimensions of Stalinist power restructuring during the FFYP, I can now extend this argument to the second phase of the Stalin revolution. The Great Purges were neither a baffling incident nor the result of Stalin's personal monstrosity and the passivity and ignorance of the Russian people. Whereas the first phase of the Stalin revolution marked the subjugation of the social forces of old Russia to the power of the Soviet party-state, the second phase marked the subjugation of communist officialdom to the power of the Stalinist state. Just as a confluence of state-sponsored social mobilization and upheaval from below propelled the restructuring of power during the FFYP, top and bottom versus the middle interactions were the centerpiece of the concluding phase of the Stalin revolution.

## The Rise of Competing Centers of Power

Some analysts have mistakenly discerned a degree of organizational stability in the Soviet system of the 1930s that was not realized until the post-Stalin period, but a spirit of "consolidation and institutionalization" was gaining momentum among Soviet political and technical elites by 1933. Having prevailed in the brutal collectivization campaign and achieved truly spectacular successes in the industrialization drive, many leaders were in fact ready for a "return to normalcy." Richard Lowenthal once observed that "economic growth achieved by politically forced development is accompanied by spontaneous social changes" as communist elites pursue their own interests in the new organizational framework and construct "new centers of social power."[123] Precisely such new centers of political and social power arose in the course of the collectivization and industrialization drives. As these power centers articulated their own interests and views and began to contest the authority of Stalin and his followers, political conflict erupted and power-restructuring processes already under way in society were brought to bear on the communist movement itself.

The rise of competing centers of power was evident in two key areas in the early and mid-1930s. Within the upper ranks of the party and state apparatus emerged a "moderate bloc" advocating a less frenetic pace of industrialization and a more conciliatory stance vis-à-vis the peasantry, old regime specialists, and inner-party oppositionists. At the regional and local levels, processes of bureaucratic encrustation and power and resource appropriation proliferated.

As Soviet and Western accounts show, there was extensive inner-party opposition to Stalin at the Seventeenth Party Congress in January–February 1934, and hundreds of delegates voted against Stalin's renomination to the Central Committee.[124] In fact, moderate tendencies had already been strong in 1932, when Stalin had insisted on the death penalty for the authors of the anti-Stalin "Riutin Platform" and been outvoted by a Politburo majority consisting of such "Stalinist" stalwarts as Sergei Kirov, Sergo Ordzhonikidze, and Ian Rudzutak.[125] By the time of the Seventeenth Party Congress, the so-called Congress of Victors, Soviet leaders standing for reconciliation, an abolition of terror, and a "return to normalcy" were clearly in the ascendancy.[126] Why did this shift occur in the direction of moderation and reconciliation on the part of top party leaders who had just presided over the brutal collectivization and industrialization drives?

In an account of the relationship between party leaders and the technical intelligentsia in the early and mid-1930s, Bailes provided an explanation for the changing attitudes of some top Soviet leaders. As early as spring 1931, there had emerged a "more moderate bloc . . . with its center of gravity among the industrial managers, headed by Ordzhinikidze, Commissar of Heavy Industry, and supported by his close friend in the Politburo, Kirov, party secretary of the heavily industrialized Leningrad region."[127] With the initial "storming" phase of the industrialization drive complete, these leaders were confronted with practical problems of economic administration; as political radicalism gave way to managerial concerns, moderate leaders sought "a restoration of order and discipline in the factories" and higher levels of productivity, efficiency, and technical proficiency. In Bailes's view, by 1931 Ordzhonikidze and his top industrial managers had recognized that attaining these ends meant stressing technical education and increasing the authority and status of the technical intelligentsia.[128] Since most of the *vydvizhentsy* were still in school, this policy shift entailed reconciliation with old technical intelligentsia, people who had only recently been the target of cultural revolution radicalism but whose skills were now deemed vital to improved economic performance.

Moderate party leaders promoted a comprehensive set of reconciliation policies. By mid-1933, many former inner-party oppositionists, including Bukharin, had been allowed to return to responsible positions in Moscow, while in the countryside private plots had been legalized, and the brutal system of high delivery quotas and low procurement prices had been relaxed somewhat.[129] But reconciliation entailed more than relaxation. Rather, a shift in worldview was under way in the party, a shift that threatened the power of Stalin, his followers, and the apparatus of coercion that had grown so rapidly over the course of the FFYP. While political radicalism gave way to managerial concerns, party leaders increasingly articulated the interests of the sectors for which they were responsible. Mary McAuley suggested that such "sectionalization" created new strains and tensions and that "within the top ranks of the party the different sectional interests jostled against each other."[130] As Soviet leaders consolidated their bases of power in the newly expanded administrative structures, sharp divisions began to split the party and pit managerial types in the industrial ministries against Stalin, his followers, and the police establishment.[131]

In a May 1934 speech that proved a harbinger of things to come, Stalin declared that the old slogan "Technique decides everything" should be replaced by a new slogan, "Cadres decide everything" and that "we must finally understand that of all the valuable forms of capital in the world the most valuable and decisive capital are people, cadres."[132] "Chiefs and leaders" had become excessively enamored of their successes and were incorrectly taking all the credit for the achievements of the FFYP; such people, Stalin remarked, were guilty of "a soulless, bureaucratic, and positively outrageous attitude towards workers."[133] A year later, Stalin spoke of "party and nonparty Bolsheviks" and asserted, "One can be a Bolshevik without being a party member," thereby undercutting the sanctity of Old Bolshevik pedigrees and serving notice that "the all-decisive cadres, the capital to be conserved, the plants to be cultivated, were especially the *little people* destined for places in a radically reconstituted ruling elite."[134]

Stalin's charges of arrogance and bureaucratism were not without foundation. Stalin and his followers were able to utilize mass hostility to the new class of communist officials and "Bolshevik grandees" as one component in a violent sociopolitical assault that destroyed real and potential opposition in the party and state apparatus. With the completion of this second phase of Stalinist power restructuring, a system of power was erected that subjected Soviet elites to unprecedented levels of central control. In the mid-1930s, however, moderate leadership elements supported by a strategically situated coalition of party leaders and technical personnel in the economic and planning ministries posed a serious challenge to the emerging Stalin system.

A second source of tension and conflict stemmed from processes of power and resource appropriation at the regional and local levels of the party and state apparatus. Even though the Soviet state had waged a largely unsuccessful war against bureaucratic encrustation in the 1920s, the state-building processes of the FFYP greatly increased the administrative functions of the party. The result was not the streamlined, disciplined, and dedicated organization of Leninist theory but a vast, raw, and unwieldy bureaucracy characterized by "lack of clarity in the division of functions, multicentrism, parallelism, enormous multiplicity of channels all the way down the line from Moscow to the *raiony* (districts), harassment and petti-fogging in supervision of the lower level by the higher, and constant delays."[135] Even more vexing than these familiar organizational difficulties was the problem of enforcing central directives at lower administrative levels. Regional and local officials did not necessarily promote moderate policies or explicitly contest Stalin-ist authority. Rather, in the customary manner of local power holders party lead-ers in the provinces and in the countryside paid lip-service to central directives, which they applied in their own fashion or ignored altogether. By the mid-1930s, Stalin was sounding a constant refrain against "family groups" in the party appa-ratus, "acquaintances, friends, home folks, personally devoted people, and masters at eulogizing their patrons," "who sought to live in peace with one another, glorify one another, and not offend one another."[136]

Recent Western accounts also depict the regional and local party organizations of the period as disorganized, corrupt, self-serving, and virtually impervious to central directives. Not only was the vastly expanded party membership cumber-some and hard to control; it also was full of careerists, opportunists, and "political illiterates," most of whom did not read the party press and "did not even know the names of the leaders of the party and government, much less the details of the po-litical platform."[137] Despite repeated purges, in which 116,000 party members were expelled in 1929–1930 and more than 1 million in 1933–1934, problems of control remained unresolved, prompting Stalin to complain at the Seventeenth Party Congress that "nine-tenths of our defects and failures are due to the lack of a properly organized system to check on the fulfillment of decisions."[138] The 1929 and 1933 general party purges were in fact impeded by the foot-dragging of re-gional and local officialdom. As Getty detailed, such leaders resisted centrally mandated efforts to disrupt family networks of power and influence; when the central authorities again attempted to clean house in 1935–1936 with a partywide verification and exchange of party documents, this effort also "foundered early on the rocks of bureaucratic inertia."[139] Within the year, Stalin and his followers would attempt to control communist officialdom and enforce central directives by reigniting a different and already proved power-restructuring strategy.

Getty suggested that the Great Purges cannot be studied as a single process since "the struggles over economic planning, treatment of the opposition, and balance of power in the territorial party apparatuses were separate problems in the 1930s," which reached "critical mass" only in 1936.[140] Yet Tucker asserted that "the Terror of the later 1930s is comprehensible as a political action only if seen in the larger setting of the revolution from above as Stalin conceived and was at-tempting to carry it out."[141] I have argued that the logic of the purges paralleled that of earlier Soviet power-restructuring processes. The sociopolitical upheaval of 1936–1938 was not solely the top-down creation of a dictatorial Stalin and his allies in the police establishment. Rather, the purges were an extension of the state-society interactions and three-way power contests that characterized the FFYP, the 1920s, and War Communism.

Elite politics in the early and mid-1930s mirrored fundamental sociopolitical developments. We have seen that an increasingly assertive group of party leaders wielding considerable economic and administrative power arose in the course of the FFYP. The moderate policies advocated by this new class of communist managers and technocrats threatened Stalin and his followers by bringing back into positions of power and influence inner-party oppositionists and old regime specialists with records of opposition to authority–social mobilization methods. Similarly, the moderate leadership's emphasis on educational credentials and technical expertise necessarily undercut the legitimacy of the coercive organizations and politically appointed personnel who had risen to power and prominence in the course of collectivization and crash industrialization. The threat to the police establishment was particularly obvious since its raison d'être was contradicted by a return to normalcy and the displacement of class struggle by managerial values and reconciliation.[142] But the sociopolitical dynamics of the purges would reveal that hostility to the new class of communist officials had deep social roots extending far beyond the police establishment and Stalinist "politicals."

However cynical the charge that chiefs and leaders were guilty of a soulless, bureaucratic, and positively outrageous attitude toward workers, Stalin's rhetoric resonated at the mass level. As McAuley noted, a new stratum of "hastily trained but well-paid" management personnel and technical specialists emerged during the FFYP; beneath this privileged group garnering the best material benefits "was a mass of unskilled, uneducated workers earning low wages."[143] Even though huge income and status differentials were sanctioned by the state and justified in terms of providing adequately for the best and brightest representatives of Soviet power, the privileged lifestyle of new class elites at a time of bitter privation for the majority was inevitably a source of resentment and hostility. In addition, the "high and mighty ways" and "communist conceit" of the new class functionaries further estranged them from the populace.[144] During the purges, economic discontent and perceptions of injustice at the mass level were fanned by Stalin and the police establishment and erupted violently.[145]

## "The Assault on the Party and State Cadres"

The attack on party and state officials during the Great Purges of 1937–1938 paralleled the power-restructuring experience of 1928–1931.[146] Whereas the cultural revolution was simultaneously a "revolution from above" and an eruption of social pressures, both occurring in a context of political conflict with overtones of class struggle, similar patterns were played out in 1937–1938. Just as old regime elites were delegitimated and attacked during the cultural revolution, new class elites were labeled class enemies and subjected to sociopolitical attack during the purges. Where the attempt to build a new "Soviet" elite underlay the upward mobility processes of 1928–1931, so, too, were targeted groups in 1937–1938 replaced en masse by younger, more politically reliable people from the lower classes.

Soviet accounts often date the actual inception of the purge process from the murder of Kirov. Evgenia Ginzburg began her account of the purges with the sentence "The year 1937 began, to all intents and purposes, at the end of 1934—to be exact, on the first of December."[147] Indeed, Kirov's murder did occur in an atmosphere of mounting political tensions stemming from both the rise of moderation and a series of unsuccessful internal organizational reform efforts, issues that remained unresolved. The first half of 1936 witnessed renewed conflict between Stalin and moderate elements in the economic and planning ministries regarding the direction and tempo of the Third Five-Year Plan; according to Bailes, the economic policy formulation process collapsed under these pressures, and the plan only took effect in 1938 after the purges.[148] The decision to reopen the Kirov case in mid-1936 must therefore be understood in light of these ongoing political struggles.

With the August 1936 show trial of the "Trotskyite-Zinovievite Center" on charges of "counter-revolutionary activity" and "terrorism," an ominous coalescence of anti-opposition and antibureaucratic rhetoric surfaced in Soviet political discourse. As *Pravda* editorials asserted that "enemies" had penetrated the apparatus, condemned local party leaders for having protected such people through "patronage and nepotism," and "called upon rank and file activists to unmask enemies in the party organizations themselves," political tensions escalated.[149] In a portentous series of speeches at the Central Committee plenum in February–March 1937, Stalin explicitly linked anti-opposition and antibureaucratic concerns and effectively put the party leadership on notice. While censuring party leaders for focusing on economic work to the neglect of political and organizational work, Stalin condemned "enemies of the people" who had penetrated "into some responsible positions"; Trotskyites, in his view, accounted for up to 10 percent of the party leadership.[150] Invoking familiar populist themes, Stalin put forward two demands. First, party leaders needed "better ideological education, and fresh forces, in line for advancement, must be added to them"; prior to attending six-month political and ideological courses, therefore, party leaders at all levels were to select several shifts of replacements capable of fulfilling their duties.[151] Second, Stalin reaffirmed the continuing need for criticism from below, whereby "the masses check up on leaders by critically noting their errors and ways of rectifying them."[152]

These statements have been subjected to very different scholarly interpretations. One commentator has maintained that Stalin's solutions were "not necessarily life-threatening" and that Stalin "urged reform rather than liquidation."[153] For Tucker, however, Stalin's call for intraparty democracy was a "smokescreen" and his speeches at the plenum "a performance by one of history's grand masters of political guile, whose capacity for evil knew no bound."[154] I suggest that Stalin's statements are most appropriately understood in light of the power-restructuring argument advanced in these pages. Like Chairman Mao's condemnation of a "small nest" of "powerholders in the party taking the capitalist road" and his call to "bombard the headquarters" in summer 1966, Stalin's demand that the party be reformed from below both legitimated and set in motion a violent sociopolitical assault on the party and state apparatus. As in the cultural revolution of 1928–1931, and the Chinese Cultural Revolution three decades later, the assault on officialdom during the Great Purges came simultaneously from above and below.

Many aspects of the Great Purges were relentlessly systematic and bore the clear mark of a central guiding force. This methodical, orchestrated quality was especially evident in the steadily expanded and always pivotal role of the police establishment. According to the memoirs of a People's Commissariat of Internal Affairs (NKVD) lieutenant colonel who defected in 1945, a comprehensive compilation of personnel dossiers was undertaken by the NKVD "under the general direction of Stalin's private *apparat*" during the 1933 general party purge; by October 1936 "NKVD purge groups" had been established in all major institutional spheres and had compiled lists of likely targets.[155] Stalin's call in February–March 1937 to root out enemies of the people was not put forward until the police establishment was fully onboard.

At the local level, the assault on the party and state cadres was methodical and inexorable. As Ginzburg detailed, the web of suspicion, denunciation, and arrest was typically first spun around relatively powerless and vulnerable members of the local elite, from whom incriminating "confessions" were extracted by a variety of means; this "evidence" was then used against their superiors, and the process was repeated in a steadily escalating pattern.[156] Or the pattern would be reversed, with top local leaders arrested first, followed by lesser officials "incriminated" by their long-standing involvement with enemies of the people.[157] In equally systematic fashion, the all-out physical assault on regional and local party leaders did not get under way until July 1937, a month after the core of the Red Army command had been summarily charged with treason on June 11 and tried and executed the next day.[158] Only after the military had been neutralized, and its connections with regional power centers severed, did representatives from the Stalin center move into the provinces and with the NKVD depose the local and regional party leaderships.[159]

The massive expansion of police activity during the purges was an extension of concentration and control processes already in motion. Just as increased central control and police power were brought to bear on peasants, old regime elites, and workers during the FFYP, this process was set in motion within the party itself in 1937–1938. Methods already successfully deployed against competing centers of social and economic power were used to attack competing centers of power in the institutions of party and state. The linkage between the purges and the power-restructuring processes of 1928–1931 was personified by NKVD chief Nikolay

Ezhov, who during the cultural revolution had been "responsible for providing radical proletarian cadres for industry and agriculture while removing 'bourgeois specialists.'"[160] This long-standing pushing-up proponent was in charge of compiling personnel dossiers in the mid-1930s and finally spearheaded the assault on the party and state cadres during the height of the Great Terror.[161]

During the purges, the NKVD emerged as a centrally controlled alternative to orthodox channels of party and state power; under "mature Stalinism" the police establishment functioned as an institutional alternative to party officialdom, which it held in check through the constant threat and periodic application of terror. Yet the NKVD itself was also subject to terror and periodic purging. As F. Beck and W. Godin related, "Members of the NKVD, from the lowest to the highest, led lives as harassed as that of every other Soviet official of corresponding rank and lived in equal or greater fear of arrest. . . . The higher an official's rank in the NKVD, the greater danger he was in."[162]

## The Revolution from Below

Why were powerful communist officials, especially regional and local party leaders who had successfully fended off earlier attempts by the Stalin center to reorganize their operations, unable to blunt the assault in 1937–1938? I have just discussed the top-down dimensions of the Great Purges and the scale and ferocity of the NKVD assault in particular; at the same time, it must be emphasized that communist officialdom and Soviet elites generally were the victims of a centrally encouraged upheaval from the bottom up. Not surprisingly, this process is the subject of sharp disagreement in the scholarly literature. While noting that "the center was stimulating criticism of local leaders" by encouraging "little people" to speak up, Getty insisted that "the February plenum awakened and unleashed this sentiment; it did not create it."[163] But Tucker unequivocally rejected this view, stating, "Lest the reader infer that the revolution from above was becoming one from below, it must be said that no 'revolt of subordinates' would or could have taken place without the permission, incitement, and pressure to denounce that came from Stalin and his accomplices."[164]

Attacks on local and regional party leaders were typically set in motion by populist appeals in the centrally controlled press, which, by urging rank-and-file party members to come out against their leaders, left local authorities "isolated," "paralyzed," and "demoralized."[165] Yet the revolution from below had real sociopolitical substance and should be understood as a manifestation of popular aspirations and interests and an eruption of smoldering suspicions, grievances, and anti-elitism at the mass level.[166] Edward J. Brown once observed that the pattern described by Ginzburg in her account of the purges and the slave labor camp system was one in which the prisoners generally tended to be intellectuals and members of the Soviet privileged classes, while "their jailers were almost all recently or barely educated workers or peasants, moral illiterates full of hatred for these alien types who had once 'eaten caviar by the spoonful' in hungry and miserable Russia."[167] This cruel and powerful alliance of top and bottom versus the middle was most graphically manifested in the slave labor camps, where educated people were singled out for the harshest treatment and camp administrators systematically favored the habitual criminal element, whom they used to terrorize and control the "politicals."[168] But popular hatred and resentment of privileged groups, the natural by-product of the usually harsh and difficult mass living conditions of the 1930s and an insistent theme in Soviet political culture in the 1920s and 1930s, pervaded the population.[169] During the Great Purges, these sentiments and interests were legitimated with the slogans of "class war" and "enemies of the people" and set in motion with devastating effect against Soviet elites of all types.

Was widespread popular hostility to the privileged orders the result of sheer "moral illiteracy"? The answer is yes only if the sociopolitical dynamics of the 1930s are viewed in the most superficial light. We have seen that the purges were an extension of the upward mobility, social engineering, and class creation processes by which the Soviet state consistently sought to bolster its power in the 1920s and 1930s. The assault on the party and state cadres was thus an extension of the pushing up processes already in motion in other institutional spheres. In industry, in the party and state apparatus, in the military, and even in the police establishment, Old Bolsheviks and many of the new class elites formed in the course of the FFYP were replaced by younger, recently educated people of overwhelmingly lower class origin.[170] People of this type, educated, promoted, and rapidly advanced in the 1930s, were the political and organizational mainstay of the system that was finally consolidated during the purges. With few ties to the classic Bolshevik tradition and very much the product of "Soviet" experience, the Stalin generation physically embodied the substantial political gains of hitherto non-privileged groups in Soviet society. My discussion has shown how the Stalinist fusion of power-concentrating and pushing-up processes simultaneously reinforced central authority, legitimated the attack on officialdom at the mass level, and provided a new corps of reliable leaders and officials. Stalinist power restructuring thus entailed not "the triumph of the bureaucracy over the masses" envisioned by Trotsky but the wide-ranging incorporation of a sizable lower-class contingent into a new ruling group.[171]

This is not to suggest that the Stalin system was participatory. It is certainly mistaken, for example, to speak of Stalin's interest in "populist control from below."[172] Once competing centers of official and elite power had been destroyed or neutralized and more reliable and pliable leaders put in place, the authority of the new leaders and their power over the masses was reaffirmed. Just as cultural revolution radicalism was abruptly terminated in June 1931, Stalin in October 1937 condemned radical "excesses," declared it wrong to persecute all leaders, and decreed that since the Soviet management cadre and intelligentsia were now of proletarian origin, they deserved the trust of the Soviet people.[173] But power relations had been fundamentally transformed by the late 1930s. The Great Purges targeted most explicitly the Soviet political elite that had come to power in the 1920s and grown mighty in the course of collectivization and industrialization.[174] As these high-ranking political, economic, and military officials were either destroyed or forcibly subjugated to a highly concentrated amalgam of Stalinist personal rulership, police power, and central ministerial hegemony, the dependent and uncertain position of all Soviet elites was underscored once and for all. As I discuss in Chapter 5, curbing the autonomy of officialdom and preventing the emergence of competing centers of power were perhaps the most important political aims of what Seweryn Bialer termed the "mature Stalinist system."[175] Yet in the decades following Stalin's death, the contest between Soviet rulers and Soviet elites would be renewed and their relationship redefined, this time with very different results.

## Notes

1. Carl J. Friedrich and Zbigniew Brzezinski, *Totalitarian Dictatorship and Autocracy* (Cambridge, Mass.: Harvard University Press, 1965), 46.

2. In Martin Malia's words, "One of the purposes of this chapter, therefore, is to derive Stalin's policies from the Soviet system rather than to work the relationship the other way around" (*The Soviet Tragedy* [New York: Free Press, 1994], 181). In Richard Pipes's version, "The leadership (in 1921) thus confronted a painful choice: whether to sacrifice unity and all the advantages that flowed from it by tolerating dissent within party ranks, or to outlaw dissent and maintain unity even at the risk of both ossification of the party's leading apparatus and its estrangement from the rank and file. Lenin unhesitatingly opted for the second alternative; by this decision he laid the groundwork for Stalin's personal dictatorship" (*Russia Under the Bolshevik Regime* [New York: Knopf, 1994], 436–437).

3. Stephen F. Cohen, "Bolshevism and Stalinism," in Robert C. Tucker, ed., *Stalinism* (New York: Norton, 1977), 3–29. See also Moshe Lewin, *Lenin's Last Struggle* (New York: Monthly Review Press, 1968), for an extended discussion of Lenin's unsuccessful effort to thwart Stalin's rise.

4. Stephen F. Cohen, *Bukharin and the Bolshevik Revolution* (New York: Oxford University Press, 1980), chap. 10. Theda Skocpol also emphasized the disjuncture between Leninism and Stalinism and argued, "In the end, triumphant Stalinism twisted and up-ended virtually every Marxist ideal, and rudely contradicted Lenin's vision of 1917 of destroying bureaucracies and standing armies" (*States and Social Revolutions* [Cambridge: Cambridge University Press, 1979], 171).

5. According to the Conference Resolutions of the Nineteenth All-Union Party Conference of the CPSU in summer 1988, "Our prime task is to fully restore the Leninist vision of democratic centralism, which implies free discussion at the stage when a particular question is being considered" ("On Democratizing Soviet Society and Reforming the Political System," in *Reprints from the Soviet Press* 47, 2 [July 31, 1988], 43).

6. Sheila Fitzpatrick, *The Russian Revolution, 1917–1932* (Oxford: Oxford University Press, 1984), 3.

7. See J. Arch Getty and Roberta Thompson Manning, eds., *Stalinist Terror: New Perspectives* (Cambridge: Cambridge University Press, 1993), for a collection of revisionist analyses of the role of social forces and input from below in the Great Purges.

8. Fitzpatrick, *The Russian Revolution,* 153, 3.

9. Moshe Lewin, *Political Undercurrents in the Soviet Economic Debates* (Princeton: Princeton University Press, 1974), chap. 4.

10. See Moshe Lewin, *The Making of the Soviet System* (New York: Pantheon, 1985), 286–314, for a critical discussion of predominantly state- and politics-oriented analytic approaches. Thus, "economic, social, and cultural phenomena have to be introduced into the analysis, even when the object of study is a powerful and arbitrary destructive despot" (288–289).

11. Kendall E. Bailes, *Technology and Society Under Lenin and Stalin* (Princeton: Princeton University Press, 1978), 8.

12. Lewin, *Political Undercurrents in the Soviet Economic Debates,* 76.

13. Cited in Cohen, *Bukharin and the Bolshevik Revolution,* 92.

14. Lewin, *Political Undercurrents in the Soviet Economic Debates,* 75.

15. Alec Nove, *An Economic History of the USSR* (Baltimore: Penguin, 1969), 59–60.

16. The events of the Civil War caused the rural population more than ever to see the city as "a complex organization of cunning people who lived off the bread and toil of the countryside, make useless things for the peasants, and who in all ways adroitly try to cheat and deceive them" (Richard Stites, *Revolutionary Dreams* [New York: Oxford University Press, 1989], 53).

17. Daniel R. Brower, "'The City in Danger': The Civil War and the Russian Urban Population," in Diane P. Koenker, William G. Rosenberg, and Ronald Grigor Suny, eds., *Party, State, and Society in the Russian Civil War* (Bloomington: Indiana University Press, 1989), 58–80. Although private traders kept the famine-stricken cities partially fed during the civil war, the urban population saw things rather differently: "The desperate search for any means to barter for food on terms set by the traders, largely peasants, represented one aspect of rural economic dominance" (74).

18. Ibid., 76.

19. James Bunyan, *The Origins of Forced Labor in the Soviet Union, 1917–1921* (Baltimore: Johns Hopkins University Press, 1967), 52.

20. As Pipes noted, this was a fateful development: "That the Communist bureaucracy should so quickly adapt old ways is not surprising, given that the new regime in so many respects continued old habits. Continuity was facilitated by the fact that a high percentage of Soviet administrative posts was staffed by ex-tsarist functionaries, who brought with them and communicated to Communist newcomers habits acquired in the tsarist service" (*Russia Under the Bolshevik Regime,* 505).

21. Daniel T. Orlovsky, "State-Building in the Civil War Era: The Role of the Lower-Middle Strata," in Koenker et al., eds., *Party, State, and Society in the Russian Civil War,* 191, 203.

22. E. H. Carr, *The Bolshevik Revolution, 1917–1923* (Harmondsworth: Penguin, 1972), vol. 2, 188–189.

23. Ibid., 191–204.

24. Cited in Bunyan, *The Origins of Forced Labor in the Soviet Union,* 134.

25. Mary McAuley, "Bread Without the Bourgeoisie," in Koenker et al., eds., *Party, State, and Society in the Russian Civil War,* 158–179. In the words of a nonparty delegate to the Petrograd soviet in 1920, "Comrades, under the bourgeoisie I wore a dirty blouse and the parasites who killed our working brothers and rank their blood wore ties and starched collars, and now our comrade members of the union organization have inherited those ties . . . and begun looking cleaner than the bourgeoisie. I suggest all bosses should be more

polite in their dealings with the working classes . . . and that all leather jackets should be handed in and be sent where they are needed" (175).

26. Stites, *Revolutionary Dreams,* 53–54. In the wake of the Soviet collapse and the ensuing crisis of central power in the early and mid-1990s, this phenomenon has reappeared.

27. Carr, *The Bolshevik Revolution,* vol. 2, 183–184. In Chapter 5, I look more closely at struggles for power and resources between the central ministerial apparatus and regional and local power centers in the late 1950s and early 1960s.

28. Nove, *An Economic History of the USSR,* 110–111.

29. Cited in Alan M. Ball, *Russia's Last Capitalists: The Nepmen, 1921–1929* (Berkeley and Los Angeles: University of California Press, 1987), 85.

30. Ibid., 104.

31. Nove, *An Economic History of the USSR,* 84.

32. Ball, *Russia's Last Capitalists,* 41.

33. Cited in Carr, *The Bolshevik Revolution,* vol. 2, 340.

34. In 1928, fewer than 1 percent of all engineers and technicians were members of the communist party. See E. H. Carr and R. W. Davies, *Foundations of a Planned Economy, 1926–1929* (New York: Macmillan, 1969), vol. 1, part 2, 578–580.

35. Thus, "workers distrusted and resented these social remnants of the ancien regime and those who prospered at workers' expense. They complained about the material privileges that these alleged class enemies enjoyed. . . . Whatever differences existed within the proletariat, widespread worker resentment (frequently fueled by the press) of 'bourgeois elements" privileges and power drew that class together" (William J. Chase, *Workers, Society, and the Soviet State: Labor and Life in Moscow, 1918–1929* [Urbana: University of Illinois Press, 1990], 129).

36. Whereas Stalin in 1927 claimed that grain marketings had fallen to 13 percent of total production, Nove cited figures indicating that 25 percent was marketed in 1909–1913 versus 21 percent in 1926–1928. In any case, "even if one allows fully for Stalin's statistical devices, the fact remains that marketings were below pre-war, while the need for grain was increasing and would obviously increase more rapidly as industrialization got underway" (*An Economic History of the USSR,* 111).

37. Chase, *Workers, Society, and the Soviet State,* 216.

38. Ibid.

39. Moshe Lewin, *Russian Peasants and Soviet Power* (Evanston, Ill.: Northwestern University Press, 1968), 185–186.

40. Leonard Schapiro, *The Communist Party of the Soviet Union,* 2d ed. (New York: Vintage, 1971), 313, 327.

41. Stites, *Revolutionary Dreams,* 140.

42. Robert V. Daniels, *The Conscience of the Revolution: Communist Opposition in Soviet Russia* (Cambridge, Mass.: Harvard University Press, 1960), 166.

43. Isaac Deutscher, *Stalin: A Political Biography* (New York: Oxford University Press, 1966), 230–234.

44. According to reports from local party organizations in 1927–1928, the ancient customs and traditions of the countryside had been "almost untouched by the revolution"; "the land community is the master," while "the village Soviet sits by one side" (E. H. Carr, *Foundations of a Planned Economy, 1926–1929* [New York: Macmillan, 1971], vol. 2, 248–249).

45. Ibid., 181.

46. Sheila Fitzpatrick, "Stalin and the Making of a New Elite," *Slavic Review* 38, 3 (1979):99.

47. Carr and Davies, *Foundations of a Planned Economy,* vol. 1, part 2, 574–604.

48. Bailes, *Technology and Society Under Lenin and Stalin,* 99. According to Carr and Davies, however, few, if any, specialists engaged in open political opposition. Rather, "active supporters of the regime were also not numerous," as most specialists "had no strong political convictions, and professed to be politically neutral, being concerned only to do a practical job" (*Foundations of a Planned Economy,* vol. 1, 580–581).

49. In the early 1920s, Lenin spoke of a few Communist leaders versus the "enormous mass of bureaucrats," and mused, "Who is leading and who is being led? I very much doubt if it can be said the Communists are leading. I think it can be said that they are being led" (cited in Lewin, *Lenin's Last Struggle,* 10). As I have noted, the early Soviet state structure was in fact heavily staffed with former czarist functionaries.

50. J. Arch Getty, *The Origins of the Great Purges: The Soviet Communist Party Reconsidered, 1933–1938* (Cambridge: Cambridge University Press, 1985), 40–41.

51. Cited in Carr, *Foundations of a Planned Economy,* vol. 2, 295.

52. These terms represent a synthesis of ideas put forward by Charles E. Lindblom, *Politics and Markets* (New York: Basic Books, 1977); and Franz Schurmann, *Ideology and Organization in Communist China* (Berkeley and Los Angeles: University of California Press, 1968). Whereas Lindblom divided the political-economic systems of the world into the two essential categories of authority oriented and market oriented, Schurmann identified two distinct economic and organizational approaches in Communist China in the 1950s and early 1960s, which he termed "social mobilization" and "material incentive" strategies. The contest between these contending strategies is a central aspect of power restructuring in the history of the Soviet Union and Communist China.

53. For a detailed and very sympathetic account of Bukharin's program, see Cohen, *Bukharin an.' the Bolshevik Revolution,* chap. 6.

54. Ibid., 182.

55. Ibid., 201–202.

56. Alexander Erlich, "Stalin's Views on Soviet Economic Development," in William L. Blackwell, ed., *Russian Economic Development from Peter the Great to Stalin* (New York: New Viewpoints, 1974), 219–220.

57. Lewin, *Russian Peasants and Soviet Power,* 143. Even at the height of NEP, Soviet authorities were ambivalent about private trade. In 1924–1926, liberal official policies were periodically punctuated with "administrative measures" and crackdowns on "speculators" (Ball, *Russia's Last Capitalists,* 44).

58. E. A. Preobrazhensky, "The Economic Policy of the Proletariat," in Donald A. Filtzer, ed., *The Crisis of Soviet Industrialization* (White Plains, N.Y.: M. E. Sharpe, 1979), 29.

59. Cohen, *Bukharin and the Bolshevik Revolution,* 136–137.

60. Lewin, *Lenin's Last Struggle,* 15–16. But Alexander Rabinowitch suggested that an all-powerful state was not implicit in the Bolshevik agenda from the outset. It was thus the "horrendous personnel losses" of the civil war that sapped the vitality and autonomy of district soviets in Petrograd; as all experienced local leaders familiar with weapons were rushed to the front, "structural distinctions between party and soviet all but disappeared" ("The Petrograd First City District Soviet During the Civil War," in Koenker et al., eds., *Party, State, and Society in the Russian Civil War,* 150).

61. Lewin, *The Making of the Soviet System,* 193.

62. Andrei Sinyavsky, *Soviet Civilization: A Cultural History* (New York: Arcade, 1990), 71.

63. Nina Tumarkin, *Lenin Lives! The Lenin Cult in Soviet Russia* (Cambridge, Mass.: Harvard University Press, 1983). When in fall 1923 Stalin proposed that "Lenin is a Russian and ought to be buried in accordance with this fact," Trotsky exclaimed, "The Russian manner, in accordance with the canons of the Russian Orthodox Church, makes relics out of its saints. Apparently we, the party of revolutionary Marxism, are advised to behave in the same way—to preserve the body of Lenin" (174–175). Trotsky's indignation notwithstanding, the creation of the Lenin cult graphically underscored the continuity in political culture between the old regime and the new state. See also Sinyavsky, *Soviet Civilization,* 112–113, for a penetrating analysis of the worship of holy relics and the religious foundations of Soviet power.

64. In January 1928, urban workers made up 56.8 percent of party membership, while state employees accounted for another 18.3 percent (Schapiro, *The Communist Party of the Soviet Union,* 316).

65. Cohen, *Bukharin and the Bolshevik Revolution,* 270.

66. Nove, *An Economic History of the USSR*; Deutscher, *Stalin.*

67. Those questioning the Marxian origins of agricultural collectivization need only consult *The Communist Manifesto,* which spoke of the "abolition of property in land," "extension of factories and instruments of production owned by the state; the bringing into cultivation of wastelands, and the improvement of soil generally in accordance with a common plan," and the "establishment of industrial armies, especially for agriculture" (Karl Marx and Friedrich Engels, *The Communist Manifesto* [New York: International Publishers, 1948], 70).

68. Lewin, *Russian Peasants and Soviet Power,* 202.

69. Cited in ibid., 205; Nove, *An Economic History of the USSR,* 148.

70. Lewin, *Russian Peasants and Soviet Power,* 200.

71. Robert Conquest, *The Harvest of Sorrow* (New York: Oxford University Press, 1986), 87, pointed to the failure of the Soviet government to build up grain reserves in good years and its unwillingness to offer favorable terms of trade to the peasants, noted that Stalin distorted grain procurement statistics, and suggested that the deficit in January 1928 did not constitute a "danger" or "crisis." But this argument is too narrow; the decision to collectivize was driven by a combination of economic considerations, ideological predilections, and social forces.

72. Ibid., 102–103.

73. Lewin, *Russian Peasants and Soviet Power,* 255–257.

74. Cited in Hiroaki Kuromiya, *Stalin's Industrial Revolution: Politics and Workers, 1928–1932* (Cambridge: Cambridge University Press, 1988), 85–86. As Kuromiya noted in this regard, "Whether Stalin's analysis of food shortages convinced the working class is arguable. What is definite is that he sought to deflect their grievances to the countryside and elicit their political support for the collectivization drive" (86).

75. Conquest, *The Harvest of Sorrow,* 154.

76. Deutscher, *Stalin,* 325.

77. Lynne Viola, *The Best Sons of the Fatherland: Workers in the Vanguard of Soviet Collectivization* (New York: Oxford University Press, 1987), 89.

78. Whereas state grain procurements totaled 10.8 million tons in 1928, the figures for 1930 and 1931 were 22.1 and 22.8 million tons, respectively; whereas 0.18 million tons of

grain were exported in 1929, the figures for 1930 and 1931 were 4.6 and 5.06 million tons, respectively (Nove, *An Economic History of the USSR,* 180).

79. Ibid., 211.

80. David J. Dallin and Boris I. Nicolaevsky, *Forced Labor in Soviet Russia* (New Haven: Yale University Press, 1947), 197–200.

81. Lewin, *The Making of the Soviet System,* 184.

82. Lewin, *Political Undercurrents in the Soviet Economic Debates,* 107.

83. Nove, *An Economic History of the USSR,* 193.

84. In Kuromiya's words, "A vicious circle emerged at this time: the overwhelming pressure for the fulfillment of plan targets inevitably led to a sharp decline in the quality of products; the lower quality of goods forced factories to consume them in greater quantity, thereby increasing demands for quantity" (*Stalin's Industrial Revolution,* 160).

85. Thus, "the peasant workers, bewildered by their new surroundings, often short of food and adequate lodging, wandered about in search of better things" (Nove, *An Economic History of the USSR,* 197).

86. Kuromiya, *Stalin's Industrial Revolution,* 93.

87. Ibid., 72.

88. Lewin, *The Making of the Soviet System,* 252–253.

89. John Scott, *Behind the Urals* (Cambridge, Mass.: Riverside Press, 1942), 74–75.

90. Ibid., 84–85.

91. Roy A. Medvedev stressed the primarily economic function of the Soviet GULAG (*Let History Judge* [New York: Knopf, 1972], 394). But Robert Conquest argued that, whereas economic aims were foremost in the late 1920s and early 1930s, by 1937 the "central aim was to kill off the prisoners" (*Kolyma* [New York: Viking, 1978], 17). In contrast to Nazi ovens and gas chambers, Soviet prisoners were worked to death, in accordance with the economic thrust of the system.

92. This aspect of the Stalin revolution was widely recognized. In an enthusiastic account of the building of the Magnitogorsk industrial complex in the early 1930s, John Scott noted that some fifty thousand workers were under police supervision; these "de-kulak-ized, well-to-do farmers" and "criminals" worked under guard and "formed the reservoir of labor power needed to dig foundations, wheel concrete, shovel slag, and do heavy work" (*Behind the Urals,* 85).

93. Dallin and Nicolaevsky, *Forced Labor in Soviet Russia,* 88–89.

94. Stephen F. Cohen, *Rethinking the Soviet Experience* (New York: Oxford University Press, 1985), 23.

95. Sheila Fitzpatrick, "The Cultural Revolution as Class War," in Sheila Fitzpatrick, ed., *Cultural Revolution in Russia, 1928–1931* (Bloomington: Indiana University Press, 1978), 12.

96. Sheila Fitzpatrick, *Education and Social Mobility in the Soviet Union, 1921–1934* (Cambridge: Cambridge University Press, 1979). See Chapter 11 for a summation of Fitzpatrick's upward mobility and elite-building thesis.

97. Kuromiya, *Stalin's Industrial Revolution,* 200.

98. In fact, systematic pushing-up policies dated from the early 1920s; during the Stalin revolution these methods were deployed on a larger scale (Medvedev, *Let History Judge,* 313–315).

99. Once again, the notion that violent struggle against the class enemy was both necessary and heroic was not new. During the struggle against counterrevolution in the civil war, "the Cheka was the dictatorship's most frightening instrument, sowing terror throughout

Russia. But Dzerzhinsky, the new government's premier executioner, fairly shone in all his blood-red, merciless glory. In the system of new ethical values, this chief hangman and jailer became the preeminent moral model" (Sinyavsky, *Soviet Civilization,* 125). In the 1930s, this kind of mentality was fused with upheaval from below, with devastating consequences.

100. Fitzpatrick, "The Cultural Revolution as Class War," 9–11.

101. Bailes, *Technology and Society Under Lenin and Stalin,* 115.

102. Robert Conquest, *The Great Terror* (New York: Macmillan, 1968), 551.

103. Medvedev, *Let History Judge,* 123, 101.

104. Fitzpatrick, *Education and Social Mobility in the Soviet Union,* 113. It would be more accurate to say that the accused were being attacked as members of an elite professional group.

105. Chase, *Workers, Society, and the Soviet State,* 275. By 1926, "workers were bringing to production meetings deepening senses of frustration, hostility, and anger. Over the past few years, the growth of their living standard had been slow and subject to reverses. During the same period, official labor policy demanded continually higher worker productivity. Yet management, which was quick to demand greater productivity and fire workers, was slow to improve work conditions that would ease their burden, reduce the accident rate, and make higher productivity possible" (277).

106. Ibid., 277.

107. Kuromiya, *Stalin's Industrial Revolution,* 114–115. Thus, "the leaders of the shock workers were mainly young and skilled males of proletarian origin who had experienced the revolution and civil war in their childhood, first entered industrial work after the revolution, and therefore had several years of work experience and some skills by the late 1920s. Predominantly party and Komsomol members, they were in a position to be critical of both the work culture of older workers and the peasant culture of new arrivals from the countryside" (323).

108. Bailes, *Technology and Society Under Lenin and Stalin,* 193. As young, working-class activists experienced rapid upward mobility, most future Soviet leaders got their start in this period. For the case of Khrushchev, see Nikita Khrushchev, *Khrushchev Remembers* (Boston: Little, Brown, 1970), 34, 56.

109. Fitzpatrick, "Stalin and the Making of a New Elite," 386–387.

110. Fitzpatrick, *The Russian Revolution,* 142–143.

111. Ibid., 3.

112. Malia, *The Soviet Tragedy,* 228.

113. Ibid., 269.

114. In the words of two of the most insightful and knowledgeable analysts of the purges: As "the new caste of officials set about enjoying fully the material advantages that went with the control of socialized property," "the central power saw the position clearly, detected the threat to its own security in the development of a new mandarin caste, and nothing was more obvious than to embark on the liquidation of these people" (F. Beck and W. Godin, *Russian Purge and the Extraction of Confession* [New York: Viking, 1951], 263).

115. Cohen, *Rethinking the Soviet Experience,* 62. As Conquest asserted in 1968, "The dominating ideas of the Stalin period, the evolution of the oppositionists, the very confessions in the great show trials, can hardly be followed without considering not so much the whole Soviet past as the development of the party, the consolidation of the dictatorship, the movements of faction, the rise of individuals and the emergence of extreme economic policies" (*The Great Terror,* 3).

116. Khrushchev, *Khrushchev Remembers,* 567; Medvedev, *Let History Judge,* 325.

117. Robert C. Tucker, *Stalin in Power: The Revolution from Above, 1928–1941* (New York: Norton, 1990), 278, 374.

118. Lewin, *Political Undercurrents in the Soviet Economic Debates,* 118.

119. Guiseppe Boffa, *The Stalin Phenomenon* (Ithaca: Cornell University Press, 1990), 194–195. Thus, "another issue that has received too little attention is the social foundation of Stalinism. In crucial periods that foundation took on a mass character, though Stalin's rule had staked its very existence on brutal conflicts with vast strata of the Soviet population" (194).

120. In Geoffrey Hosking's words, "In Soviet society of the 1930s, as we have seen, the number of young, ambitious, and upwardly mobile people was unusually high. Doubtless many of them were envious of their seniors" (*The First Socialist Society: A History of the Soviet Union from Within* [Cambridge, Mass.: Harvard University Press, 1985], 196). In Pipes's view, the most fundamental affinity of communism, fascism, and Nazism was their appeal to "hate" and "class resentment" as a means of winning mass support (*Russia Under the Bolshevik Regime,* 262).

121. Tucker, *Stalin in Power,* 445.

122. Dimitri Volkogonov, *Stalin: Triumph and Tragedy* (New York: Grove Press, 1991), 263.

123. Richard Lowenthal, "Development Versus Utopia in Communist Policy," in Chalmers Johnson, ed., *Change in Communist Systems* (Stanford: Stanford University Press, 1970), 47–48.

124. According to Volkogonov, nearly 300 of 1,225 delegates voted against Stalin (*Stalin,* 200). Tucker put the number a bit lower: "The fact that only 1,059 ballots have turned up in the party achives (166 less than the number of delegates to the Seventeenth Congress with the right to vote) strongly suggests that something like that number were destroyed, as Stalin demanded" (*Stalin in Power,* 261).

125. Conquest argued that this vote confirms the existence of a "moderate bloc" commanding a Politburo majority (*The Great Terror,* 28–29).

126. Boris I. Nicolaevsky, *Power and the Soviet Elite* (Ann Arbor: University of Michigan Press, 1975), 32–35.

127. Bailes, *Technology and Society Under Lenin and Stalin,* 174.

128. Ibid., 175.

129. Cohen, *Bukharin and the Bolshevik Revolution,* 345.

130. Mary McAuley, *Politics and the Soviet Union* (Middlesex: Penguin, 1977), 119–120.

131. Although Ordzhonikidze put an end to specialist baiting, imposed higher standards of technical education, arranged the rehabilitation of "bourgeois engineers" convicted in the 1930 Industrial Party trial, and actively shielded technical personnel from police interference in his areas of jurisdiction, the 1935 model curriculum for heavy industry sharply increased specialized engineering courses at the expense of political indoctrination. See Bailes, *Technology and Society Under Lenin and Stalin,* 226–227; Getty, *The Origins of the Great Purges,* 129.

132. Cited in Tucker, *Stalin in Power,* 320.

133. Cited in Getty, *The Origins of the Great Purges,* 102–104.

134. Cited in Tucker, *Stalin in Power,* 320–321. Tucker noted that Stalin's "partiality for the young and unsung" was evident in the early 1920s. Of course, partiality for nonprivileged and low-status groups is essential for central rulers seeking to preserve and expand their power at the expense of established elites.

135. Lewin, *The Making of the Soviet System,* 238.

136. Tucker, *Stalin in Power,* 427. In Tucker's view, Stalin disliked "family groups" because they obstructed the purge process by protecting one another. But the corrupt behavior of patron-client networks was real enough. The Smolensk Archive described the drunkenness and thievery of one local party leader, who "surrounded himself with relatives, of whom there are many, both in the kolkhoz and also in the village soviet, in responsible and leading positions, and naturally he protects them in all their abuses" (Merle Fainsod, *Smolensk Under Soviet Rule* [New York: Vintage, 1958], 151).

137. Getty, *The Origins of the Great Purges,* 21.

138. Cited in David Lane, *State and Politics in the USSR* (New York: New York University Press, 1985), 78. See also Getty, *The Origins of the Great Purges,* 25.

139. Getty, *The Origins of the Great Purges,* 90; see also chaps. 2, 3.

140. Ibid., 3, 25.

141. Tucker, *Stalin in Power,* 319.

142. Nicolaevsky argued that the police establishment murdered Kirov and spearheaded the attack on moderation because Kirov stood "for the idea of abolition of terror, both in general and inside the party," and advocated the "abolition of the police departments of the Machine-Tractor Stations; these political departments were the tentacles of the police apparatus reaching into the very depths of the countryside" (*Power and the Soviet Elite,* 32, 95).

143. McAuley, *Politics and the Soviet Union,* 119.

144. For high and mighty ways, see Evgenia Ginzburg, *Journey into the Whirlwind* (New York: Harcourt, Brace and World, 1967), 122. For communist conceit, see Medvedev, *Let History Judge,* 414.

145. Victor Kravchenko's chilling memoir contains a poignant account of an impoverished woman worker attacking an Old Bolshevik plant manager for living "in grand style" while "ignoring the hardships of the proletariat" (*I Chose Freedom* [New York: Charles Scribner, 1946], 258–259). But we have seen that eruptions of popular hostility at old and new elites were recurrent in the first decades of Soviet power, extending back to the FFYP, the cultural revolution, NEP, War Communism, and the Revolution of 1917.

146. This section's heading is the title of chap. 6 in Medvedev, *Let History Judge.*

147. Ginzburg, *Journey into the Whirlwind,* 3. In Volkogonov's view, "Kirov's murder marked the approach of a sinister era. . . . December 1, 1934 at once sharply raised the 'significance,' as Stalin would say, of the NKVD's punitive personnel, who began to grow rapidly in number" (*Stalin,* 209).

148. Bailes, *Technology and Society Under Lenin and Stalin,* 270–271.

149. Cited in Getty, *The Origins of the Great Purges,* 125.

150. Ibid., 138–140.

151. Cited in Tucker, *Stalin in Power,* 426.

152. Cited in ibid., 428–429.

153. Getty, *The Origins of the Great Purges,* 149. Thus, "regional secretaries were to withdraw from direct economic administration, bone up on political education, subject themselves to new elections, and cease persecution of rank-and-file party members. . . . Such measures, if successfully carried out, would have revolutionized local party administration by forcing local leaders to toe the line in all their activities" (149).

154. Tucker, *Stalin in Power,* 431. Tucker surely erred in this regard. Stalin was a longstanding proponent of bringing popular pressure to bear on officialdom. In a letter to

Maksim Gorky in January 1930, Stalin wrote, "We cannot do without self-criticism. . . . Without it, stagnation, corruption of the apparatus, growth of bureaucracy, and sapping of the creative initiative of the working class are inevitable. . . . Self-criticism provides material (and a stimulus) for our advancement, for unleashing the constructive energies of the working people, for the development of competition, for shock brigades, and so on" (cited in Kuromiya, *Stalin's Industrial Revolution,* 76).

155. Bailes, *Technology and Society Under Lenin and Stalin,* 281–282.

156. Ginzburg, *Journey into the Whirlwind,* 128–131.

157. Medvedev provided examples of "from the top down" and "from the bottom up" purge processes; in either case, "the business would end with the destruction of the victim selected by Stalin and the NKVD" (*Let History Judge,* 306–307).

158. Conquest, *The Great Terror,* 201.

159. Getty, *The Origins of the Great Purges,* 167–173.

160. Ibid., 117.

161. According to Tucker, Stalin from start to finish "was the Terror's general director"; Ezhov "remained throughout a subservient underling" (*Stalin in Power,* 444). A more complex picture is presented by Boris A. Starkov, "Narkom Ezhov," in Getty and Manning, eds., *Stalinist Terror,* 21–39.

162. Beck and Godin, *Russian Purge and the Extraction of Confession,* 153.

163. Getty, *The Origins of the Great Purges,* 161.

164. Tucker, *Stalin in Power,* 461.

165. Medvedev, *Let History Judge,* 307.

166. Noting that "various accounts portray workers more as actors in the Great Terror of 1936–8 than as victims," Robert Thurston concluded that "workers' aspirations, grievances, and suspicions constituted an important part of the forces that drove pursuit forward" ("The Stakhanovite Movement: Background to the Great Terror in the Factories, 1935–1938," in Getty and Manning, eds., *Stalinist Terror,* 158–159).

167. Edward J. Brown, *Russian Literature Since the Revolution* (Cambridge, Mass.: Harvard University Press, 1982), 288–289.

168. See Conquest's harrowing account of "the social order of Kolyma," where "enemies of the people" were given the heaviest work and the least food, while ordinary criminals were allowed a free hand to conduct a reign of terror, theft, extortion, etc. (*Kolyma,* 78–83).

169. The Smolensk Archive contains a letter addressed to the regional party secretary and signed by twenty-one workers that expresses the confluence of Stalinist rhetoric and mass anti-elitism: "All of us . . . hope that such 'Communists' who have become bureaucratized, who have become puffed up with conceit, have become great magnates, who did not want to hear anything, although they knew and were informed a thousand times, we feel that those who allowed the accursed enemy into the ranks of the Leninist-Stalinist Party, will not remain unpunished" (cited in Fainsod, *Smolensk Under Soviet Rule,* 237). The letter was written in 1936.

170. Fainsod cited "a list, dated September 16, 1937 of comrades recommended by the Party organization of the Oblast court for leading work," including a thirty-six-year-old worker with an elementary education and no legal training who became chief of the cadres division of the regional court and a twenty-seven-year-old woman of peasant origin "who had supplemented an elementary education with a one-year law course and had also served as a Komsomol organizer" and was appointed to the regional court (*Smolensk Under Soviet Rule,* 192).

171. Leon Trotsky, *The Revolution Betrayed* (New York: Pathfinder, 1972), 105.

172. Getty, *The Origins of the Great Purges,* 162.

173. Ibid., 179.

174. A quantitative analysis of the "purge rate by bureaucratic rank" indicates that political elites were most explicitly targeted. Thus, "those in the elite *outside* politics, for example, scientists, educational administrators, and artists, regardless of their 'alien' class background, party status, age, or old regime education, were *relatively* safe from arrest. Personal attributes that *increased* risk or vulnerability in the elite were functions of political and administrative position. Statistically, it was a purge of politicians" (J. Arch Getty and William Chase, "Patterns of Repression Among the Soviet Elite in the Late 1930s: A Biographical Approach," in Getty and Manning, eds., *Stalinist Terror,* 243).

175. Seweryn Bialer, *Stalin's Successors* (Cambridge: Cambridge University Press, 1980), 10.

# 5

# Reform and Reaction in the Khrushchev Era

Power dynamics from the time of Stalin's death in March 1953 until the overthrow of Khrushchev in October 1964 are considered in this chapter. While viewing the Khrushchev era in light of the power-restructuring argument advanced thus far, my discussion focuses on the fundamental shifts in power relations and political process that occurred in the 1950s and 1960s. Power-restructuring initiatives that in time would undercut and overturn the Stalinist legacy in the Soviet Union and Communist China were first manifested on a significant scale during the Khrushchev era. Khrushchevian power restructuring took two related but distinct forms: power decentralization and power deconcentration. Post-Stalin power restructuring under Khrushchev was a fascinating and constantly evolving synthesis of historical continuity and historical change as the Soviet leader first sought to ameliorate especially oppressive aspects of the Stalin system, and subsequently turned to the more complex, difficult, and dangerous task of fundamentally reforming the Stalinist political economy. Even though Khrushchev was defeated in the latter undertaking, the consequences of this initial foray into post-Stalin power restructuring were nonetheless profound.

I begin with a brief discussion of Soviet internal politics during World War II and the period of mature Stalinism and conclude with an assessment and a critique of power and politics in the Brezhnev era, 1964–1982. But my main concerns are twofold. First, the profound restructuring of power that occurred during the first phase of the Khrushchev period must be set forth and examined. The period from Stalin's death until the late 1950s witnessed a general loosening of police controls, the political revitalization of the Communist Party of the Soviet Union (CPSU), and a wide-ranging restoration of the sociopolitical status of Soviet elites in general. Khrushchev played the leading role in spearheading and implementing these changes.

Second, in the late 1950s power dynamics in the Soviet Union experienced another fundamental shift. As familiar phenomena of bureaucratic encrustation and official power and resource appropriation were manifested in new and more assertive form, Khrushchev assumed an increasingly adversarial stance vis-à-vis the

Soviet political elite, and he attempted a restructuring of power at the expense of party and state officialdom. Many of the economic, institutional, and political reforms that Khrushchev sought to enact in the late 1950s and early 1960s presaged comparable and more extensive post-Stalin power-restructuring processes under Mao and Gorbachev. Yet Khrushchevian power restructuring was rooted in Stalinist antecedents. In this chapter, I ponder these linkages, consider patterns of continuity and change, and delineate the sociopolitical contours of the era. In the end, Khrushchev was overthrown by the political elite he sought to reform, a counterrevolution that set the stage for the unprecedented ascendancy of Soviet officialdom in the Brezhnev era.

## Conceptualizing Khrushchev and Khrushchevism

When Khrushchev was suddenly ousted in October 1964, Western analysts were caught flat-footed. As Merle Fainsod, the dean of U.S. sovietology, had written only a year or two earlier, "Khrushchev, like Stalin before him, tolerates no derogation of his own authority, permits no opposition to raise its head within the Party, and insists that the Party function as a unit in executing his will."[1] Yet the abrupt demise of the supreme leader at the hands of his subordinates irrevocably undercut the totalitarian image of uncontested and depoliticized state domination of political life and social forces and underscored the need for new ways of conceptualizing power relations and political process in the Soviet Union.[2] By 1966, Carl A. Linden could write that "the Khrushchev era came to be characterized by a loss of the kind of firm discipline within the leading group that Stalin imposed. . . . Contention between the various elements of the upper echelons pervaded the environment in which Khrushchev worked."[3] While emphasizing the conflict and instability of the era, however, subsequent conceptualization of Khrushchev and Khrushchevism was varied and contradictory.

Three images are recurrent in firsthand and scholarly accounts of the period: Khrushchev as a ruler, Khrushchev as a reformer, and Khrushchev as a transitional figure.[4] These images are not mutually exclusive; satisfactory conceptualization of Khrushchev and Khrushchevism necessarily incorporates elements of all three. Yet the prevailing tendency to draw on a variety of overlapping perspectives blurs the distinctive thrust of power restructuring under Khrushchev.

Accounts stressing Khrushchev's role as a ruler focused on his rise to power and the means by which he consolidated and exercised authority and tried to show how this process resembled power-concentrating processes under Lenin, Stalin, and Brezhnev. Thus, totalitarian theorists such as Fainsod saw Khrushchev as a ruler in the classic Soviet mode. While detailing the incessant political conflict of the period and Khrushchev's ally-building strategy, Roman Kolkowicz also argued that the fall of Marshal Georgy Zhukov in October 1957 was "only a matter of time," as Khrushchev and his associates, having removed their main opponents in the party, then put an end to Zhukov's self-aggrandizing and impolitic public behavior and relegated him to obscurity.[5]

More recent interpretations also noted the many parallels that linked Khrushchev's rule to familiar patterns in Soviet power politics. Harry Rigby and Martin McCauley pointed out that Khrushchev's rise mirrored that of Stalin in many ways:

> Both started as dark horses; their power base was the Party Secretariat; through it they promoted their allies and demoted their opponents; by placing these nominees in key Party positions they built up support in the Central Committee and in so doing put pressure on the majority of the Presidium which opposed them; they widened the arena of Party discussion by taking the average Party member into their confidence; and they formed temporary policy alliances with their main political opponents.[6]

Alternatively, George W. Breslauer sought to demonstrate the essential continuity of policy goals and power dynamics under Khrushchev and Brezhnev. Hence, even though "the Khrushchev and Brezhnev administrations shared a broad regime consensus on behalf of breaking with the extremes of Stalinism and tackling new tasks"; "the key to power consolidation was still the accumulation of patronage and cultivation of the party apparatus and military-industrial complex as bases of support."[7]

But the foregoing approach obscured the radicalism of Khrushchevian power restructuring. Khrushchev did rise to power as a ruler wielding power in the classic Soviet manner; yet he sought to address the familiar dilemmas of the Soviet system in new and potentially revolutionary ways. While deploying political techniques partially reminiscent of Stalinism, Khrushchev pursued policies and attempted to enact reforms that sharply contradicted the Stalinism of the past and the Brezhnevism to come. With his advocacy of egalitarian educational reform, administrative decentralization, increased mass participation in decisionmaking, and power devolution, Khrushchev, according to Alastair McAuley, should be viewed as an "original leader" who "tried fundamentally to change Soviet society."[8] In McAuley's assessment, "The Khrushchev period witnessed a crucial shift in social priorities" over the course of which "the rigid and joyless system that Khrushchev inherited in 1953 was changed radically."[9] Nor were Khrushchev's reforms of purely historical significance. Noting the "Khrushchevian echoes" in Gorbachev's policies, Sidney I. Ploss showed how both leaders pursued programs of internal innovation, economic decentralization, more rapid turnover of leading personnel, less secrecy in the conduct of public affairs, and anti-Stalinism.[10]

Interpretations that view Khrushchev as a transitional leader are the most problematic, given their premise that Khrushchev's impetuous tenure marked the necessarily bumpy transition from the instability and violence of Stalinism to the "normalcy" and "institutionalization" of the Brezhnev period. In a controversial rewrite of Fainsod's *How Russia Is Ruled,* Jerry F. Hough characterized the Brezhnev period as "the return to normalcy," when Khrushchev's "harebrained" organizational schemes were restructured "along lines more congenial to administrators in each area" and greater emphasis was given to "scientific decision-making," "a phrase which now implied a weighing of alternatives, an understanding of limitations, a reliance on data and evidence."[11] Similarly, Graeme Gill suggested that the decisive factor in Khrushchev's fall was "the existence of strong pressures for institutionalization in the structure of the Soviet system"; it was "higher levels of institutionalization along bureaucratic lines," "resting upon considerations of rationality and efficiency in government . . . which carried the day and led to the rejection of Khrushchev and the activist style of leadership with which many of his actions are associated."[12] But these interpretations are untenable. As the rhetoric, revelations, and denouement of the Gorbachev reform period made clear, the Brezhnev era was a time of mounting stagnation, decay, and dysfunction, when the seeds were sown for the collapse and disintegration of the Soviet system.

In the present discussion, Khrushchev is depicted as a ruler and as a reformer, roles that he would combine with varying degrees of success and vigor from the start to the finish of his tenure as head of state. But I do not subscribe to the transitional image or to notions of Khrushchev-Brezhnev "regime consensus" and continuity.[13] Rather, I underscore the many parallels that link Khrushchev's attempted reforms to subsequent processes of post-Stalin power restructuring in the Soviet Union and China. Khrushchevian power restructuring addressed the sociopolitical and institutional challenges of the post-Stalin era, and Khrushchev chose to grapple with these challenges in ways that most closely resembled future Maoist and Gorbachevian power-restructuring initiatives. At the same time, the events of the Khrushchev era must be understood in the broad context of power relations and political process in Russian and Chinese history. I see the Khrushchev era, and the late 1950s and the early 1960s in particular, as a time when power-restructuring themes—three-way power contests, processes of decentralized power and resource appropriation, attempts to restructure Soviet institutions and redefine the status of Soviet elites, and the historic collision between the ruler and his subordinates—once again came to the fore in the Soviet Union. These recurrent patterns and processes were manifested with special salience in the post-Stalin era. By viewing Khrushchev and Khrushchevism in light of my general perspective on power and politics in China and Russia, we see that he was the first communist ruler to grapple with the particular complexities and requirements of post-Stalin power restructuring.

## Internal Politics During World War II

An extended discussion of the cataclysmic Soviet experience in World War II is beyond the scope of this book. But the internal politics of the Soviet Union from

1941 to 1945 are closely related to my concerns in two key respects. First, despite the devastation and chaos inflicted by the Nazi invasion, power relations and political process displayed marked continuity with patterns in the late 1920s and 1930s. Power-concentrating processes, regime attempts to find allies and build constituencies, purging and pushing up, and increasingly assertive behavior on the part of Soviet military elites all figured prominently during these years of national disaster, mobilization, and triumph. Second, a fundamental change occurred in the sociopolitical stature of the Stalin system. A coercive system that had been erected at the expense of substantial segments of the Soviet population and that depended for its existence primarily on the support of its beneficiaries was transformed in the course of World War II into an unassailable embodiment of national salvation and national greatness. Victory over Nazi Germany conclusively legitimated the Stalin system at all levels of Soviet society, thereby reinforcing Stalinism and Stalin's personal rulership in ways that would complicate and vitiate subsequent reform efforts.

The shock of the Nazi invasion on June 22, 1941, and the horrific decimation of the Red Army and staggering losses of population, territory, and infrastructure that followed appeared to augur the collapse of the system of power that had been erected in the 1930s. As collectivized peasants, subjugated nationalities, and anticommunists of all types seized on the opportunity to overthrow communist rule, the Soviet system came under political as well as military attack.[14] Yet in the end, Soviet rulers were able to turn back this challenge by relying on familiar power-building mechanisms, deploying the considerable economic and technological strengths of the system built up in the 1930s, and drawing on previously untapped sources of national unity, pride, and perseverance.[15]

Stalin and the central leadership reacted to the initial Nazi onslaught by tightening political and administrative controls. The Stavka, the General Headquarters of the Soviet Supreme Command, was set up; the commissar system, which reported cases of "unworthiness" among officers and political personnel to the Supreme Command, was reinforced; and a military, as opposed to a political, purge of the Red Army was set in motion, in which inept and incompetent commanders were swept aside.[16] But the system was on the verge of collapse, and the political hold of the Soviet state was shaky. The regime was thus forced to find allies and build support in ways that would have been unacceptable in less desperate times. Especially notable were Stalin's "Holy Russia" speeches on November 6 and 7, 1941, the occasion of the twenty-fourth anniversary of the October Revolution, with the Nazis some forty miles from the gates of Moscow. Explicitly appealing to Russian national pride rather than to Marxism-Leninism, Stalin vowed that the Germans would be defeated and driven from Russia just as the Teutonic Knights, Tatars, Poles, and Napoleon had been.[17] As Alexander Werth noted, "The glorification of Russia—and not only Lenin's Russia—had a tremendous effect on the people in general, even though it made perhaps a few Marxist-Leninists squirm. However, even these realized that it was this patriotic, nationalist propaganda which identified the Soviet Regime and Stalin with Russia, Holy Russia, that was most likely to create the right kind of uplift."[18]

During the life-and-death struggle with Nazi Germany, power contests between Soviet military elites and Soviet central rulers moved to center stage. While Stalin and the Stavka high command attempted to maintain their decisionmaking monopoly, they also had to build up the prestige, authority, and operational abilities of Soviet military commanders and develop a new generation of military leaders. In a move directly paralleling the pushing-up processes of the late 1920s and 1930s, younger and more talented officers were promoted en masse during the war and took the place of the purged and fallen.[19] During the perilous fall 1942 leading up to the climactic Battle of Stalingrad, numerous measures were taken to build up the morale and authority of the Red Army: The system of military commissars was abolished, the full authority (*edinonachalie,* or one-man management) of military commanders was established, and Stalin "showered the military with new status symbols, ranks, medals, and other accolades."[20] In Werth's view, "All this was, in a sense, a clear victory of the 'Army' over the 'Party.'"[21] Although Stalin had intended the relaxation of controls as a "temporary tactical expedient," "it had enabled the military to ascend to a highly privileged status, and had created a large elite of military officers who, for the first time, were enjoying the glory and prestige of victors, and the freedom to make many (albeit only tactical) decisions without having to consult their political 'advisors.'"[22]

Once the war turned in favor of the Soviet Union, therefore, central efforts to curb and roll back the autonomy of Soviet military elites were resumed. By mid-1943, measures to facilitate closer political control and ideological indoctrination of the military had been implemented; by early 1944 a highly centralized system of command and control, in which all important decisions, orders, and documents went through the Stavka, was fully in place.[23] When the victory over Nazi Germany was finally won, the center launched an even more determined effort to "put the Red Army in its place."[24] But it was not only the reassertion of familiar Stalinist power-concentrating and policing mechanisms that made possible the reimposition of political controls over a military establishment that had just won a historic victory of overwhelming proportions. As Aleksander Wat eloquently described, "No one in Russia ever had the popularity that Stalin had in the brief period between Stalingrad and the end of the war. . . . Suddenly all of Stalin's bestial features were smoothed over in people's minds, disappeared. . . . Stalingrad changed everything. . . . It was hysteria, but the hysteria of people melting in patriotic emotion, incredibly fervent."[25] Legitimated on a scale never achieved in the 1930s, the aging and increasingly despotic Stalin system was able to reassert an unchallenged dominion over all levels of Soviet society in the postwar period.

## The Politics of Mature Stalinism

The Soviet economy and society suffered massive devastation in World War II— tens of thousands of villages, towns, and factories burned to the ground and laid waste, tens of millions of people dead, wounded, orphaned, homeless. After four years of war, suffering, and sacrifice, "the Russian people liked to think that life would soon be easier, and that Russia could 'relax' after the war."[26] Instead, "Stalin was already of the view that only by maintaining the people's mood in a state of permanent tension and mobilization, akin to civil war, could all these difficulties be overcome."[27] By mid-1946, a "hardening of the regime" was under way; a tightening of controls in economics, culture, and politics was in place; and the stage was set for the ascendancy of a mature Stalinist system.[28]

Soviet rulers were initially concerned with reestablishing authority in areas that had been under extended Nazi occupation, such as Ukraine, White Russia, and the Baltic states; military operations against nationalist groups and campaigns to reimpose agricultural collectivization were conducted in all these areas. Even as Ukraine suffered a massive drought and crop failure in 1946, the screws were tightened, and "all possible measures were taken to supply enough grain to the State."[29] While famine claimed thousands of lives, the Central Committee and the Council of Ministers "issued a joint decree which condemned abuses by kolkhozes, especially their allowing *kolkhozniki* to illegally expand their private plots, and established a Council for Kolkhoz Affairs to supervise kolkhozes and prevent such abuses."[30] In the realm of culture, Andrey Zhdanov spearheaded an attack on "counter-revolutionary," "anti-Soviet," "individualist," "escapist," and "slavishly" pro-Western manifestations in Soviet poetry, literature, philosophy, music, and cinema.[31] But it was the tightening of controls over Soviet political elites in the postwar period that most directly concerns us here.

Along with the crackdown in culture and agriculture, a far-reaching, centrally mandated reorganization of CPSU operations was launched in late 1946. Citing "errors in cadre work" and "ideological laxness" on the part of regional and local party organizations, a new "Administration for Checking Party Organs" was set up and charged with inspecting the work of regional, district, and republican party committees and their fulfillment of Central Committee decrees. As Werner G. Hahn noted, "Having been given considerable authority, the new inspectors proceeded to tackle prominent regional leaders."[32] Containing the aspirations of the Soviet political elite and curbing the rise of new centers of power were, of course, primary functions of the system erected in the 1930s. Even the most powerful and privileged Soviet officials were not exempted from the all-encompassing attentions of the police establishment, which routinely examined their papers, held the combination to their "private" safes, and maintained full-time personal surveillance.[33] In the distinctly nonrevolutionary atmosphere of the postwar period, Soviet political elites were targeted in a series of violent purges.

Especially notable was the still-murky Leningrad Affair of 1949–1950, during which the leadership of the regional apparatus was decimated and numerous rising young officials executed. Various explanations of the affair have been advanced: the independent-minded behavior of the Leningrad party organization, economic administrator and theorist N. A. Voznesensky's advocacy of a partial reform of the system of centralized resource allocation, cordial contacts between the

Leningraders and the Yugoslavs, and factional conflict at the top.[34] Whatever the actual facts of the matter, the Leningrad Affair underscored the ferocity with which the Stalin system continued to combat even the most tentative manifestations of independence on the part of Soviet political elites.

Among the key characteristics that Bialer enumerated in his conceptualization of the mature Stalinist system were "the system of mass terror," "the extinction of the party as a movement," "the extreme mobilizational model of economic growth," "the end of the revolutionary impulse to change society," and "the system of personal dictatorship."[35] In such a system, terror functioned as a "normal method of rule and governance" and coercion as the "foundation stone on which the Stalinist leadership was able to base its economic growth strategy."[36] All these elements were magnified in the years preceding Stalin's death. In Khrushchev's inimitable words, "Those last years with Stalin were hard times," when the "government virtually ceased to function."[37] At the top, as Stalin maintained his power by playing one faction of the ruling group off against another and periodically purging potential upstarts, power relations and political process had in fact come to resemble court intrigue in the "Oriental despotic" manner. At the mass level, the early 1950s witnessed a further tightening of central economic controls. In 1950, the size of collective farms was enlarged and their number reduced, and in 1952 Stalin's definitive "economic theses" repudiated any notion of economic reform and envisioned the elimination of market exchanges altogether by a system of centralized resource control and distribution.[38]

Yet even in this apparently totalitarian situation, the Stalin system was not solely reliant on terror and coercion. As Vera S. Dunham demonstrated, the regime, which had "chosen and nurtured certain allies in the past," looked for support in the postwar period to the Soviet "middle class," "totally Stalinist, born out of Stalin's push for industrialization, reeducation, and bureaucratization of the country, flesh of the flesh of Stalin's revolutions from above in the thirties."[39] Under mature Stalinism, however, the dynamic power-restructuring processes of the 1930s had long since evolved into a rigid, dogmatic, and repressive system that had manifestly run out of ideas and solutions. With the personal ruler's death in March 1953, the tensions and pressures so harshly contained by the Stalin system began to erupt, triggering a series of ambitious and tumultuous attempts at organizational change, economic restructuring, social liberalization, and political reform.

## Khrushchev and the Revitalization of Party Power

In the immediate wake of Stalin's death, the Soviet political leadership acted to ameliorate the oppressive and uncertain conditions in which the Soviet people and Soviet elites lived and worked. As Fedor Burlatsky related, "The first speeches by Khrushchev, Malenkov, and other leaders already sounded different. They spoke about the people and their needs, about food, the problem of housing and a pardon for those who had been prisoners of war. They said that the aim of social-ism could not lie only in industrial growth."[40] And the new leaders moved rapidly to behead and rein in the powers of the terroristic police establishment.[41] But it was one thing to ameliorate particularly oppressive and distasteful features and quite another to attempt the restructuring of the system built up in the 1930s. The Stalin system rested on a complex of economic, social, political, and ideological controls; how was such a system to be reformed and revitalized without precipi-tating crisis and collapse? This challenge, on which Gorbachevian power restruc-turing would founder in the late 1980s, was already at the forefront of the Soviet political agenda in 1953.

Breslauer suggested that two responses emerged in the mid-1950s. The first, premised on "an accommodation with officialdom" and put forward by the head of the central ministerial apparatus, Georgy Malenkov, envisioned the retention of the existing system of centralized decisionmaking and administration *without* the constant purging and arbitrary intervention characteristic of Stalinism. The sec-ond, advanced by Khrushchev, advocated the decentralization of political and especially economic decisionmaking authority to regional and local party organi-zations while also denouncing "that great evil—bureaucratism."[42] Khrushchev's approach to political participation, Breslauer suggested, was characterized by a populist "trust in society," a "core belief that problems of economic growth could not be solved without eliciting authentic mass initiative," and an abiding interest in expanding "mass political participation."[43] During Khrushchev's first years as a post-Stalin leader, however, he focused primarily on the extension of more trust to the regional and local centers of CPSU power that had been suppressed by the Stalin system of centralized command and control. In Khrushchev's hands, decen-tralizing power to regional and local party organizations was both a way of rein-vigorating CPSU leadership and activism at the lower levels and a means of un-dercutting his political opponents in the central ministerial apparatus.

In the first instance of what was to prove a recurrent power-restructuring strat-egy, Khrushchev in fall 1953 implemented a far-ranging decentralization of power in Soviet agricultural administration. Operational command was shifted from the Ministry of Agriculture to ministries at the republican level, key ministerial ac-counts were transferred to previously subordinate party units, and at the district level "formal structural units were broken up in order to push administrative per-sonnel into the field."[44] Power decentralization entailed greatly expanded roles for the district party committees *(raikomy)*, which were now charged with both polit-ical and economic leadership functions. As Robert F. Miller noted, although Khrushchev "was clearly wedded to the idea that Party secretaries *should by right* occupy the leading positions in the management of the country . . . he qualified this enhancement of Party responsibilities with the requirement that Party leader-ship be based on managerial and technical competence, rather than on mere po-litical authority."[45] At the same time, the decentralization of power to regional and

local party organizations cut the "ministries off from their grassroots in the countryside," ensured that "Khrushchev was the best informed person on rural affairs,"
and "provided him with the ammunition to attack the central government bureaucracy."[46]

This effort to increase the power and authority of the party at the local level
continued to be manifested in organizational initiatives in the mid-1950s. In 1954,
Khrushchev began to call for the reform of the hitherto sacrosanct edifice of central control in the countryside, the Machine Tractor Station (MTS). Noting that
MTS staff specialists as paid agents of the state were not "materially interested" in
the economic performance of the collective farms to which they were attached, he
argued that control of the MTS should be transferred to the kolkhoz itself.[47] In
March 1955, the central authorities announced that "centralized agricultural planning was being replaced by a system which would permit the kolkhoz management some discretion in production planning"; "by permitting local officials a
greater voice in plan formulation," authorities would, or so they argued, enable
local peculiarities to be taken into account and productivity increased.[48]

Yet Khrushchev was not a consistent proponent of power decentralization. Indeed, the policy initiative that propelled him to the top, the Virgin Lands campaign, was a classic authority–social mobilization program conceived and set in
motion from the top. In an effort to open up millions of hectares of new agricultural land, hundreds of thousands of Young Communists were mobilized, hundreds of new settlements and state farms were erected, and tens of thousands of
tractors, combines, seeding machines, and trucks were deployed in spring and
summer 1954.[49] In contrast to the reforms I have just discussed, this campaign
featured strong central controls over resource allocation and funding. Khrushchev, in his memoirs, discussed the central leadership's fears that investments
would wind up in the hands of the regional administration in Kazakhstan and the
decision to channel funds so as to bypass the regional authorities.[50] The complex
and ambiguous relationship between Soviet central rulers and centers of regional
and local power remained unsettled up to the very end of the Khrushchev period;
until the late 1950s, however, Khrushchev continued to advocate and implement
increases in the power and authority of the party at the regional and local levels.
As always, this stance was motivated by a combination of political considerations
and reformist convictions.

## The Twentieth Party Congress and the
## Politics of Economic Reform

Khrushchev's determination to restore the party organization to its rightful place
at the center of Soviet political life was most forcefully manifested in his historic
indictment of Stalin at the Twentieth Party Congress in February 1956. The message of the Secret Speech was unambiguous and straightforward: By "allowing

himself many abuses, acting in the name of the Central Committee, not asking for the opinion of Committee members nor even of members of the Politburo"; by "showing brutal willfulness toward Party cadres"; and by "using mass terror against the Party cadres," "Stalin ignored the norms of Party life and trampled on the Leninist principle of collective leadership" and thereby "caused tremendous harm to our country and to the cause of socialist advancement."[51] Khrushchev never mentioned the equally painful and more widespread sufferings of the common people under Stalin. Stalin's personal crimes and transgressions were thus carefully distinguished from the "achievements" of collectivization and industrialization. Hence, "our historical victories were attained thanks to the organizational work of the Party, to the many provincial organizations, and to the self-sacrificing work of our great nation."[52] But the impact of the Secret Speech was nonetheless cataclysmic. By so openly and explicitly denouncing Stalin, Khrushchev opened up to discussion and criticism the Soviet system as a whole and set in motion systemwide processes of political conflict and organizational change. As Burlatsky related, "It was clear that the country had to reject its old methods. It was unclear what the new methods would be and how quickly the new decisions would produce results. Everyone wanted to go further and faster, but many were apprehensive that the search for new methods would destabilize the situation and rock the boat."[53]

De-Stalinization was a comprehensive process encompassing the final breakup of the slave labor camp system, intellectual liberalization, economic reforms, and social initiatives. Inevitably, this was a tumultuous process, which Khrushchev actually sought to accelerate by means of a series of power-decentralizing measures. When outbreaks in Hungary and Poland in summer and fall 1956 underscored the perils of this loosening of controls and strengthened the hand of conservative forces, Khrushchev employed top and bottom versus the middle tactics and bypassed opposition at the ministerial level by expanding the power of the party organization at the regional and local levels. In August 1956, the position of CPSU Central Committee party organizer, the local representative of central power in Soviet institutions, was abolished "in order to extend democracy in the party still further and to heighten the responsibility of local party organs for the work of large enterprises and the most important institutions."[54] Six months later, more extensive efforts to empower, reform, and revitalize local government were launched.[55] But the centerpiece of post–Twentieth Party Congress Khrushchevian power restructuring was the *sovnarkhozy* (regional economic councils) reforms.

Citing the rigid and constricting effects of central ministerial economic administration, the February 1957 plenum of the Central Committee called for "an increased role for the local economic, party, and trade union organs in the management of the economy"; stipulated that "the centre of gravity for the operative management of industry and construction must be transferred to the local level"; and laid the groundwork for the subsequent establishment of more than one hundred "regional economic councils."[56] To be sure, this decentralization of economic decisionmaking authority both undercut Khrushchev's conservative opponents in the central ministries and was enthusiastically supported by the regional and local party organizations that stood to gain by such a restructuring of power. In the words of one contemporary analyst, "By stumping the country, by sending out the message via his own Party network, Khrushchev, while his colleagues glumly schemed against him in Moscow, offered to key men of all kinds throughout the provinces the promise of undreamed-of advancement, increased scope and promotion for tens of thousands."[57]

When Malenkov, Lazar Kaganovich, Molotov, and other top leaders attempted in June 1957 to oust Khrushchev in a "Kremlin coup," it was precisely such regional party leaders who rallied to Khrushchev's defense and enabled him to prevail.[58] Once this Anti-Party Group was defeated, regional party leaders received even more tangible rewards as a wide range of previously centralized financial and organizational powers were devolved to the republican level in August 1957.[59] So pivotal were regional and local party leaders in strengthening Khrushchev's hand in spring and summer 1957 that Fainsod in 1963 was moved to write that "the victory of Khrushchev symbolized the ascendancy of party bureaucracy in its quintessential form."[60] In fact, spring and summer 1957 marked the amicable high point of political relations between Khrushchev and the party organization. For the remainder of his tenure as leader, Khrushchev boldly and no doubt recklessly attacked the organizational and social defects of the Soviet system. This ambitious power-restructuring agenda in short order collided with the interests of the party organization that Khrushchev supposedly led and represented.

## The Eruption of Localism and the Dilemma of Reform

At a time when most Western analysts were focusing on the political dimensions of the *sovnarkhozy* reforms, Nove observed that "it would be misleading to regard the reorganization as solely a power maneuver, for such a view ignores its intrinsic importance as an attempt to deal with the real problems that beset the Soviet economy."[61] Indeed, the *sovnarkhozy* reforms represented an extension of policies Khrushchev had long championed in the agricultural realm and were consistent with his long-standing belief that economic performance could be improved by more closely involving the party organization in direct production at the regional and local levels. This logic was applied on a sweeping scale, in the course of which specialized ministries in Moscow were shut down, thousands of state functionaries and specialists were forced to move to the provinces, and central economic decisionmaking powers were decentralized into the hands of economic councils at the regional (oblast) level. Although deeply resented by officials removed from the privileges and pleasures of the capital, the *sovnarkhozy* reforms were more widely viewed at the time as a positive attempt "to bring the leaders closer to the people and as a step toward democracy, reducing the disparities in living standards between public officials and ordinary people, and making the pyramid of power a more gently sloping structure."[62]

Some analysts viewed the expansion of regional and local party power that ensued in a favorable light. In *The Soviet Prefects,* Hough depicted the *sovnarkhozy* reforms as part of the ongoing effort of the Soviet leadership to more closely involve local party organs in vital administrative and leadership functions. The expansion of regional and local party power yielded a variety of benefits, Hough argued, by increasing the technical competence of *obkom* (regional party committee) secretaries, improving regional economic cooperation and coordination, facilitating personnel selection and promotion at the lower levels, and involving the local party organization in day-to-day problemsolving.[63] These findings led Hough to conclude that local party organs were not "an intrusive element that interferes with the effective operation of the administrative, but an integral part of the system—one which, in fact, has played an important role in promoting its effective operation."[64] Yet Hough himself documented that the propensity of higher Soviet leaders to view administrative officials at the lower levels as "incorrigible representatives of localism" was not without foundation.[65]

As Nove observed, "An authority with power over the resources of a given area is bound to direct them to the needs of the area, which is its area of knowledge and responsibility, unless prevented from doing so by orders from some superior authority."[66] With the decentralization of economic decisionmaking came an eruption of localism, a familiar decentralized appropriation of power and resources. Within months of Khrushchev's power-decentralizing "theses" of March and April 1957, the official press began to fill with complaints about "tendencies toward autarky," arbitrarily cut deliveries of contracted supplies, defaults in interregion deliveries, misuse and waste of investment funds, and a variety of familiar localist abuses.[67]

Moreover, the habitual tendency of local officials to promote local interests at the expense of "outsiders" was exacerbated by the politics of the *sovnarkhozy* reforms. One notable feature of the new system was the large number of economic regions, as many as 105, the boundaries of which had nothing to do with economic rationality but instead coincided "with existing administrative boundaries, or, in political-personal terms, with the areas of influence of local party secretaries, who have always been the key personalities at the *oblast* level."[68] Even though Khrushchev's decentralization of economic administration had been intended to win the political support of the regional and local apparatus *and* improve economic performance at the local level, only the former objective was accomplished. Whereas the Stalin system was premised on central ministerial intervention and hegemony, the *sovnarkhozy* reforms simply redistributed and devolved these functions by concentrating them in the hands of regional and local party leaders.

This restructuring of power was not what Khrushchev had in mind, and he soon aired his dissatisfaction with the unintended consequences of the *sovnarkhozy* reform. Apparently fearful of the "harmful effects of direct administration by MTS zone party secretaries and their instructors," who were "unduly interfering in the management of the kolkhozes and usurping the prerogatives of the kolkhoz chairman and primary party organizations," Khrushchev attempted to decentralize power still further by abolishing the MTS system in January 1958.[69] Yet many of the supervisory and coordinating powers of the central economic ministries were partially restored in the late 1950s. In the early 1960s, it was precisely this apparently paradoxical combination of decentralizing and centralizing processes that would emerge as the centerpiece of Khrushchevian power restructuring. In the late 1950s, however, Khrushchev still looked to the party to provide dynamic sociopolitical leadership. In his report to the Twenty-first Party Congress in January–February 1959, Khrushchev called for "a comprehensive development in the country's productive forces . . . as will make possible a decisive step forward in creating the material-technical base of communism and ensuring the victory of the USSR in peaceful competition with the capitalist countries." He later stipulated, "The fundamental task of all party and Komsomol organizations is the thorough study and elucidation of the report" and "many-sided party political work among the masses to mobilize everyone's efforts to implement these decisions."[70] It was only as the failure and inability of the regional and local party organizations to provide such dynamic leadership became fully evident that Khrushchev altered his political tactics and attempted a more radical restructuring of power.

## The Critique of Elitism and Bureaucratism

Khrushchev's economic reforms and his ongoing effort to more closely involve the party organization in daily life reflected a broader concern with problems of elitism and bureaucratism in the Soviet system. In his memoirs, Khrushchev was critical of the indifference of Stalin and Soviet officialdom to the material needs of the peasantry and linked this kind of official insensitivity to the sorry condition and low productivity of Soviet agriculture.[71] An attempt to remedy the social and organizational defects of the Soviet system by bringing officialdom and elite groups generally into closer contact with the harsh realities of life at the mass level was thus recurrent in Khrushchev's pronouncements and policies throughout his post-Stalin career. In Breslauer's assessment, "Khrushchev echoed the Stalinist distrust of bureaucrats" and was a consistent proponent of criticism from below and the "mobilization of the masses against officials of both the party and the state."[72] But these themes only came to the fore in the early 1960s. Unlike Stalin, moreover, Khrushchev was interested in more than simply controlling officialdom with pressure from above and below; he also sought to reshape and revitalize the structure of power by behaviorally transforming officialdom.

Along with the unremitting political pressure and pervasive physical insecurity that the Stalin system imposed on Soviet elites, by the 1940s there was in place a "rigid system of social stratification, in which the upper classes would remain upper, the lower classes lower, and the twain would rarely meet."[73] Among the numerous manifestations of this system were a highly differentiated wage structure, elite access to goods and services unavailable at any price to the ordinary citizen, stiff tuition fees at educational institutions preparing students for administrative and professional careers, elegant uniforms, and elaborate titles—in short, all the attributes of the newly arisen Soviet aristocracy that Trotsky complained of in the 1930s and that Milovan Djilas popularized for Western audiences in the 1950s.[74] Whereas Stalin used a combination of terror and privileges to keep elite aspirations in check, Khrushchev pursued a more ambitious and perilous course in attempting to dismantle many of the more blatant features of the system.

Khrushchev's critique of elitism and bureaucratism was multifaceted and ranged from attempts to restrict the material perquisites enjoyed by Soviet elites to fundamental challenges to the assumptions and processes underpinning the system of special privilege. The salaries of top ministerial, military, and party functionaries and those of the technical and professional middle classes were reduced in 1960; at the same time, there were "criticism of the practice of assigning chauffered cars to officials; a pervasive, if still partial change in the method of awarding medals and orders; a demand that the Soviet fashion journal concern itself less with furs and gowns and more with 'everyday' clothes."[75] Of course, such attempts to curb the special privileges and perquisites enjoyed by Soviet elites aroused resentment and grumbling and were derailed more often than not.[76]

More profoundly, Khrushchev attempted to implement far-reaching changes in the structure and function of the Soviet educational system. Under the rubric of making the system more democratic, tuition fees at higher educational institutions were abolished, the curriculum was shortened and simplified, preferential quotas for workers' and peasants' children were established, preference was given at the higher levels to applicants with two years of work experience or military service, and a general effort was made to bring academic training "closer to life."[77] As Bialer observed at the time, these policies amounted to a "war on permanent privilege" and "had as their common target the perpetuation of privileged status without regard to performance, the bequest of such status from one generation to another, and the companion tendency in Soviet society towards class immobility."[78]

Khrushchev's reforms were always motivated by practical concerns, and labor shortages in the post-Stalin period no doubt spurred his interest in simplifying education and bringing it closer to life. But educational reform was just as importantly a manifestation of Khrushchev's growing inclination to link elite privilege and detachment from everyday concerns with the organizational shortcomings and behavioral defects that continued to thwart the economic and social initiatives launched in 1957–1958. Khrushchev increasingly harped on this theme and in fall 1962 criticized the young people who on joining Gosplan "did their work honestly, but gradually detached themselves from life."[79] These "people have never heard the hum of a motor, and already they are uttering economic maxims and trying to plan production in a country as huge as the Soviet Union," which "is why it might be better to think about replacing these entrenched officials and hire new ones who, after graduating from the Institute, have actually worked on a factory or on a farm."[80]

In 1960, a Western analyst noted that many aspects of Khrushchev's educational reforms and attempt to increase equality displayed an unmistakably Stalinist spirit. The arrogant and apparently unreformable deportment of Soviet officialdom, Robert A. Feldmesser observed, "was simply the obverse side of the arbitrary power delegated to local officials for the sake of allowing them to carry out their instructions from above without interference from below."[81] Yet "by being freed from criticism from below, administrators were able to free themselves of supervision from above. . . . Stalin, in other words, forgot his Stalinism; and Khrushchev is not repudiating Stalinism; he is, if anything, reinstating it."[82] We have seen that the thrust of Khrushchevian power restructuring in the 1950s differed qualitatively from that of the Stalinist variant, and this was even more the case in the early 1960s. But Feldmesser very accurately anticipated the fundamental shift in Khrushchev's political tactics that occurred in 1960–1961. With the apparent failure of power decentralization to improve economic performance and energize the system, subsequent Khrushchevian power restructuring would combine power-concentrating and purging processes partially reminiscent of Stalinism with radical, new forms of power deconcentration.[83] In his last four years as leader, Khrushchev engaged in mounting political conflict with important and increasingly wide segments of the Soviet political elite. In the course of what Yanov termed this "establishment crisis," Khrushchev deployed some of the very power-restructuring methods he had denounced less than a decade before in his role as champion of the party organization.[84] At the same time, Khrushchev attempted to deconcentrate and thereby broaden the structure of power in the Soviet Union to a degree unprecedented since the 1920s.

## The Twenty-Second Party Congress and the Collision with Officialdom

The most interesting and significant aspect of Soviet internal politics from the period of the *sovnarkhozy* reforms to October 1964 is surely the transformation of Khrushchev from proponent and revitalizer of party power into taskmaster of an increasingly embittered and recalcitrant political elite. But, as Hough observed, "of course, ultimately Khrushchev was removed. Perhaps in historical perspective this is the most important fact about the Khrushchev era, together with the gradual developments that made it possible."[85] What were these gradual developments?

Western commentators have conventionally linked Khrushchev's ouster to his impetuous and confrontational political style; to his extravagant claims and initiatives, and subsequent defeats and humiliations, on the domestic economic front and in the international arena; and to his penchant for organizational "tinkering" and personnel shake-ups.[86] I suggest that Khrushchev and the political events of the Khrushchev era should be viewed in comparative and historical perspective and that his transformation from champion of the party organization into its taskmaster and his subsequent fall be understood in light of power restructuring. In the closing years of the Khrushchev era, the struggle between the central ruler and the elite resurfaced, and processes of bureaucratic encrustation and official power and resource appropriation collided with processes of personal rulership and power deconcentration set in motion from the top. Although partially reminiscent of Stalinism, Khrushchevian power restructuring was distinctly post-Stalinist.

The mounting tension between Khrushchev and the party organization at the regional and local levels especially burst into the open at the end of 1960 with the Riazan oblast scandal. Amid the campaign fervor of the late 1950s and under pressure from above for impressive results, the Riazan party organization managed to double and then quadruple regional meat production in 1959. The oblast was initially held up for national acclaim and emulation, but it soon became evident that a deception had been perpetrated and that the regional and local party organizations were rife with corruption, falsification, and malfeasance.[87] In Yanov's view, the Riazan scandal "became the symbol of the corruption of the Soviet prefects and signalled the beginning of what I call the 'Soviet Watergate'—i.e., a general purge of corrupt party professionals."[88] The scandal made it clear, moreover, that power decentralization had simply reinforced the capacity of regional and local authorities to evade and distort central policy without producing any offsetting improvement in economic performance.[89] From early 1961 until Khrushchev's removal from power in October 1964, he increased the political pressure on Soviet officialdom in ways both familiar and unprecedented.[90]

From 1958 onward, "Khrushchev enforced a high turn-over of the political elite and does not appear to have been concerned about a possible political backlash."[91] This process was massively accelerated in the early 1960s and reached a crescendo at the Twenty-second Party Congress in October 1961. At the regional level, "between October 1960 and October 1961, 55 of 114 provincial and territorial party first secretaries were either replaced or transferred," while in the Russian Republic two-thirds of the regional party leaders who had acquired power in the mid-1950s were removed.[92] High rates of personnel turnover were also evident in the composition of the ruling bodies elected at the congress as 74 of 175 full Central Committee members, 113 of 155 alternate members, and 45 of 65 Auditing Commission members were completely new—that is, "had not figured in the principal bodies as constituted in previous Congresses (1956, 1952, 1939)."[93] This purge of the political elite was accompanied by another familiar phenomenon—personal rulership and the emergence of a Khrushchev "personality cult." Among the various trappings of the cult, which still paled in comparison to that of Stalin, were the appearance in 1960 of a long film documentary of Khrushchev's life, the publication of a fictionalized biography, and the naming of various collective and state farms after the great man. More significantly, Khrushchev played an overwhelmingly dominant role at the congress, delivered two marathon reports, took the floor on every issue, and garnered voluminous amounts of praise from his senior "colleagues."[94]

While employing these apparently Stalinist methods, however, Khrushchev also revived the rhetoric and revelations of de-Stalinization at the congress and renewed the denunciation of the Anti-Party Group for attempting to "maintain discredited forms and methods of leadership and to slow down the development of the new in our life."[95] Was this an essentially political move, as Michel Tatu argued, with de-Stalinization as a "singularly dangerous weapon in the hands of the First Secretary, who was using it to purge his would-be rivals and consolidate his power"?[96] Only in part. While Khrushchev purged rivals and consolidated power in an apparently Stalinist manner (minus the violence), he also offered unprecedented solutions to the familiar problem of bureaucratic encrustation. The rhetoric and resolutions of the congress were replete with populist imagery and provisions, and the notion of "public control" was repeatedly invoked. The congress was attended by 4,408 voting delegates, almost four times the number attending the Twenty-first Party Congress. Of course, Stalin in the 1930s and during the Great Purges especially also spoke of control from below. In diametric contrast to Stalin's extensive reliance on police methods, violence, and terror, Khrushchev in his final years at the top would attempt to reform and energize the Soviet system with a complex of power-restructuring initiatives containing truly participatory and even "democratic" dimensions.

## Power-Restructuring Initiatives

Perhaps the most striking power-restructuring initiative of the early 1960s was the "three-terms rule." As a means of institutionalizing curbs against bureaucratic encrustation, the "Programme of the CPSU" put forward at the Twenty-second Party Congress called for the "systematic renewal of the leading bodies" and sought to "introduce the principle that the leading officials of the union, republican, and local bodies should be elected to their offices, as a rule, for not more than three consecutive terms."[97] At the same time, "so that fresh millions of working people may learn to govern the state . . . it is advisable that at least one-third of the total number of deputies to a soviet should be elected anew each time." These provisions, the "Programme" further stated, were intended to keep Soviet government "free of bureaucracy, formalism, and red tape" and to ensure the "regular accountability of soviets and deputies to their constituents and the right of the electorate to recall ahead of term deputies who had not justified the confidence placed in them."

The three-terms rule has been subjected to conflicting interpretation. Whereas Tatu argued that Khrushchev's opponents intended the new rules to curb the "excessive concentration of power" in his hands, Yanov viewed these measures as a victory for the managerial elite, who were not subject to the process, over party professionals.[98] According to Burlatsky, "The idea of the rotation of cadres, which had come directly from Khrushchev, provoked the most arguments, and underwent a series of changes."[99] Even Malia, whose entire analysis was premised on the "tragedy" and unreformability of the Soviet system, acknowledged that "these new rules, if applied, would have ended the virtual life tenure that all *apparatchiki* had enjoyed since Stalin's death."[100] In fact, the three-terms rule was emblematic of Khrushchev's overall effort to broaden the structure of power both within the party and in Soviet society generally. Particularly significant was his revival of a top and bottom versus the middle strategy that often resembled the processes of the 1930s. Whereas Khrushchev in the 1950s used "mass consumer expectations" and pressure from the top as means of controlling and energizing the Soviet political elite, the power-restructuring initiatives of the early 1960s were more radical and wide-ranging.

The attempted implementation of the three-terms rule was closely followed in 1962 by measures intended to reduce the monopolistic power of regional and local party leaders and then deconcentrate power beyond the party itself. In January 1962, it was announced that rank-and-file, or "non-staff," party members were to be drawn into investigations of new party admissions and charges against members for rule violations,[101] a policy in keeping with Khrushchev's long-standing interest in more directly involving citizens in the maintenance of law and order. By enlisting ordinary party members on a part-time, unpaid basis, this measure undercut the power of the full-time party professionals who normally held sway. In November 1962, the monolithic power of party leaders was radically reduced by the bifurcation of the oblast party hierarchies into separate industrial and agricultural committees. Khrushchev argued that "such a restructuring will vitalize all aspects of the party's activities . . . by concentrating attention primarily on production problems" and by furthering "the party's general policy of reducing the administrative apparatus and improving its operation."[102] At the same time, rural district party committees were eliminated and replaced by "production directorates" staffed by professional managers.[103]

If all these power-restructuring initiatives were effective means of removing or curbing political opposition at the regional and local levels, they were also motivated by Khrushchev's determination to bring party professionals closer to life and to involve ordinary party members and technical-managerial professionals in political and economic decisionmaking processes previously monopolized by CPSU elites. The rhetoric of the Twenty-second Party Congress was dominated by themes of economic development and expansion, processes that were explicitly connected with extending "the operative independence and initiative of enterprises" and "giving the most capable people leading posts at enterprises."[104] To be sure, Khrushchev was a long-standing opponent of marketization and privatization and in the late 1950s presided over a crackdown on private plot cultivation in the Soviet countryside.[105] Yet by early 1962, he was criticizing the intervention of rural party leaders in the daily affairs of collective farms and calling for the replacement of political professionals by technically proficient professional managers. Significantly, Khrushchev sponsored the first tentative experimentation with the "link system," a form of agricultural organization wherein peasants organized themselves into groups of subcontractors, operated independently, and worked for profit.[106]

And there is evidence that Khrushchev was pushing for more radical changes in the structure of power on the eve of his ouster in October 1964. In the words of Sergei Khrushchev:

> The problem of political power greatly disturbed Father. He worried about who would succeed him and how, and about how to create guarantees against concentration and abuse of power. How to elect deputies was another key issue. Instead of the existing one candidate system, Father proposed nominating several candidates. That way people would be able to express their preferences, and the deputies would really depend on those who elected them. For the moment, this was just an idea, but it might well have been adopted during consideration of a new constitution, which was scheduled for late 1964.[107]

## Assessing Khrushchev and Khrushchevism

Like the man himself, Khrushchevian power restructuring was an intriguing mix of old and new. Khrushchev was a ruler in the classic Russian and Soviet mode: He was a vigorous practitioner of personal rulership who concentrated increasing power in his own hands, eliminated rivals and promoted followers, and autocratically implemented, and if necessary imposed, his own policies, often in the face of official hesitation, noncompliance, and opposition.[108] Especially reminiscent of Stalinism were Khrushchev's policies of massive official personnel turnover and purging, on the one hand, and populist appeals and threats, on the other. As his repeated recourse to top and bottom versus the middle tactics attested, Khrushchev was very much a product of the political culture of the 1930s. But Khrushchev was no Stalin. As Edward Crankshaw observed in 1959, "On the face of it his rise to power has in so many ways resembled Stalin's before him: many are still convinced that he is simply another Stalin in sheep's clothing. But in fact the differences quite outweigh the similarities. Certainly he learnt a great deal about political tactics from Stalin, and put his learning to good use. And yet, I believe, it would be hard to find two men more unlike."[109] Crucial differences distinguished Khrushchev from Stalin, differences that both explain his fall from power and underscore his stature as the first communist leader to confront the political challenges of post-Stalin reform.

Khrushchev's refusal to use violence against his political opponents stands in direct contrast to Stalinist bloodletting. Whereas Stalin physically destroyed thousands of real and imagined political rivals, Khrushchev consciously set out to change power relations and political process in the Soviet system. When Khrushchev outmaneuvered the Anti-Party Group in 1957, he refrained from the kind of violent retaliation that Stalin had routinely employed and that his opponents no doubt would have inflicted on him had they prevailed.[110] When Khrushchev heard of official scheming against him in 1964, he remarked, "We mustn't devote ourselves to settling scores. That would provoke a new wave of violence and hate."[111] When confronted with the reality of the plot to remove him from power in October, he took pride and solace in having changed the style of leadership at the top.[112]

While repudiating Stalinist violence, however, Khrushchev was unable to duplicate or recast Stalin's power-building accomplishments. As we have seen, it was Stalin's enduring achievement in the 1930s to recruit, train, and put in place an entire generation of officials, managers, and engineers devoted to his policies and system. The Stalin generation, a new, fully Soviet elite, was the political and organizational mainstay of the Stalin system, a reliable social base to which Stalin was able to turn on repeated occasions. We have also seen that central rulers engaged in power contests with political and bureaucratic elites must build alternative channels of power and foster institutional competitors to established bases of official power. In Khrushchev's initial struggle with the central ministerial apparatus and the Anti-Party Group, he accomplished this feat by allying with and empowering regional and local party leaders. In his subsequent attempt to reform the structure of party power itself, however, Khrushchev was unable to build or locate sociopolitical alternatives and organizational counterweights sufficient to oppose established bases of CPSU power. Indeed, Khrushchev was an inveterate practitioner of patron-client relations and as a founding member of the new Soviet elite preferred to work through long-standing associates and allies in his personal entourage and within the party apparatus.[113]

Both the aversion to Stalinist bloodletting and the failure to build effective alternatives to the established structure of party power can be attributed to Khrushchev's essential faith in and loyalty to the party organization. In Breslauer's view, "Both Khrushchev and Brezhnev were 'party men,' who defended the primacy of political-mobilizational approaches to public administration . . . and ·forged programs that relied heavily on party activism and intervention for their realization."[114] Yet Khrushchev attempted to reshape the structure of power in the Soviet Union in ways that sharply contradicted both the Stalinist legacy and the record of his successors. From his stewardship of agricultural affairs in the immediate aftermath of Stalin's death, to his administrative reforms and personal triumph in 1957 and his power restructuring initiatives of the early 1960s, the most important and recurrent feature of Khrushchevism was an effort to decentralize and finally deconcentrate political power. The party organization, so fiercely stifled and repressed by Stalin, gladly embraced the decentralization of power into its own hands, but Khrushchev's aims were more ambitious. In his attempt at a radical restructuring of power, Khrushchev in the early 1960s began to attack the root cause of bureaucratic encrustation and power and resource appropriation in the Soviet system—the power monopoly of the political elite—and was over-thrown.

As the record of his successors confirmed, it was Khrushchev's policies of organizational change, personnel turnover, and power deconcentration that precipitated his downfall. (In my discussion of the Chinese Cultural Revolution and the period of perestroika, I consider the momentous consequences of more wide-ranging and radical assaults on the power monopoly of the communist party.) Understood in this light, Khrushchev's defeat was an opportunity lost for the Soviet system, when avenues of change, reform, and revitalization were foreclosed that would be re-opened only decades later under different and more adverse conditions.

## Brezhnevian Counterrevolution

The power dynamics of the Brezhnev era bear scant resemblance to the tumultuous power-restructuring initiatives and organization upheavals of the preceding decade. Two comparisons suffice to underscore the very different trajectory of power and politics under Khrushchev and Brezhnev: The political style of the Brezhnev regime and its internal policies contrast sharply with those of the Khrushchev era.

The Brezhnev era has long been characterized as conservative, with "its antireformist spirit and policies expressed in a galaxy of refurbished conservative catchphrases, cults, and campaigns—'stability in cadres,' 'law and order,' 'the strengthening of organization, discipline, and responsibility in all spheres.'"[115] Similarly, analysts have conventionally spoken of Brezhnev's consensual approach to leadership and his "decisionmaking style[,] which emphasized consensus and a lowest common denominator approach in the Politburo."[116] These characterizations are accurate but do not go nearly far enough. When the power relations and political process of the Brezhnev era are compared to the patterns in the preceding decades of Soviet power, it becomes evident that an elite counterrevolution occurred under Brezhnev. In contrast to the brutal but effective pressure that the Stalin system brought to bear on the Soviet political elite, pressure that Khrushchev for much of his tenure attempted to bring to bear in new ways, Brezhnev and Brezhnevism manifested an untroubled and complacent ascendancy of officialdom unprecedented in the history of the Soviet Union. Brezhnev was an assiduous consensus builder, who started his working day with several hours of telephone calls to other central and regional party leaders, but his style of political leadership consisted first and foremost of pork barrel politics and the dispensing of patronage, favors, and resources. In Burlatsky's telling observation, "In general it was not production that Brezhnev preferred to be engaged in, but distribution. This was what Brezhnev-style politics consisted of. Such people are not very competent at deciding important economic, cultural, or political issues, but to make up for it they know exactly whom to appoint and where to appoint him to; whom to reward for services rendered, when and how."[117] Over the course of the Brezhnev years, corrupt politics became increasingly pervasive throughout the Soviet system, and political elites at the central, regional, and local levels, provided they did not directly challenge the rulers at the top, were allowed free rein to build "independent kingdoms" and to enrich themselves, their families, and their followers.[118]

Yet the corrupt politics of Brezhnevism went hand in hand with the strengthening of party controls over society and the economy at large. Significantly, the first major policy decision of the new rulers was to reverse Khrushchev's bifurcation initiative and restore the monolithic economic powers of regional party committees.[119] Whereas Khrushchev attempted to curb the privileges and arbitrary powers of the Soviet political elite, the new rulers persistently sought to upgrade the status and prerogatives of the CPSU. In sharp contrast to Khrushchev's attempt to increase party membership and broaden the internal distribution of power, new restrictions on party admissions were imposed in 1965 and the process made more selective.[120] Whereas Khrushchev was troubled by arbitrary power wielding by party leaders and sought to involve more people in decisionmaking processes, Brezhnev strengthened the interventionist powers of the party organization.[121] Most telling of all, whereas the Khrushchev years witnessed vigorous personnel turnover and limits on tenure in office, the Brezhnev era was a time of "unparalleled bureaucratic stability and, first and foremost, of personnel stability."[122] In Bialer's classic summation, "If Khrushchev brought the Soviet elite the gift of life, Brezhnev assured it security of office. Soviet high officials do not fade away; they die in office."[123]

It is the unbridled ascendancy of officialdom under Brezhnev that most strikingly distinguishes Brezhnevism from Khrushchevism and from Stalinism as well. Freed of the terroristic controls of the Stalin system, the Soviet political elite successfully contested Khrushchev's attempts to restructure its power and curb its privileges. This elite counterrevolution was the central reality and most enduring legacy of Brezhnevism. Just as an elite counterrevolution in the wake of the Revolution of 1905 undercut the possibility of reform and sealed the fate of the imperial system, the consequences of the Brezhnevian counterrevolution proved similarly detrimental to the Soviet system. In 1983, Ken Jowitt wrote, "What was a tendency in 1934 became a reality in 1965. With Brezhnev, Kirov triumphed. The remarkable emphasis on cadre tenure signals the success of organizational corruption and political routinization in the Soviet Union."[124] In retrospect, we can see that Brezhnevism proved less enduring than Jowitt supposed. When Gorbachev attempted to reform and revitalize the Soviet system with a complex of radical power-restructuring initiatives in the late 1980s, the system, now more rickety and corrupt than ever, was unable to take the strain and disintegrated.

## Notes

1. Merle Fainsod, *How Russia Is Ruled,* rev. ed. enl. (Cambridge, Mass.: Harvard University Press, 1965), 583.

2. See Chapter 1 for my assessment of the totalitarian versus interest group theory debate. *How Russia Is Ruled* was the last major conceptual statement of the totalitarian school

prior to the collapse of the Soviet Union, when such commentators as Malia and Pipes attempted to resurrect totalitarian theory.

3. Carl A. Linden, *Khrushchev and the Soviet Leadership, 1957–1964* (Baltimore: Johns Hopkins University Press, 1966), 218. For a detailed and illuminating post-Khrushchev account of factional politics in the Soviet elite, see Roman Kolkowicz's discussion of factions and patron-client networks in the Soviet military and the role of Khrushchev's faction, the "Stalingrad Group," in particular. (*The Soviet Military and the Communist Party* [Princeton: Princeton University Press, 1966], chap. 7).

4. Martin McCauley argued that Khrushchev could be viewed in three basic ways: "1) as a transitory leader; 2) as a transitional leader; 3) as an original leader" ("Khrushchev as Leader," in Martin McCauley, ed., *Khrushchev and Khrushchevism* [Bloomington: Indiana University Press, 1987], 24). The first view, that of Khrushchev's successors who sought to denigrate his harebrained schemes, does not merit discussion.

5. Kolkowicz, *The Soviet Military and the Communist Party*, 252–253.

6. McCauley, "Khrushchev as Leader," 11–12.

7. George W. Breslauer, *Khrushchev and Brezhnev as Leaders: Building Authority in Soviet Politics* (London: George Allen and Unwin, 1982), 4, 7. Breslauer's "broad regime consensus" included "increased consumer satisfaction; greater material incentives for the masses; deconcentration of public administration; expanded political participation by social activists and specialists; a narrower definition of political crime; an end to mass terror; and greater collective leadership" (4). My discussion, which highlights the differences between the Khrushchev and Brezhnev eras, shows that this interpretation is untenable.

8. McCauley, "Khrushchev as Leader," 26–27.

9. Alastair McAuley, "Social Policy," in McCauley, ed., *Khrushchev and Khrushchevism*, 138, 143.

10. Sidney I. Ploss, "A New Soviet Era?" *Foreign Policy* 62 (Spring 1986):46–60.

11. Jerry F. Hough and Merle Fainsod, *How the Soviet Union Is Governed* (Cambridge, Mass.: Harvard University Press, 1979), 252, 255.

12. Graeme Gill, "Khrushchev and Systemic Development," in McCauley, ed., *Khrushchev and Khrushchevism*, 31, 41, 44. Thus, "institutionalization means the regularization of operating procedures, the development of patterns of action which are accepted as the norm, and through which the institution functions" (30). Therefore, "the clash between pressures for institutionalization and for the dominant leader model constituted the major dynamic of the Khrushchev period" (41).

13. In 1982, Breslauer wrote, "The evidence brought forth in this book suggests that Soviet elite politics since Stalin have been marked by substantial continuity and consensus on the need to increase consumer satisfaction, rationalize the administrative structures, and expand political participation (relative to Stalinist levels)" (*Khrushchev and Brezhnev as Leaders*, 269). These lines obviously could not be written in the 1990s!

14. In Geoffrey Hosking's words, "Peasants hoped the Germans would dissolve the collective farms and reopen the churches; Ukrainians, Bielorussians, and the Baltic peoples hoped they would permit them to establish national states of their own; and everybody hoped that the Germans, as a 'cultured' nation, would at least allow them to lead a more secure and settled existence than they had known under Stalin's terror. They were to be disappointed, but that was not immediately apparent" (*The First Socialist Society: A History of the Soviet Union from Within* [Cambridge: Cambridge University Press, 1985], 270–271).

15. As William C. Fuller noted in this regard, "The creation of a new military system based on industrial might was to be Stalin's achievement" (*Power and Strategy in Russia, 1600–1914* [New York: Free Press, 1992], 463).

16. Alexander Werth, *Russia at War, 1941–1945* (New York: Dutton, 1964), 226–227.

17. Ibid., 248–249. Thus, "be worthy of this great mission! The war you are waging is a war of liberation, a just war. May you be inspired in this war by the heroic figures of our great ancestors, Alexander Nevsky, Dimitri Donskoi, Minin and Pozharsky, Alexander Suvorov, Mikhail Kutuzov!" (249).

18. Ibid., 249; see part 4, chap. 6, for a discussion of the modus vivendi established between the Soviet state and the Russian Orthodox Church during the war.

19. In the words of one contemporary observer, "Stalin had carried out sweeping purges, especially in the higher command, but these had less effect than is sometimes believed, for he did not hesitate at the same time to elevate younger and more talented men; every officer who was faithful to him and to his aims knew that his ambitions would meet with encouragement" (Milovan Djilas, *Conversations with Stalin* [New York: Harcourt, Brace and World, 1962], 49–50).

20. Kolkowicz, *The Soviet Military and the Communist Party*, 67.

21. Werth, *Russia at War*, 428.

22. Kolkowicz, *The Soviet Military and the Communist Party*, 68.

23. In a critique repeatedly echoed by subsequent reformers of the Stalin system, Chief Marshal of Artillery N. N. Voronov noted, "The excessive centralization was extremely vexing. It not only robbed one of a great deal of time and prevented one from concentrating on the main thing, but it fettered the initiative of subordinates, slowed things down, and lowered efficiency" ("The Vexations of Centralization," in Seweryn Bialer, ed., *Stalin and His Generals: Soviet Military Memoirs of World War II* [New York: Pegasus, 1969], 367).

24. Wertl., *Russia at War*, 999. See Werth's discussion of Marshal Zhukov's immense popularity as the victor of the Battle of Berlin and his subsequent eclipse and posting to the minor position of commander of the Odessa Military District (995–1000).

25. Aleksander Wat, *My Century: The Odyssey of a Polish Intellectual* (Berkeley and Los Angeles: University of California Press, 1988), 352.

26. Werth, *Russia at War*, 941; see part 7, chap. 8, for a description of the relatively easy-going cultural atmosphere and "soft" economic policies that briefly prevailed.

27. Dimitri Volkogonov, *Stalin: Triumph and Tragedy* (New York: Grove Press, 1991), 504.

28. For the hardening of the regime, see Alexander Werth, *Russia: The Post-War Years* (New York: Taplinger, 1971), chap. 6.

29. Nikita Khrushchev, *Khrushchev Remembers* (Boston: Little, Brown, 1970), 229. Nikita Khrushchev was in charge of Ukraine at this time. In his memoirs, Khrushchev expressed sympathy for the suffering of the people and described how he attempted to buffer the population from Stalin's relentless demands. But it was Khrushchev who spearheaded the drive to reestablish Soviet power in Ukraine (228–235).

30. Werner G. Hahn, *Postwar Soviet Politics: The Fall of Zhdanov and the Defeat of Moderation, 1946–53* (Ithaca: Cornell University Press, 1982), 59. The issue of private plots was fiercely debated and contested in China in the 1950s and 1960s, and the outcome was very different.

31. Werth, *Russia,* chaps. 11, 16.

32. Hahn, *Postwar Soviet Politics,* 55. Thus, it was the local and regional party organizations that were held responsible for "shortcomings" and "violations" in agriculture.

33. Victor Kravchenko, *I Chose Freedom* (New York: Charles Scribner, 1946), 395.

34. See Robert Conquest, *Power and Policy in the USSR* (New York: Harper, 1961), 103–110; Hahn, *Postwar Soviet Politics,* 123–124; Khrushchev, *Khrushchev Remembers,* 251. It is probable that factional politics was key since the assault on the Leningrad party organization followed the political defeat and subsequent death of Zhdanov, whose major rivals were Malenkov, head of the central ministerial apparatus, and police chief Beria. We have seen that the fomenting of interelite factional conflict is a control device regularly employed by central rulers, including Stalin.

35. Seweryn Bialer, *Stalin's Successors* (Cambridge: Cambridge University Press, 1980), 10, 12, 20.

36. Ibid.

37. Khrushchev, *Khrushchev Remembers,* 297. For a vivid and still unrivaled description of the treacherous and deadly atmosphere in which Stalin and his top subordinates worked and partied, see 296–315.

38. Harry Schwartz, *Russia's Soviet Economy,* 2d ed. (Englewood Cliffs, N.J.: Prentice-Hall, 1958), 310–311. In Stalin's words, "It is necessary . . . by means of gradual transitions, to replace commodity circulation by a system of products-exchange, under which the central government, or some other social-economic center, might control the whole product of social production in the interests of society" ("Concerning the Errors of Comrade Yaroshenko," in *Economic Problems of Socialism in the USSR* [Peking: Foreign Languages Press, 1972], 69).

39. Vera S. Dunham, *In Stalin's Time: Middle-Class Values in Soviet Fiction* (Cambridge: Cambridge University Press, 1976), 13. While discussing the "embourgeoisement of Soviet manners, values, attitudes," Dunham's analysis is centered on the "new legion of productive engineers, organizers, administrators, and managers" that was recruited and trained in the 1930s and continued its ascent in the 1940s (4–5).

40. Fedor Burlatsky, *Khrushchev and the First Russian Spring* (London: Weidenfeld and Nicolson, 1991), 13.

41. Beria was arrested in June 1953; charged with "the criminal goal of using the organs of the Ministry of Internal Affairs against the Communist Party and the Government of the USSR, and placing the Ministry of Internal Affairs over the Party and Government in order to seize power"; and executed along with a half dozen top associates in December. See Robert Conquest, "Announcement on the Trial of Beria" in *Power and Policy in the USSR,* 444–447; and a colorful account in Khrushchev, *Khrushchev Remembers,* 322–341.

42. Breslauer, *Khrushchev and Brezhnev as Leaders,* 45. Burlatsky cast considerable doubt on this interpretation. In mid-1953, Malenkov gave a speech with all the familiar Stalinist denunciations of the "degeneration" and "corruption" of the "state apparatus," thereby terrifying his audience and inducing a "deathly silence." Only after Khrushchev retorted, "But the apparatus is our buttress" did "friendly, stormy, and prolonged applause break out" (*Khrushchev and the First Russian Spring,* 13–14).

43. George W. Breslauer, "Khrushchev Reconsidered," in Stephen F. Cohen, Alexander Rabinowitch, and Robert Sharlet, eds., *The Soviet Union Since Stalin* (Bloomington: Indiana University Press, 1980), 50–53.

44. Robert F. Miller, "Continuity and Change in the Administration of Soviet Agriculture Since Stalin," in James R. Millar, ed., *The Soviet Rural Community* (Urbana: University of Illinois Press, 1971), 81–82.

45. Ibid., 80.

46. McCauley, "Khrushchev as Leader," 15. McCauley asserted that the "driving force behind the 1953 reform was political, not administrative or economic" (15). In fact, Khrushchev's power-restructuring initiatives were usually motivated by a combination of genuine reform convictions and hard-nosed power politics considerations.

47. See Nikita Khrushchev, *Khrushchev Remembers: The Last Testament* (Boston: Little, Brown, 1974), 125–126.

48. Howard R. Swearer, "Agricultural Administration Under Khrushchev," in Roy D. Laird, ed., *Soviet Agricultural and Peasant Affairs* (Lawrence: University of Kansas Press, 1963), 24.

49. "On the Further Increase of Grain Production in the Country and the Development of Virgin and Unused Lands," Plenum of the Central Committee, March 2, 1954, in *Resolutions and Decisions of the Communist Party of the Soviet Union, 1898–1981*, vol. 4, *The Khrushchev Years,* ed. Grey Hodnett (Toronto: University of Toronto Press, 1974), 30–33.

50. Khrushchev, *Khrushchev Remembers: The Last Testament,* 124.

51. Khrushchev, *Khrushchev Remembers,* 570, 572–573, 584.

52. Ibid., 612.

53. Burlatsky, *Khrushchev and the First Russian Spring,* 64–65.

54. "On the Party Organizers of the Central Committee of the CPSU," August 7, 1956, in *Resolutions and Decisions of the CPSU,* vol. 4, 72–73.

55. "On Improving the Work of the Soviets of Workers' Deputies and Strengthening Their Ties with the Masses," January 22, 1957, in ibid., 73–81; see also Ronald J. Hill, "State and Ideology," in McCauley, ed., *Khrushchev and Khrushchevism,* 48–49.

56. "On Further Improving the Organization and Management of Industry and Construction," Central Committee Plenum, February 14, 1957, in *Resolutions and Decisions of the CPSU,* vol. 4, 85.

57. Edward Crankshaw, *Khrushchev: A Career* (New York: Viking, 1966), 247.

58. The Anti-Party episode involved great political drama. Outnumbered by opponents in the Presidium, Khrushchev insisted that only the full Central Committee could decide his fate. When Khrushchev's allies in the military flew in Central Committee members from the provinces, who then demanded to know what was going on, Malenkov et al. "found themselves in the position of an insignificant minority" and "Khrushchev took complete command of the plenum." See Khrushchev's account as related to the Yugoslav ambassador in Veljko Micunovic, *Moscow Diary* (Garden City, N.Y.: Doubleday, 1980), 270–271.

59. "On Granting to the Central Committees of the Union Republic Parties the Right to Resolve Certain Party-Organizational and Budgetary-Financial Questions," August 2, 1957, in *Resolutions and Decisions of the CPSU,* vol. 4, 98–100.

60. Fainsod, *How Russia Is Ruled,* 175.

61. Alec Nove, "The Soviet Industrial Reorganization," in Abraham Brumberg, ed., *Russia Under Khrushchev* (New York: Praeger, 1962), 189.

62. Roy A. Medvedev and Zhores A. Medvedev, *Khrushchev: The Years in Power* (New York: Norton, 1978), 83.

63. Jerry F. Hough, *The Soviet Prefects* (Cambridge, Mass.: Harvard University Press, 1969), 66, 121, 168, 214.

64. Ibid., 289.

65. Ibid., 265–266.

66. Alec Nove, "Industry," in McCauley, ed., *Khrushchev and Khrushchevism*, 65.

67. Nove, "The Soviet Industrial Reorganization," 197–198.

68. Ibid., 194.

69. Swearer, "Agricultural Administration Under Khrushchev," 24–25. The Central Committee decree "On the Further Development of the Kolkhoz System and the Reorganization of the MTSs," February 26, 1958, noted, "In many cases, this form has started to hamper the continued advance of leading kolkhozes, hindering the initiative of the kolkhoz cadres and of all kolkhozniks in the better exploitation of kolkhoz production reserves" (*Resolutions and Decisions of the CPSU*, vol. 4, 112).

70. "On the Report by Comrade N. S. Khrushchev 'Control Figures for the Development of the Economy of the USSR in the Years 1959–65,'" February 5, 1959, and "On the State of Mass Political Work Among the Toilers of Stalino Oblast and Measures for Improving It," March 11, 1959, in *Resolutions and Decisions of the CPSU*, vol. 4, 124, 133.

71. Khrushchev, *Khrushchev Remembers: The Last Testament*, 112–113.

72. Breslauer, *Khrushchev and Brezhnev as Leaders*, 44.

73. Robert A. Feldmesser, "Equality and Inequality Under Khrushchev," in Brumberg, ed., *Russia Under Khrushchev*, 223.

74. Milovan Djilas, *The New Class* (New York: Praeger, 1957), chap. 3.

75. Feldmesser, "Equality and Inequality Under Khrushchev," 234. See also Michel Tatu, *Power in the Kremlin* (New York: Viking, 1970), 115.

76. See Burlatsky's account of Khrushchev's unsuccessful attempt to close the Moscow "feeding trough," "a unique club for the upper ranks of the Communist Party" "where good food supplies were handed out at very moderate, subsidized prices" (*Khrushchev and the First Russian Spring*, 197–198).

77. Feldmesser, "Equality and Inequality Under Khrushchev," 230–233. This effort to favor low-status and nonprivileged groups at the expense of established elites is familiar.

78. Seweryn Bialer, ". . . But Some Are More Equal Than Others," in Brumberg, ed., *Russia Under Khrushchev*, 251.

79. Tatu, "Khrushchev's Agricultural Speeches," in *Power in the Kremlin*, 288.

80. Ibid. Once again, these comments strikingly parallel Maoist ideas about "sending down" students and intellectuals to the countryside and factories to "learn from the masses."

81. Feldmesser, "Equality and Inequality Under Khrushchev," 236–237.

82. Ibid.

83. In a communist system, the thrust of power decentralization and that of power deconcentration differ fundamentally. Whereas the former entails the redistribution of power *within* the power monopoly of the communist party, the latter involves the redistribution of power *beyond* the power monopoly of the party. This conceptual distinction was first articulated by Franz Schurmann in his discussion of economic decentralization in China in the 1950s. Whereas Schurmann's "decentralization I" involved power transfers from the center to the party organization at the regional and provincial levels, "decentralization II" was market oriented and involved power transfers to household and individuals (*Ideology and Organization in Communist China* [Berkeley and Los Angeles: University of California Press, 1970), 175–176, 297.

84. Alexander Yanov, *The Drama of the Soviet 1960s* (Berkeley: Institute of International Studies, University of California at Berkeley, 1984), 74.

85. Hough and Fainsod, *How the Soviet Union Is Governed,* 236.

86. Breslauer, *Khrushchev and Brezhnev as Leaders;* Tatu, *Power in the Kremlin.* Hough suggested that Walter Lippman's notion of the "tinkering reformer . . . a man who is forever trying to make the existing machinery of government function perfectly in terms of some abstract ideal" aptly characterized Khrushchev ("A Harebrained Scheme in Retrospect," *Problems of Communism* 14 [July–August 1965]:26–32).

87. The regional party leadership was able to achieve a spectacular onetime increase in meat production by ordering the slaughter of virtually all livestock in the area, including milk cows, breeding herds, and household animals forcibly purchased from peasants. When meat deliveries plummeted the next year, the fraud was exposed, the oblast party secretary committed suicide, and a terrible scandal ensued (Medvedev and Medvedev, *Khrushchev,* chap. 9).

88. Yanov, *The Drama of the Soviet 1960s,* 72.

89. Thus, when "local officials, party and government, saddled with the responsibility of meeting overambitious agricultural goals and fortified by some administrative autonomy as a result of decentralization in agricultural planning and management, took refuge in falsification of all kinds," in 1961 a "reversal [occurred] of the trend toward administrative decentralization in agriculture" (Swearer, "Agricultural Administration Under Khrushchev," 27).

90. Martin Malia suggested that mounting political resistance to Khrushchev's reforms in 1961 "had its roots in the affair of the Anti-Party Group of June 1957" and the "hostility of the orthodox" toward Khrushchev's loosening of controls and abolition of the MTSs in the late 1950s *(The Soviet Tragedy: A History of Socialism in Russia, 1917–1991* [New York: Free Press, 1994], 336). In fact, Soviet elites in the provinces benefited from Khrushchev's power-decentralizing reforms, and it was only when the Soviet leader attempted to deconcentrate power that widespread resistance within the political elite began to mount.

91. McCauley, "Khrushchev as Leader," 21.

92. Breslauer, *Khrushchev and Brezhnev as Leaders,* 99; McCauley, "Khrushchev as Leader," 21. See also Yanov's account of this "purge of regional dictators unprecedented in its proportions in the post-totalitarian era" *(The Drama of the Soviet 1960s,* 73–74).

93. Tatu, *Power in the Kremlin,* 191–192.

94. Ibid., 177–180.

95. "On the Report of the Central Committee," October 31, 1961, in *Resolutions and Decisions of the CPSU,* vol. 4, 164.

96. Tatu, *Power in the Kremlin,* 142.

97. "Programme of the CPSU," October 31, 1961, in *Resolutions and Decisions of the CPSU,* vol. 4, 236–237. (All quotes in this paragraph are from this source.) In his "Report," Khrushchev spoke of the necessity for "striking a proper balance between the old and experienced party workers and young, energetic, and capable organizers," and he stated, "There is no room for out-of-date and conceited persons who have lost their feel for life, who are devoid of ideas and principles" (165).

98. Tatu, *Power in the Kremlin,* 183; Yanov, *The Drama of the Soviet 1960s,* 87–88.

99. Burlatsky, *Khrushchev and the First Russian Spring,* 129–130. Burlatsky, who participated in the drafting of the three-terms proposal, concluded, "In the final text the whole plan to create a new procedure for the replacement of cadres became unrecognizable. What

remained concerned almost without exception the lower structures and soon turned out to be useless in practice" (130).

100. Malia, *The Soviet Tragedy*, 338.

101. "On the Creation in City and Raion Party Committees of Non-Staff Party Commissions for the Preliminary Examination of Questions of Admission to the Party and Personal Affairs of Communists," January 11, 1962, in *Resolutions and Decisions of the CPSU*, vol. 4, 282–283.

102. "On the Development of the National Economy of the USSR and the Reorganization of Party Leadership of the Economy," November 23, 1962, in ibid., 294. Hence, "in struggling against deception, embezzlement, bribe taking, red tape, and other negative phenomena alien to the spirit of the socialist system . . . the plenum of the CPSU Central Committee emphasizes that a radical restructuring of the operations of party, soviet, and economic organs will not lead to a rise in the number of administrators but, on the contrary, will reduce their number and also reduce the cost of their upkeep" (294–295).

103. Yanov, *The Drama of the Soviet 1960s*, 88–94.

104. "Programme of the CPSU," 225–226. Yet no diminution of central planning was envisioned. Rather, "democratic principles of management" were to be coupled "with a strengthening and improvement of centralized economic management by the state" and the "determined elimination of elements of localism."

105. Karl-Eugen Wadekin, *The Private Sector in Soviet Agriculture* (Berkeley and Los Angeles: University of California Press, 1973), chap. 9.

106. Yanov, *The Drama of the Soviet 1960s*, sec. 1.

107. Sergei Khrushchev, *Khrushchev on Khrushchev: An Inside Account of the Man and the Era* (Boston: Little, Brown, 1990), 23. Burlatsky's account confirms that Khrushchev was developing and getting ready to implement a set of new constitutional provisions in 1964 (*Khrushchev and the First Russian Spring*, 200–201).

108. Burlatsky saw Khrushchev as an exemplar of patrimonial rulership: "In the mind of Khrushchev and of a whole generation of leaders the traditional model of a patriarchal peasant household was preserved. . . . Paternalism, the right to interfere in any matter or relationship, the infallibility of the patriarch, intolerance of dissenting views—this was the typical age-old notion of power in Russia" (*Khrushchev and the First Russian Spring*, 135).

109. Edward Crankshaw, *Khrushchev's Russia* (Baltimore: Penguin, 1959), 50–51.

110. When the Anti-Party Group was defeated, Kaganovich phoned Khrushchev and tearfully "told him that he hoped he was not going to revert to the ways of the past which Khrushchev had so strongly condemned (he was thinking of reprisals, prison, and executions). Khrushchev replied that it was in order to prevent the past being repeated that he, Kaganovich, and the others were being thrown out of the Central Committee (Micunovic, *Moscow Diary*, 275).

111. Cited in S. Khrushchev, *Khrushchev on Khrushchev*, 15.

112. In Sergei Khrushchev's recollection of his father's remarks: "I've done the main thing. Relations among us, the style of leadership, has changed drastically. Could anyone have dreamed of telling Stalin that he didn't suit us anymore, and suggesting that he retire? Not even a wet spot would have remained where we are standing. Now everything is different. The fear's gone and we talk as equals. That's my contribution" (*Khrushchev on Khrushchev*, 154).

113. In Burlatsky's words, "When we spoke of the First's weaknesses we would say, 'He's got used to walking in his worn-out slippers.' That was his reputation even when he

was in the Ukraine and later when he came to Moscow: that he preferred to work with an apparatus which had been handed down to him from his predecessors and rarely replaced those around him" (*Khrushchev and the First Russian Spring,* 131).

114. Breslauer, *Khrushchev and Brezhnev as Leaders,* 13.

115. Stephen F. Cohen, *Rethinking the Soviet Experience: Politics and History Since 1917* (New York: Oxford University Press, 1985), 138.

116. Gill, "Khrushchev and Systemic Development," 44. See also Breslauer, *Khrushchev and Brezhnev as Leaders,* 12.

117. Burlatsky, *Khrushchev and the First Russian Spring,* 217–218. Hence, "Leonid Ilyich worked hard to place people like himself in leading posts. They were 'little Brezhnevs'— unhurried, bland, uninspiring, not very concerned about work, but skillful at distributing largesse" (218).

118. For firsthand accounts of official corruption in the Brezhnev years, see Michael Voslensky, *Nomenklatura* (Garden City, N.Y.: Doubleday, 1984), 185–197; and Konstantin Simis, *USSR: The Corrupt Society* (New York: Simon and Schuster, 1982), chap. 2.

119. At the same time, the monolithic powers of the district (*raion*) party committee were restored. See "On the Unification of Industrial and Agricultural Oblast and Krai Party Organizations," November 16, 1964, in *Resolutions and Decisions of the Communist Party of the Soviet Union, 1898–1981,* vol. 5, *The Brezhnev Years,* ed. Donald V. Schwartz, (Toronto: University of Toronto Press, 1982), 41–42.

120. "On Serious Errors Committed by the Kharkov Oblast Party Organization with Respect to the Admission of Young Communists into the Party and Their Education," July 20, 1965, in *Resolutions and Decisions of the CPSU,* vol. 5, 45–49, stated, "In selecting people for the party it must be borne in mind that the admission of even a few persons unworthy of the lofty title of communist is harmful to the party, chokes its ranks, lowers its authority, and weakens the fighting efficiency of party organization" (48).

121. "On the Work of the 'Mikhailov' Sovkhoz Party Committee in the Panin Raion of Voronezh Oblast," February 18, 1967, in ibid., 89–93, charged state farm party organizations with the responsibility and the right to intervene in a wide range of daily operational, organizational, economic, political, and ideological activities.

122. Bialer, *Stalin's Successors,* 91.

123. Ibid. It is now conventional to speak of the "internal arteriosclerosis" that occurred during the Brezhnev era; e.g., Malia, *The Soviet Tragedy,* 382. But Bialer's pioneering analysis of organizational stability and "ossification" under Brezhnev is still the best (81–96).

124. Ken Jowitt, "Soviet Neotraditionalism: The Political Corruption of a Leninist Regime," *Soviet Studies* 35, 3 (July 1983):297.

# 6

# Chinese Communism, Maoism, and the Origins of the Cultural Revolution

Power restructuring in Communist China is comparable in sociopolitical scale and world-historical significance to power restructuring in the Soviet Union. In this chapter, I chart power-restructuring dynamics during the first two decades of Chinese Communist rule, 1949 to 1966. My discussion encompasses the nationwide consolidation of CCP power in the early 1950s, the momentous campaigns and sociopolitical collisions of the late 1950s, power relations and political process in the early 1960s, and the eruption of the Cultural Revolution in summer and fall 1966. I demonstrate that power dynamics during the first two decades of Chinese Communist rule often paralleled those of the Soviet 1920s and 1930s and of the Soviet 1950s and early 1960s as well. While exploring these similarities, I also identify the crucial differences that distinguish Chinese Communist power restructuring from the Soviet experience. In this chapter, I focus special attention on processes of concentration and control, contending developmental strategies, the deconcentration and decentralization of power, political conflict at the top and at the societal level, and top and bottom versus the middle power-restructuring processes.

In the early 1950s, CCP power was successfully established at all levels of Chinese society, and a national program of social, economic, and technological transformation was set in motion. In contrast to the limited reach of the Soviet state in the 1920s, the mobilizational and coercive capacities of China's new rulers in the 1950s were formidably well developed and far-reaching. Even as they presided over massive structural transformations, however, China's leaders faced developmental dilemmas and became divided by policy disputes that closely paralleled those of the Soviet 1920s. In the late 1950s, these dilemmas and disputes were manifested in two pivotal sociopolitical upheavals—the Hundred Flowers Movement and the Great Leap Forward. While delineating these cataclysmic events and their aftermath, I consider the origins of the most fateful power-restructuring episode in the history of Chinese communism—the Cultural Revolution. My discussion in this chapter concludes with an analysis of the preliminary stages and opening salvoes of this watershed event. In Chapter 7, I undertake a more extended analysis of the Cultural Revolution, delineate its unintended consequences, and assess its historical significance.

Power restructuring in the first two decades of Chinese Communist rule should be viewed from three complementary perspectives: the historical experience of Chinese communism; the dilemmas of building a new political, economic, and social order; and the challenge of reforming a communist system. As a revolutionary movement based in the countryside, drawing on peasant support, and built up over more than two decades, Chinese communism differed in its experience and worldview from those of the Bolsheviks. During the CCP's protracted sojourn in the Chinese countryside, the party developed power-restructuring methods that would be deployed with potent effect on the party's ascent to national power. Yet as Marxist-Leninists, the Chinese Communists looked to the Soviet Union for support and inspiration and sought to emulate Soviet economic and institutional achievements. In the course of building up a communist system, Chinese Communist leaders were faced with many of the dilemmas that Soviet rulers had confronted three decades earlier. While engaged in the familiar task of erecting a system of concentrated power, however, the CCP in the late 1950s also encountered the changed circumstances of the post-Stalin era and the problem of post-Stalin reform. It was in this setting that the sociopolitical upheavals of the late 1950s and 1960s occurred and left their mark on the historical trajectory of Chinese communism.

## Conceptualizing Chinese Communism

Although Western analysts have relied on a variety of models and devices to conceptualize the first two decades of Chinese Communist rule, two divergent analytic approaches stand out. Both in the 1950s and today, some accounts have taken an essentially monolithic view of Chinese communism and accented the far-reaching capacity of the communist party-state and its leadership to assert power and implement policy in a sweeping and unified fashion. But the more prevalent analytic tendency has been to accent problematic aspects of Chinese Communist rule and focus on the series of unresolved and often traumatic political conflicts, social transformations, and economic upheavals that occurred in the 1950s and 1960s. With largely contradictory emphases on the primacy of control versus the primacy of conflict, these divergent views of power dynamics under Chinese communism broadly approximate the totalitarian versus revisionist divide in Soviet studies.

In the 1950s, some analysts adopted Fainsod's totalitarian terminology and spoke of Chinese communism as a "Soviet-style police state" functioning primarily on the basis of coercion, police controls, "raw power," and "terror as a system of power."[1] As Jurgen Domes observed, however, "This tendency approached unthinking anti-Communism, which obscured not only the emerging Sino-Soviet dispute but also the extensive social changes that were taking place in China in the 1950s."[2] While avoiding the excesses of totalitarian rhetoric, important analyses of power relations and political process under Chinese communism continued to underscore the all-encompassing reach and unchallengeable power of the unified party-state and its leadership.

In a discussion of political structure under Maoism, Hong Yung Lee spoke of the "enormous discretionary powers" wielded by the leading cadres at all institutional levels. Thus, "the Leninist principle of democratic centralism created a pseudo-military command structure with authority flowing from the Politburo down to the secretary of each party cell," wherein "as agents of the state, the cadres were expected to carry out every policy faithfully, regardless of its popularity with the masses or its conformity to the perceived interests of the masses."[3] Andrew G. Walder made the same point in his account of institutional structure in Chinese Communist factories by delineating the formidable network of "overlapping political organizations that serve both to prevent organized political opposition and to recruit and coopt members of the workforce."[4]

Utilizing the vocabulary of contemporary political science, Avery Goldstein argued that the Chinese Communist political system from 1949 until the eruption of the Cultural Revolution in 1966 was a "hierarchically ordered political realm" characterized by "bandwagon politics." In this setting, political actors rallied around perceived political victors rather than engage in factional politicking or "anarchic self-help"; in these conditions of concentrated political power, policies were decisively formulated and rapidly implemented and were unlikely to be contested and obstructed.[5] An extreme variant of this argument was put forward by Frederick C. Teiwes, who drew on the "imagery of the imperial palace, of the emperor surrounded by anxious courtiers seeking to gain or retain his favor, to obtain his backing for their various projects and political interests" and posited a "Mao-centered political process" wherein opposition to Mao's policies was "rare" and political opposition "unheard of."[6]

Goldstein also suggested that it was only with the advent of the Cultural Revolution that the dominant scholarly "portrait of a regime effectively managed by a basically consensual central elite was replaced by an emphasis on conflict both among the elite and within society."[7] In fact, in work predating the Cultural Revolution, Franz Schurmann showed how policy disputes, contending developmental strategies, center-region rivalries, and state-society tensions were recurrent in the 1950s and early 1960s.[8] By the late 1970s and early 1980s, however, many Western analyses of power and politics in the first two decades of Chinese Communist rule were emphasizing intraparty and state-society conflict. Whereas Harry Harding detailed the many and varied ways CCP leaders had attempted to control and transform communist officialdom "ever since the founding of their movement," Richard Kraus suggested that "the political apparatus used to destroy old inequalities had itself given rise to a new set of social distinctions."[9] Parris H. Chang argued that the Great Leap Forward was a struggle between "two distinct strategies or approaches to economic development" entailing fundamentally different conceptions of state-society relations and the role of party officials, whereas Mark Selden emphasized the recurrent policy oscillations and "at times reciprocal, but often conflictual, even explosive" state-society relationships that have defined China's "developmental trajectory."[10]

My discussion of the first two decades of Chinese Communist rule integrates control and conflict perspectives. The capacity of the CCP and its leadership to assert power and implement policy was formidable indeed. Yet it was precisely the vast coercive and mobilizational powers of the communist party-state that gave rise to new conflicts and tensions and set in motion a series of political, social, and economic upheavals. Far from being mutually exclusive, the processes of control and conflict that triggered the Hundred Flowers Movement, the Great Leap Forward, and, most important, the Cultural Revolution interacted.

As we saw in Chapter 2, the Chinese Communists rode to victory on a potent combination of CCP-sponsored concentration and control and popular upheaval. In the 1950s, these processes of social revolution and mass mobilization were fused with imported Soviet state-building and developmental techniques to create massive momentum on the side of the party-state. Even as these power-building achievements were being realized, however, phenomena of bureaucratism, routinization, and developmental disparities were coming to the fore. Chinese Communist leaders, Mao in particular, chose to respond to these challenges by launching power-restructuring initiatives. These efforts drew on the CCP base area experience and the Soviet experience of the 1930s and the 1950s while also prefiguring future power-restructuring processes in China and the Soviet Union.

Power restructuring in the first two decades of Chinese Communist rule pivoted on high levels of state-society interaction. In the course of establishing nationwide authority, conducting a comprehensive land reform, and implementing far-reaching programs of industrialization, social control, and agricultural collectivization, the CCP made effective use of its well-honed mobilizational capacities and successfully elicited high levels of popular support for its policies. By the late 1950s and 1960s, however, the interaction between the concentrated power of the communist party-state and the rest of Chinese society was becoming strained. Mounting state-society conflict was evident in the unforeseen eruption of popular opposition to communist rule during the Hundred Flowers Movement and, on a much broader scale, in the social and economic devastation of the Great Leap Forward. Both these events set the stage for the climactic power-restructuring event of Chinese Communist history, the Cultural Revolution. During the initial phases of this sociopolitical upheaval especially, the cardinal themes of this book—three-way power contests, top and bottom versus the middle power-restructuring attempts, and decentralized processes of power and resource appropriation—were manifested with unprecedented clarity.

## Chinese Communism and the
## Dilemmas of State Power

Unlike the Bolsheviks in 1917, the Chinese Communists came to power in 1949 equipped with mighty political and organizational advantages. Already an established presence in much of the countryside, in firm control of the newly conquered cities, and at the head of a battle-honed army, the CCP imposed its power in the manner of a vigorous new dynasty. The early 1950s witnessed the far-ranging application of methods and policies proved successful in the party's long rise to power. In a nationwide extension of the communist power-restructuring strategy of the 1930s and late 1940s, the CCP program centered on the destruction of old elites and institutions and their replacement by new structures of political, economic, and social power. While describing the imposition of CCP power in Guangdong Province, Ezra Vogel observed that unlike the Manchus, "the Communists from the north penetrated thoroughly into all important party and government organs, from the very highest to the very lowest," "and "formed personal relationships which cut across regional ties, thus narrowing the gap between local cadres and outsiders. Never in Chinese history had Kwangtung localism been so thoroughly infiltrated."[11]

In the countryside, the long-standing CCP strategy of using agrarian revolution to destroy competing centers of power was manifested in the massive transformations and bloodletting of the Land Reform Movement of 1950–1953. With the "extermination of the landlord class" set in motion by CCP leaders, and "struggle meetings" *(douzheng hui)* as the essential mechanism, landlords and rich peasants were brought before mass rallies, denounced and forced to surrender their property, and often tortured or killed. Even though estimates of the dead range from 1 million to "no less than five million," by 1953 the landlord class had been completely expropriated, and nearly 40 percent of the cultivated land had changed ownership.[12] Land reform was a cataclysmic social revolution that physically destroyed the rural gentry, which for centuries had mediated the relationship between local society and the state.[13] At the same time, the CCP in the early 1950s launched an equally violent and wide-ranging assault on representatives of the old order in the cities, and hundreds of thousands of "counterrevolutionaries" *(fan geming)* were arrested, brought before mass rallies and tribunals, denounced, and executed.[14]

The attack on the old institutional and political order was paralleled by the rapid building up of a new order by means of a comprehensive resource mobilization, social control, and collectivization drive. While "the transformation from private and capitalist ownership to state and collective ownership of agriculture, industry, handicrafts, and commerce was basically completed in the years 1953–1956," "the state established mechanisms to control population movement, particularly to bind peasants to their collective village, and to regulate and restrict entry to the cities."[15] In 1953, peasant households were required to sell their grain in fixed quantities and at fixed prices to state procurement agencies; at the same time, the new rulers pushed the formation of multihousehold production units as a further means of controlling and mobilizing agricultural production.[16] As the central authorities "transferred significant resources out of the agricultural sector" and "an agricultural procurement system and retail price policy enabled the state to generate significant resources through the profits of light industry," resources were mobilized, accumulated, and channeled into state-building and industrial development.[17] The macroeconomic effects of these restructuring processes were profound, resulting in nothing less than the industrial transformation of the Chinese economy in a few short years.

As in the Soviet 1920s, however, Chinese Communist state building and industrialization were complicated by shortages of qualified technical and professional people. However adept in the politics of class war and mass mobilization, only some 720,000 out of 4.5 million party members at the end of 1949 possessed the technical skills and intellectual training to serve as cadres and officials.[18] Nonparty intellectuals and ex-KMT officials were therefore recruited in large numbers into the state apparatus, a process that worried communist leaders from the start. Historically, the CCP had relied on rectification campaigns when organizational expansion and increased recruitment resulted in problems of political reliability and corruption.[19] In 1951–1952, the Sanfan (Three-Anti) campaign against corruption, waste, and bureaucratism in the state apparatus was set in motion and, when revelations of widespread bribery of public officials surfaced, was followed by the Wufan (Five-Anti) campaign against "lawless industrialists and merchants."[20] But even though party leaders were aware of the threat of organizational corruption and the need to control officialdom, specific remedies and responses differed markedly.

The problem of controlling officialdom was further complicated by the wholesale introduction of Soviet organizational and developmental methods in the 1950s. The Chinese Communists eagerly sought Soviet managerial and technical assistance and saw Soviet institutions and methods as a quick fix to China's industrial underdevelopment and technical backwardness and a means of ensuring unified party leadership and control in national reconstruction and development.[21] As I discussed in Chapters 4 and 5, however, a central feature of the Stalin system was the subordination of the party organization to central ministerial hegemony. The propensity of the Soviet system to favor central ministerial rule over party leadership, to strengthen the authority of the enterprise manager against that of the party secretary, and to promote bureaucratic domination in general was soon viewed with alarm by many CCP leaders. These fears were confirmed in the Gao Gang affair in 1955 when the chairman of the State Planning Commission and his associates were purged and charged with building "independent kingdoms" *(duli wangguo)* in Manchuria and the industrial ministries and thereby attempting to seize power from the party.[22] Finally, the Chinese Communist leadership became increasingly aware of a fundamental economic defect in the course of implementing the Soviet developmental model—a pro–heavy industry bias manifestly out of accord with China's overwhelmingly rural economy. By the mid-1950s, sharp developmental disparities had appeared between the rapidly growing, Soviet-assisted, capital-intensive heavy industrial sector and the light industrial sector, which lagged far behind, and agriculture, which remained little changed from its pre-1949 condition.[23]

## Contending Strategies in China

Beginning in 1956, the means of remedying these organizational, political, and economic dilemmas were sharply disputed by the top leadership. As in the Soviet 1920s, two very different views of developmental strategy and political-economic organization came to the fore in China. Whereas one approach stressed the primary importance of state control and planning mechanisms and viewed dynamic party leadership as the decisive element in accelerated economic development and increased systemic vitality, the contending approach stressed the importance of market mechanisms and advocated more reliance on material incentives to motivate peasants and increase agricultural production.[24] While engaging issues the Bolsheviks had debated three decades before, the Chinese dispute was simultaneously shaped by Khrushchev's denunciation of Stalin at the Twentieth Party Congress, which had "raised the larger questions of the relationship of the supreme leader of the Party to Party institutions and the relationship of the Party to the people."[25]

But the clash between these contending approaches was more complex than that which pitted Stalinist central planners and heavy industrialists against Bukharinist propeasant consumer advocates in the Soviet 1920s. Rather, CCP policy conflicts featured distinctively Chinese elements, as well as elements reminiscent of the Soviet 1920s, 1930s, and 1950s. Two complementary, yet dissimilar authority–social mobilization approaches emerged in China in the mid-1950s—the first an essentially orthodox central planning–heavy industry Soviet approach, the second an approach championed by Mao and the party organization that, ironically, more closely resembled the developmental and organizational strategy advocated by Khrushchev in the late 1950s. In opposition to these divergent but equally mobilizational approaches, some important CCP leaders, notably Vice Premier and economic administration specialist Chen Yun and Vice Premier and agriculture specialist Deng Zihui, persistently advocated an approach that combined market mechanisms and material incentives in the countryside with central ministerial coordination, light industrial development, and expert management in the factories. David Bachman analyzed the three approaches and documented their interaction in the period leading up to and during the Great Leap Forward.[26]

Chinese Communist efforts to develop alternatives to the Soviet model sometimes obscure the pivotal role of Soviet methods in the economic development

and industrialization of China, especially in the 1950s. As noted, the effects of Soviet resource mobilization techniques on agriculture and rural living standards
were deleterious. Yet the 1950s was a period of remarkable achievement, in which
the assistance of the Soviet Union played an indispensable part. While hundreds
of industrial plants were imported from the Soviet Union, Soviet methods of economic control and resource extraction keyed increased savings and investment
and the formation of new physical and human capital. As the state used its monopolistic economic control to keep the prices of industrial goods high while costs
fell as production revived, and the ensuing profits were channeled into industrial
and infrastructural development, the first two decades of Chinese Communist
rule witnessed unprecedented rates of capital formation.[27] As Nicholas R. Lardy
observed, "Estimated at about 5 percent for the 1930s and much less for the civil
war years, capital formation rose to 10 percent by 1952 (the beginning of the first
5-year plan), to 20 percent by 1957 (the end of the first 5-year plan), to 25 percent
or more in the early 1970s."[28] In Thomas G. Rawski's view, "The return of domestic peace and political integration for the first time in forty years produced a
growth spurt in the 1950s that largely reflected the unfulfilled potential of China's
prewar economy."[29]

But this suggestion is implausible. In Chapter 2, I discussed the extreme political and fiscal weakness of the Chinese central state in the 1930s, a condition in no
way conducive to dynamic processes of state-directed development and industrialization. In fact, the phenomenal rates of capital formation achieved under Chinese communism, which created "400,000 industrial and transport enterprises
with total assets of $500 billion in three decades," were the result of Soviet meth-
ods of resource extraction and investment established and enforced by the communist party-state.[30] Throughout the struggle between contending strategies that
commenced in the mid-1950s and continued into the 1960s and 1970s, therefore,
core features of the Soviet system were put in place and exerted a powerful and enduring effect on the Chinese economy.

The alternative to the Soviet model put forward by Mao and other CCP leaders
remained fundamentally authority–social mobilization in spirit and in substance.
Whereas the Soviet system hinged on the absolute primacy of central economic
controls, however, the Chinese variant was premised on expanded party leadership at the regional, provincial, and local levels. Reflecting both the CCP heritage
of guerrilla warfare, decentralization, and adaptation to local conditions and an
awareness of the rigidities and imbalances of the Soviet model, the Maoist strategy
sought to accelerate economic development and social transformation in the
countryside with a dynamic combination of party leadership, collective organization, and mass mobilization. Unlike established Soviet practice, this approach implied political decentralization and the promotion of multiple centers of decisionmaking.

Not coincidentally, the emergence of the Maoist organizational and developmental strategy closely paralleled Khrushchev's effort to decentralize the Soviet

economy and promote economic development by reenergizing party leadership at the regional and local levels. Although Khrushchev would later denounce the Great Leap Forward and compare Mao to Stalin, Roderick MacFarquhar noted the similarity of Khrushchev's and Mao's attitudes toward economic development and suggested that Mao's Great Leap ideas were reinforced and inspired by Khrushchev's "grandiose plans" of 1957.[31] Moreover, just as Khrushchev's *sovnarkhozy* reforms were intended to perform the dual function of revitalizing the economy and destroying the power bases of his political opponents in the central economic ministries, Mao was motivated by similar considerations.[32]

In contrast to the Maoist approach, the market–material incentive alternative to the Soviet model entailed a significant measure of power deconcentration. Whereas the Maoist strategy was consistent with the CCP's mass-mobilizing heritage, market–material incentive proponents insisted that agricultural production could not be increased by direction from above, outside regulation, or ideological exhortation. Instead, proponents argued that producing units "will increase output only if they can gain something in return" and that increased material incentives, market mechanisms, and consumer goods availability were essential to the success of development policy in the countryside.[33] Hence, whereas the Maoist approach pivoted on a decentralization of power into the hands of the party organization at the regional, provincial, and local levels, the market–material incentive approach implied a significant deconcentration of economic power and a regulation of relatively autonomous lower-level producing units by the market.

While advocating the deconcentration of economic power, however, market–material incentive proponents envisioned no comparable deconcentration of political power. As Bachman noted, the "break with a traditional Soviet model of development should not be overstated. The budgeteers wanted the market to remain subordinate to the plan, relatively more resources to be devoted to light industry and agriculture, and continued significant investment in heavy industry. Budgeteers never denied the importance of party leadership."[34] As Chen Yun's slogan "Big planning and small freedoms" indicated, while the central ministerial apparatus would continue to administer vital commercial activities and industrial enterprises, direct state controls were to be loosened at the lower levels of the economy.[35] In contrast to the Maoist emphasis on the primacy of party leadership and mass mobilization, the market–material incentive approach hinged on a combination of market forces in the countryside and expert management at the top. Mao consistently opposed this policy and sought during the Cultural Revolution to destroy it forever. Ironically, it was precisely the scale and ferocity of the Maoist assault that set the stage for the ascendancy of the Chen Yun approach in the post-Mao period.

## Collectivization, the Hundred Flowers Movement, and Power Deconcentration

As in the Soviet Union, agricultural collectivization was seen as key by authority–social mobilization advocates. But unlike the Soviet experience, in the early

1950s the Chinese Communists were able to impose state controls and increase the size of agricultural production units without encountering widespread peasant resistance or noncompliance. Yet while Chinese industry expanded massively in the early and mid-1950s, agriculture paid the price and lagged behind. By mid-1955, the CCP rulers, with Mao in the lead, had concluded that full-scale collectivization was the solution to the problem of agricultural production. Compared to the Soviet case, the less violent and relatively smoother pace of collectivization in China was the result of the CCP's deeply rooted organizational presence at the village level, on the one hand, and still fresh memories of land reform violence, on the other.[36] It was in the course of collectivizing agriculture, however, that the first important collision between contending organizational and developmental approaches in China occurred.

In what MacFarquhar termed the "first Leap Forward," an intense "big push" was set in motion in late 1955. As provincial and local party organizations stepped up their activities, the pace of agricultural collectivization was accelerated; ambitious plans, target figures, and completion dates were issued from on high; large numbers of peasants were mobilized for public works projects; and numerous new industrial enterprises were funded.[37] Significantly, Mao played the key role in initiating these processes by deploying top and bottom versus the middle methods. On July 31, 1955, the chairman delivered a speech at an unprecedented meeting of county party secretaries in which he derided proponents of gradual, voluntary collectivization in the Central Committee and the CCP rural work department as "women with bound feet hobbling along" and personally called on local party leaders to take the lead in pushing the pace of collectivization and mass mobilization.[38]

In bypassing top party and state institutions and directly appealing for political support to the lower levels of the system, Mao previewed power-restructuring tactics that he would more sweepingly deploy in the years to come. And in an equally telling preview of events to come, when the big push encountered popular resistance in the countryside and in the cities, precipitated economic imbalances and organizational problems, and produced less than anticipated gains in agricultural production, both orthodox Soviet-style planners and market–material incentive proponents were quick to criticize policies of "reckless advance," to point up the decisive importance of expert management and central coordination, and to underscore the key role of material incentives.[39] The disappointing aftermath of the first Leap Forward left CCP leaders, especially Mao, searching for answers; it was in the course of this search that the familiar issue of power deconcentration first came to the fore in China.

The less than impressive results of the first Leap Forward apparently convinced Mao that party leadership by itself was unable to resolve China's organizational and developmental dilemmas. In early 1957, Mao delivered a series of speeches and informal talks that acknowledged CCP errors, solicited suggestions and criticism from people outside the party, and called for a loosening of the CCP power monopoly. Especially notable was his insistence that sustained economic and social development could be achieved only through a dynamic synthesis of genuine popular input and enthusiasm and party leadership and organization. Understood in my terms, Mao was advocating a deconcentration of political power.

Mao articulated this message in his most famous Hundred Flowers statement, "On the Correct Handling of Contradictions Among the People," delivered to an audience of leading communists and noncommunists at the Supreme State Conference in February 1957. The Chinese people, he declared, were now united as one in the "great task of building socialism," counterrevolutionaries had been essentially cleared out, agricultural cooperatives were supported by the "overwhelming majority of the poor peasants and lower middle peasants," and most Chinese intellectuals had "expressed themselves in favor of the socialist system."[40] Yet "while welcoming the new system, the broad masses of people are not yet quite accustomed to it"—hence the importance of correctly handling "contradictions among the people."[41] Most important, this meant trusting nonparty people and soliciting their input, especially intellectuals whose contributions were so vitally needed. The party was lacking in this respect, for "many of our comrades are not good at uniting with intellectuals. They are too crude in dealing with them, lack respect for their work, and interfere in certain matters of scientific and cultural work where interference is unwarranted. We must do away with all such shortcomings."[42]

The conciliatory thrust of Mao's speech and his public admission of CCP errors and call to improve the party's work style especially had a tremendous impact. In a succession of informal talks to CCP cadres in February and March 1957, Mao went further still and put forward a strikingly liberal view of the relationship between the party and the people. Political controls should be loosened since "it is incorrect not to allow workers to strike. . . . Putting up posters is the freedom of speech; holding meetings is the freedom of assembly. . . . Since there are problems, it's good to have a bit of disturbance."[43] Public criticism of the CCP was desirable since "only by letting a hundred schools contend and compete with one another, only through criticism and discussion, can we develop what is correct. We mustn't fear these things. Don't be afraid. Instead of staying in houses with heating facilities, we must go out into the open air."[44] Instead of "simply resorting to administrative decree," the CCP should "specially invite some people to supervise us, and (to partake in) long-term coexistence. . . . It can be argued that it would be better if some democratic parties put on a rival show and made sarcastic comments, revealing our shortcomings with sarcastic comments several times a year. Therefore, instead of tightening up (control) now, we must loosen up more."[45] Mao specifically juxtaposed his views against Stalinist practice, when "under an increasingly dictatorial government, criticism was no longer to be tolerated. If someone made a criticism, or a hundred flowers were to bloom, that was something very much to be feared. . . . Whoever caused the slightest trouble would be branded a counterrevolutionary and thrown into jail or executed."[46]

In arguing that the CCP could be revitalized, its "commandism" overcome, and its ties to society reaffirmed by a loosening of controls and increased political participation by nonparty people, Mao outlined a power-restructuring vision and strategy that he would more fully deploy a decade later. During the Cultural Revolution, Maoist pronouncements proclaimed that "to 'open wide' *[fang]*, means to let everybody express their suggestions, so that the people dare to speak, dare to criticize, and dare to debate."[47] In March 1957, the idea of deconcentrating political power and inviting outsiders to participate in the rectification of the party itself was unprecedented and, in the eyes of most CCP leaders and cadres, confusing and bizarre. When the *People's Daily* failed to endorse the Hundred Flowers line, such top party leaders as Liu Shaoqi clearly indicated their disapproval of Mao's contradictions speech, and Peking mayor and CCP Secretariat member Peng Zhen warned of the unstable political atmosphere and the probability of mass disorders, Mao was placed on the defensive and forced to lobby for his ideas.[48] Although the opposition and resistance of CCP leaders at the top and throughout the apparatus to the deconcentration of power were natural enough, these reactions plainly contradict the "bandwagon" and "Mao-centered political process" theses suggested by Goldstein and Teiwes. As Teiwes himself acknowledged, "Mao's lobbying efforts of spring 1957 were clearly designed to win over a Party membership that was confused and fearful over where the Hundred Flowers might lead, as well as uncomprehending as to why the victors of the Chinese revolution should be subjected to criticism from suspect bourgeois intellectuals."[49]

The painful denouement of the Hundred Flowers episode is well known. When nonparty intellectuals unleashed a torrent of anticommunist censure and questioned the legitimacy of CCP rule, which some likened to that of Hitler, a violent backlash ensued, hundreds of thousands of critics were labeled "rightists" *(youpai)* and denounced, and many were jailed and exiled to labor camps. This pattern, in which people were urged to speak out in the interests of "democracy" and China's development and then punished when their criticism went too far, is recurrent in the history of Communist China.[50] Less well known is the proliferation of strikes and labor unrest that occurred in Chinese cities in spring 1957, as workers in "newly formed joint-ownership enterprises protested against the deterioration in economic securities and political voice which accompanied the socialization of these firms."[51] This eruption of popular grievances and social tensions underscored a fundamental power-restructuring dilemma: Deconcentrating a system of concentrated power means suspending the established mechanisms of party and state control, in the course of which a Pandora's box is opened wide. This dilemma, on which Mao's power-deconcentrating initiatives of February and March 1957 foundered, would resurface in even more intractable form during the Cultural Revolution.

The expert-oriented market–material incentive approach was the leading casualty of the Hundred Flowers debacle. Angered and frightened at the hostility of the old society intellectuals and professionals on which this strategy was premised, the CCP shifted to a "developmental strategy in which the role of intellectuals (such as scientists, engineers, technicians, managerial and planning staff), who were now politically tainted, was to be deemphasized in the course of socialist construction."[52]

While repudiating the idea of power deconcentration, the CCP from 1958 to 1960 attempted a very different but nonetheless radical restructuring of power. During the Great Leap Forward, a comprehensive decentralization of political power and economic decisionmaking authority into the hands of regional, provincial, and local party organizations occurred. With decentralized party leadership in the lead, this authority–social mobilization campaign was intended to effect major economic and social transformations.

## The Great Leap Forward and Power Decentralization

The ideology of the Great Leap Forward harked back to the glory days of the revolution and sought to accelerate economic development and the building of communism by reviving the self-sacrificing spirit and self-reliant ways of the CCP base area experience. In Mao's words:

> The rural work style and guerrilla practices are, after all, better. In twenty-two years of war we were victorious: Why is it that building communism doesn't work? . . . In the past during the revolution numerous people died without asking anything in return. Why can't it be like that now? Probably in about ten years our production will be very bountiful (and the people's) morality will be very noble; (then) we can practice communism in eating, clothing, and housing.[53]

Inevitably, this attempt to revive the "revolutionary-heroic" ideology and methods of the base area period in the changed and more complex circumstances of the late 1950s was fundamentally problematic.

At the same time, broader dilemmas of power decentralization were revealed during the Great Leap Forward. While drawing heavily on the CCP's historical experience, the logic of Great Leap Forward policies paralleled that of Khrushchev's *sovnarkhozy* reforms. In both cases, a wide range of economic decisionmaking functions were decentralized to lower-level party organizations on the assumption that this redistribution of power would rekindle party activism at the local level and inject new, politically charged dynamism into an economic system that was performing inadequately. Both efforts sought to escape the rigidities and imbalances of the system developed under Stalin by reaffirming the principle of vanguard party leadership in organizational and developmental policy. Given these parallels, it is not surprising that the Great Leap Forward and the *sovnarkhozy* reforms encountered similar difficulties, in type, if not in degree. Simply put, central leaders exchanged one set of political and organizational problems for a different but nonetheless vexing set. In both cases, decisionmaking and resource allocation by central ministerial experts, planners, and managers were superseded by "departmentalism," redundancy, and chaos as regional, provincial, and local party organizations formed autonomous power centers; pursued individual, often overlapping economic agendas; and constructed independent kingdoms.[54] Power decentralization accentuated the concentrated power of the party and its authoritarian tendencies. In contrast to the centralized dictatorship of the Stalin system, however, edicts and decrees were now issued in an often haphazard manner by competing party organizations at the regional, provincial, and local levels. While undercutting central ministerial economic coordination, power decentralization concentrated power in the hands of lower-level party organizations more firmly than ever.

This combination of organizational fragmentation and official authoritarianism was manifested with lethal consequences during the Great Leap Forward. As party organizations in the provinces rushed to build self-sufficient industrial complexes, and "people's communes" also attempted to "go in for industry in a big way," disastrous economic imbalances occurred, as did transportation bottlenecks and waste and misallocation of scarce resources.[55] The most grievous example of the latter was the backyard steel furnace fiasco, which consumed large amounts of capital and energy and produced little of use. At the same time, the voluntarism and authoritarianism of the party organization took a heavy toll. As Mao was warning against "bourgeois ideological work styles" and denigrating specialists and experts, CCP cadres in the countryside were promoting the slogan *ren you duo da dan, di you duo da chan* (However much daring people have, that's how much output the land has).[56] The economic leap forward was paralleled by an all-out push to effect major social transformations in the countryside especially. While urging the organization of labor along military lines, Mao envisioned the commune "as the basic unit of socialist social structure, combining industry, agriculture, commerce, education, and military (affairs)," the establishment of which he linked to the abolition of the "patriarchal (family) system (that derives) from history."[57] In fact, the structure of Chinese peasant society was subjected to a massive battering, as collective kitchens and group mess halls were set up, graves and temples moved and destroyed, rural markets and fairs shut down, and so many men sent away on construction projects that women were forced to bring in the harvest.[58]

But the attempt to rekindle the dynamic synthesis of party leadership, mass mobilization, and social revolution that had propelled the CCP to power failed massively in 1958–1960. Although party cadres spoke of a historic transformation of "antiquated production relationships," the militarization of the peasantry during the "high tide" of 1958 more closely resembled the corvée labor systems that imperial rulers had historically imposed on the peasantry.[59] As "decisions from on high" were issued "without regard for property rights, even the collective property rights of production teams and brigades, and without regard for mutual benefit," William Hinton chronicled, "higher bodies asked large numbers of people to supply materials for and work on projects that brought no benefit at all to their local communities."[60] At the same time, the party cadres mounting the big push were themselves pressured for results, while "the fear of punishment, heightened by the 1957 anti-rightist campaign, meant that it was difficult to report the truth to higher authority."[61] A vicious cycle was thereby set in motion wherein political loyalty was measured by "daring," "overtaking," and stupendous feats, which resulted in the setting of unrealistic targets, grueling work schedules, inevitable shortfalls, and grossly inflated output claims that distorted perceptions throughout the CCP chain of command.[62] When top Chinese Communist leaders finally acknowledged the full scope of these problems, the economic losses, organizational damage, and political disarray were already extensive.

"The Great Leap Forward precipitated the most devastating famine in China's modern history and the collapse of the economy," in the course of which per capita food grain production and nutrient availability plummeted, millions of people starved to death in the countryside, and urban areas experienced widespread malnutrition and privation.[63] In the assessment of some of the most knowledgeable Western researchers, "The Great Leap death toll was not a sudden, one-time error resulting from unique policy blunders in 1958, 1959, and 1960. . . . A generalized disaster was made more likely when the state foreclosed ways that villagers could earn money and expand the economy, ending grain markets, eliminating rural handicrafts, sidelines, and processing, and imposing large, alienating, abstract collectives."[64] The disruptive effects of these processes were further magnified by the abrupt withdrawal of Soviet economic and technical assistance in 1959.[65] Understood in my terms, when decentralized authority–social mobilization methods were given full rein during the Great Leap Forward, and economic decisionmaking power was decentralized into the hands of local and provincial party organizations, powerful, uncontrollable, and destabilizing forces were unleashed, and the result was economic and social devastation on a nationwide scale.

While less far-reaching, the political fallout of the Great Leap Forward was nonetheless profound. Within the ranks of the leadership, Marshal Peng Dehuai leveled an unprecedented attack on Mao's authority at the Lushan plenum in June 1959 by suggesting that the chairman's policies of "petty-bourgeois fanaticism" had contributed to the disaster.[66] Mao rallied the top leadership behind him and mercilessly crushed his accuser, but the issue of Mao's responsibility for the Great Leap policies would figure pivotally in the mounting political tensions at the top in the early 1960s. At the mass level, the Great Leap disaster badly damaged the legitimacy of the CCP in the villages; "according to the testimony of hundreds of refugees interviewed in Hong Kong in this period, Mao Zedong lost the credibility as a new living god that he had gained with many peasants during 1950–1952."[67] Yet though damaged, corrupted, and in popular disrepute, the CCP power monopoly remained intact and its power structures strong.[68] It was only when Mao attempted an even more radical restructuring of power during the Cultural Revolution that a political and institutional upheaval comparable to the economic and social devastation of the Great Leap Forward occurred.

## The Rise of Moderation in the Early 1960s

As in the Soviet Union in the 1930s, the peasantry bore the brunt of authority–social mobilization policies in China during the Great Leap Forward. But crucial differences separate the Chinese and Soviet experiences. Whereas Soviet rulers pressed ahead and forcefully subjugated the peasantry in the 1930s, a shift to more moderate organizational and developmental policies occurred in China in the early 1960s. This shift was driven in large measure by necessity rather than choice. Faced with famine, social and organizational breakdown, and mass alienation and outrage in the villages, CCP leaders at the top and at the local level had little choice but to take a more tolerant stance vis-à-vis the market and material incentives. Although private plots had been eliminated in 1958, "in 1960 they were restored and, in some cases, expanded to 5 to 10 percent of villages," as villagers pushed to expand household plots.[69] By 1962, the *sanzi yibao* (three freedoms and one guarantee) system, which permitted peasants to cultivate private plots, to engage in sideline occupations, and to sell their production on the open market but also held each household responsible for certain quotas on the public land assigned to it, was prevalent in many rural areas. Indeed, as "collective lands were divided up among peasants on a long-term basis in the 1962 period, and some peasants were even permitted to leave communes to engage in private farming," the market-oriented "household responsibility system" that would figure so pivotally in the post-Mao reform period was already in place.[70]

As market–material incentive policies superseded authority–social mobilization methods in the villages, central ministerial economic coordination at the top and expert management in the factories were revived. The early 1960s witnessed a sharp diminution of the economic decisionmaking authority of the factory party committee and a corresponding increase in Soviet-style one-man management. While obligated to fulfill centrally mandated output and profit targets, factory managers commanded considerable operational autonomy in the prevailing conditions of economic crisis and disarray.[71] At the same time, the social status of previously denigrated "bourgeois intellectuals," technical experts, and professionals was elevated and restored. Thus, South-Central Regional CCP Bureau chief Tao Zhu, in a September 1961 speech to "higher intellectuals" that would be used as "evidence" against him during the Cultural Revolution, declared, "I apologize to the comrades who have been wronged. . . . We should refrain from using the term 'bourgeois intellectual' again. . . . Struggle meetings to carry out ideological criticism should be banned. . . . We should unite with the higher intellectuals and show respect for their expertise, integrity, and views."[72]

Tao's speech underscored a key sociopolitical development stemming from the Great Leap disaster—a rapprochement between top CCP leaders and both party and nonparty professional and technical elites. With the manifest defects of decentralized authority–social mobilization methods so plainly and painfully revealed, many Chinese Communist leaders who had earlier promoted such methods fundamentally reassessed their views. This process was evident as early as November 1959 when newly designated chief of state Liu Shaoqi, previously a proponent of Great Leap Forward voluntarism, sponsored and participated in an economics seminar featuring a long-standing advocate of expert management and market–material incentive methods, former vice chairman of the State Planning Commission and head of the State Statistical Bureau Xue Muqiao.[73] Whereas Xue's defense of technical standards and professionalism had cost him both jobs in 1958, his reemergence signaled an important policy shift at the highest levels.

The rapprochement between political and technical-professional elites in China in the early 1960s paralleled to a striking degree events in the Soviet Union in the early and mid-1930s. Just as specialist baiting and class war were set aside and respect for professionalism and technical expertise established in the Soviet Union in the early 1930s, previously villified technical-professionals were welcomed back to positions of authority, their views solicited, and their special status and privileges restored in China. Whereas putatively Stalinist leaders such as Kirov and Ordzhonikidze sought to moderate radical authority–social mobilization tactics and cope with the economic chaos of the FFYP and the accompanying disaster in the countryside by implementing rational managerial methods, respect for technical expertise, and a policy of reconciliation with society, top CCP leaders increasingly shifted to organizational and developmental policies of this type after the collapse of the Great Leap. Of course, Stalin was a consistent proponent of professional management and technical expertise, and it was only when a new generation of Stalinist experts was waiting in the wings that class war was used to destroy the power of the Soviet "red-expert" coalition.

Like Stalin, Mao came to view the Chinese red-expert coalition as a challenge to his personal authority, policy preferences, and revolutionary vision. A crucial turning point in this process was the "seven thousand cadres conference" in January 1962, where Liu delivered the keynote report in which he "articulated what was, in effect, a systematic critique of the leap and outlined the various measures being taken to save the situation."[74] This was a watershed event in which the authority–social mobilization policies that Mao had championed and with which he was inextricably associated were openly censured and repudiated. However adulatory the praise still lavished on the chairman at the conference, it was at this juncture that Mao's ideas were impugned, his authority undercut, and the ascendancy of market–material incentive methods underscored before an audience of thousands of important CCP leaders.[75]

## The Socialist Education Movement and the Cultural Revolution

The political tensions that appeared to so suddenly erupt during the Cultural Revolution were built up in the course of the Socialist Education Movement of

1962–1966. This campaign, initially aimed at combating cadre corruption and re-vitalizing party leadership in the villages, was marked by serious intraparty policy disputes, which culminated finally in Mao's estrangement from much of the top CCP civilian leadership. These disputes revolved around the familiar issues of power concentration versus power deconcentration, the relationship of the party to society, and the role of mass mobilization. As Mao and other top CCP leaders put forward increasingly divergent analyses and responses to these problems, po-litical tensions mounted, and themes that would figure prominently in the Cul-tural Revolution were aired. According to Deng Xiaoping's 1980 recapitulation of events, whereas Mao in early 1962 was "sincerely rectifying 'leftist' errors," by the summer of 1962 he had "reversed course and promoted class struggle," and in early 1965 he put forward the fateful slogan "Power holders in the party taking the capitalist road" *(dangnei zou zibenzhuyi daolu de dangquanpai)*.[76] How and why did events develop in this direction?

The CCP was able to launch the Great Leap Forward in the countryside because of its formidable organizational presence and the large reservoir of popular good-will accruing from land reform; by the same token, the economic and social disas-ters induced by Great Leap tactics precipitated a widespread breakdown in party leadership, morale, and legitimacy in the villages. As a result, rural party organiza-tions were no longer able to effectively confront a variety of previously unaccept-able political, economic, and social challenges. Such "unhealthy tendencies" included a prevailing peasant preference for "private plots and family sideline oc-cupations rather than less profitable collective undertakings," a reemergence of "feudal" beliefs and practices, a general decline in cadre morale and increasing cadre susceptibility to corruption, and an unprecedented boldness of class ene-mies seeking to take advantage of the party's disarray and "reverse the verdict."[77] Although all CCP leaders, including Mao, saw the need for some form of organi-zational rectification, however, two very different and ultimately antagonistic re-sponses to the threat of "capitalist restoration" emerged in the Socialist Education Movement.

In Mao's view, the widespread corruption of basic-level cadres and their corre-sponding failure to provide vigorous political leadership constituted the crux of the organizational crisis in the countryside. In May 1963, Mao put forward the "First Ten Points," which linked the revitalization of the party to accelerated mass mobilization and increased nonparty input and criticism. Thus, the "long-dor-mant poor and lower-middle peasant associations in the countryside" were to be activated and a social movement set in motion, in the course of which "the masses must be given every opportunity to air fully their views, make criticisms of errors and shortcomings, and expose evil people and evil deeds."[78] By more regularly participating in "collective productive labor," holding fewer conferences and com-piling fewer reports, and spending less time in the office and more in the field, rural party organizations would be revitalized and their ties to society reaffirmed. These were familiar ideas, dating back to the base area and land reform periods; by calling for mass participation in the rectification of the party, Mao was also attempting to revive the power-deconcentrating processes that had backfired so badly during the Hundred Flowers episode.

It was a measure of Mao's estrangement from the CCP civilian establishment that the First Ten Points were soon discarded and the problem of cadre corruption addressed with a very different set of political and organizational policies. No doubt determined to avoid another chaotic upwelling of popular discontent, CCP secretary general Deng Xiaoping issued a new directive in September 1963 that sharply curtailed the power-deconcentrating dimensions of the campaign. "Work teams" *(gongzuo dui)* were dispatched en masse to the villages to "make suggestions, carry out guidance and assistance, and enlighten basic-level cadres in the analysis of problems and the determination of policies and methods."[79] Most important, the rectification of cadres was to remain an internal affair. As Richard Baum noted, peasants were prohibited from conducting mass struggle meetings and judging or determining the punishment of errant cadres; peasant organizations were allowed to participate in the formation of local administrative policies on a consultative, nonvoting basis only; cadres were shielded from popular scrutiny and investigated and criticized behind closed doors; and all verdicts had to be approved by higher-level party committees before being carried out.[80] When hundreds of thousands of rural cadres were purged in the latter part of 1964, moreover, "the impetus came not from below, with the organization of the poor and lower-middle peasant masses, but from above, with the organization of huge teams of cadres who came down to ride herd on those below them."[81]

The countermanding of the First Ten Points and the transformation of a mass movement into a top-down purge brought political tensions at the top to a head. In January 1965, Mao responded with the "Twenty-three Points," which reformulated the question of cadre corruption by putting forward the fateful concept of power holders in the party taking the capitalist road. In Hinton's assessment, "The target, then, was not simply grafters, not simply bureaucrats, not simply those with mistakes, but Party members in power who followed a bourgeois line, promoted careerism, individualism, private enterprise and private gain, and undermined the socialist system of ownership and the socialist system of production and exchange."[82] Point seven was especially portentous: "In cases of a serious nature, where the leadership has been seized by alien class elements or degenerate elements, struggles should be waged to get it back. First struggle with them and then remove them from office."[83] These ideas would be set in motion with explosive and unforeseen consequences during the tumultuous opening phases of the Cultural Revolution.

## Opening Salvos

The Cultural Revolution was launched in late 1965 with an apparently esoteric campaign in the Shanghai media against so-called poisonous weeds *(du cao)* in intellectual and academic circles. In fact, this attack on leading Peking intellectuals Wu Han and Deng Tuo revolved around the recent experience of the Great Leap Forward and the increasingly acrimonious policy disputes of the early 1960s. When Mao proxy Yao Wenyuan denounced "comrade" Wu Han's thinly veiled criticism of Great Leap voluntarism and Mao's leadership style in the play *Hai Rui Dismissed from Office*, Yao fired the first shots in a campaign that within months would culminate in a sweeping political and ideological indictment of the red-expert moderate coalition.[84]

In the welter of venom, rhetoric, and recrimination of Yao's call to arms in May 1966, "Critique of 'Three-Family Village,'" one theme emerged clearly: The policies of moderation, reconciliation, expert management, and political retrenchment of the early 1960s constituted nothing less than "a single black line" *(yi tiao heixian)*—an erroneous policy.[85] Thus, Deng Tuo's advocacy of "fostering labor power" and praise of the ancients for mastering the "objective laws of the efficacy of labor power" were repudiations of the achievements of the Great Leap Forward, admissions that the policies of "aiming high" and "self-reliance" were "beyond one's ability" *(li bu sheng ren)*, and denigrations of such feats as opening the Daqing oil field and developing the atomic bomb. Similarly, Yao denounced Deng's call to "unite with those who are stronger" and "learn from those with more knowledge" as an attempt to emulate the "path of the Soviet revisionist clique" and slander China's national dignity. And Deng was charged with slandering Mao and the policies of the Great Leap with such reproaches as "big empty talk" *(da kong tan)*, "words confounded by deeds," and "failure to keep faith."

In a consideration of mounting political tensions at the top in 1965, Teiwes spoke of Mao's "petulant outbursts," "extraordinary expressions of irrationality," and "a Chairman more occupied with perceived personal slights and a sense of his own vulnerability than policy issues per se."[86] But this trivialization of Mao's decision to launch the Cultural Revolution is unacceptable. However polemical, Yao's indictment underscored the relatively unconstrained opposition of some influential and well-connected intellectuals and professionals to the authority–social mobilization policies of the Great Leap and Mao's leadership generally. By the end of summer 1966, such people would be linked to power holders in the party taking the capitalist road and the Maoist assault on the red-expert coalition unleashed in full fury. But this was a gradual process and occurred only in the course of intra-party maneuvers and countermaneuvers in spring and early summer. As in the Socialist Education Movement, Maoist mass-mobilizing and power-deconcentrating impulses collided with Leninist concentration and control as the campaign against the black line of Wu Han and Deng Tuo unfolded. When Mao attempted to induce popular ferment in the Peking university and middle school system, the leaders of the party organization in the capital countered with equally familiar tactics. This collision was described from the Maoist perspective in the historic "big-character poster" *(dazibao)* that marked the beginning of the attack on the authority and legitimacy of the CCP during the Cultural Revolution.

# The Assault on the Authority and Legitimacy of the Party

In late May 1966, Nie Yuanzi and a group of junior professors and instructors in the philosophy department of Peking University put up a big-character poster attacking the administration and party committee of the university and the Peking municipal party committee. This big-character poster, which was quickly endorsed by Mao, published in the *People's Daily*, and broadcast nationwide, aggressively put forward and provocatively expanded an array of Maoist power-restructuring themes.[87] Especially fateful was the idea that time-honored CCP methods of power concentration and social control now constituted antiparty, antisocialist revisionism. Thus, it was precisely the attempt of the university and municipal party organization to "strengthen leadership" (*jiaqiang lingdao*) and "guide the movement to develop in the correct direction" (*yindao yundong xiang zhengque de fangxiang fazhan*) that constituted a black line. In a radical, and no doubt hopelessly confusing, organizational and ideological reformulation, the familiar attempt of the party leadership to provide guidance was denounced as "suppressing and opposing mass revolution." Furthermore, the big-character poster substituted the authority and legitimacy of the Central Committee and Chairman Mao for that of the party organization. Aligning with the "center," Nie et al. vowed to "protect the Central Committee" and to "protect Mao Zedong Thought" but omitted any reference to the CCP as such.[88]

In fact, this attack on the authority and legitimacy of the party organization echoed themes that Mao had already introduced into the policy process. Although not made public until a year later, a May 16 "Notice" of the Central Committee of the CCP was widely distributed throughout the party in late spring and early summer 1966. Subsequently proclaimed as Mao's personal statement, this document asserted the existence of a "large group of anti-party, anti-socialist bourgeois representatives" at all levels of the party and state apparatus, denounced some CCP leaders for conducting the struggle against these elements incorrectly, and provided the theoretical rationale for the ouster of errant intellectuals *and* errant officials.[89] In retrospect, however, the most salient features of the Notice were its violent and uncompromising rhetoric, denigration of party control, and glorification of unconstrained social ferment and political upheaval. Explicitly invoking his Hundred Flowers advocacy of *fang* (opening wide), Mao attacked certain party leaders for distorting the true meaning of the concept. Whereas *fang* meant "allowing everybody to speak up," this process had been short-circuited by the party organization's insistence on "leadership," "prudence," and "caution." This stifling of the mass movement amounted to nothing less than "intolerance of proletarian revolution," an "attack on the Left," "opposition to Mao Zedong Thought," and the "path of modern revisionism and capitalist restoration." In these uncompromising terms, the Notice advanced a power-restructuring strategy that would be massively accelerated in the coming months—legitimation from on high of attacks from below, which were now to extend beyond errant intellectuals to "bourgeois representatives" in the party and state apparatus.

In early June 1966, a series of strident *People's Daily* editorials openly aired the inflammatory rhetoric of the May 16 Notice and turned the now-familiar charges against bourgeois experts and scholars into a struggle of epic proportions. Simply because "we have overthrown their rule and confiscated their property," the editorial "Sweep Away All Freaks and Monsters" pronounced, "this does not mean that we have confiscated the reactionary ideology in their minds."[90] A life-or-death struggle to determine the fate of today's youth and that of coming generations was both necessary and inevitable. While asserting the fundamentally "critical" and "revolutionary" essence of Marxism, other editorials proclaimed, "Struggle is life" and hailed the persistence of contradictions for "a thousand years, ten thousand years, a hundred million years."[91]

This militant and incendiary rhetoric would soon be embraced by the emerging Red Guard movement in Peking and enshrined in the leitmotif slogan *zaofan youli* (Rebellion is justified). With the spirit of rebellion expressed in such formulations as "Daring to rebel is the most fundamental and precious trait of the proletarian revolutionary," "To not rebel is 100 percent revisionism," and "Promote disorder, the more disorderly, the better," the sociopolitical temperature in the universities and middle schools of the capital rose sharply throughout June.[92] But this process from the outset was both encouraged and legitimated by proclamations from above. While denouncing as "revisionist and counterrevolutionary" the "party spirit" and "organizational discipline" of the Peking University Party Committee, *People's Daily* editorials asserted that "700 million people are all critics" and that only when ⸱he "broad masses" themselves swept clean the legacy of thousands of years of oppression could the success of China's socialist revolution be assured.[93] These familiar power-deconcentrating and mass-mobilizing themes were paralleled by a mounting insistence on the centrality of Mao Zedong Thought. Directly contradicting the vanguard party's historic insistence on mediating popular upheaval and mass mobilization, Maoist proclamations in June 1966 depicted the "great awakening" of the Cultural Revolution as a union of Mao Zedong Thought and the masses.

The party organization reacted to the Maoist assault on its authority and legitimacy by mounting a vigorous and sophisticated defensive effort. As part of the reorganization of the Peking municipal and Peking University party organizations in early June, CCP work teams were dispatched to the universities and middle schools of the capital to "lead the socialist cultural revolution and carry out the functions of the Party Committee."[94] Although hailed as "the new victory" of Mao Zedong Thought at the time, the deportment of the CCP work teams proved decisive in Mao's decision in early August to more vigorously confront the party organization as a whole. In a reprise of concentration and control tactics deployed during the Socialist Education Movement, the work teams banned public meetings and big-character posters, prohibited interschool communication, denounced some especially active Red Guard groups as "illegal," arrested as counterrevolutionaries some "outside agitators," and generally attempted to reimpose order in the school system.[95]

Although these methods were nothing more "than a standard response to organizational disruption precipitated by extra-Party mass agitation," the effect was to blunt the emerging Red Guard movement and direct its thrust away from the party organization.[96] More ominously, the work teams also sought to contain the mounting ferment by "directing the spearhead downward" *(ba maotou zhi xia).* As Hong Yung Lee noted, "Compelled by the 'May 16 Notice,' which unequivocally called for the purge of power holders, the party organization moved with reluctance to comply with Mao's wishes. It approached the unpleasant task in a purely organizational way, relying exclusively on the existing leadership at the various institutions and on the inner-party regulations regarding 'management and evaluation of cadres.'"[97] Naturally unwilling to indict senior figures, the work teams purged lower-level cadres only, especially those from "bourgeois" family backgrounds or with a history of trouble with the party leadership. Deflecting mass pressure away from power holders by focusing attention onto politically vulnerable bourgeois types or "troublemakers" would figure importantly in the subsequent CCP "survival strategy" and in the factional conflict, bloodshed, and terror that engulfed China in late 1966 and 1967.

## Top and Bottom Versus the Middle

The eruption of the Red Guard movement and the full-scale onset of the Cultural Revolution in July and August 1966 were an interactive process in which Maoist personal rulership and upheaval from below coalesced with explosive effect. In June and early July, rebel students in the elite universities and middle schools of the capital repeatedly clashed with the work teams and challenged their authority. At Peking University, members of the disgraced administration and party committee were forcibly brought in front of a struggle meeting by radical students in mid-June, whereupon "the work team labeled the affair a counter-revolutionary act, and many participants who were Party or Youth League members were expelled from these organizations. All radical students were required to make self criticism, some as many as five times. Less radical students were organized to struggle against the rebel students."[98] In early July, the Red Guards of Qinghua University Middle School defied the work team's attempt to "cool" the situation and in a big-character poster declared, "Has the black line and the black gang in all areas and all units now been entirely annihilated? It has not! Does destroying the black line and the black gang now mean there can be no new birth of a black line and a black gang in the future? It does not!"[99]

Yet youthful rebels in the Peking school system from the outset justified their defiant behavior by invoking the authority of the Central Committee and Chairman Mao.[100] This linkage was made explicit in late July and early August when Mao openly legitimated the Red Guard upheaval with a series of appearances and pronouncements. Especially striking was Mao's swim down the Yangtze at Wuhan, a classic gesture of symbolically charged personal rulership. By prevailing over the swift current of the river, the chairman demonstrated to the nation his own "radiant vigor and buoyant spirits" and commanded the people to "set their sights on the future, riding on the winds and waves as they advance."[101] Dramatically enveloped in this heightened personal aura, Mao returned to the capital and in a series of political maneuvers definitively unleashed the Red Guard movement. In late July, Mao's personal representatives visited Peking University, approvingly examined big-character posters, and then disbanded the work team and conferred official recognition on the rebel group.[102] On August 5, Mao himself wrote a big-character poster with the inflammatory title "Bombard the Headquarters," which denounced the recent deportment of the work teams in the schools and likened their methods to erroneous CCP tactics deployed in the Socialist Education Movement.[103] In this remarkable turn of events, the people of the capital were presented with the spectacle of the supreme leader of the CCP calling forth and conferring his blessings on an assault from below on the party organization he personified and headed up.

Finally, Mao's personal intervention was formalized in the "Decision of the Central Committee of the CCP Concerning the Great Proletarian Cultural Revolution" of August 8, 1966. Subsequently known as the "Sixteen Points," this set of guidelines contained radical ideas and instructions that were both familiar and profoundly ambiguous. The Sixteen Points opened with a ringing endorsement of the Red Guard phenomenon: "Unavoidable defects" notwithstanding, "a group of previously unknown revolutionary youth have become heroic pathbreakers" and have taken the lead in using "big-character posters, criticism, exposure, and debate to attack bourgeois representatives."[104] As "considerable evidence shows," only such a "full activation of the masses" could overcome the stubborn obstruction of power holders in the party taking the capitalist road and eradicate the influence of the "habits of the old society." With the exception of the military, party organizations at all levels were instructed to promote big-character posters and debate and to "encourage the masses to criticize the defects in their own work" by "freely activating the masses" (*fangshou fadong qunzhong*) and "allowing the masses to themselves teach themselves in the midst of the movement" (*rang qunzhong zai yundong zhong ziji jiaoyu ziji*).

During the Hundred Flowers episode and in the Socialist Education Movement as well, Mao had linked the vitality of the CCP to power deconcentration and increased input and criticism from below. Yet as his tactics during the Great Leap Forward underscored, Mao never questioned the principle of vanguard party leadership and hegemony. In the Sixteen Points, Mao sought to reinvigorate the CCP and reinforce the socialist enterprise by using his personal authority to sanction a far-reaching popular upheaval. This attempt to revitalize the mechanism of concentrated power by means of its temporary suspension was problematic and contradictory from the start and was immediately enveloped in complex and in-tractable power-restructuring dilemmas.

## Ambiguous Messages, Conflicting Interpretations

Mao's authoritative interventions vindicated and reignited the Red Guard move-ment in Peking and were broadcast nationwide, thereby triggering Red Guard re-sponses in the provinces.[105] As set forth in a big-character poster at the First Peking Municipal Girl's Middle School, "The Central Committee and Chairman Mao have turned over great power to us," and "we must quickly assume mastery of the house, and with the attitude of the master of the house vigorously plunge into the midst of the revolution."[106] This now-legitimated mastery was manifested in an eruption of youthful exuberance as Red Guard groups demonstrated in the schools and paraded in the streets, published newspapers and proclamations, and ecstatically rallied in Tiananmen Square for a series of Olympian personal appear-ances by Mao.

In a more foreboding taste of things to come, these Red Guard groups took to the streets and attacked bourgeois representatives of a particular type—intellectuals educated in the West, former capitalists, persons with ties to the old regime, and various and sundry "bad elements" with tainted "class backgrounds." The resi-dences of such people were raided; their antiques, artifacts, and memorabilia were seized as evidence of suspect sympathies, put on display, and destroyed; and they were denounced, humiliated, or beaten, often severely.[107] At Peking University Middle School, I personally witnessed the fatal stomping of a "hoodlum" (liu-mang) who had made the mistake of wandering into a Red Guard rally attired in flashy, Westernized garb. In the elite universities and middle schools of the capital, Red Guard mastery was expressed in a theory of "natural redness," whereby the student body was divided into the politically correct "five red categories" (the chil-dren of workers, peasants, soldiers, revolutionary cadres, and martyrs) versus the politically incorrect "five black categories" (the children of landlords, rich peas-ants, counterrevolutionaries, bad elements, and rightists), and politically incorrect students were persecuted by the politically correct.[108]

This Red Guard reign of terror, which would soon be condemned by the "cen-ter" as "royalist and reactionary," was in part the by-product of the ambiguous Maoist message. While legitimating the upheaval in the schools, the political tar-gets put forward in the Sixteen Points were complex, overlapping, and poorly de-fined. Were the young heroic pathbreakers to direct their fire against power hold-ers in the party taking the capitalist road, "reactionary bourgeois academic authorities," or those parts of the "superstructure that do not correspond to the socialist economic base," all targets that were stressed in the Sixteen Points?[109] On the crucial question of CCP cadre rectification, point eight simultaneously called for the exposure and removal of antiparty, antisocialist rightist elements, stipulated that the majority of cadres were "good" or "comparatively good," and held out the possibility of forgiveness and rehabilitation for the worst offenders.[110] As for bourgeois academic authorities, point five stressed that a "strict distinction" was to be made between antiparty, antirightist elements and people who "support the party and socialism but had said some wrong things, done some wrong things, or written some bad things." Similarly, there was also to be a strict distinction between persons with "regular bourgeois academic ideology" and "reactionary academic overlords and authorities." Of course, these were the kinds of distinctions and labels historically deployed by the CCP for purposes of mass mobilization and political control. When the established mechanisms of CCP power were suspended in late 1966 and 1967, these labels were exploited and manipulated in freewheeling power contests at all levels of Chinese society.

However problematic the definition of targets in the Sixteen Points, the treatment of power relations and political process was murkier still. While demanding that the party organization abandon its efforts to guide the mass movement, the Sixteen Points imposed no similar requirements on the Chinese military. But the PLA immediately emerged as a key actor in the Cultural Revolution, with direct effects on the power-restructuring processes unleashed in summer and fall 1966. While deconcentrating political power and legitimating unprecedented popular involvement in the internal affairs of the party, the Sixteen Points stressed the role of Mao Zedong Thought as a "guide to action" *(xingdong zhinan)*. Yet Maoist autocracy and deployment of a Mao cult of astounding proportions would prevail in the months and years to come. By late 1967, "revolutionary transformation" would be defined not by mass participation in political action but by the memorization and repetition of Maoist catch phrases long since devoid of any substantive meaning.

But the ambiguous content and conflicting interpretations of the Sixteen Points were most tellingly encapsulated in Mao's injunction *fangshou fadong qunzhong,* a slogan I translate as "freely activating the masses" and that others translate as "freely mobilizing the masses" and "boldly arousing the masses." In fact, none of these translations adequately conveys the profoundly equivocal quality of this peculiarly Maoist utterance. Since the literal meanings of the words *fang* and *shou* are "to let go" and "hand(s)," the slogan is most accurately rendered as "hands-off activation of the masses." Given the party's traditions and history, this guideline was incomprehensible, for we have seen that CCP mobilizational practices were nothing if not hands-on. Yet the ambiguity of the slogan exemplified Mao's insistence that a cultural revolution would reconcile the populist and Leninist strains in Chinese communism and the Chinese Revolution.

## Notes

1. Richard L. Walker, *China Under Communism: The First Five Years* (New Haven: Yale University Press, 1955), 25. Thus, "much of the power of the Communist regime in China is based on terror which is designed to paralyze the will of all its subjects to resist. In their application of terror as a system of power the Chinese Communists have demonstrated

that they have learned much from their schooling in the land of the big brother, as well as utilizing some aspects of their own traditional despotism" (215).

2. Jurgen Domes, *China After the Cultural Revolution: Politics Between the Two Party Congresses* (Berkeley and Los Angeles: University of California Press, 1977), 3.

3. Hong Yung Lee, *From Revolutionary Cadres to Party Technocrats in Socialist China* (Berkeley and Los Angeles: University of California Press, 1991), 395–397. While conceding that cadres always attempt to protect their personal interests and neutralize conflicting pressures, Lee also spoke of their "blind subscription to the Leninist principle of democratic centralism" (397) and concluded, "The revolutionary cadres generally acted as the state's agents" (396).

4. Andrew G. Walder, *Communist Neo-Traditionalism* (Berkeley and Los Angeles: University of California Press, 1986), 19–20. Although paternalistic ties of of obligation and reciprocity link managers and workers, "as representatives of the state, communist managers are extraordinarily unified and well-organized" (19). For a far-reaching assessment and critique of Walder's argument, see Brantly Womack, "Transfigured Community: Neo-Traditionalism and Work Unit Socialism in China," *China Quarterly* 126 (June 1991):313–332.

5. Avery Goldstein, *From Bandwagon to Balance-of-Power Politics* (Stanford: Stanford University Press, 1991), 9–11, 49–51. Goldstein attempted to demonstrate his point by showing that "Mao's initiatives before 1966 triggered a rush to demonstrate enthusiastic support for his preferred outcome" (9). This notion is more than a little far-fetched; yet Goldstein's insistence that 1966 is the fundamental line of demarcation in the politics of Chinese communism is important.

6. Frederick C. Teiwes, *Politics and Purges in China*, 2d ed. (Armonk, N.Y.: M. E. Sharpe, 1993), lxii, xv. While insisting on his thesis of a Mao-dominated political process, Teiwes qualified his argument beyond recognition by conceding the importance of policy disputes in 1956, during the Great Leap Forward, and throughout the early 1960s and speaking unconvincingly of "conflict without opposition" (xxxvi).

7. Goldstein, *From Bandwagon to Balance-of-Power Politics,* 5.

8. Franz Schurmann made his classic distinction between material incentive and social mobilization policies, or decentralization I and decentralization II, in *Ideology and Organization in Communist China*, enl. ed. (Berkeley and Los Angeles: University of California Press, 1968), 196–197. For an early discussion of NEP-style policies, center versus region rivalries, and tensions between the CCP and intellectuals in the years preceding the Cultural Revolution, see Franz Schurmann, "China's 'New Economic Policy'—Transition or Beginning?" in Roderick MacFarquhar, ed., *China Under Mao: Politics Takes Command* (Cambridge, Mass.: MIT Press, 1966), 211–237.

9. Harry Harding, *Organizing China: The Problem of Bureaucracy, 1949–1976* (Stanford: Stanford University Press, 1981), 1; Richard Kraus, *Class Conflict in Chinese Socialism* (New York: Columbia University Press, 1981), 178.

10. Parris H. Chang, *Power and Policy in China*, 2d, enl. ed. (University Park: Pennsylvania State University Press, 1981), 9; Mark Selden, *The Political Economy of Chinese Socialism* (Armonk, N.Y.: M. E. Sharpe, 1988), 3.

11. Ezra Vogel, *Canton Under Communism: Programs and Politics in a Provincial Capital, 1949–1968* (Cambridge, Mass.: Harvard University Press, 1969), 123.

12. The figure of 5 million was provided by Jurgen Domes, *The Internal Politics of China, 1949–1972* (New York: Praeger, 1973), 37–38. Estimates of between 1 and 4 million

were suggested by Valerie Strauss and Dan Southerland, "How Many Died? New Evidence Suggests Far Higher Numbers for the Victims of Mao Zedong's Era," *Washington Post,* July 17, 1994, 22. For a sympathetic account of land reform, see Isabel Crook and David Crook, *Ten Mile Inn: Mass Movement in a Chinese Village* (New York: Pantheon, 1979).

13. Schurmann, *Ideology and Organization in Communist China,* 437.

14. Walker, *China Under Communism,* 219–221.

15. Tiejun Cheng and Mark Selden, "The Origins and Social Consequences of China's *Hukou* System," *China Quarterly* 139 (September 1994):653.

16. Edward Friedman, Paul G. Pickowicz, and Mark Selden, *Chinese Village, Socialist State* (New Haven: Yale University Press, 1991), 154. Viewing events from the perspective of the rural population, these commentators took a dim view of the state grain monopoly and emphasized the inefficiencies, disincentives, and inequities of the process. Understood in macroeconomic terms, however, it was the capacity of the state to mobilize and channel resources in desired directions that keyed the industrialization of China in the 1950s.

17. Nicholas R. Lardy, *Agriculture in China's Modern Economic Development* (Cambridge: Cambridge University Press, 1983), 127.

18. Harding, *Organizing China,* 35.

19. "From the beginning, the party knew that rapid expansion would introduce many undesirable elements. It instructed local committees to use the 'wave style' of recruiting members: to 'recruit some, immediately train them, and then recruit another group.' This pattern of expansion, immediately followed by a rectification campaign, was a well-established procedure" (Lee, *From Revolutionary Cadres to Party Technocrats in Socialist China,* 41).

20. During the Wufan campaign, CCP leaders spoke of "a systematic attack of the bourgeois class (carried out) against party and state cadres over the past three years" (Harding, *Organizing China,* 51).

21. Schurmann, *Ideology and Organization in Communist China,* 257–260.

22. Ibid., 271. For a more complex interpretation underscoring the role of intraparty factional conflict, see Teiwes, *Politics and Purges in China,* xvii–xxii.

23. Domes, *The Internal Politics of China,* 74.

24. Chang, *Power and Policy in China,* 9–10. Some top leaders questioned the relevance of basic aspects of the Soviet system. In the words of Vice Premier Deng Zihui, "As the USSR possessed the necessary conditions for collectivization at the time, it was right for her to act thus. We, however, have not the necessary conditions. . . . Moreover, the Chinese peasants' conception of private ownership is relatively deep" (10).

25. David Bachman, *Bureaucracy, Economy, and Leadership in China: The Institutional Origins of the Great Leap Forward* (Cambridge: Cambridge University Press, 1991), 17. Bachman noted the connection between Khrushchev's liberalizing efforts and subsequent attempts in China and suggested that Mao in 1956 probably "supported most elements of Khrushchev's analysis of Stalin" (17).

26. For the Chen Yun, central planning–heavy industry, and Mao-party organization approaches, see ibid., chaps. 4–6.

27. See Barry Naughton, "The Pattern and Legacy of Economic Growth in the Mao Era," in Kenneth Lieberthal, Joyce Kallgren, Roderick MacFarquhar, and Frederic Wakeman Jr., eds., *Perspectives on Modern China* (Armonk, N.Y.: M. E. Sharpe, 1991), 229–233.

28. Nicholas R. Lardy, "Recent Chinese Economic Performance and Prospects for the Ten-Year Plan," in *Chinese Economy Post-Mao* (Washington, D.C.: Joint Economic Committee, Congress of the United States, 1978), vol. 1, 49.

29. Thomas G. Rawski, *Economic Growth in Prewar China* (Berkeley and Los Angeles: University of California Press, 1989), 348.

30. Robert F. Dernberger, "The Chinese Search for Self-Sustained Development in the 1980s," in *China Under the Four Modernizations* (Washington, D.C.: Joint Economic Committee, Congress of the United States, 1982), 24–25.

31. Roderick MacFarquhar, *The Origins of the Cultural Revolution 2: The Great Leap Forward, 1958–1960* (New York: Columbia University Press, 1983), 15–17. In Nikita Khrushchev's words, "The Great Leap Forward and the creation of the communes caused a great decline in China's industry and agriculture, leading literally to famine. It was necessary for Mao to recognize his mistakes. But that was no more possible for him than for Stalin" (*Khrushchev Remembers: The Glasnost Tapes* [Boston: Little, Brown, 1990], 159).

32. In the assessment of Chang, "Mao's inclination to sponsor decentralization appears to have been motivated by political considerations. . . . His political tactic was to balance different political groups, and play the provincial forces off against the centrally based leaders" (*Power and Policy in China*, 52).

33. Schurmann, *Ideology and Organization in Communist China*, 198.

34. Bachman, *Bureaucracy, Economy, and Leadership in China*, 93.

35. Chang, *Power and Policy in China*, 54.

36. On the one hand, rural party organizations convened cadre meetings, people's delegates meetings, and mass meetings amid intense propaganda and education appeals. On the other hand, "the revolutionary terror was still fresh in the minds of the rural population. Neither the peasants nor the regime wished a repetition of these events" (Schurmann, *Ideology and Organization in Communist China*, 453).

37. Roderick MacFarquhar, *The Origins of the Cultural Revolution 1: Contradictions Among the People* (New York: Columbia University Press, 1974), chap. 2.

38. Chang, *Power and Policy in China*, 15. I am indebted to Mark Selden for bringing the full dimensions of this portentous event to my attention.

39. MacFarquhar, *The Origins of the Cultural Revolution 1*, chaps. 5, 7; Chang, *Power and Policy in China*, 26–29. For a groundbreaking account of worker unrest in 1956–1957, see Elizabeth J. Perry, "Shanghai's Strike Wave of 1957," *China Quarterly* 137 (March 1994): 1–27.

40. Mao Zedong, *On the Correct Handling of Contradictions Among the People* (Peking: People's Publishing, 1957), 1, 20, 23, 29.

41. Ibid., 17.

42. Ibid., 30.

43. "Talk at Yinian Tang," February 16, 1957, in Roderick MacFarquhar, Timothy Cheek, and Eugene Wu, eds., *The Secret Speeches of Chairman Mao: From the Hundred Flowers to the Great Leap Forward* (Cambridge, Mass.: Harvard University Press, 1989), 122.

44. "Talk at a Conference of Party Member Cadres at Tianjin Municipality," March 17, 1957, in ibid., 294.

45. "Talk at a Conference of Party Member Cadres of Shandong Provincial Organs," March 18, 1957, in ibid., 303.

46. "On Ideological Work (Talk at a Conference Attended by Party Cadres from People's Liberation Army Units Under the Nanjing Command and from Jiangsu and Anhui Provinces)," March 19, 1957, in ibid., 327.

47. "Tongzhi zhongguo gongchandang zhongyang weiyuanhui" (May 16 notice of the central committee of the CCP), *Renmin ribao* (People's daily), May 18, 1966, 1. This key Cultural Revolution document placed special emphasis on Mao's invocation of the concept of *fang* in 1957.

48. MacFarquhar, *The Origins of the Cultural Revolution 1,* 191–204.

49. Teiwes, *Politics and Purges in China,* xxiii. Incomprehensibly, Teiwes did not believe that widespread official resistance to Mao's ideas contradicted his low conflict thesis and apparently failed to ask himself, Why would Mao have to "win" people over in a political process centered around his preferences?

50. Both Mao and China's rulers in the 1980s understood "democracy" in instrumental terms and viewed it first and foremost as a means of building and strengthening Chinese socialism. As Mao also stated in March 1957, although "criticism surely is allowed, the result and purpose of it must be the consolidation of democratic centralism and the leadership of the party" ("On Ideological Work," in MacFarquhar et al., eds. *The Secret Speeches of Chairman Mao,* 339).

51. Perry, "Shanghai's Strike Wave of 1957," 8.

52. Chang, *Power and Policy in China,* 37.

53. "Talks at the Beidaihe Conference (Draft Transcript)," August 17–30, 1958, in Mac-Farquhar et al., eds., *The Secret Speeches of Chairman Mao,* 417, 419.

54. In Bachman's words, "As the Great Leap Forward would reveal, when given the chance these leaders pushed decentralization to the maximum and attempted to build up the heavy industrial base of their provinces" (*Bureaucracy, Economy, and Leadership in China,* 144). We have seen that regional party organizations responded to the *sovnarkhozy* reform in identical fashion.

55. Chang, *Power and Policy in China,* 106–107; MacFarquhar, *The Origins of the Cultural Revolution 2,* 163.

56. In Mao's words, "This time we must restore our military tradition—the tradition of the Red Army, the Eighth Route Army, (and) the PLA—the tradition of Marxism; (and we) must get rid of bourgeois ideological workstyles. We may be a bit 'uncouth,' but (our ways) are genuine and most civilized. The bourgeoisie appear a bit more civilized, (but) in reality they're hypocritical and uncivilized" ("Talk at the Beidaihe Conference," in MacFarquhar et al., eds., *The Secret Speeches of Chairman Mao,* 418).

57. "Talks at the First Zhengzhou Conference," November 6, 1958, in ibid., 452, 456.

58. Friedman et al., *Chinese Village, Socialist State,* 238–239. These commentators spoke of a "cultural revolution that made war on Chinese culture" (238) during the Great Leap Forward.

59. Schurmann, *Ideology and Organization in Communist China,* 479–480.

60. William Hinton, *Shenfan* (New York: Random House, 1983), 233.

61. MacFarquhar, *The Origins of the Cultural Revolution 2,* 199.

62. Ibid., 79. We have seen that the same pattern emerged in the course of Khrushchev's economic campaigns in the late 1950s. It should be noted that Mao was aware of and warned against overexertion, inflated claims, and production falsification in November 1958 ("Talks at the Wuchang Conference," November 21–23, 1958, in MacFarquhar et al., eds., *The Secret Speeches of Chairman Mao,* 494, 507).

63. Selden, *The Political Economy of Chinese Socialism,* 17. Estimates of famine deaths stemming from the Great Leap Forward by Western demographers and Chinese analysts

range from 20 million to 30 million to a recent high of 43 million. See Strauss and Southerland, "How Many Died?"

64. Friedman et al., *Chinese Village, Socialist State,* 240.

65. For an account showing how disagreements between Mao and Khrushchev on
geopolitical strategy and the subsequent Soviet refusal to share nuclear weapons technology with China were key in the Sino-Soviet split, see John Wilson Lewis and Xue Litai,
*China Builds the Bomb* (Stanford: Stanford University Press, 1988), 66–72.

66. MacFarquhar, *The Origins of the Cultural Revolution 2,* 216.

67. Jon L. Saari, *Legacies of Childhood—Growing Up Chinese in a Time of Crisis, 1890–
1920* (Cambridge, Mass.: Harvard University Press, 1990), 15.

68. For example, the *hukou* population registration and control system was strongly
and successfully reinforced beginning in 1960 as part of the central effort to reestablish
economic and social control (Cheng and Selden, "The Origins and Social Consequences of
China's *Hukou* System," 666).

69. Friedman et al., *Chinese Village, Socialist State,* 254.

70. Chang, *Power and Policy in China,* 138–139.

71. Schurmann, "China's 'New Economic Policy,'" 222–226.

72. "Tao Zhu's Report to Higher Intellectuals," in *Survey of the China Mainland Press
(SCMP)* 4200 (August 1969):12–15.

73. MacFarquhar, *The Origins of the Cultural Revolution 2,* 293–295; Schurmann, *Ideology and Organization in Communist China,* 197.

74. Teiwes, *Politics and Purges in China,* xl. Teiwes attempted to salvage his low-con-
flict, Mao-centered political process thesis by noting that "in his own speech to the conference Mao endorsed the whole set of policies which would be attacked as revisionist during
the Cultural Revolution" (xl). But the implication that Mao actually accepted these policies
is clearly contradicted by events to come.

75. Teiwes stressed the emotional impact of the conference on Mao and suggested that
it was at this time that the chairman began to "harbor unspoken resentments" against Liu
(*Politics and Purges in China,* xli). But fundamental policy differences were the key.

76. Deng Xiaoping, "Suggestions on Drafting 'Resolution of Various Questions of Party
History Since 1949,'" in Deng Xiaoping, *Selected Works of Deng Xiaoping (1975–1982)* (Beijing: Foreign Languages Press, 1984), 259–260. Deng spoke approvingly of Mao's willingness to acknowledge his mistakes at the seven thousand cadre conference and then criticized Mao's renewed insistence on the importance of class struggle at the subsequent
"Beidaihe conference" in summer 1962 (nn. 96–97).

77. Richard Baum, *Prelude to Revolution* (New York: Columbia University Press, 1975),
12–13. To "reverse the verdict" (*fanan*) is to challenge and overturn the sociopolitical label,
e.g., "class enemy" or "counterrevolutionary," affixed to a person. The affixing of labels
was a standard CCP practice, and label affixing and overturning were central to power contests during the Cultural Revolution.

78. Ibid., 23–24.

79. Ibid., 47.

80. Ibid., 58–59.

81. Hinton, *Shenfan,* 318.

82. Ibid., 347. Hence, "Of those who support these elements, some are in the lower levels and the rest are in the higher levels. . . . Of those in the higher levels, some are anti-socialist elements working in the organs of the communes, districts, counties and prefectures,

and even in the provincial and central departments. Among them are some who have always been alien class elements; others are degenerates; and still others are persons who have received bribes and are collaborating in violating law and discipline" (347).

83. Cited in ibid., 350.

84. Yao Wenyuan, "Ping xinpian lishiju 'Hai Rui baguan'" (Critique of the new historical play "Hai Rui dismissed from office"), *Wenhui bao* (Literary digest), November 10, 1965, in Chi Wen-shun, ed., *Readings in the Chinese Communist Cultural Revolution* (Berkeley and Los Angeles: University of California Press, 1971), 3–15.

85. Yao Wenyuan, "Ping 'San jia cun'" (Critique of "Three-family village"), *Hongqi* (Red flag), May 11, 1966, in Chi, *Readings in the Chinese Communist Cultural Revolution,* 114. (All quotes in this paragraph are from this source.)

86. Teiwes, *Politics and Purges in China,* xliii.

87. The origins of this big-character poster are murky. It went up on May 24, 1966, and then, according to Lowell Dittmer, "on June 1, Nie's poster came to Mao's attention and he called Kang Sheng to request that it 'should at once be broadcast and published in the newspapers'" (*Liu Shao-ch'i and the Chinese Cultural Revolution* [Berkeley and Los Angeles: University of California Press, 1974], 78). But Nie was already a member of Mao's inner circle and a Jiang Qing confidante.

88. Nie Yuanzi et al., "Song Shuo, Lu Ping, Peng Peiyun zai wenhua da geming zhong jiujing gan xie sheme?" (Whatever are Song Shuo, Lu Ping, and Peng Peiyun doing in the great cultural revolution?), *Wuchanjieji wenhua da geming dazibao xuan (Selected big character posters of the great proletarian cultural revolution)* (Peking: People's Press, 1966), 1–4.

89. "Tongzhi zhongguo gongchandang zhongyang weiyuanhui," 263. (All quotes in this paragraph are from this source.)

90. "Hengsao yiqie nuigui sheshen" (Sweep away all freaks and monsters), *Renmin ribao,* June 1, 1966, in *Hengsao yiqie nuigui sheshen* (Sweep away all freaks and monsters) (Peking: People's Press, 1966), 3.

91. "Chuji renmin linghun de da geming" (A great revolution touching the souls of people), *Renmin ribao,* June 2, 1966, in *Hengsao yiqie nuigui sheshen,* 9.

92. Thus, "gan zaofan, zhe shi wuchanjieji gemingjia zui jiben zui kegui de pinzhi"; "bu zaofan jiushi baifen zhi yibai de xiuzhengzhuyi"; "da de luan luan de, yue luan yue hao!" (Daring to rebel, this is the proletarian revolutionary's most basic and most precious quality; not to rebel is one hundred percent revisionism; strike up great chaos, the more chaotic the better!) ("Wuchanjieji de geming zaofan jingshen wan sui" [Long live the proletarian revolutionary rebellion Spirit]) in *Wuchanjieji wenhua da geming dazibao xuan,* 10–12.

93. "Zuo wuchanjieji geming pai, hai shi zibenzhuyi baohuang pai?" (To be proletarian revolutionaries or to be bourgeois royalists?), *Renmin ribao,* June 5, 1966, 23; "Women shi jiu shijie de pipan zhe" (We are the critics of the old world), *Renmin ribao,* June 8, 1966, 1.

94. "Mao Zedong sixiang de xin shengli" (The new victory of Mao Zedong thought), *Renmin ribao,* June 4, 1966, 17.

95. Dittmer, *Liu Shao-ch'i and the Chinese Cultural Revolution,* 78–83. At Peking University Middle School, many of my fellow students defied the restrictions, climbed over the walls at night, and returned with tantalizing accounts of big-character posters and Red Guard activity at other schools.

96. Ibid., 80.

97. Hong Yung Lee, *The Politics of the Chinese Cultural Revolution* (Berkeley and Los Angeles: University of California Press, 1978), 48.

98. Victor Nee, *The Cultural Revolution at Peking University* (New York: Monthly Review Press, 1969), 62.

99. "Zailun wuchanjieji de geming zaofan jingshen wan sui" (Once again, long live the proletarian revolutionary rebellion spirit), in *Wuchanjieji wenhua da geming daziboa xuan,* 13–14.

100. For a consideration of the social psychology of the rebel youth in the opening phases of the Cultural Revolution, see Mark Lupher, "Revolutionary Little Red Devils: The Social Psychology of Rebel Youth, 1966–1967," in Anne Behnke Kinney, ed., *Chinese Views of Childhood* (Honolulu: University of Hawaii Press, 1995).

101. "Chairman Mao Swims in the Yangtze," *Peking Review,* July 29, 1966, 3, 7. This piece is notable for the charismatic Mao imagery prevalent during this period. Thus, "just as the competition was starting, a fast launch cut through the waves and sailed toward the swimmers from the east where the sun was rising. One of the swimmers first caught sight of the great leader on the launch. Hardly able to contain his joy, he immediately shouted out: 'Chairman Mao has arrived! Long live Chairman Mao!' Instantly, the swimmers, holding hundreds of red banners high above the water, swam towards Chairman Mao. The eyes of thousands upon thousands of people on the banks and in the river, which became red with the reflections of the banners, were turned on Chairman Mao" (3).

102. Nee, *The Cultural Revolution at Peking University,* 65.

103. "Bombard the Headquarters," *Peking Review,* August 11, 1966, 3.

104. "Zhongguo gongchandang zhongyang weiyuanhui guanyu wuchanjieji wenhua da geming de jueyi" (Decision of the central committee of the CCP on the great proletarian cultural revolution), *Renmin ribao,* August 11, 1966, in Chi, *Readings in the Chinese Communist Revolution,* 224. (All subsequent quotes in this paragraph are from this source.)

105. See Liang Heng and Judith Shapiro, *Son of the Revolution* (New York: Vintage, 1983), 43–45, for the powerful impact of Mao's statements and gestures as they were transmitted to the provinces.

106. "Nachu zhuren weng de taidu lai" (Sally forth with the attitude of the master of the house), in *Wuchanjieji wenhua da geming dazibao xuan,* 17–18.

107. In the words of one of Anita Chan's informants, "It was the beginning of the Cultural Revolution. . . . We were trying to take the train from the Peking railway station, and we saw those secondary school students beating people, completely out of hand. Whap! Whap! They were whipping some former landlords and whatnot. Blood all over" (*Children of Mao: Personality Development and Political Activism in the Red Guard Generation* [London: Macmillan, 1985], 169).

108. Lee, *The Politics of the Chinese Cultural Revolution,* 68–75. This cleavage was key at my middle school, where the student body was composed primarily of children of the CCP civilian and military elite and children of the old Peking intelligentsia.

109. K. H. Fan, *The Chinese Cultural Revolution* (New York: Grove Press, 1968), 165–170.

110. "Zhongguo gongchandang zhongyang weiyuanhui guanyu wuchanjieji wenhua da geming de jueyi," 226. (All subsequent quotes in this paragraph are from this source.)

# 7

## The Cultural Revolution and the Origins of Post-Mao Reform

The Cultural Revolution is the analytic centerpiece of this book. This focus stems in part from my personal experience as a student at Peking University Middle School from the fall of 1965 until its closure a year later during the tumultuous opening phases of the Cultural Revolution. During that time, and then as a resident of Peking for two more years, I observed firsthand, and sometimes participated in, the unfolding, eruption, and ebbing of this great political and social upheaval.[1] But the significance ascribed to the events of the Cultural Revolution in these pages is no mere reflection of my personal history. Rather, I understand the Cultural Revolution in light of the general view of power relations and political process put forward in this book. The Cultural Revolution was a power-restructuring event of unprecedented scope and intensity, in the course of which the central themes of my discussion were revealed with striking clarity and detail. This view of China's Cultural Revolution both modifies and contradicts prevailing Chinese and Western perspectives.

In 1980, Deng Xiaoping rendered the official Chinese verdict on the Cultural Revolution and pronounced, "During the ten years of the 'Great Cultural Revolution,' Comrade Mao Zedong was in error," and the "floodgates of anarchism and ultra-individualism were opened wide."[2] This official verdict was buttressed in the 1980s by a great outpouring of "scar literature" (shanghen wenxue), which documented the sufferings of members of the political elite and the intelligentsia and depicted the Cultural Revolution as a "calamity" during which "democracy was trampled, law was smashed, persons were humiliated, and power was usurped."[3] In the 1980s, official Chinese analyses always depicted the post-Mao reforms as a decisive break with the conflict, chaos, and violence of the Cultural Revolution.[4]

Just as sympathetic Western observers of Communist China in the 1960s often accepted the official Maoist version of events, many Western analysts in the 1980s echoed the prevailing Chinese view and depicted the Cultural Revolution as a cruel tragedy and inexplicable aberration. At one extreme, Merle Goldman likened the victimization of elites and intellectuals during the Cultural Revolution to the devastation that European Jews suffered at the hands of the Nazis during

World War II. Hence, the Chinese victims of this "pointless and absurd" movement "use the language of the Holocaust to descibe the sense of abandonment and isolation they felt. Likewise they 'bear witness,' so that the Cultural Revolution will never happen again."[5] This comparison both trivializes the Holocaust and sheds little light on the momentous power-restructuring events of the Cultural Revolution decade.

Other analysts attempted to explain the violence of the Cultural Revolution in terms of the "reactive extremism" that provided the "rationale for Stalin's mass murders." In Andrew G. Walder's view, Maoist variations on the old Stalinist themes of class warfare and subversion from within precipitated "the inquisitions, witch hunts, cruel and vindictive persecutions of individuals, and unprincipled and often incoherent factionalism" of the Cultural Revolution.[6] Hong Yung Lee stated that "the Cultural Revolution represented a noble attempt to resolve an ironical situation in which the Communist Party, initially established to carry out the Communist Revolution, became itself the object of revolution."[7] But when viewed historically and comparatively, Mao's decision to launch the Cultural Revolution appears more familiar. I suggest that the logic of the Cultural Revolution should be understood in light of the revolutionary experience of Chinese communism, the Soviet experience under Stalin and Khrushchev, and power restructuring.

As I discussed in Chapter 2, it was the synthesis of vanguard party concentration and control processes with popular aspirations and energies that propelled the CCP to power in 1949. Both Mao and the leaders of the party establishment sought to re-create these dynamic sociopolitical interactions during the Socialist Education Movement; yet they attempted to do so with methods premised on increasingly divergent and contradictory visions of the revolutionary experience and the role of the party. By persistently linking the political and organizational vitality of the party to mass enthusiasm and the deconcentration of political power, Mao sought to revive the vibrant populist traditions of the base area period. By insisting on the primacy of party leadership and coordination from above, CCP leaders Liu Shaoqi and Deng Xiaoping embraced the equally potent and well-established tradition of Leninist concentration and control. As commentators have long noted, tensions between Maoist populism and Leninist vanguard party hegemony are recurrent in the history of Chinese communism.[8] Although the greatest successes of Chinese communism pivoted on the dynamic synthesis of these political and organizational approaches, the formula was eroded and finally collapsed in the early 1960s.

At the same time, processes of stabilization and bureaucratization resulted in the ascendancy of a red-expert moderate coalition in the early 1960s. Like Stalin, Mao viewed the rise of moderation as a challenge to his political leadership and to the authority–social mobilization policies he championed. Like Stalin, Mao sponsored an attack from above and below on the rising moderate coalition, which he attempted to displace with a new group of younger, more politically reliable people, often recruited from the lower classes. Yet Mao attempted this restructuring by deconcentrating power in ways that have few analogs in the Soviet 1930s and that more closely resembled the power-restructuring methods of post-Stalin Soviet reformers. These differences both distinguish Maoist power restructuring from Stalinist power restructuring and explain Stalin's "success" and Mao's "failure" in achieving their power-restructuring objectives.

Finally, I understand the Cultural Revolution as a three-way power contest and a manifestation of the perennial struggle of central rulers against decentralized power and resource appropriation. In the manner of Chinese and Russian central rulers in imperial times, under communism, and today, Mao attempted during the Cultural Revolution to combat processes of appropriation "from the top-down, with assertive personal rulership and the deployment of centrally-controlled power structures; and from the bottom-up, with appeals to the masses and alliances with non-privileged social strata."[9] Because the Maoist top and bottom versus the middle power-restructuring initiative was set in motion by means of a radical deconcentration of political power, freewheeling and violent struggles to control power and resources immediately broke out in the capital and in the provinces, and a sociopolitical upheaval of historic proportions ensued.

## The Political Sociology of the Cultural Revolution

The societal response to the deconcentration of political power, the suspension of administrative controls, and the sanctioning of mass criticism of the party was tumultuous and soon assumed forms that the initiators of the Cultural Revolution neither anticipated nor desired. By mid-fall 1966, a variety of Red Guard organizations, leaders of the local party organizations and their supporters, and various and sundry "rebel" groups had become involved in a welter of rapidly escalating and increasingly violent conflicts. This eruption of violence and conflict was only partly the result of the ambiguous messages and conflicting interpretations conveyed by Maoist directives. Even though Maoist power-restructuring initiatives were set in motion from above, contests over power and resources at the societal level forthwith emerged as the primary driving force.

In contrast to commentators who depicted the Cultural Revolution as a "pointless Holocaust" of "witch-hunts" and "incoherent factionalism," other Western analysts took a more systematic approach and attempted to explain the eruption of violence and conflict in light of the political, ideological, and sociostructural conditions of Chinese Communist society in the 1960s. Thus, some observers argued that the violence of the Cultural Revolution stemmed directly from long-standing Chinese Communist ideology and administrative policies. In Anita Chan's view, the brutal Red Guard "authoritarian personality" was the by-product of two interrelated processes: the pre–Cultural Revolution "educational system[,] which gave precedence to iron discipline and competitive submission to collective and higher authority," and "the black and white Manichean worldview of Maoist teachings; the militancy and lack of compassion students were supposed to exhibit when confronting the people's enemies; the pernicious class line prejudice that was taught."[10] Similarly, Lynn T. White III asserted that the "arbitrary violence" and "destructive chaos" of the Cultural Revolution were the result of "bad" CCP administrative policies. Hence, "the main roots of the Cultural Revolution's violence lie in previous measures undertaken by the state. From 1949 to 1966 three administrative policies—which can be summed up in the words *labeling, monitoring,* and *campaigning*—influenced Chinese urbanites' attitudes toward each other and toward their local leaders."[11]

In a related but more persuasive vein, Hong Yung Lee and Stanley Rosen argued that the violent conflicts of the Cultural Revolution were linked to political, social, and economic cleavages in Chinese Communist society. In their work, they showed how factional divisions mirrored sociostructural cleavages whereby beneficiaries of the status quo, such as the children of CCP officials and workers with permanent state jobs, took up "conservative" positions, while nonprivileged groups, such as the children of "bourgeois" intellectuals and temporary contract workers, adopted a "rebel" stance.[12] In Lee's words, "The radical mass organizations were largely composed of underprivileged social groups, whereas the conservatives were heavily drawn from the better-off groups. The radicals attempted to change the political status quo as much as possible, whereas the conservatives strenuously defended the status quo."[13] While focusing on sociostructural cleavages instead of CCP ideology and administrative policies, however, Lee and Rosen also linked the violent conflicts of the Cultural Revolution to preexisting conditions in Chinese Communist society.

Yet Avery Goldstein perceptively noted that, although cleavages among students and workers "provided the immediate cause of much of the early conflict," "these tensions do not provide a sufficient explanation for the politics of the decade of the Cultural Revolution" since "before the Cultural Revolution these alleged causes . . . had not produced the effects observed after 1966."[14] Nor had CCP administrative policies and Maoist ideology before the Cultural Revolution resulted in the kind of open-ended political conflict that suddenly erupted in summer and fall 1966; rather, campaign violence had been tightly orchestrated and closely focused, in typically Leninist fashion. Of course, as White himself acknowledged, the crucial difference was the deconcentration of political power: "Mao's personal role in encouraging the Cultural Revolution—especially in relaxing police controls during August 1966, and also in stirring the Red Guards or soldiers to seize power—was a necessary condition for the whole event."[15]

I view the political sociology of the Cultural Revolution and the violent conflicts thereof in light of three key factors. First, CCP administrative policies were important, but not in the way White argued. As in the Soviet 1930s, it was the turning of the mechanisms of party dictatorship against the officials of the party and state apparatus themselves that precipitated the eruption of violent conflict. Second, the tables were turned on officialdom in ways that Stalin never countenanced or considered—through the suspension of the party dictatorship itself and the wholesale relaxation of political, administrative, and police controls in late summer and fall 1966. It was only Mao's deconcentration of power, a political act unprecedented in the history of Soviet and Chinese communism, that turned highly structured and tightly focused CCP administrative policies into White's "policies of chaos." Yet however chaotic, open-ended, and violent the power contests that subsequently erupted, these events cannot be understood in light of the "anarchic, self-help, balance-of-power" model of political process that Goldstein suggested for the Cultural Revolution decade.[16] Even though various privileged, underprivileged, and nonprivileged social strata all mobilized in defense of their perceived interests, this was an unequal contest from the start. Third, the party organization mounted a determined and sophisticated defense of its power, position, and privileges. Even as the CCP power monopoly was subjected to an unprecedented sociopolitical battering, this process was already under way by fall 1966.

## The Battle for Power and Resources

The Cultural Revolution has long been depicted as a tragedy for all concerned, variously characterized by the random terrorization of hapless intellectuals, old regime survivors, and party officials and by an all-encompassing Maoist dictatorship. In Tang Tsou's assessment, the Cultural Revolution marked the "arbitrary use by a minority of political leaders of the authority of the state and the power of the mob to harass, attack, detain, arrest, and incarcerate a large number of other leaders and to oppress most social strata." So extreme and uncontested was this combination of Maoist dictatorship and "mob" terror that Tsou was moved to describe it as a system of "revolutionary-'feudal' totalitarianism" and to pose the question "Why did the resistance by various groups and strata prove to be so weak and easily crushed?"[17] According to Lee, the Cultural Revolution was both a "total failure" that "produced many losers and very few winners" and a "chaotic mass movement" in which "confusion, cruelty, viciousness, deception, and distrust ran riot."[18] Other analysts augmented these themes of mass terror, chaos, and tragedy with more conventionally totalitarian images of an all-encompassing Maoist dictatorship. During the Cultural Revolution decade, Andrew J. Nathan suggested, "Power was tightly concentrated in the leader's circle, while all aspects of life were controlled by vast bureaucracies of economic management, police surveillance, political supervision, and propaganda."[19]

But imagery of this type obscures crucial dimensions of the social conflict and political violence that broke out in summer and fall 1966, extended into 1967 and 1968, and continued sporadically throughout the Cultural Revolution decade. I have argued that Mao's deconcentration of political power in summer and fall 1966 was the key to the violent conflicts of the Cultural Revolution. This political act triggered an eruption of previously muted or suppressed conflicts and pitted law and order advocates against rebels; defenders of the established party organization against a variety of opponents; privileged groups against less privileged groups; central rulers against power holders at the regional, provincial, district, town, and village levels; and proponents of authority–social mobilization methods against market–material incentive advocates.

But this was no anarchic free-for-all. Although political violence and terror were widespread during the first years of the Cultural Revolution especially, intellectuals, old regime types, and party officials were hardly the only victims. Rather, the party organization resisted the attack from above and below, skillfully deployed its accumulated political experience and organizational skills, and was able to enlist powerful allies on its behalf. I assert that much of the violence, bloodshed, and persecution of the Cultural Revolution occurred in the course of battles over power and resources in which the embattled Chinese Communist political elite was an active, effective, and ultimately victorious participant.

The violent and protracted power contests of the Cultural Revolution produced clear winners and losers: Law and order advocates prevailed over rebels, the party organization survived the attack from above and below, privileged groups were able to hold onto their privileges, central power was eroded and the power of local elites expanded, and authority–social mobilization tactics were successfully contested and displaced by market–material incentive methods. The violence and terror of the Cultural Revolution were neither random nor incoherent; rather, factional conflicts at the mass level revolved around real issues of power and access to resources. Moreover, leaders of the embattled party organization were both overtly and covertly engaged in these conflicts and in most cases were aided and protected in their efforts by the Chinese military establishment. Finally, although Maoist aspirations of "dictatorship" *(zhuanzheng)* were real enough, Mao's radical power-restructuring initiative was contested from the outset of the Cultural Revolution and in the end resulted in a restructuring of power that the chairman never envisioned or desired.

In sum, I understand the Cultural Revolution as a power contest in which Mao, Maoist policies, and Maoist goals, along with the social forces mobilized on their behalf, were defeated by a more powerful array of political, institutional, and social forces. But the tumultuous power contests of the Cultural Revolution did not result in a restoration of the status quo ante; instead, the Chinese Communist system underwent a series of massive and wholly unforeseen changes. As I discuss in Chapter 8, this conclusion necessitates a fundamental rethinking of the origins and significance of post-Mao reform.

## Maoist Power Restructuring Versus the Party Organization

In Lee's view, "One of the most amazing aspects of the Cultural Revolution is that despite ten years of chaos and ruthless purging, the majority of the pre–Cultural

Revolution elite managed to regain their political power," a result he attributed to Maoist unwillingness to "execute the losers in a power struggle."[20] In fact, embattled CCP officials in Peking and in the provinces engaged in a wide-ranging and generally effective countermobilization and actively contested the assault from above and below. Just as Maoist rebels attempted to turn the mechanisms of vanguard party dictatorship against the apparatus, embattled officials were often able to turn Maoist power-restructuring tactics and rhetoric against their opponents. The pre–Cultural Revolution political elite did not survive because of Maoist magnanimity or squeamishness; rather, it was the party organization and its allies that finally prevailed in the violent and protracted power contests set in motion by Maoist power deconcentration.

Official resistance to Maoist power restructuring took many forms, beginning with the dispatch of work teams to the Peking school system in May and June 1966. When the Red Guards were unleashed in all their fury in August, CCP leaders bent with the wind and deftly rallied the early Red Guard movement to the defense of orthodox officialdom. In an ironic and ingenious twist, the Maoist call for an attack on the bourgeoise and the "four olds" (si jiu—old customs, old habits, old culture, old thinking) was used as a means of deflecting pressure away from the party organization and "directing the spearhead downward." While Red Guard groups made up exclusively of the high-and-mighty "naturally red" offspring of senior civil and military officials savaged powerless bourgeois intellectuals and other old regime remnants in the streets of Peking, their parents remained untouched for the time being.

In fall 1966, this sociopolitical phenomenon took a ferocious and revealing turn in Peking University Middle School and other elite educational institutions in the capital with the formation of the paramilitary Red Guard organization Lianhe xingdong weiyuanhui (United Action Committee), popularly known as Liandong or "United Action." The members of Liandong, who were the children of especially high-ranking (and therefore especially "red") CCP leaders, affected military garb and insignia, elaborately calligraphed armbands and glinting Mao badges, and Sam Brown belts, which they used to beat their victims. As the self-anointed "proletarian representative," United Action took on itself the responsibility of checking the "class background" (jieji chusheng) of other students, limited participation in the Cultural Revolution to students with the appropriate bloodline criteria, specifically exempted "old cadres" and "old revolutionaries" (lao ganbu, lao gemingpai) from scrutiny, and imposed "proletarian dictatorship" on the politically and socially incorrect.

I personally witnessed many violent incidents during the first two years of the Cultural Revolution, including "struggle meetings" where senior CCP officials were manhandled and abused and factional siege warfare that resulted in deaths and serious injuries. But the earliest outbreaks of political violence that I recall were perpetrated by elite Red Guard groups and United Action members especially, and the victims were not party officials or high-ranking professional-technical types.

Instead, in a pattern characteristic of "conservative" Red Guard behavior through-out China from August to December 1966, United Action and other elite Red Guard groups concentrated their fire on "smashing the four olds" *(po si jiu)* and mounted violent attacks on politically and socially incorrect groups. At Peking University Middle School, this assault took many forms, ranging from the brow-beating and bullying of classmates of "impure" class origin, to violent "struggle meetings" conducted against low-ranking, "bourgeois" teachers, to the systematic capture, imprisonment, and torture of "hoodlums" from the Xidan District.[21]

The United Action ascendancy, which itself proved short-lived, underscored a pattern of more enduring significance. If elite Red Guard groups were the first to violently defend their privileged position under the guise of upholding proletar-ian dictatorship, it was the leaders of the embattled party organization who sup-ported and promoted such tactics. Thus, Zhao Ziyang, a leading reformer in the late 1970s and 1980s, as first party secretary of Guangdong Province in 1966 "con-gratulated the Red Guards in late August for vandalizing the homes of the bour-geoisie."[22] Similarly, when United Action formations arrived in Changsha and engaged in "search raids" and intellectual bashing, the local party organization praised as "revolutionary heroism" their attack on the four olds.[23]

But party leaders were not simply passive supporters of conservative Red Guard action. In the provinces especially, many CCP cadres, themselves veteran practi-tioners of class warfare and mass mobilization, quickly put these skills to use in their own defense, and deployed a variety of sophisticated survival strategies. In Parris H. Chang's words, "The incumbent provincial power-holders did not wait for their political demise with folded arms. On the contrary, many of them used all the leverage provided by their positions and resorted to various ingenious de-vices for self-preservation."[24] Most important, leaders of the embattled party or-ganization sponsored conservative or "royalist" *(baohuang pai)* mass organiza-tions, which actively contested the Maoist assault. These organizations, made up of politically correct five red category students or more privileged workers, en-gaged in violent confrontations with militant, antiestablishment Red Guard groups composed of politically less favored or underprivileged social strata, a process that foreshadowed the ferocious factionalism that soon enveloped all Chi-nese institutions.[25] The Sixteen Points had specifically prohibited such behavior and warned against "inciting masses to struggle against masses, students to strug-gle against students" *(tiaodong qunzhong dou qunzhong, xuesheng dou xuesheng)*. But the notion of mobilizing "masses" against power holders was vitiated from the start by the party organization's successful appeal for support from more privi-leged political, social, and economic groups.

In October 1966, Mao attempted to counter the conservative Red Guard ascen-dancy with a series of proclamations. The central media announced for the first time that the main target of the Cultural Revolution was the "bourgeois reac-tionary line" of power holders in the party taking the capitalist road. On October 5, a central directive explicitly challenged the "structural legitimacy" of the CCP by decreeing that adherence to Mao Zedong Thought was the sole criterion for participation in the Cultural Revolution.[26] These proclamations weakened the hand of embattled party leaders, demolished their supporters' claims of natural redness and political correctness, and legitimated attacks on the CCP from all comers, provided the appropriate Maoist slogans were invoked.

For the politically incorrect groups that had borne the brunt of work team harassment and conservative Red Guard terror, these directives represented vindication. At the same time, the lifting of controls galvanized underprivileged social and economic groups into action and allowed "people who disliked their labels or their bosses" to rise up to change both.[27] In a stunning reversal of fortune that occurred in all institutions involved in the Cultural Revolution, hitherto politically and socially impure students at Peking University Middle School formed their own Red Guard groups and, as righteous defenders of Mao Zedong Thought, turned on their tormentors, who suddenly stood condemned from above as defenders of a black line. In Peking municipality, the Red Guard Third Headquarters was formed, which immediately outstripped in prestige and activism the First and Second Headquarters, staffed by the children of high-ranking cadres and now tainted by their support of the "bourgeois reactionary line."[28] In the factories of the capital, underprivileged contract and temporary workers united with the burgeoning rebel movement to attack factory party committees and became involved in conflicts with other groups of workers, generally those with permanent jobs, higher wages, and more extensive social welfare benefits.[29] As the persecuted and the disadvantaged turned on the persecutors and the more advantageously situated, the newly activated "revolutionary rebels" spearheaded an assault on party authority that by December would culminate in the denunciation and purge of hundreds of top political leaders, the virtual collapse of formal government in Peking, and the suspension of normal CCP functions nationwide.

Yet the leaders of the battered party organization still managed to contest the rebel onslaught by employing yet another ingenious survival strategy, that of "economism." Coopting the Maoist policy of spreading the radical message to the provinces by providing Red Guards with free transportation and travel expenses, CCP leaders in many large industrial centers supplied funds to workers in their jurisdiction, who thereupon went to Peking by the hundreds of thousands to demand improvement in wages and conditions.[30] In addition to undermining the Maoist appeal to underprivileged workers, economist tactics induced massive transportation bottlenecks nationwide and virtual economic paralysis in the cities, thereby blunting the rebel assault. Indeed, this attempt to win political support at the mass level with material concessions was successful and finally goaded Mao into a fateful broadening of the power deconcentration process.

The determined and sophisticated countermobilization of the party organization presaged the intractable dilemmas on which Maoist power restructuring would founder in the coming months. However complex the challenge of making the CCP itself the object of revolution, the eruption of political conflict and social tensions underscored the perils of deconcentrating a system of concentrated power. As in the Hundred Flowers episode, power deconcentration in fall 1966 undercut established mechanisms of control in Chinese society and precipitated an apparent sociopolitical free-for-all. If underprivileged groups were thereby allowed unprecedented freedoms, so, too, were opportunities afforded to the opponents of communist rule and to CCP leaders seeking to preserve their power as well. Yet Mao's intention in launching the Cultural Revolution was the revitalization of the Chinese Communist system, not its destruction or civil war. How was the party to be revitalized and the resistance of officialdom overcome while at the same time communist rule and the socialist enterprise were strengthened? In late 1966 and early 1967, Mao, his associates in the Central Cultural Revolution Group (CCRG), and Maoist allies at the top of the military establishment attempted to resolve these dilemmas by further extending the deconcentration of political power, intensifying Maoist personal rulership, and engaging the People's Liberation Army in the Cultural Revolution.

## Power Seizures and Mass Movements

The "January Power Seizure" *(Yiyue duoquan)* was an astounding and bewildering political spectacle. On January 4, 1967, radical mass organizations supported by Maoist leaders at the top overthrew the party committee and municipal government in Shanghai. In the following weeks, mass "power seizures" *(duoquan)* were attempted throughout China. Even if we allow for the rhetorical bombast of the day, the *People's Daily* editorial of January 22, 1967, "Proletarian Revolutionaries, Form a Great Alliance to Seize Power from Power-Holders Taking the Capitalist Road," was not far wrong when it proclaimed, "This is an extremely great pioneering undertaking in the international communist movement, an event without precedent in mankind's history."[31] As Lee observed, "In this period a so-called totalitarian regime governing a quarter of the world's population ordered its people to seize power from itself," an act that ranks as "the most daring undertaking Mao had ever attempted, whether or not he intended to let power remain in the hands of the masses."[32]

This radical call to arms sought to overcome the party organization's countermobilization by drastically extending Mao's long-standing belief that power deconcentration and the fomenting of mass movements were effective means of revitalizing the CCP. Frustrated by the "strong, unprecedented resistance of the class enemy" and the "new large-scale counter-attacks by the bourgeois reactionary line and a flood of counter-revolutionary economism," Maoist publicists deployed some truly incendiary rhetoric in January 1967.[33] Because "the revolution suffered these setbacks for no other reason than that they did not seize in their own hands the seals of power," the populace was now exhorted to "Seize power! Seize Power! All the party power, political power, and financial power held by the counter-revolutionary revisionists must be recaptured!"[34] Perhaps, as subsequent events suggest, mass power seizures were viewed by Maoists at the top in tactical, rather than strategic, terms. Yet as the deconcentration of political power was broadened and radical new visions of power relations and political process in socialist society were put forward, power seizure rhetoric was taken seriously and acted on by millions of newly activated Cultural Revolution participants.

January Power Seizure radicalism was most emphatically articulated in the CCRG pamphlet "The Dictatorship of the Proletariat and the Great Proletarian Cultural Revolution."[35] Ridiculing the "revisionist" notion of "socialist-society-without-contradictions," Wang Li et al. put forward the familiar Stalinist, and now Maoist, argument that classes continue to exist and class struggles continue unabated in socialist society. In the intense class struggles of the Cultural Revolution, victory could be ensured only through the creation of new forms of power and new methods of control with a strong participatory content. Precisely such a Paris Commune–style redistribution of power was now unfolding, whereby "the masses have the right to criticize and raise suggestions about party and state policies and every aspect of the state apparatus. The masses have the right to criticize leading cadres at all levels no matter how meritorious their service, how high their position, or how senior their qualifications. . . . The masses have the power to replace through election or recall any elected member at any time."

Contrary to Walder's assertion that Cultural Revolution radicalism was "firmly grounded in the sadly familiar political mentality" of "Stalinist reactive extremism," the suspension of political and police controls and mass power seizures would have been unthinkable in the emerging Stalin system and were never remotely approximated in the Soviet 1930s.[36] In China, the idea of mass power seizure was taken seriously, acted on, and manifested in such forms as the Peking People's Commune, a "form of state power led by the working class" in which "the revolutionary masses may take part directly in the administration of the state" and officials "must be responsible to the people[;] otherwise the masses may remove them from office any time."[37]

However outlandish such notions as institutionalized popular supervision of officialdom and accountable government would appear in light of subsequent events, there can be no denying the powerful impact of these ideas in January and February 1967. With CCRG representatives also calling for training and bringing up a contingent of working-class intellectuals as new leaders, January Power Seizure rhetoric apparently entailed a radical restructuring of power in Chinese society, to be realized by the deconcentration of political power and sharply increased mass participation in basic decisionmaking processes. Variously moved by idealistic acceptance of the Maoist vision, political and personal grievances, hopes of alleviating the pressures of an unequal and often oppressive system, or the pursuit of opportunities and benefits in a chaotic and rapidly changing situation, tens of millions of urban Chinese became involved in power seizures in early 1967. In a massive cresting of the sociopolitical upwelling that had been building for months, thousands of mass organizations literally "seized the seals of power" from the leaders of the party organization.

In the words of one prominent rebel proclamation, "The greatest fact of the storm of the January revolution was that 90 percent of the senior cadres were made to stand aside."[38] In fact, the January Power Seizure marked the high tide of the radical assault on the power and authority of the party organization. As contending mass organizations attempted power seizures and were countered by conservative organizations in various guises, governmental, educational, technical-scientific, and manufacturing and commercial institutions throughout China were enveloped in political turmoil and virtual civil war; the state apparatus succumbed to almost total paralysis; and existing control structures broke down. With practically all senior leaders in the capital and in the provinces under attack and threatened with political extinction, normal administrative functions were suspended or ground to a halt. While many cadres were arrested by rebel organizations and "struggled against," others abandoned their posts and took refuge with relatives and allies; at the same time, regular party meetings, dues collections, and the induction of new members ceased altogether.[39] As a measure of the "devastating impact of the Cultural Revolution on formal authority," Lee calculated that between 73 and 77 percent of such top party and government leaders as CCP Central Committee members, ministers and vice ministers, and provincial party secretaries were purged in 1967–1969.[40]

Underprivileged social and occupational groups with ample grievances against the status quo were especially active during the January Power Seizure. The "contract worker" *(hetong gong)* movement in Peking was symptomatic of the "sudden surfacing of various social groupings during the Cultural Revolution."[41] Denied the social welfare benefits, decent wages, and security of employment enjoyed by permanent workers in state factories, these downtrodden people were quick to blame their plight on "capitalist roaders." I attended contract worker rallies in Peking in December 1966 and January 1967 and was struck by the wrathful rhetoric and palpable hatred of CCP officialdom that permeated these meetings. In a pattern closely paralleling the Hundred Flowers episode, contract worker rhetoric soon moved beyond criticism of capitalist roaders to an indictment of the previous seventeen years and communism per se. And in a familiar sign of things to come, the contract workers' organization was one of the first mass organizations to be labeled "counterrevolutionary."[42]

## The Role of the PLA

As chaos, breakdown, and conflict spiraled out of control in January and February, Mao called on the PLA to intervene in support of mass power seizures. With its hallowed history of sacrifice, service, and struggle against the people's enemies, the PLA occupied a position of unassailable revolutionary legitimacy; its intervention on behalf of the rebels appeared to sound the death knell of the party organization's countermobilization. In the early 1970s, Western commentators concluded that "it was the use of military forces that finally brought down the recalcitrant, well-entrenched provincial party leaders," as "the generals almost everywhere forced the provincial party leaders to resign and made themselves heads of the provisional governing bodies."[43] In retrospect, it is evident that PLA intervention was a decisive turning point in the Cultural Revolution insofar as it marked the end of radical power deconcentration and the beginning of a shift for the better in the fortunes of the beleaguered party organization.

In Lee's view, the role of the army was obscured in 1967 and for some time thereafter by "its rhetorical commitment to revolution" versus the reality of "its conservative institutional interests."[44] In fact, the army was fragmented into different political and regional alignments and was never a reliable instrument for the implementation of radical power-restructuring policies. Even at the height of the January Power Seizure, however, the rhetoric emanating from the PLA differed markedly from that of "revolutionary rebel" radicalism. While editorializing "The People's Liberation Army Firmly Backs the Proletarian Revolutionaries" on January 25, the PLA newspaper argued that the army as "the mainstay of the dictatorship of the proletariat" necessarily had to "become the bulwark of defending the Great Proletarian Cultural Revolution."[45] By mid-February 1967, a conservative backlash was under way, spearheaded by the military in coalition with remnants of the battered party organization and conservative mass organizations. This backlash, subsequently termed by CCRG radicals the "February Adverse Current," was manifested in numerous, if not all, central proclamations and directives.

Initially somewhat ambivalent and uncertain, the conservative shift rapidly gained momentum and became increasingly assertive. In a paradoxical and no doubt confusing reformulation, *Red Flag* commentators thus sought to combine radical Paris Commune imagery with a newfound emphasis on the virtues of order, discipline, and respect for the authority of the CCP. While noting in passing that "the Marxist principle of smashing the state machinery must be put into practice in the struggle for the seizure of power," the article "On the Proletarian Revolutionaries' Struggle to Seize Power" first cautioned readers that "to regard all persons in authority as untrustworthy is wrong" and warned against "departmentalism, small-group mentality, excessive decentralization, the disregard of organizational discipline, liberalism, subjectivism, and individualism."[46] Similarly, the more suggestively titled article "On Revolutionary Discipline and Proletarian Revolutionary Authority" noted that "we must bear in mind the lesson that the Paris Commune made too little use of its authority" and concluded with the conventionally Leninist injunction, "Without authority there will be no organized revolutionary action, let alone victory in the revolution."[47] But the mounting conservative backlash was most unequivocally put forward in the pivotal article "Cadres Must Be Treated Correctly."

Advancing the slogan "Cure the sickness to save the patient" *(zhibing jiuren)*, the article's commentators declared, "It must also be recognized with open eyes that most cadres are good, and that the alien class elements who have wormed their way into the ranks of the cadres are very few. Most of the cadres who have made mistakes, even serious mistakes, can make amends under the education of the party and the masses." Explicitly contradicting the capitalist roader rhetoric and imagery with which CCP officialdom had been battered for months, the article praised the special qualities of "revolutionary leading cadres," who were "more politically mature," "more experienced in struggle," "more organizationally skilled," and thus better able to "exercise power and administer work for the state of proletariat." In contrast, although veteran cadres were not to make light of them, "of course the young revolutionary fighters have shortcomings and mistakes. They lack experience in struggle, are not yet mature politically, and at crucial turning points in the course of the revolution, they frequently cannot see the direction clearly." These defects, the article concluded, "all stem from a bourgeois world outlook. Young revolutionary fighters, too, must seriously remold their world outlook."[48] By February 1967, then, the fortunes of the revolutionary rebels had been abruptly reversed, as central directives decreed that it was the heroic pathbreakers who now needed to reform themselves.

The erosion of rebel power was formalized in March when central commentators declared that the January Power Seizure had produced a new power structure, the "revolutionary committee" *(geming weiyuanhui)*. This "revolutionary 'three-in-one' provisional organ of power" was to be made up in equal parts of representatives of mass organizations, the PLA, and the party organization.[49] In Lowell Dittmer's view, two competing organizational models emerged out of the January Power Seizure—the Paris Commune and the revolutionary committee.[50] In fact, this competition took place on a sharply skewed playing field, with the organizational clout, armed might, and unassailable legitimacy of the PLA unambiguously backing the revolutionary committee concept and the shift in cadre policy it represented. By February and March 1967, military representatives occupied dominant positions at all institutional levels, thereby "robbing the Cultural Revolution Left of the fruits of its victory."[51]

While paying lip-service to shaky notions of mass political participation, central directives in February and March stressed the authoritative role of the PLA and its "glorious revolutionary traditions." In the hands of military commentators, Maoist slogans such as "The masses are the real heroes" were drastically reformulated. Thus,

> we must help the genuine revolutionary mass organizations develop and expand quickly, help them with their self-education, step up their revolutionization, destroy the concept of self-interest, foster devotion to the public interest, and thus promote the great alliance of various revolutionary organizations on the basis of a common general orientation. We must guide them to a correct understanding and implementation of the cadres policy formulated by Chairman Mao.[52]

While the PLA intervened in and interpreted the power seizure process, would-be opponents were warned of the consequences of such actions. Hence, "the attitude

towards the People's Liberation Army is in fact an attitude towards the dictatorship of the proletariat and it is an important criterion for distinguishing whether
or not one is of the genuine revolutionary Left."[53]

## Civil War and the Defeat of
## Revolutionary Rebellion

Yet the sociopolitical upheaval set in motion in the preceding months was not so
readily reined in. The radical mass organizations that had come into existence in
late 1966 and early 1967 were numerically large, in possession of significant financial resources and some military equipment, and loaded with political momentum. Equally important, radical mass organizations were backed by the CCRG
and, intermittently, by Mao himself. The result was a stand-off from February
until summer 1967 that pitted the still highly charged rebel groups and their backers at the top against a formidable but as-yet-unconsolidated law and order coalition that included most elements of the PLA, conservative mass organizations, the
battered remnants of the party organization at the local and provincial levels, and
a few top leaders who had managed to weather the "January Storm," notably Premier Zhou Enlai.

The final offensive of the radical mass organizations and their backers in the
CCRG was launched on May 18, 1967, with the publication in *People's Daily* and
*Red Flag* of the well-known but previously restricted May 16, 1966, Central Committee "Notice" on the Cultural Revolution. By publicizing and promoting anew
the directive that a year earlier had signaled the attack on "a large group of anti-
party, anti-socialist bourgeois representatives" at all levels of the party and state
apparatus, the "Left" sought to reignite the attack on officialdom and to rekindle
the radical power-restructuring drive of the preceding year.

But Cultural Revolution radicalism was in difficult straits by late spring and
early summer 1967. Faced with a formidable military presence that in most cases
explicitly or indirectly favored the party organization, radical mass organizations
were also engaged in intense factional conflict with determined royalist opposition. In the universities, middle schools, and research institutes of Peking, the factional conflict that I witnessed during this time took the form of "loudspeaker
wars" in which the contending parties attempted to drown each other out with
constant barrages of broadcast rhetoric and invective. The din would be periodically punctuated by armed forays into the opposition's territory, which often resulted in bloodshed and the taking of prisoners or ended inconclusively. A similar
pattern prevailed in the provinces, usually more violent but no less inconclusive
and debilitating. As a letter writer from Sichuan Province complained in June
1967, "In the *xian* (district) town of Mapian which has only two streets and a population of about 6,000, there are two broadcasting stations, one belonging to the
party *xian* organization and the other to the revolutionary mass organization. The
loudspeakers of these two broadcasting stations are installed opposite to each

other in the same street, so that their sound waves interfere with each other and the effect of propaganda is reduced."[54] Meanwhile, radical mass organizations, conservative forces, and the PLA were involved in power seizures, counter–power seizures, armed clashes, and violent struggle meetings throughout the provinces.[55]

In summer 1967, elements of the CCRG in association with some radical mass organizations attempted power seizures in institutional spheres untouched thus far, namely, the military establishment and Premier Zhou's Foreign Ministry. Viewed from a January Power Seizure perspective, this development was both logical and inevitable. As the Hunan shengwulian (Hunan Province Proletarian Alliance) radicals asserted, if "90 percent of the senior cadres were forced to stand aside" in January 1967, "the January storm has not touched in any way the vital problem of all revolutions—the problem of the army."[56] Thus, "the unanimity of the interests of the capitalist roaders in the army and those of the local capitalist roaders prevents the army from carrying out Chairman Mao's revolutionary line. . . . Some of the armed forces in the revolution have not only changed their blood-and-flesh relations with the people that obtained before liberation, but have even become tools for suppressing revolution."[57] Predictably, attempts to seize power from "power holders in the army taking the capitalist road" (junnei zou zibenzhuyi daolu de dangquanpai) precipitated a fateful collision between the military establishment and Cultural Revolution mass radicalism that ended in the conclusive defeat of the latter.

The mounting tension between the PLA and the Left came to a head in a region where the authority of Peking was relatively weak and the power of local leaders correspondingly strong, the sprawling Wuhan industrial and commercial complex in south-central China. Garrison commanders in the Wuhan Military Region were especially active and open in their support of royalist forces, and in mid-July CCRG representatives went to Wuhan and attempted to intervene on behalf of the radical side. When representatives Wang Li and Xie Fuzhi arrived on the scene and rendered a verdict in favor of the suppressed rebel organization, they were kidnapped by the conservative mass organization Baiwan xiongshi (One Million Heroic Troops) with the acquiescence of the local PLA commander, Chen Caidao, and were freed only when an airborne division and naval vessels were dispatched from Peking.[58]

Lee noted that the "Wuhan Incident" was more than a mutiny by local military commanders and should be understood as a calculated confrontation in which the military establishment sought to demonstrate its strength and challenge that of the CCRG.[59] In late July and August 1967, CCRG-sponsored mass radicalism and PLA-sponsored law and order collided violently in the capital and throughout the provinces. On July 22, Jiang Qing responded to events in Wuhan by putting forward the inflammatory slogan "Attack with words and defend with weapons" (wengong wuwei). On July 31 a People's Daily editorial hailed the historically progressive role of armed mass insurrection and called for "dragging out the handful of capitalist roaders in the army."[60] In the wake of the Wuhan Incident, this provocative renewal of January Power Seizure rhetoric triggered what the Hunan shengwulian radicals would term "the local domestic revolutionary war of August," when "gun-seizing became a movement," "for a short time the cities were in a state of 'armed mass dictatorship,'" and "a short-lived and unstable redistribution of 'assets and powers' took place for a second time."[61] As some CCRG leaders denounced the "collaboration of leaders of local armed forces with local capitalist roaders" and proclaimed, "It is necessary to mobilize hundreds of millions of people to drag them out and topple them," radical mass organizations attempted to seize power from army units.[62] In August 1967, violent factional conflict escalated sharply, lethal weaponry was brought to bear, a virtual civil war erupted in many provinces, and thousands of people were killed or wounded in the carnage.

But this was a civil war between very unequally matched adversaries. Indeed, as in January and February 1967, the outcome of the collision between the forces of mass radicalism and the forces of law and order in August was a forgone conclusion. The disparity between CCRG power seizure rhetoric and the vastly superior power position of the military was clearly revealed in the radical call to arms itself, "The Proletariat Must Take Firm Hold of the Gun." Even as it called for "dragging out the handful in the army," this editorial glorified the "revolutionary heritage of the people's army," appealed to the PLA for political support, promised complete forgiveness for past transgressions, and spoke yearningly of "the unity of the army and the masses."[63]

Of course, these appeals were unsuccessful. As Jurgen Domes observed, the Wuhan Incident demonstrated that "the Centre could no longer completely rely on the loyalty of the regional commanders if it was not prepared to make concessions to their growing concern about the need for a return to law and order."[64] In a definitive move that marked the end of the Maoist attempt to effect systemic revitalization by the deconcentration of political power and the fomenting of mass movements, a central directive on September 5, 1967, ruled in unequivocal favor of the army and law and order. Bearing Mao's personal imprimatur, the directive termed the PLA a "peerless people's army" and the "pillar of the dictatorship of the proletariat," warned against attempts to "weaken or lower the PLA's fighting strength and prestige," and prohibited mass organizations from seizing any materials whatsoever from PLA units.[65] Although the armed forces were ordered to dissuade and to reason with potential offenders, people attempting seizures would be guilty of counterrevolution and dealt with accordingly.

As the accusations leveled against Wang Li et al. in the purge of the CCRG that followed the September 5 directive made clear, the radical attempt to undermine the position of the PLA and "split our Great Wall" threatened the very foundations of Chinese Communist power.[66] Mao, mindful of his own maxim "Political power grows out of the barrel of a gun," was unwilling to sanction power seizures against a military establishment that in any case occupied the high ground. Even though factional conflict in the schools, violent clashes between the PLA and radical mass organizations, and all-out warfare between contending factions in some provinces continued into summer 1969, the events of August and September 1967 underscored the fundamental shift in power-restructuring tactics at the top. With the dangers and uncertainties of radical power deconcentration so clearly manifested, January Power Seizure rhetoric was definitively superseded by a language of power concentration, militarized social control, and personal rulership. As revolutionary rebels were suppressed and "disciplined" in late 1967 and over the next few years and the mass radicalism of 1966–1967 subsided, power contests among contending elites at the top and in the provinces moved to the fore. Frustrated by the outcome of the radical power-restructuring initiatives, Mao in the years remaining to him would attempt to deploy power-restructuring methods of a different and more familiar type.

## The Extent of Maoist Dictatorship

If the notion of Maoist revolutionary-feudal totalitarianism has any historical relevance, it is in the years 1968–1970, when Maoist power restructuring assumed a harshly dictatorial and overtly militaristic form. As enunciated by the chairman's anointed successor, Marshal Lin Biao, the Cultural Revolution was "a great political revolution personally initiated and led by our great leader Chairman Mao" that aimed "to smash revisionism, seize back that portion of power usurped by the bourgeoisie, exercise all-round dictatorship of the proletariat in the superstructure, including all spheres of culture, and strengthen and consolidate the economic base of socialism."[67] This program was to be realized by unremitting struggle against "revisionism" and "bourgeois restoration" *(zibenzhuyi fubi)*; reliance on Mao Zedong Thought and the PLA, that "mighty pillar of the dictatorship of the proletariat"; and revitalization of the party through the "absorbing [of] fresh blood."[68] In the late 1960s, personal rulership and military power were the means by which radicals at the top sought to revive the Maoist power-restructuring agenda.

Mao's September 5 directive initiated de facto military rule in the schools, factories, and government institutions disrupted by the upheavals of the previous year and a half. In January 1968, a *Liberation Army Newspaper* editorial clearly and uncompromisingly set forth the role of the army: As a "highly proletarianized and militant people's army" and "the most important mainstay of the great proletarian cultural revolution," it was the PLA's responsibility to "promote the formation of the revolutionary great alliance between the two revolutionary groups" and prevent "renegades," "special agents," "the handful of diehard capitalist roaders in the Party and other class enemies in society" from stirring up and using "reactionary bourgeois and petty bourgeois factionalism to incite discord and sow dissension among the revolutionaries in order to split their ranks."[69] By decreeing that all political competition would henceforth be viewed as "bourgeois factionalism" *(zibenzhuyi paixing)*, the army served notice on would-be challengers to the new order. As Lee noted, the PLA strategy was one of verbally supporting the Cultural Revolution while methodically and ruthlessly suppressing rebel organizations.[70]

With the hold of the PLA tightened and legitimated, Maoist personal rulership was reinforced. Just as the chairman had used his personal authority and charisma to unleash the upheavals of 1966–1967, the disciplinary campaigns of 1968–1970 were marked by an intensified Mao personality cult. Of course, deification of Mao had been a defining feature of the Cultural Revolution from the start; from 1968 onward, however, Cultural Revolution radicalism was eclipsed by an all-pervasive Mao cult. In a massive expansion of processes already in motion, Mao's works and "quotations" *(Maozhuxi yulu)* were printed by the hundreds of millions, Mao statues and portraits became ubiquitous in public and private, people high and low dared air their views only when prefaced by an appropriate Mao quote, and "Chairman Mao's supreme instructions" *(Maozhuxi de zuigao zhishi)* were construed as absolute truth in matters great and small. These Olympian pronouncements, issued from on high and studied by millions of people, were sweeping and all encompassing.[71]

The flavor of Maoist dictatorship and its characteristic mix of personalism and militarism are fully conveyed in the famous July 28, 1968, "Dialogue" *(tanhua)* between Mao and "responsible persons" of the violently feuding Peking Red Guard movement. Indeed, this dialogue was no such thing. Rather, Mao held forth at length, reprimanded the Red Guard leaders for their factional fighting, insisted on the absolute primacy of political unity, meditated aloud on the complexities of the situation and the vagaries of history, and offered a stream of sympathy, verdicts, and threats, all the while echoed by an approving chorus from Lin Biao, Zhou Enlai, various CCRG leaders, PLA generals, and police chiefs. More than anything, the encounter resembled an imperial audience, with the Red Guard leaders cast in the role of misguided but obedient subjects being chastised for their shortcomings and instructed on proper future conduct. Lest any doubts remain regarding Mao's determination to put an end to the political turmoil in the capital and in the provinces, he finally decreed, "Now, a nation-wide public notice is again issued. If anyone still continues to defy or attack the PLA, destroy means of transportation, kill people, or set fires, this is committing a crime. Those few who won't listen to persuasion and continue unreformed, are bandits or KMT elements and will be encircled. If they continue to resist, annihilation *(xiaomie)* will be carried out."[72]

Mao's violent language and class enemy imagery underscored the coercive measures that the central rulers used to stabilize the situation in 1968–1970. In these years, PLA power was uncompromisingly deployed throughout China, campaigns against "May 16 elements" and "class ranks" in need of "purification" were launched, and militant Red Guard groups and radical mass organizations were "disciplined," disbanded, and smashed. Social and political order was forcefully reimposed, with the outright suppression of radical groups by military power, the extraction of "confessions" by force, the supposedly voluntary "rustication" *(xiafang)* of urban youth, and the occupation of the Peking school system by "Mao

Zedong Thought Propaganda Teams" comprising workers from politically reliable factories.[73] Students who had been members of "oppose the army" radical factions were singled out for especially harsh treatment by the PLA; as May 16 elements their confessions were extracted by torture, they were exiled to the most backward rural areas, and they were driven to suicide in large numbers.[74] While some sixty thousand to seventy thousand Red Guard leaders were taken to military camps and farms run by the army, millions of demobilized youths were effectively deported to the countryside, there to learn "revolutionary discipline" from the peasants and to settle for the rest of their lives.[75] Sheer physical repression was paralleled by efforts to provide an ideological rationale for the new course. In CCRG ideologue Yao Wenyuan's words, "Throughout the entire process, the great proletarian cultural revolution has been under the sole leadership of one class only, the working class. . . . The proletarian headquarters headed by Chairman Mao represents in a concentrated way the interests of the working class, the poor and lower-middle peasants, and the masses of laboring people."[76]

Maoist dictatorship, with its ruthless deployment of militarized autocracy, may have resembled revolutionary-feudal totalitarianism in intent. Under central rulers who sought to revitalize the structure of power by absorbing fresh blood from the proletariat, while elevating Mao to godlike stature and imposing all-encompassing ideological and social controls, an apparently "total" system emerged in the late 1960s and seemingly replicated both traditional Chinese imperial autocracy and Stalinist despotism. But this totalitarian facade masked the profound political and structural changes that were taking place at the regional, provincial, and local levels at this time. The Maoist dictatorship was contested, undercut, and vitiated from the outset by power contests, policy disputes, and a fundamental erosion of central power.

## Power Contests and Policy Disputes During Military Domination

However harsh and apparently formidable, the system of personal rulership and military rule that took shape in the late 1960s was unstable and, in the end, ineffective. Beset by political conflicts and factional cleavages throughout the chain of command, radical leaders at the top were unable to enforce their policy preferences at the regional, provincial, and local levels. This was especially true in the economic realm, where in the course of the authority crisis and administrative breakdown of late 1966 and 1967 a massive decentralization of economic decisionmaking power had occurred. Even as controls at the mass level were being reimposed, party and state leaders who had been purged in 1966–1967 were mounting a political comeback and attempting to "reverse the verdict" (fanan). With a foothold already in the revolutionary committees being set up nationwide, veteran officials were aided in their quest for restoration and vindication by political cleavages and policy disputes in the PLA and by the unsettled relationship between the central military establishment and its putative "supreme commander."

A characteristically authoritarian bent and commitment to institutional interests notwithstanding, the PLA in the late 1960s was divided by political, regional, and personal cleavages. In fact, the Chinese Communist military establishment had been divided into different "loyalty groups" ever since the late 1940s.[77] But the divided loyalties of the military were increased in the course of the mass upheavals of 1967 and the subsequent involvement of PLA commanders in daily administration. When the PLA moved to fill the power vacuum left by the suspension of normal CCP functions, military leaders at the regional, provincial, and local levels found themselves unencumbered by the usual constraints of party supervision and civilian control. Although this "militarization and regionalization" of power amounted to a "de facto military seizure of power in the majority of China's provinces," the PLA itself was split by policy disputes that pitted elements of the central military apparatus under Lin Biao against an array of virtually autonomous regional military commanders.[78]

At issue was the perennial contest between authority–social mobilization and market–material incentive developmental and organizational approaches. In 1968, and especially after the formal designation of Marshal Lin Biao as Mao's successor at the Ninth Party Congress in April 1969, radical military and civilian leaders at the top attempted to revive the policies of the Great Leap Forward in the countryside.[79] As Dazhai, a village in arid and poverty-stricken northwest China, was being held up as a national model, the central leadership was launching a series of authority–social mobilization campaigns that sought to combine political and ideological ferment, appeals for sacrifice, class struggle, and self-reliance with increased production and grain deliveries to the state. Among the familiar features of the "In Agriculture, Learn from Dazhai" *(Nongye xue Dazhai)* campaign were the attempted imposition of higher levels of collective economic organization; restrictions on private plot cultivation and sideline activities; reliance on ideological exhortation, rather than material incentives, as motivating mechanisms; and an overall contempt for private property and individual profit.[80]

The Dazhai campaign encountered widespread peasant resistance, both overt and passive, and never took root in most villages. In Guangdong Province, hardly an area of CCP strength in any case, central directives to emulate Dazhai were received without enthusiasm, implemented hesitantly and with little success, and reversed as soon as possible.[81] In Hinton's more politically responsive Long Bow village, situated in the historical CCP base areas of Shanxi Province, attempts to imitate Dazhai cultivation techniques and organizational forms proved difficult and ultimately impractical.[82] Nor was the problem simply one of adapting Dazhai methods to areas that differed in climate, topography, and tradition; rather, peasants resented and resisted the coercive thrust of the Dazhai campaign.

Moreover, if peasants were unable to effectively resist extractive central policies in the 1950s and early 1960s, the structure of power that had previously enforced resource transfers at the expense of the countryside was significantly eroded by the events of the Cultural Revolution. On the one hand, as Jean C. Oi observed, the "factionalism" and the "uncertainty" of the Cultural Revolution undercut effective policy implementation at the local level. Thus, even though many directives were issued from on high and team leaders had numerous reports to fill out, "few cadres were sent to see that the policies were implemented. . . . Consequently, team leaders were sometimes left with more autonomy than the pile of directives would indicate."[83]

Equally important, the peasantry now found allies in the newly regionalized structure of power. As PLA commanders suddenly found themselves charged with popular welfare and economic stability in the areas under their control, they no longer so readily spoke in their usual capacity as enforcers of central policy. Hence, whereas "the central military apparat around Lin Biao wanted to enforce a return to Mao's political ideas of 1958 and to a concept of development through mobilization campaigns," "the majority of regional military commanders saw the role of the armed forces as being particularly one of safeguarding law and order, and furthering pragmatic growth and consumption-oriented concepts."[84]

At the same time, the leaders of the civilian apparatus mounted a political comeback and energetically contested the radical attempt to implement authority–social mobilization policies. As David Zweig detailed, a major debate on agricultural policy got under way in summer and fall 1970 as numerous press articles attacked the attempt to impose higher levels of collectivization and stressed the importance of cash crops; in October "Xu Shiyou, head of the Nanking Military Region and a conservative Politburo member, sharply attacked leftist agricultural policies."[85] In March 1971, *People's Daily* ran a series of articles praising production teams, private plot cultivation, private livestock raising, and sideline production and pointing to the very different conditions that prevailed from place to place.[86] By 1970, and increasingly in 1971, radical power-restructuring initiatives encountered the potent opposition of a coalition of regional military commanders and veteran party and state officials with a shared commitment to stabilization, normalization, and market–material incentive developmental and organizational approaches.

This moderate coalition was the primary victor in yet another power contest played out in 1971—the eternal struggle between the aging ruler and his designated successor, in this instance a power-hungry general. As the official indictment of Lin Biao after his demise in fall 1971 made clear, the supposed coup against Mao was driven by power politics rather than policy differences. It was thus dissatisfaction with Mao's personal rulership and a desire to "establish another mountaintop," rather than substantive differences regarding the efficacy of authority–social mobilization methods, that set Lin and his associates on a collision course with the chairman.[87] Even though Mao sought to depict the conflict as the latest of "ten major struggles in the Party concerning line," it was Lin's refusal to obey central commands, his "arrogance," and his assumption of "the style of the warlord" that were finally singled out as the cardinal offenses.[88] Yet Mao was able to deflect Lin's warlord challenge only by accommodating the moderate coalition's demands for a muting of authority–social mobilization tactics and a further decentralization of power.[89]

The political effects of Lin's fall were wide-ranging. In the countryside, the anti-Lin campaign launched in early 1972 provided the opportunity to reject unpopular aspects of the Dazhai campaign and radical policies in general.[90] As the recent national guideline "In Industry, Learn from Daqing; in Agriculture, Learn from Dazhai; the Entire Nation Learns from the PLA" was displaced by the slogan "The PLA Learns from the Entire Nation," authority–social mobilization methods were manifestly downgraded in favor of policies more in accord with local conditions and requirements. Although Dazhai continued to be held up as a national model until Mao's death in 1976, the campaign from 1972 onward downplayed "politics in command" in favor of popular measures such as farmland capital construction, agricultural mechanization, and improvements in living standards.[91] At the same time, Lin's fall accelerated improvements in the political fortunes of the pre–Cultural Revolution political elite. In the years 1972–1974, large numbers of senior cadres who had been attacked and purged in the preceding years were formally rehabilitated and returned to office.[92] As always, this process occurred in a setting of ongoing power contests and policy disputes.

## The "Theory and Program" of Resurgent Officialdom

I have argued that the resistance and countermobilization of party and state officialdom against Maoist power restructuring were strong and remarkably effective from the outset of the Cultural Revolution. Even at the height of the radical onslaught in early and mid-1967, leaders of the embattled party organization were able to rely on the support or benevolent neutrality of most army units and to secure a foothold in the new structures of power being erected. In October 1968, radicals in Shanghai were already complaining that most revolutionary committees were afflicted by a "tendency to restore the old"; "in these units, the leading groups are composed entirely of former personnel, have not drawn in proletarian blood, and are not a revolutionary three-in-one combination. Even if in form they have absorbed revolutionary fresh blood, they have done everything they could to get rid of fresh blood."[93] Six months later, Mao himself noted the difficulty of dislodging the old guard at the local level and conceded, "Our foundation is not solid. In my observation, neither all, nor the absolute majority, but, I'm afraid, a considerable number of factories are not under the leadership of genuine Marxists and the masses of workers. . . . They have followed Liu Shaoqi's line by advocating material incentives and putting profit in command."[94]

In the course of the last-stand radical counteroffensive against resurgent officialdom in early 1976, a *People's Daily* editorial pronounced, "Their [resurgent officials] activities to reverse previous verdicts were well organized on the basis of a theory and a program."[95] In fact, this theory and program were already fully manifested in the policies pushed by the moderate coalition that successfully contested the authority–social mobilization campaigns of 1969–1971. With the demise of Lin Biao, this coalition moved into high gear. Three policies keyed the theory and program of resurgent officialdom: a return to the market–material incentive policies of the early 1960s, a regionalization and decentralization of political and economic power, and a restoration of veteran officials and a "purge of the purgers."

As Domes detailed, the "New Course" that emerged after the fall of 1971 featured familiar ideas and policies. Regional leaders were granted more autonomy in economic administration and planning; the powers of management at the enterprise level were strengthened; the principle of material incentives was revived; the production team was reinforced, and private plots, private livestock raising, and private sideline activities were guaranteed and encouraged; and remuneration of peasants and workers was organized in relation to productivity. Thus, "as during the first readjustment phase in the early 1960s, the New Course brought a change of political priorities in favor of growth-oriented principles."[96] In the detailed analysis and assessment of Hsu Tak-ming, "Even before 1971, the internal and external policies of the Chinese Communists had already been restored to 90 percent of the pre–Cultural Revolution situation."[97] This shift to more moderate, pragmatic, and flexible policies was headed up and personified by Premier Zhou, whose "Report" to the Tenth Party Congress in August 1973, while replete with quotations from the Marxist-Leninist–Mao Zedong Thought canon, repeatedly attacked Lin's advocacy of authority–social mobilization campaigns, exhorted party organizations to "pay close attention to questions of economic policy and concern themselves with the well-being of the masses," and noted, "Our country's industry, agriculture, transportation, finance and trade are doing well. We have neither external nor internal debts. Prices are stable and the market is flourishing."[98]

But the final confrontation between resurgent officialdom and its would-be successors, the "newborn things" *(xinsheng shiwu)* of the Cultural Revolution, was only beginning to come to a head. On the one hand, large numbers of veteran officials were returned to office in 1972–1973, a process that Mao both condoned and encouraged.[99] With Lin's demise, the rehabilitation of the pre–Cultural Revolution political elite accelerated, beginning with venerable Marshal Zhu De in January 1972, extending to the leaders of the Wuhan Incident in August 1972, and culminating with the reappointment of arch "capitalist roader" Deng Xiaoping to his former post as vice premier in March 1973.[100] On the other hand, radical forces at the top, with Mao's support, mounted a vigorous effort to appoint to office and promote large numbers of younger people who had been active in the Cultural Revolution. The tension between resurgent officialdom and the "revolutionary successor" *(geming jiebanren)* generation was fully evident at the Tenth Party Congress. While Premier Zhou stipulated that "all cadres, veteran and new alike, must maintain close ties with the masses, be modest and prudent, guard against arrogance and impetuosity, and go to any post as required by the Party and people," radical leader Wang Hongwen emphasized the "training of millions of successors for the cause of proletarian revolution in the course of mass movements," and asserted, "We must . . . lay stress on selecting outstanding persons from among the workers and poor and lower middle peasants and placing them in leading positions at all levels."[101]

The Politburo and the Central Committee elected at the Tenth Party Congress appeared to reflect a "delicate political balance," with both "a significant rise in party and government bureaucrats, including a number of leading figures purged during the Cultural Revolution," and the promotion of "radical-leftists, and for the first time, representatives of model workers and peasants."[102] In fact, an intense power contest was under way in which the forces of Cultural Revolution radicalism sought to restructure the party by recruiting large numbers of politically reliable people from lower-class and nonprivileged backgrounds and accelerating the promotion of younger officials and were fiercely resisted by veteran officials, especially at the provincial and local levels.[103] As in 1967, however, this was an unequal contest with a predictable outcome. Indeed, by 1973–1974 the disparity between radical power-restructuring efforts and the political realities of the situation was acute.

At the Tenth Party Congress, Wang Hongwen had publicly complained that "there are still a small number of cadres, especially some leading cadres, who will not tolerate differing views of the masses inside or outside the Party. They even suppress criticism and retaliate, and it is quite serious in some individual cases."[104] In his famous "Secret Speech" in January 1974, Wang painted a far bleaker picture of frustration and defeat at the hands of resurgent officialdom. Thus, "some comrades even today are no different than seven or eight years ago when they did not understand the Cultural Revolution, did not take it seriously, and did not work hard for it. Some are even confusing right and wrong, calling black white, and describing the Cultural Revolution as all black, likening it to a flood of beasts."[105] Moreover, "the directives of Mao and the Central Committee have been blocked by certain individuals, preventing them from being passed on to the masses. Sometimes the masses are given directives without being told which have been issued by Mao, which have been issued by the Central Committee, and which have been issued by the individuals themselves."[106] But the final indignity was the unfolding purge of the purgers. "In some localities, errant veteran cadres are watched and helped and allowed to atone for their wrong doings, but new cadres found to be delinquent are finished off with one blow. Why is it that errant veterans can be educated, while errant new cadres cannot be educated and are shot down? This is not fair! It is not helping Party unity!"[107]

## The Last Stand of Cultural Revolution Radicalism

In 1974–1975, resurgent officialdom accelerated the push to implement its theory and program, a process highlighted at the Fourth National People's Congress in January 1975, where Premier Zhou proclaimed the goal of accomplishing "the comprehensive modernization of agriculture, industry, national defence, and science and technology before the end of the century, so that our national economy will be advancing in the front ranks of the world."[108] As Domes detailed, "This goal was soon to be known as the 'Four Modernizations' *(sige xiandaihua)* and, as such, became the central slogan for anti-leftist policies," thereby setting the stage for Deng Xiaoping's attempt for "an all-out return to pre–Cultural Revolutionary policies" in spring 1975.[109] In the final years of the Cultural Revolution decade, radical leaders at the top and their remaining supporters at the mass level mounted a last stand to contest the ascendancy of resurgent officialdom.

With the suppression of the mass radicalism of 1966–1967, we have seen how the forces of Cultural Revolution radicalism were increasingly confronted by various formidable constellations of military and civilian power. Lacking the coercive and organizational resources of their opponents and significant bases of power at the local level in most cases, radical leaders sought to counter resurgent officialdom in three ways—by launching an ideological counterattack from their strongholds in the central media and propaganda apparatus, by reactivating mass radicalism in areas still subject to their political influence, and by soliciting the intervention and support of the aging personal ruler.

Throughout the Cultural Revolution decade, radical leaders were able to promote their ideas and artificially inflate the true extent of their power through their control of the central media and propaganda apparatus. In the wake of the Tenth Party Congress, radicals at the top launched a series of ideological initiatives, including the promotion of Legalist doctrine; the glorification of China's "totalitarian" historical unifier, Qin Shi Huangdi; and an anti-Confucius campaign. These radicals also sought to counter resurgent officialdom by extolling the historically progressive role of central power and the attendant effort to subdue landed and bureaucratic elites in traditional China. In September 1973, a *People's Daily* article on Qin Shi Huangdi's "book burning and burying alive of scholars" rejected the conventional view that this was a "tyrannical atrocity and reactionary act that directly caused the downfall of the Qin Dynasty." Instead, "the act of 'burning books and burying alive learned scholars' was by nature a progressive measure aimed at 'stressing the present and deemphasizing the past' in order to prevent the restoration of old rules by the usurpation of power."[110] In early 1974, radical leaders attempted to coopt resurgent officialdom's anti–Lin Biao campaign by linking it to a campaign against Confucius, both of whom supposedly embodied the threat of "usurpation" and "restoration."[111] In late 1974, a group at Peking University wrote approvingly of the Legalist philosopher Hanfeizi's attempt to curb the powers of "notables" *(zhongren)* and pointed to the propensity of local potentates to "weaken central power and the authority of the prince" for their own benefit and at the expense of the people.[112]

At the same time, a briefly successful effort to revive the mass radicalism of 1966–1967 was mounted in one of the last areas of radical political and organizational strength, Zhejiang Province.[113] As Keith Forster detailed, "In the first half of 1974, power appeared to pass out of the hands of the provincial Party leadership and into the hands of worker and Red Guard rebel leaders who had been prominent in the upheavals of 1967–1969. The administration lost the initiative and was outmaneuvered by the rebels, who utilized mass campaign tactics . . . and exerted pressure . . . to induct supporters into the CCP and place them in key bureaucratic posts."[114] As in 1966–1967, the radical attack came from above and below, as Wang Hongwen encouraged rebel leaders to resume their earlier struggles and as rebel leaders appealed to and sought to recruit underprivileged workers and marginal groups to their cause. But this attempt to reactivate Cultural Revolution mass radicalism was forcefully countered by familiar forms of official resistance. In early 1975, Deng Xiaoping condemned "factionalism," which "now seriously jeopardizes our overall interests," and stated, "Persons engaging in factional activities should be re-educated and their leaders opposed. . . . If they correct their mistakes, then we will let bygones be bygones, but if they refuse to mend their ways, they will be sternly dealt with."[115] By July 1975, political and military pressure had been brought to bear: "Rebel leaders and their supporters were banished, sent to the countryside, or enrolled in study classes to review their mistakes and receive ideological and political reeducation," and "outside troops, uninvolved in the lengthy and bitter local squabbles" were sent "into the factories of Hangzhou to pacify workers and supervise the resumption of normal production."[116]

The death of Premier Zhou in January 1976 brought the struggle between resurgent officialdom and radicals at the top to a climax as radical forces mounted a "counterattack against the rightist storm of reversal of verdicts" and were resisted by mass demonstrations in support of Zhou in Tiananmen Square and in other urban centers. On April 7, 1976, with Mao's personal intervention, radical forces appeared to win a major political victory and were able to force Deng's removal from office.[117] But the second purge of Deng was the last stand of Cultural Revolution radicalism. When Mao died in September, the so-called Gang of Four was purged and imprisoned forthwith, and the implementation of the theory and program of resurgent officialdom was begun in earnest.[118]

## Notes

1. I arrived in Peking in September 1964 with my mother, Nancy Dall Milton; my stepfather, David Milton; my brother, Grant Lupher; and my stepbrother, Christopher Milton. For our family story, see David Milton and Nancy Dall Milton, *The Wind Will Not Subside* (New York: Pantheon, 1976). After a year of intensive Chinese-language instruction, I was

enrolled in Peking University Middle School (Beida fuzhong). Following the lead of students at Peking University, students at my middle school were active participants in the early phases of the Cultural Revolution and founded some of the first and most militant Red Guard organizations. Like other schools in the capital, Peking University Middle School was shut down in summer 1966, not to reopen for many years. With my fellow students, with other young members of the foreign community in Peking, and on my own, I witnessed struggle meetings and Red Guard rallies, spent time working in the countryside, and worked in a Peking machine tool factory for several months. I returned to San Francisco with my brother in September 1968.

2. Deng Xiaoping, "Suggestions on Drafting 'Resolution of Various Questions of Party History since 1949,'" in Deng Xiaoping, *Selected Works of Deng Xiaoping 1975–1982*) (Peking: Foreign Languages Press, 1984), 288.

3. Zhou Mong, ed., *Lishi zai zheli chenci* (Meditate on history here) (Beijing: Huaxia Publishing, 1986), 1. As the tone of affronted dignity suggests, these words come from the memoirs of children of high-ranking officials attacked during the Cultural Revolution.

4. Xue Muqiao, *Zhongguo shehuizhuyi jingji wenti yanjiu* (Research on economic questions in Chinese socialism) (Beijing: International Books, 1981), 207.

5. Merle Goldman, "Mao Made Us Do It," *New York Times Book Review*, February 22, 1987, 31.

6. Andrew G. Walder, "Cultural Revolution Radicalism: Variations on a Stalinist Theme," in William A. Joseph, Christine P.W. Wong, and David Zweig, eds., *New Perspectives on the Cultural Revolution* (Cambridge, Mass.: Harvard University Press, 1991), 61.

7. Hong Yung Lee, *The Politics of the Chinese Cultural Revolution* (Berkeley and Los Angeles: University of California Press, 1978), 59.

8. For an early account of Maoist populism versus orthodox Leninist tactics in the Rectification Movement of 1942–1944, see Boyd Compton, *Mao's China: Party Reform Documents, 1942–1944* (Seattle: University of Washington Press, 1952), 211. For a discussion of Mao's advocacy of "unleashing" mass energies versus Liu Shaoqi's efforts to secure results through party leadership during the Great Leap Forward, see Roderick MacFarquhar, *The Origins of the Cultural Revolution 2: The Great Leap Forward, 1958–1960* (New York: Columbia University Press, 1983), 53–55.

9. Mark Lupher, "Power Restructuring in China and the Soviet Union," *Theory and Society* 21, 5 (October 1992):668.

10. Anita Chan, *Children of Mao: Personality Development and Political Activism in the Red Guard Generation* (London: Macmillan, 1985), 17, 184.

11. Lynn T. White III, *Policies of Chaos: The Organizational Causes of Violence in China's Cultural Revolution* (Princeton: Princeton University Press, 1989), 306, 3; Lynn T. White, "The Cultural Revolution as an Unintended Result of Administrative Policies," in Joseph et al., *New Perspectives on the Cultural Revolution*, 84.

12. Lee, *The Politics of the Chinese Cultural Revolution*, 5–6; Stanley Rosen, *Red Guard Factionalism and the Cultural Revolution in Guangzhou (Canton)* (Boulder: Westview Press, 1982), 95–97.

13. Lee, *The Politics of the Chinese Cultural Revolution*, 5.

14. Avery Goldstein, *From Bandwagon to Balance-of-Power Politics* (Stanford: Stanford University Press, 1991), 179.

15. White, "The Cultural Revolution as an Unintended Result of Administrative Policies," 93. Or as Goldstein put it, "Only when the political structure was altered, the suggested underlying cause for the patterns of conflict observed during the Cultural Revolu-

tion, were such diverse interests politically consequential" (*From Bandwagon to Balance-of-Power Politics,* 179).

16. Goldstein, *From Bandwagon to Balance-of-Power Politics,* 251. In Goldstein's view, "After 1966, in short, the Chinese polity had become an anarchically ordered realm populated by self-regarding actors, a structural context for political action that would persist, despite the diminution of social chaos, until 1978" (251).

17. Tang Tsou, "Back from the Brink of Revolutionary-'Feudal' Totalitarianism," in Victor Nee and David Mozingo, eds., *State and Society in Contemporary China* (Ithaca: Cornell University Press, 1983), 73, 82.

18. Hong Yung Lee, *From Revolutionary Cadres to Party Technocrats in Socialist China* (Berkeley and Los Angeles: University of California Press, 1991), 163–165. In Lee's view, the Cultural Revolution "ruined Mao's position in Chinese history," destroyed radical leaders such as Lin Biao and Jiang Qing, induced "profound disillusionment" among ordinary Chinese and the Red Guard generation, and inflicted terrible sufferings on members of the old CCP elite and their children (163).

19. Andrew J. Nathan, *Chinese Democracy* (New York: Knopf, 1985), xii.

20. Lee, *From Revolutionary Cadres to Party Technocrats in Socialist China,* 163.

21. As one of the elite middle schools, Peking University Middle School was a United Action bastion, and many of my classmates were members. For a scholarly account of the conservative Red Guard milieu in Peking, see Lee, *The Politics of the Chinese Cultural Revolution,* 84–92.

22. Neale Hunter, *Shanghai Journal* (New York: Praeger, 1969), 209.

23. Liang Heng and Judith Shapiro, *Son of the Revolution* (New York: Vintage, 1983), 67–70.

24. Parris H. Chang, "Provincial Party Leaders' Strategies for Survival During the Cultural Revolution," in Robert Scalapino, ed., *Elites in the People's Republic of China* (Seattle: University of Washington Press, 1972), 502.

25. Hence, "power-holders in the provinces" "exploited critical divisions in Chinese society." As a provincial party secretary exhorted conservative Red Guards in September 1966: "You are all the sons and daughters of the five red categories; the regime relies on you for protection. Many of those in the liaison teams from Peking have bad backgrounds. Before, we struggled against their parents and established our regime. Today, obviously, their parents are not reconciled to this and are using their children to struggle against us. You must battle against them" (ibid., 514–515).

26. Lee, *The Politics of the Cultural Revolution,* 111–112.

27. White, *Policies of Chaos,* 49.

28. Lowell Dittmer, *Liu Shao-ch'i and the Chinese Cultural Revolution* (Berkeley and Los Angeles: University of California Press, 1974), 141.

29. Lee, *The Politics of the Chinese Cultural Revolution,* 129–131.

30. Jurgen Domes, *The Internal Politics of China, 1949–1972* (New York: Praeger, 1973), 176. White erred in suggesting that "economism was mostly a matter of workers coercing cadres to approve demands for higher pay and other privileges" (*Policies of Chaos,* 239). In fact, economism was only one of the many successful defensive tactics employed by embattled party leaders.

31. "Wuchanjieji gemingpai, da lianhe, cong zou zibenzhuyi daolu de dangquanpai duoquan" (Proletarian revolutionaries, form a great alliance to seize power from power-holders taking the capitalist road), *Renmin ribao,* January 22, 1967; in *On the Proletarian Revolutionaries' Struggle to Seize Power* (Peking: Foreign Languages Press, 1968), 1.

32. Lee, *The Politics of the Chinese Cultural Revolution*, 140.

33. "Wuchanjieji gemingpai, da lianhe, cong zou zibenzhuyi daolu de dangquanpai duoquan," 17.

34. Ibid., 17. In China historically, under communism, and today, all official documents bear an official seal; to seize the seals of power, therefore, was truly a revolutionary proposition.

35. Wang Li, Jia Yixue, and Li Xin, "Wuchanjieji zhuanzheng he wuchanjieji wenhua da geming" (The dictatorship of the proletariat and the great proletarian cultural revolution) (Peking: People's Press, 1967), 9. (All quotes in this paragraph are from this source.)

36. Andrew G. Walder, "Cultural Revolution Radicalism: Variations on a Stalinist Theme," in Joseph et al., eds., *New Perspectives on the Cultural Revolution*, 61.

37. "Beijing renmin gongshe wan sui" (Long live Peking people's commune), *Beijing hongqi* (Peking red flag) (Peking Aviation Institute), February 10, 1967, 37, 38.

38. "Whither China," *Hunan shengwulian* (Hunan Province proletarian alliance), January 8, 1968, in *SCMP* 4190 (June 4, 1968):3. Hunan Shengwulian was a radical, "ultraleft" group that was suppressed in fall 1967. In the assessment of the Hunan radicals, the power seizures of January 1967 transferred power "to the hands of the people, who were full of boundless enthusiasm and who were organized to take over the urban administration and the Party, government, financial, and cultural powers in the industrial, commercial, communications and other systems. What the editorial called for, i.e., that the masses should rise up to take control of their socialist country, and to manage the cities, industry, communications and economy, was truly realized" (3).

39. Jurgen Domes, *China After the Cultural Revolution: Politics Between the Two Party Congresses* (Berkeley and Los Angeles: University of California Press, 1977), 47.

40. Lee, *From Revolutionary Cadres to Party Technocrats in Socialist China*, 81–82. Lee also calculated that the damage was somewhat less extensive in the provinces, where some 54 percent of top leaders were purged during 1967–1969.

41. Milton and Milton, *The Wind Will Not Subside*, 189.

42. Ibid., 190.

43. Chang, "Provincial Party Leaders' Strategies for Survival During the Cultural Revolution," 537; Domes, *China After the Cultural Revolution*, 11.

44. Lee, *The Politics of the Chinese Cultural Revolution*, 183.

45. "Renmin jiefangjun jianjue zhichi wuchanjieji gemingpai" (The PLA firmly supports the proletarian revolutionaries), *Jiefangjun bao* (Liberation Army newspaper), January 25, 1967, 1.

46. "Lun wuchanjieji gemingpai duoquan de douzheng" (On the proletarian revolutionaries' struggle to seize power) *Hongqi* 3 (1967), in *On the Proletarian Revolutionaries' Struggle to Seize Power*, 7, 5.

47. "Lun geming jilu he wuchanjieji geming quanli" (On revolutionary discipline and proletarian revolutionary authority), *Hongqi* 3 (1967), in ibid., 31.

48. "Bixu zhengque duidai ganbu" (Cadres must be treated correctly), *Hongqi* 4 (1967), in *On the Revolutionary "Three-in-One" Combination* (Peking: Foreign Languages Press, 1968) 24, 42.

49. "Lun geming 'sanjiehe'" (On the revolutionary "three-in-one Combination"), *Hongqi* 5 (1967), in ibid., 1.

50. Dittmer, *Liu Shao-ch'i and the Chinese Cultural Revolution*, 151.

51. Domes, *China After the Cultural Revolution*, 12.

52. "Jianjue zhichi he yonghu geming de 'sanjiehe' zhengce" (Firmly carry out and uphold the revolutionary "three-in-one" policy), *Jiefangjun bao,* March 23, 1967, 48.

53. "Lun geming 'sanjiehe,'" 12.

54. "Masses Demand Stop to the Use of Broadcasting Vans and Deafening Loudspeakers," *Renmin ribao,* June 16, 1967, in *SCMP* 3697 (August 10, 1967):3.

55. William Hinton provided this example of factional conflict in Shanxi Province during this period: "On July 21 another group of demonstrators, assembled around a militant core of Huai-hai Arsenal workers, surrounded the Regional Medical School, a United stronghold, and tried to break in. In the fighting that ensued, United later charged, Huai-hai workers beat up 200 of the defenders, injured more than ninety, seventeen of them seriously, and damaged property up to 100,000 yuan. On July 22 Red units surrounding the Army Subdistrict Headquarters demanded that Commander Wu Tianming come before them for criticism. They questioned him roughly for several days and, United said, 'conducted a struggle' against him" (*Shenfan* [New York: Random House, 1983], 571). Factional clashes of this type, often on a much broader and more deadly scale, occurred throughout China in spring and summer 1967.

56. "Whither China," 6.

57. Ibid., 7.

58. Lee, *The Politics of the Chinese Cultural Revolution,* 244–246.

59. Ibid., 247.

60. "The Proletarian Must Take Firm Hold of the Gun," *Renmin ribao,* July 31, 1967, in Chi Wen-shun, ed., *Readings in the Chinese Communist Cultural Revolution* (Berkeley and Los Angeles: University of California Press, 1971), 280. White translated *wengong wuwei* as "civil offense and armed defense" and suggested that it involved reviving militias to "monitor units that the Revolutionary Committee wanted to control better" (*Policies of Chaos,* 257). In fact, "Attack with words and defend with weapons" was an incendiary radical slogan that was used to justify the arming of rebel groups and the seizure of weapons from the army. For a more detailed account, see Lee, *The Politics of the Chinese Cultural Revolution,* 247–248.

61. "Whither China," 8.

62. "Towering Crimes Committed by Counter-Revolutionary Clique of Wang Li, Kuan Feng, Lin Chieh, Mu Hsin, and Wu Ch'uan-ch'i," *Canton Open Warfare Bulletin,* March 1968, in *SCMP* 4158 (April 16, 1968):8.

63. "Wuchanjieji bixu laolao zhangwo qiangganzi" (The proletariat must take firm hold of the gun), *Renmin ribao,* July 31, 1967, 1.

64. Domes, *China After the Cultural Revolution,* 12.

65. "Party and Government Circular of September 5, 1967," *Communist China Digest,* November 24, 1967, 55.

66. In fall 1967, CCRG representatives who had taken the lead in attempting to "drag out the handful in the army" were purged, labeled "May 16 elements" (*wuyaoliu fenzi*), and denounced as a "counter-revolutionary clique" that "oppose[s] the Chinese People's Liberation Army and undermine[s] and split[s] our Great Wall, in a vain attempt to take advantage of the great cultural revolution to usurp the powers of the Party and the State and restore capitalism" ("Towering Crimes Committed by Counter-Revolutionary Clique of Wang Li, Kuan Feng, Lin Chieh, Mu Hsin, and Wu Ch'uan-ch'i," 1).

67. Lin Biao, "Report to the the 9th Party Congress," *Renmin ribao,* April 28, 1969, in James T. Myers, Jurgen Domes, and Milton D. Yeh, eds., *Chinese Politics—Documents and*

*Analysis,* vol. 2, *Ninth Party Congress (1969) to the Death of Mao (1976)* (Columbia: University of South Carolina Press, 1989), 64, 75.

68. Ibid.

69. "Earnestly Implement the Principle of 'Supporting the Left, But Not Any Particular Faction,'" *Jiefangjun bao,* January 28, 1968, in *Peking Review,* February 2, 1968, 8.

70. Lee, *The Politics of the Chinese Cultural Revolution,* 274.

71. In the "18-point Instruction" of May 1968, Mao ruled on the "general orientation of the current movement," declared that cadres were 95 percent "good or comparatively good," judged "intellectuals and young undergraduates" to be susceptible to the "bourgeois worldview" and therefore unfit as "revolutionary successors," passed judgment on several controversial articles and the fate of Foreign Minister Chen Yi, and finally stated, "By all means don't throw our army units into disarray. If there are problems in the Liberation Army, they may be discussed in one province and later in another" ("Chairman Mao's Latest 18-Point Instructions," *SCMP* 4201 [June 19, 1968]:1–7).

72. "Zhaojian shoudu hongdaihui fuzeren de tanhua" (Dialogue with responsible persons of the capital red guard congress), *Joint Publications Research Service (JPRS)* 61269-2 (February 20, 1974):481. The imperial nature of this encounter is explicit in Chinese: The proceedings were termed *zhaojian,* a "summons."

73. See Hinton, *Shenfan,* 636–639, for a description of the methods used by the army to suppress radical mass organizations in Shanxi. Harsh measures were routinely employed, and "revolutionary rebels" were executed when they refused to recant and to acknowledge their "errors."

74. Anne F. Thurston, *Enemies of the People* (New York: Knopf), 196–205.

75. Domes estimated that by the beginning of 1970 "fifteen million young people throughout China were affected by the deportations" (*China After the Cultural Revolution,* 64). Yet many of my classmates went willingly at first, fully accepting the necessity and desirability of "learning from the workers and peasants."

76. Yao Wenyuan, "The Working Class Must Exercise Leadership in Everything," *Peking Review,* August 30, 1968, 3.

77. Domes noted the "existence of five Field Army Loyalty Groups which had existed since the last phase of the Civil War (1947–1949) and dominated military behavior in politics to a considerable extent ever since" ("Introduction," in Myers et al., eds., *Chinese Politics,* 6).

78. Domes, *China After the Cultural Revolution,* 35–36.

79. See ibid., chap. 4.

80. For a definitive discussion, see David Zweig, *Agrarian Radicalism in China, 1968–1981* (Cambridge, Mass.: Harvard University Press, 1989). As Zweig noted, "The reintroduction of family farming in the early 1960s and the radicals' intense fears of retrogression to capitalism" led them to advocate "production brigade" (*shengchan da dui*) as opposed to "production team" (*shengchan dui*) ownership and accounting systems in the villages (98).

81. Anita Chan, Richard Madsen, and Jonathan Unger, *Chen Village* (Berkeley and Los Angeles: University of California Press, 1984), 239–240.

82. Hinton, *Shenfan,* chap. 84.

83. Jean C. Oi, *State and Peasant in Contemporary China: The Political Economy of Village Government* (Berkeley and Los Angeles: University of California Press, 1989), 126–127.

84. Domes, "Introduction," 8. This is precisely the policy formula that Chinese Communist leaders advocated throughout the 1980s and in the wake of the June 4, 1989, crackdown.

85. Zweig, *Agrarian Radicalism in China,* 60–61.

86. Domes, *China After the Cultural Revolution,* 114–116.

87. Michael Y.M. Kau, ed., *The Lin Biao Affair* (White Plains, N.Y.: International Arts and Sciences Press, 1975), 89, 72. For a no doubt unreliable but very colorful account of this murky episode, see Yao Mingle, *The Conspiracy and Death of Lin Biao* (New York: Knopf, 1983).

88. "Document No. 12 of the Central Committee of the CCP," *Issues and Studies* (September 1972):7.

89. In Domes's assessment, "The majority of regional commanders stood for a continuation of the policy of decentralization which had been introduced in the early 1960s and which they had fully implemented during the crisis of the Cultural Revolution," while in regard to "social policies in the agricultural sector . . . the civilian administration around Zhou Enlai supported the view of the majority of regional commanders" ("Introduction," 18–19).

90. Chan et al., *Chen Village,* 250.

91. Henry J. Groen and James A. Kilpatrick, "China's Agricultural Production," in *Chinese Economy Post-Mao* (Washington, D.C.: Joint Economic Committee, Congress of the United States, 1978), vol. 1, 616.

92. Lee, *From Revolutionary Cadres to Party Technocrats in Socialist China,* 93.

93. "Oppose Restoration of the Old," *Wenhui bao,* October 18, 1968, in *SCMP* 4300 (November 18, 1968):1.

94. "Mao Zedong's Speech to the 1st Plenary Session of the 9th Central Committee of the CCP," April 28, 1968, *Issues and Studies* 6 (March 1970):95.

95. "It Is Contrary to the Will of the People to Reverse Previous Verdicts," *Renmin ribao,* March 10, 1976, in Myers et al., eds., *Chinese Politics,* 353.

96. Domes, "Introduction," 19–20.

97. Hsu Tak-ming, *Wenge hou de zhonggong jingji* (The Chinese communist economy after the cultural revolution) (Hong Kong: Union Research Institute, 1974), 907.

98. "Report to the Tenth National Congress of the Communist Party of China," August 23, 1971, in *The Tenth National Congress of the CCP (Documents)* (Peking: Foreign Languages Press, 1973), 34, 8. While attacking Lin at length, Zhou's "Report" was especially critical of Lin's contention that the "main contradiction" was "between the advanced socialist system and the backward productive forces of society" (5).

99. Thus, "some good cadres have not yet been rehabilitated. Most of our cadres are good; the bad ones are in the minority. Those who have been liquidated amount to no more than one percent and the figure will not exceed three percent when taking all questionable persons in consideration" ("Document No. 12 of the Central Committee of the CCP," 71).

100. Domes, *China After the Cultural Revolution,* 144–148; Tillman Durdin, "Purged Army Men at Fete in Peking," *New York Times,* August 2, 1972, 10.

101. *The Tenth National Congress of the CCP (Documents),* 36, 50, 51.

102. A. Doak Barnett, "Chou Is Reassembling the Nation's Shattered Unity," *New York Times,* September 2, 1973, 4.

103. The radicals made a deliberate effort to build up low-status social groups. People under thirty-five, women, and national minorities were most actively recruited during this period. See Lee, *From Revolutionary Cadres to Party Technocrats in Socialist China,* 128–129.

104. *The Tenth National Congress of the CCP (Documents),* 54. Wang therefore sought to revise the CCP constitution to read, "It is absolutely impermissible to suppress criticism and to retaliate" (55).

105. "Comrade Wang Hung-wen's Report at the Central Study Class, January 14, 1974," in Myers et al., eds., *Chinese Politics,* 177.

106. Ibid., 179.

107. Ibid., 183.

108. Zhou Enlai, "Report on the Work of the Government to the 4th NPC," in Myers et al., eds., Chinese Politics, 296.

109. Domes, "Introduction," 28–29. "Beginning in late May, the media again stressed the importance of material incentives and economic growth, and occasionally, there were even statements legitimizing the peasant's side-line occupations. At the same time, more than 60 prominent purgees of the Cultural Revolution were appointed to leading positions, particularly on the provincial level" (29).

110. "An Analysis of 'Book Burning and Burying Alive of Learned Scholars,'" *Renmin ribao,* September 28, 1973, 3.

111. "Carry the Struggle to Criticize Lin Biao and Confucius Through to the End," *Peking Review,* February 8, 1974, 4.

112. "Hanfei pingzhu" (Annotations and commentary on Hanfeizi), in *Fajia zhuzuo xuandu* (Selected readings from the famous works of the legalists) (Peking: China Books, 1975), 10–11. In the 1930s, Soviet commentators made a similar argument for Ivan IV and spoke of his historically progressive struggle against local magnates.

113. The political situation in Zhejiang Province was unusual. Adjacent Shanghai was a bastion of Cultural Revolution radicalism from the start, and radical leaders Zhang Chunqiao and Wang Hongwen continued to command significant political and organizational resources in Shanghai and Zhejiang into the mid-1970s. See Keith Forster, "Factional Politics in Zhejiang, 1973–1976," in Joseph et al., eds., *New Perspectives on the Cultural Revolution,* 116–117.

114. Ibid., 113. Rebel leaders "did not want as members of the militia workers who were obedient to the Party, who were conscientious in their jobs, or who accepted the system's social and political norms," preferring instead "those who had less of a stake in the system and would therefore be less hesitant in flouting accepted rules of behavior" (124).

115. "The Whole Party Should Take the Overall Interest into Account and Push the Economy Forward," in Deng, *Selected Works of Deng Xiaoping,* 16.

116. Forster, "Factional Politics in Zhejiang," 114. Forster noted, "This was probably the largest mobilization of troops in China to quell domestic violence since the famous Wuhan Incident of July 1967" (114).

117. Domes, "Introduction," 30. Yet "on the very afternoon of April 7, however, while the Politburo was still in session, soldiers commanded by officers of the former Third Field Army took Teng from his Peking residence, and from there escorted him via Nanking to Canton. There, he was protected from all possible attacks by Hsu Shih-yu and Wei Kuoch'ing and lived in the resort of Ts'ung-hua for almost a year" (30–31).

118. I do not employ the term *Gang of Four* in this discussion and have instead relied on the phrase "radical leaders at the top." The Gang of Four is a label used by the post-Mao CCP leadership to blame the turmoil of the Cultural Revolution on a small group of radical leaders. As we have seen, millions of people, in pursuit of different and often contradictory aims, were involved in the upheavals of the Cultural Revolution. These upheavals were set in motion by the ultimate radical leader at the top, Chairman Mao, without whose support and interventions the activities of the Gang of Four would never have come into play.

# 8

# Continuity and Change in
# Post-Mao China

In the late 1970s and 1980s, the Chinese economy and society underwent a series of historic changes. By the early 1990s, agriculture had been decollectivized, large segments of industry had been marketized and privatized, the coastal provinces had become engaged in international trade on an unprecedented scale, and China's gross domestic product (GDP) was growing at an annual rate of 12 percent.[1] At the same time, China experienced a wide-ranging commercial and cultural opening to the capitalist world in the form of direct foreign investment, joint ventures with Western corporations, the introduction of capitalist management and marketing techniques, and the wholesale importation of foreign movies, videos, television programs, consumer products, rock and roll, blue jeans, and so on[2] Virtually all Western analysts saw the momentous changes of the 1980s as a historic break with the conflict, chaos, and repression of the Cultural Revolution decade and spoke of "post-Mao reform." Depicted in this light, the reforms of the late 1970s and 1980s appeared to stem solely from the vision and decisions of reform-oriented leaders at the top and were thereby disconnected from conditions in China during the preceding decade.[3] In 1987, Harry Harding maintained that the "surprisingly smooth and rapid" post-Mao changes were the result of "extraordinary political engineering by a coalition of reform-minded leaders led by Deng Xiaoping," and in 1994 Joseph Fewsmith stressed "the degree to which reform policies are propelled, constrained, and warped by the political dynamic at the top of the regime."[4]

Other commentators reached more sweeping conclusions. In the early 1980s, Tang Tsou wrote that the post-Mao reforms of December 1978 signaled a "new historic era for China," a "decisive break with those ideological and political lines of Mao which culminated in the Cultural Revolution," and an "end of nearly three-quarters of a century of revolutionary ferments and upheavals."[5] Specifically, Tsou spoke of "a retreat of political power (i.e., the party-state) from its increasingly deeper penetration of civil society and the economy" and a corresponding rise of processes of "institutionalization," increases in "input and feedback from society to the uppermost levels of politics," and a "strengthening of the legislative branch of government at all levels, and the adoption of an electoral system in which there are more candidates than positions to be filled."[6] In the 1980s, the notion that China was becoming less authoritarian and more legal-rational, democratic, and recognizably "modern" was widely aired by Western analysts.

According to Victor Nee's "theory of market transition," "As markets replace redistributive mechanisms in the allocation and distribution of goods, there is a shift in the sources of power from the redistributive sector to the marketplace."[7] In the legal realm, R. Randle Edwards suggested that "the progressive elaboration of a comprehensive legislative structure, the training of thousands of defense lawyers, and the launching of a major public legal-education movement have made the Chinese citizen perhaps more aware of his rights and of his remedies in case of violation than ever before in Chinese history."[8] In Hong Yung Lee's view, the CCP itself became institutionalized and rationalized in the post-Mao period. Accordingly, "revolutionary cadres have been gradually displaced by bureaucratic technocrats. Selected from among the best educated segments of the population, the new Chinese leaders have their academic training mainly in engineering and production-related fields and their career backgrounds in specialist positions at functional organizations." These new officials, "have a better understanding of and better qualifications to deal with such prerequisites of industrialized society as functional specialization, the coordination of parts, rational decision-making, and problem solving."[9]

Two sets of assumptions informed these images of post-Mao China and post-Mao reform. The first set of assumptions were those of modernization theory, "which claims that progress follows a single course toward a market economy and political democracy."[10] Therefore, the more complex, industrialized, and modern a society is, the more institutionalized, rationalized, marketized, and politically pluralistic it necessarily becomes. As Edwards put it, "In other areas of civil, political, economic, social, and cultural rights, the scope of expectations to which the average Chinese citizen feels entitled has expanded in an evolutionary fashion with the increasing complexity and prosperity of society."[11] Yet modernization theory is premised on the assumption that Western historical, institutional, and developmental patterns alone constitute modernity. I reject this assumption and in this chapter show how post-Mao China and post-Mao reform cannot be understood in light of the modernization model posited by Tsou and other Western commentators.

The second set of assumptions concerned the relationship between the Cultural Revolution and the post-Mao reforms. Proponents of the institutionalization-rationalization-democratization view of post-Mao China depicted the Cultural Revolution as a negative learning experience from which the Chinese people, and China's post-Mao political leadership in particular, derived many painful, yet salutary lessons. In Nathan's words, "The experience of the Cultural Revolution has given every PRC citizen, especially the leaders, a new appreciation for the importance of legal and institutional arrangements to protect individuals from arbitrary persecution."[12] Depicted in this light, post-Mao reform could be viewed as the chastened and now-enlightened CCP leaders' repudiation of the chaos, violence, and lawlessness they had themselves suffered during the Cultural Revolution.

This argument was first put forward by Tsou and subsequently echoed by other Western commentators. In Tsou's view, members of the CCP political elite were "reeducated by the Cultural Revolution," in the course of which they experienced "the political system created by themselves both from the top and from the bottom, both from inside and from outside, both as its beneficiaries and its victims"; were forced to engage in "self-examination" and "soul-searching"; and in the end underwent a "second liberation" and emerged as "reborn revolutionaries."[13] In the early 1990s, Lee reiterated Tsou's formulations and stated, "The impetus for reform can thus be traced back to the senior leaders' personal experience of humiliation, imprisonment, and purges. As victims of the very system they had, until 1966, helped to create, they now saw its flaws. . . . Consequently, the former-victim-now-rehabilitated cadres became born-again reformers."[14] As a result, White suggested in 1989, "extensive mass violence is now unlikely, because Cultural Revolution experiences have disinclined Chinese local leaders, especially in the cities, to permit very forceful use of policies that categorize, control people, and scare people."[15]

But it is all too evident that the foregoing sets of assumptions were invalidated and undercut by the events of June 4, 1989. The violent behavior of the Deng regime, its disdain for democracy and the rule of law, and, especially, its willingness to resort to large-scale mass repressions especially, contradict both the proposition that post-Mao reform was a manifestation of inexorable processes of institutionalization, rationalization, and democratization and the suggestion that the sufferings of the CCP political elite during the Cultural Revolution caused its members to be born again in more liberal, law-abiding, and nonviolent form. For Western China scholars generally, the Tiananmen crackdown clearly necessitates a fundamental rethinking of the origins and significance of post-Mao reform and the effects of the Cultural Revolution on the contemporary Chinese political order.

I undertake precisely such a rethinking in this chapter. Rather than viewing post-Mao reform as a reaction against the Cultural Revolution, I argue that the power-restructuring events of 1966–1976 established the political preconditions and created the structural context for the changes of the late 1970s and 1980s. While locating the origins of post-Mao reform in the power-restructuring events of the Cultural Revolution, I then examine the evolving power dynamics of the 1980s and focus attention on the changing relationship between center and locality, official power and privilege in the post-Mao period and processes of conflict and control in contemporary China.

## Rethinking Post-Mao Reform

We have seen how resurgent officialdom and its theory and program were able to blunt and finally prevail over the forces of Cultural Revolution radicalism in

1966–1976. But there was no possibility of restoring the status quo ante of the early 1960s, for the convulsions and conflicts of the Cultural Revolution did result in a fundamental restructuring of power, albeit not of the type envisioned by Mao in 1966. The Cultural Revolution did not deconcentrate power; it did decentralize and devolve power. In the course of political crises, factional violence, power contests, and policy disputes of the late 1960s and early 1970s, previously centralized political and administrative power devolved into the hands of military and civil officials at the regional, provincial, and local levels. With this restructuring of political power ensued a devolution of previously centralized economic decisionmaking and resource allocation power to provinces, localities, enterprises, and even individual peasant households. Understood in my terms, decentralized appropriations of power and resources were the major consequence of the convulsions and conflicts of the Cultural Revolution decade. This massive de facto restructuring of power set the stage for the formal implementation of the post-Mao reform package in December 1978 and was subsequently manifested in a series of momentous economic, social, and cultural changes. In the 1980s and the 1990s, the devolution of power to the regional, provincial, and local levels continued to accelerate, profoundly affecting power dynamics in contemporary Chinese society.

It is unconventional to speak of the continuity of post-Mao reform with the events of the preceding decade and a half. We have seen how Western analysts linked post-Mao reform to the suffering and enlightenment that the Chinese Communists experienced in the Cultural Revolution. In a related vein, Harding argued that "the political crisis confronting China at the time of Mao's death led a group of reformers, under the leadership of Deng Xiaoping, to conclude that political change was both essential and urgent."[16] In my view, however, there is a continuity of post-Mao reform and post-Mao politics; these processes are directly descended from the theory and program of resurgent officialdom. Mao's death did not present resurgent officialdom with a political crisis but rather with the opportunity to consolidate power, fully implement its program, and destroy the Maoist opposition once and for all. The theory and program of resurgent officialdom were always premised on a combination of economic liberalization and political authoritarianism; indeed, the moderate coalition of regional military commanders and veteran party leaders who contested the attempt to revive authority–social mobilization methods in the late 1960s and early 1970s were committed from the outset to "safeguarding law and order, and furthering pragmatic growth and consumption-oriented concepts."[17] The Deng regime's commitment to this long-standing formula was unambiguously manifested in the course of the June 4 crackdown and its aftermath.

While rooted in the events of the Cultural Revolution decade, the changing power dynamics of the 1980s were accelerated by the economic, social, and cultural changes of the post-Mao period. In the 1980s, power relations and political process were reshaped in three important areas. First, the interaction between center and locality changed, as evidenced by the rise of new centers of power at the regional and local levels, and the corresponding decline in the capacity of central authorities to enforce their policy preferences in the provinces. Second, the power and privileges of party and state officialdom increased in the post-Mao period, as evidenced by the proliferation of official corruption and the accelerated appropriation of resources, on the one hand, and the reinforcing of single-party rule, on the other. Third, processes of conflict and control assumed both familiar and new forms in the post-Mao period. Even though classic mechanisms of state control, such as communist ideology and cradle-to-grave dependence on state-run institutions, were eroded, other familiar mechanisms of control and coercion remained in place. At the same time, post-Mao reform gave rise to new conflicts and exacerbated old and latent tensions.

Along with these wide-ranging internal changes, China's economic, commercial, and cultural interaction with the outside world intensified in the post-Mao era. In the 1980s, a fusion occurred of processes of economic and political decentralization, marketization and privatization, cultural liberalization and opening up to the outside world, and political authoritarianism and nationalism. These interrelated developments constitute a transition from socialism.

## The Consequences of Maoist
## Power Restructuring

The crucial act of Maoist power restructuring in fall 1966 and January 1967 was a historically unprecedented deconcentration of political power and suspension of control mechanisms. In Chapter 7, I discussed the political conflicts that erupted and showed how veteran CCP officialdom, usually in tacit alliance with the PLA, was able to contest Cultural Revolution radicalism and advance its own theory and program. I also argued that the upheavals of the Cultural Revolution resulted in a profound restructuring and redistribution of power, and I discussed the fundamental erosion of central power. How did this erosion of central power, the antithesis of Maoist dictatorship, occur? Carl Riskin observed that China's economic performance during the Cultural Revolution decade "was largely the product of the political stalemate that characterized the Chinese leadership for much of this period."[18] I suggest that power-devolving processes during the Cultural Revolution decade should be understood in light of three key factors: the authority crisis of 1966–1967, Maoist policies and reforms, and decentralized processes of power and resource appropriation.

Power devolution was in part the logical consequence of the authority crisis and central administrative paralysis that occurred in 1966–1967. Thus, when "a large part of the staff that prepared, implemented, and supported planning was attacked and purged," "planning was virtually abandoned and the economy left without a coordinating mechanism" for much of the Cultural Revolution decade.[19] But the devolution of economic power was accelerated by Maoist economic policy, with its familiar emphasis on the organizational and developmental merits of decentralization, local self-reliance, and rural industrialization. According to Barry Naughton, decentralization in industrial administration can be traced back to 1967, when local authorities began to retain enterprise depreciation allowances instead of relying on central budgetary allocations.[20] In the early 1970s, a broad decentralization of administrative and financial controls occurred, and enterprise control was transferred to localities, responsibility for capital construction was placed under local jurisdiction, and central tax collection procedures were relaxed. At the same time, Maoist resource allocation policies in the late 1960s and 1970s afforded localities easy and abundant access to state funds for investment in such priority areas as chemical fertilizer production and farm machinery manufacturing.[21]

Yet, as David Zweig observed, "national elites could put radical policies onto local agendas, but without their direct intervention into local politics the critical factors in policy implementation were local interests, the local environment, and the way individual radical policies affected those interests."[22] We have seen that the forces of Cultural Revolution radicalism were never able to establish themselves at the local level in a manner remotely comparable to CCP grassroots power building during the 1930s and 1940s. Hence, although Maoists at the top could decree policies and reforms, their political and organizational presence at the local level was typically weak, contested, or nonexistent. As the implementation of Maoist policies was thereby circumvented or distorted, the way was simultaneously opened up for processes of decentralized power and resource appropriation. In Christine Wong's assessment, though the financial system remained highly centralized during the Cultural Revolution decade, investment decisions and materials allocation were "substantially decentralized," thereby allowing local authorities to "pass along all losses to the state budget" while retaining output and "privatizing" profits.[23] In a related vein, Zweig showed how officials at the district and commune levels were able to turn radical policies to their own advantage and to "steal peasant resources and strengthen the economic basis of their political power" in the name of local self-reliance.[24] In the industrial realm, Walder suggested that Maoist antibureaucratic reforms, which reduced staff departments in industrial enterprises, "had the effect of concentrating power in the hands of the hierarchy of leaders that started with the plant director and stretched down to the shop floor."[25]

Power devolution in the Cultural Revolution decade was the further consequence of the deconcentration of power and suspension of political controls in 1966–1967. We have seen that Maoist power restructuring precipitated freewheeling power contests at all levels of Chinese society, as privileged groups mobilized in defense of their position and less privileged or nonprivileged groups sought to advance their interests and appropriate power and resources held by more advantaged groups. When veteran officials were forced to fight for their political lives, many were able to successfully defend themselves by competing for popular support and rebuilding their constituencies and in the process became more powerful at the local level. In the struggle to reposition and relegitimate themselves, embattled officials' primary vehicles were the advocacy of local interests and the promotion of patron-client networks. By the same token, when disadvantaged groups were able to prevail, they relied on similar methods to bolster their power.[26] In either case, Maoist power deconcentration moved the struggle for power and resources to the fore, and the power contests that ensued wound up reinforcing the authority of local officials and power brokers. Many accounts suggest that official corruption took a significant turn for the worse during the Cultural Revolution decade, a development that must be understood in light of the processes of adminstrative decontrol, localism, and power and resource appropriation unleashed in 1966–1967.[27]

## The Third Plenum and the Victory of Resurgent Officialdom

In 1977–1978, Mao's designated successor, Hua Guofeng, sought to resist and reverse power-devolving processes. When the central leadership denounced municipal and provincial leaders for attempting to implement independent kingdom policies and disregard central resource allocation processes in early 1977, their behavior was depicted as a manifestation of residual Cultural Revolution radicalism. Hence, it was followers of the "Gang of Four" who "forced the central departments concerned to give their approval to intercept crude oil in Shanghai harbor destined for fraternal provinces and municipalities."[28] As events soon confirmed, however, processes of power devolution were being driven by sociopolitical forces far more potent than the remnants of Cultural Revolution radicalism.

In 1977, Hua attempted to maintain essential features of the post-1967 Maoist system while jettisoning its politically objectionable and untenable aspects. In his "Political Report" to the Eleventh National Congress of the CCP, Hua blamed all the turmoil and suffering of the preceding decade on the "Gang of Four" and its deliberate defiance of Mao's wishes and admonitions. It was therefore this "sinister clique of old and new counter-revolutionaries who sneaked into our party" and pursued the "vicious attack on our Party's veteran cadres and shameless vilification of our Party's character and history," thereby directly violating Mao's instructions on "curing the sickness to save the patient" and "uniting with 95 percent of the cadres . . . including those comrades who have made the mistake of taking the capitalist road, but are willing to correct it."[29] While repudiating the attack on officialdom, however, Hua still clung to classic Maoist power-restructuring themes. Thus, even though "our Party has a contingent of old, middle-aged, and young cadres steeled in struggles from the time the Party was founded all the way to and through the Cultural Revolution," it was vital that old and young officials work together and "watch out lest we foster a bureaucratic style of work and grow into an aristocratic stratum divorced from the people."[30]

In the economic realm, Hua affirmed the validity of authority–social mobilization methods, spoke of the "tremendous power" that could be generated by "class struggle and revolutionary mass movements," and vowed to combat the "capitalism that has been rampant in recent years in a number of places and units" and to "solve the problem of capitalist tendencies in the ranks of the people."[31] Hua even sought to emulate Mao's style of personal rulership, and the setting of the Eleventh Party Congress was replete with large portraits of Hua arrayed next to those of Mao and constant references by other leaders to "our wise leader Chairman Hua."[32] Such time-honored rhetoric and imagery notwithstanding, the Hua Guofeng platform was already under fire and disintegrating. Although Hua invoked well-worn Maoist power-restructuring themes, the proceedings of the Eleventh Party Congress marked the full-scale restoration of veteran officialdom to the Central Committee and the onset of an all-out assault on officials appointed during the Cultural Revolution.

In July 1977, at the insistence of civilian and military leaders at the top and in the provinces, Deng Xiaoping was restored to all his previous positions: member of the standing committee of the Politburo, vice chairman of the CCP, vice chairman of the Military Affairs Commission, and chief of staff of the PLA.[33] According to Lee's calculations, while mass organizations saw their share of representation in the Central Committee elected at the Eleventh National Congress decline from 37 percent to 29 percent, cadre representation climbed from 33 percent to 42 percent, and cadres accounted for 56 percent of all full Central Committee members.[34] Already vitiated by the resistance of resurgent officialdom at the top and processes of devolution and appropriation at the regional, provincial, and local levels, the last remnants of Maoist power restructuring were conclusively jettisoned by the Chinese Communist leadership in the next year and a half.

At the Third Plenum of the Eleventh Central Committee in December 1978, the theory and program of resurgent officialdom were confirmed and vindicated, and power-devolving processes already in motion were formalized and accelerated. Although the policies put forward at the Third Plenum were wholly consistent with those advocated by market–material incentive proponents ever since the 1950s and early 1960s, the Deng Xiaoping reform package also reflected both the changes in power relations that had occurred from 1966 to 1976 and the explicit political goal of eradicating the organizational remnants of Maoism. I have argued that three policy goals were key to the theory and program of resurgent officialdom during the Cultural Revolution decade—a return to the market–material incentive policies of the early 1960s, a regionalization and decentralization of political and economic power, and a restoration of veteran officials and a purge of the purgers. These themes were recurrent in Deng's historic speech at the Third Plenum, "Emancipate the Mind, Seek Truth from Facts, and Unite as One in Looking to the Future."

Under the rubric of "economic democracy," Deng criticized the prevailing system of economic management as "overcentralized" *(guoyu jizhong)* and called for a "bold devolution" *(dadan xiafang)* of power, albeit in a "planned way" *(you jihua de)*.[35] Deng then advanced the familiar market–material incentive argument and asserted that the devolution of economic decisionmaking power and the prospect of more material gains would energize localities, enterprises, and individual work-ers and give full scope to their "spirit of initiative and creativity" *(zhudong chuangzao jingshen)*. In fact, the loosening of central economic controls in the post-Mao period triggered a massive upsurge in economic growth and entrepre-neurial activity at all levels of Chinese society. Thus, his observation that "once a production team has been empowered to make decisions regarding its own oper-ations, its members and cadres will lie awake at night so long as a single piece of land is left unplanted or a single pond unused for aquatic production, and they will find ways to remedy the situation" was validated on a scale that must have sur-prised Deng himself.[36]

Deploying the same logic, Deng also pushed for the further regionalization and decentralization of political power and spoke of the need for more democracy. In contrast to the "bureaucratism of over-centralized power" *(quanli guoyu jizhong de guanliaozhuyi)* that "often masquerades as 'Party leadership,' 'Party directives,' and 'Party discipline,' but actually is designed to control people, hold them in check, and oppress them," Deng spoke approvingly of "home-grown policies" *(tu zhengce)* grounded in reality and supported by the populace at the local level.[37] But Deng was especially concerned with mending the damage that overcentralized power had inflicted on the party; he asserted, "In political life within the Party and among the people we must use democratic means and not resort to coercion and attack." Contrary to the expectations of some Western commentators, however, the democracy and rule of law championed by Deng did not entail political liber-alization or political pluralism. Rather, the essential conditions for the practice of democracy were the "three don'ts"—"Don't pick on others for their faults" *(bu zhua bianzi)*, "don't put labels on people" *(bu kou maozi)*, and "Don't use a big stick" *(bu da gunzi)*.[38] In Deng's formulation, democracy and "socialist legality" meant protecting people, particularly party officials, from the kind of attacks and pressures they had experienced at the hands of the overcentralized power of Maoist dictatorship and Cultural Revolution radicalism.

Central to the policies put forward at the Third Plenum were a final restoration of veteran officialdom and an accelerated purge of the purgers. Many verdicts were reversed at the Third Plenum, or, as Deng put it, "Remedies have been made for a number of major cases in which the charges were false or which were un-justly or incorrectly dealt with." Hence, unjustly accused and incorrectly treated cadres were to be rehabilitated, while "comrades" who had made mistakes were to be given time to think "so that they can recognize those mistakes and correct them."[39] Regarding officials recruited, appointed, and promoted during the Cul-tural Revolution decade, Deng was naturally less lenient. In December 1977, Deng had already called for "resolutely striking" *(jianjue daji)* Gang of Four adherents and had stated, "We should not entrust important jobs to persons who have made grave mistakes and whose attitude remains bad; they should be deprived of their current rank and perquisites."[40] At the Third Plenum, Deng more forcefully expanded on this theme, warning, "We must never assign important posts to persons who have engaged in beating, smashing, and looting, who have been obsessed by factional ideas, who sold their souls by framing innocent comrades, or who disregard the Party's vital interests."[41] While pushing for the comprehensive rehabilitation and restoration of veteran officialdom, Deng's policy statements throughout the late 1970s and early 1980s were permeated with warnings that Gang of Four adherents had to be harshly dealt with, lest they again rise up and attempt to seize power.[42]

## The Logic of Post-Mao Reform

The new course articulated at the Third Plenum represented vindication for the moderate market–material incentive policies of the early 1960s and the theory and program that resurgent officialdom had pushed since the late 1960s and early 1970s. But I have also suggested that the major consequence of Maoist power restructuring during the Cultural Revolution decade was to accelerate processes of power devolution and resource appropriation. This potent combination of old and new forces shaped the trajectory of post-Mao reform in the 1980s.

In summer 1981, the leadership of the CCP affirmed the "Resolution on Certain Questions in the History of the Party Since the Founding of the PRC." Put forward as the definitive ruling on the Cultural Revolution and Mao's place in history, the "Resolution" both commended Hua for his role in "smashing the Jiang Qing counter-revolutionary clique" and condemned him for a variety of "left" errors. Chief among Hua's left errors in political and economic policy were his "delay" and "obstruction" in the "business of restoring the old cadres" (huifu laoganbu gongzuo) and his "over-haste in quest of results" (qiucheng guoji), a reference to Hua's attempt to affirm authority–social mobilization methods and strengthen central economic controls in 1977–1978.[43] While formally condemning the last remnants of the Maoist power-restructuring program, the "Resolution" termed the Third Plenum a "great turning point of far-reaching significance in the history of our Party since the founding of the People's Republic."[44] We have seen that the new course articulated at the Third Plenum was prefigured in the theory and program of resurgent officialdom and the moderate policies of the early 1960s. In the course of legitimating and implementing these familiar ideas and policies, however, the post-Mao leadership unleashed and energized forces that in a few short years would transform the face of the Chinese economy and society.

In the late 1970s and the 1980s, China's central rulers either abandoned altogether or began to phase out control mechanisms that were integral to the Soviet and Chinese Communist systems but that had been undercut, discredited, and delegitimated during the Cultural Revolution decade. The attempt to impose ideological controls, an essential feature of Chinese communism and an even more important aspect of Maoism, was in large measure discontinued in the 1980s.[45] More important, authority–social mobilization organizational and developmental methods, both of the Soviet variety (central economic planning and centralized resource allocation) and of the Maoist variety (mass mobilization campaigns), were either reduced in scope or abandoned altogether. Overall, the classic Soviet and Chinese Communist insistence on exercising authoritative central economic control was deemphasized. In its place emerged a decentralized material incentive system.

At the Third Plenum, Deng pushed the idea of a "responsibility system" *(zeren zhi)*. This system, subsequently dubbed the "economic responsibility system" *(jingji zeren zhi)* or "production responsibility system" *(shengchan zeren zhi)*, was the economic centerpiece of post-Mao reform. The logic of the responsibility system was familiar and straightforward: Rewards and penalties, profits and losses, and promotions and demotions were to be based on economic performance. Economic units and individuals were to reap the benefits of good performance and to suffer the consequences of bad performance. Instead of looking to the state for handouts and subsidies, localities, factory managers, workers, and peasants were to assume an ownership stake in their enterprises, along with personal responsibility for the results. Accordingly, some localities, some factories, some workers, and some peasants would make more money than others because of superior economic performance. As Deng put it, "In economic policy, I think we should allow some regions and some enterprises and some workers and some peasants to earn more and enjoy more benefits sooner than others, in accordance with their hard work and greater contributions to society. . . . This will help the whole national economy to advance wave upon wave and help the people of all our nationalities to become prosperous in a comparatively short period."[46]

The responsibility system achieved its earliest and most impressive successes in the countryside, where market–material incentive policies had a proved record dating back to the early 1960s and had been strongly supported all along by the local population and the local leaders. We have seen that the history of Maoist agrarian radicalism was one of constant frustration in the face of an apparently ineradicable market–material incentive orientation at the village level. By the early 1980s, the individual peasant family had reemerged as the basic unit of production, and a highly effective system of material incentives was in place. The essential ingredient in this process was the "household contract" *(baochan daohu/baogan daohu)* system whereby individual peasant families signed contracts with state agencies to deliver fixed amounts of produce for fixed prices and thereby received exclusive rights to plots of land as well. Once the produce under contract was delivered and the taxes due paid, all remaining production became the private property of the peasant family, to be consumed, sold on the open market, or sold to the state at above-quota prices.[47] In essence, the household contract system was a market–material incentive arrangement fully reminiscent of the policies of the early 1960s. Yet by the mid-1980s, the policies of the late 1970s had resulted in the wide-ranging decollectivization and privatization of Chinese agriculture. How had this transformation occurred so rapidly and on such a huge scale?

In fact, the household contract system was not among the policies adopted at the Third Plenum. While urging that responsibility system policies be implemented in accordance with practical conditions at the local level, the Central Committee in April 1979 also decreed that "there is little difference between the household contract system and dividing up the land and working on one's own, and this is a form of retrogression."[48] But the pressure from below for the restoration of household contracting was unrelenting and mounted irresistibly. In September 1980, the Central Committee affirmed household contract system policies in remote and poverty-stricken areas and eased restrictions in other areas. By early 1981, the leadership had extended its overall endorsement in the name of "protecting the activism of the peasants, and protecting the development of productivity."[49]

The results are well known. Throughout the 1980s, Chinese agriculture experienced average annual growth rates in excess of 10 percent, and an economic boom of massive proportions unfolded in the villages. At the same time, a wide-ranging decollectivization and privatization of land and property occurred in the countryside. As William Hinton detailed, "In many cases, collective assets were simply broken up and sold to individual bidders; when it became clear that the collective's property was going to be contracted out, people came and dismantled whatever belonged to them jointly, including the headquarters, school, any publicly owned machinery, and so on."[50] I suggest that the onset of household contracting, decollectivization, and privatization in the 1980s must be understood in light of the decentralized processes of power and resource appropriation set in motion and reinforced over the course of the Cultural Revolution decade.

Similar developments occurred in Chinese industry in the late 1970s and the 1980s. At the Third Plenum, Deng spoke explicitly of the need to "expand the authority of the managerial personnel" *(kuoda guanli renyuan de quanxian)* and put them in important positions, raise their political status, and increase their material benefits.[51] These were familiar ideas dating back to the mid-1950s and early 1960s. As in the countryside, however, post-Mao reform in industry was accelerated by processes of power devolution and resource appropriation set in motion during the preceding decade.

In the spirit of the decentralized, material incentive logic put forward at the Third Plenum, central authorities in the late 1970s and early 1980s attempted to reform the financial relationship between industrial enterprises and the state. According to Naughton, three policies were implemented in succession: "profit retention," whereby enterprises were allowed to retain more profits from increased production; "profit-contracting," whereby enterprises delivered a base figure of profits to the state and kept the rest; and "tax-for-profit," whereby enterprises paid taxes directly to the state instead of channeling profits through superordinate bodies.[52] All three policies were designed to energize and increase the productivity of industrial enterprises by altering the incentive structure and giving factory managers more operational autonomy. Similarly, the materials allocation and investment decisionmaking process was reformed in the late 1970s, and the scope of central planning and central resource allocation was reduced, the number of central ministerial commands was cut, and enterprises were given more leeway in making production and investment decisions.[53] But industrial administration, investment decisionmaking, and materials allocation had already been substantially decentralized during the Cultural Revolution decade. As Wong therefore noted, "Having gained control over vast amounts of resources, local governments were, by the end of the Cultural Revolution, in a powerful position to push reforms along lines of further decentralization and to resist efforts to reassert central control."[54]

The results of industrial reform in the post-Mao period are also well known. Industrial output surged in the late 1970s and 1980s, and some sectors experienced growth rates comparable to or in excess of those in agriculture. But many state-owned factories continued to lose money and remain dependent on state subsidies and bailouts, and in November 1992 it was estimated that half of all state-owned firms still operated at a loss, while subsidies to money-losing firms consumed some 20 percent of central revenues.[55] Even as state-owned enterprises depleted state finances, however, the capacity of central authorities to tap the profits of successful enterprises and to influence investment decisions at the local level declined throughout the 1980s.[56]

The impact of post-Mao reform on the Chinese economy was profound, and I have argued that the extent and rapidity of change in the late 1970s and 1980s must be understood in light of the power-restructuring events of the preceding decade. At the same time, post-Mao processes of decentralization, decollectivization, and privatization accelerated the pace of change and affected power relations and political process in ways both new and familiar.

## The Changing Relationship Between Center and Locality

The validation and extension of decentralized material incentive policies at the Third Plenum triggered a huge surge in economic activity, spending, and consumption at the provincial and local levels in the late 1970s and early 1980s. Spurred by market forces and entrepreneurial energies pent up during the Cultural Revolution decade, and by government policies that sharply increased agricultural procurement prices, average per capita peasant incomes rose by some 20 percent in 1979 alone.[57] By 1980, government pronouncements were explicitly linking national economic development with increased local initiative and economic decisionmaking autonomy. Thus, *People's Daily* commentators urged localities to "Give Full Play to Advantages" since "the natural resources and natural economic conditions of localities are varied in myriad ways, and various local areas all have their own branches and products that are most conducive to economic development."[58] Local leaders were therefore urged to take the lead in identifying and promoting the comparative economic advantages of the areas under their jurisdiction. But this was to be a mutually beneficial and complementary process. Rather than constructing at great cost "large and complete" *(da er quan)* industrial complexes, regions historically strong in one area (e.g., Shanxi coal production) were urged to develop mutually beneficial relations with regions with other strengths (e.g., Shanghai consumer goods production).

The validation and extension of local initiative and economic decisionmaking autonomy were especially pronounced in agriculture. In line with the logic of comparative economic advantage, central controls over the peasantry were sharply downscaled in the late 1970s in favor of "measures suited to local conditions" *(yindi zhiyi)* and "home-grown policies." According to *People's Daily,* not only "must every province attentively give full play to its advantages, so too must every district, every commune, and every production brigade also attentively give full play to their individual advantages. "Regionalization" *(quyu hua)* and "specialization" *(zhuanye hua),* it was asserted, would result in myriad benefits, including increased per unit production, improved cultivation techniques, better labor productivity, more efficient utilization of resources, and more marketable agricultural products.[59]

Even as the official media championed local initiative and economic decisionmaking autonomy, central commentators warned against and sought to curb potential excesses. Containing runaway investment and capital construction at the local level remains one of the most vexing problems confronting central authorities in China in the mid-1990s. Yet in June 1980, *People's Daily* had already cautioned, "In certain areas, there presently exists such irrational phenomena as only paying attention to building new factories and not paying attention to thoroughly using old factories, only paying attention to expanding basic construction and not paying attention to tapping the reserves of, renovating, and transforming old factories."[60] But local managers and leaders continued to use their expanded economic decisionmaking powers in ways unacceptable to the central authorities. In the early 1980s, economic protectionism *(jingji fengsuo,* literally economic blockade) became increasingly common as managers and officials at the provincial level and below attempted to exclude less expensive, higher-quality, or more efficiently produced goods from their territory.[61] At the same time, the expansion of authority at the enterprise level precipitated a variety of operational and fiscal woes, including a broad decline in the quality of manufactured goods and a rise in unit costs, as managers sought to increase production, sales, and profits, and a surge in wage increases, capital construction, and investment expenditures, as managers and workers alike sought to capitalize on their newly enhanced fiscal autonomy.[62]

In late 1981 and early 1982, the central authorities attempted to reassert and reinforce central economic controls. Under the rubric of the old central planning slogan "the entire nation as a single chessboard" *(quanguo yi panqi)*, Premier Zhao Ziyang denounced the "trend of departmentalism and dispersionism" *(ben-weizhuyi he fensanzhuyi de qingxiang)* and reaffirmed central prerogatives in four key areas. Central controls were to be tightened in foreign trade; "localities, departments, and enterprises" were to adhere to central resource allocations; "localities and departments" were not to engage in "economic blockade" or to interfere with the free flow of goods; and the administration of prices and taxes was to be "centralized and unified" *(jizhong tongyi)*, while all "localities, departments, and enterprises" were to refrain from themselves assessing taxes, lowering tax rates, or raising and lowering prices.[63] As this litany of prohibitions suggests, the central authorities in the early 1980s were already having difficulties enforcing their policy preferences at the regional, provincial, and local levels.

The rise of local economic power was a manifestation of the power-devolving and resource-appropriating processes set in motion during the Cultural Revolution decade and accelerated by the policy shifts of the late 1970s. At the same time, the attempt to reimpose central economic controls in the early 1980s was undercut by more reformist policies. As early as mid-1981, some commentators were arguing that the solution to the newly arisen problems in enterprise management and fiscal discipline lay in the further extension of local economic decisionmaking authority and the economic responsibility system. According to the pronouncements of the Conference on Enterprise Readjustment in July 1981, it was "egalitarianism" *(pingzhunzhuyi)*, whereby enterprises and workers received the same subsidies and wages whether they performed well or poorly, that constituted the root cause of problems at the enterprise level. Such ills as waste, inflated prices, shoddy work, poor labor discipline, and "violations of financial discipline" *(weifan caijing jilu)* could be eliminated not by more control from above but by a "distribution system" *(fenpei zhidu)* that rewarded success and penalized failure.[64] Similarly, a *People's Daily* editorial in August 1981 maintained that the answer to the increase in surplus labor in the countryside lay in the further expansion of rural industry, more locally funded capital construction, and fiscal self-sufficiency at the local level. Hence, because the "financial strength of the state is limited," surplus labor in the villages could be effectively absorbed only by developing industrial and commercial operations on the spot with local resources and initiative.[65]

Throughout the 1980s and into the early 1990s, the most striking aspect of power relations between center and locality was not the often-commented-on tension between market and plan but rather the regularity with which attempts to reimpose central economic controls were undertaken and then failed or were sharply reduced in scope.[66] By 1985, as capital construction investment in the first half increased 44 percent from the year before and massively exceeded the 1.1 percent budgeted and rural industrial production rose 50 percent, central authorities concerned about energy shortages and inflationary pressures again sought to contain spending at the local level.[67] Less than a year later, however, a five-year plan calling for the accelerated transfer of administrative power to local governments and a broad reduction in state supervision at all levels of industry and commerce was adopted.[68] In 1987, central authorities again demanded that provincial agencies and local enterprises cut back and targeted capital construction for zero growth; yet capital construction rose by 25 percent in the first quarter of the year alone. By 1988–1989, the Chinese economy had become badly overheated, the cities especially were experiencing measurable increases in inflation, and Western analysts were asking "whether Li Peng or any national leader has the power to rein in an economy that is careening out of control."[69]

This buildup in inflationary pressures was one of the key contributing factors in the events leading up to the June 4, 1989, crackdown. In the period following the repression, the central authorities imposed a variety of stringent economic controls, the economy went into recession, and Western observers spoke of the regime's attempt to "turn back the political clock, suppress dissent, tighten the party's ideological control, and crack down on private Chinese businesses and flourishing rural industries."[70] But these dire warnings were wide of the mark, and by late 1990 and 1991, propelled by surging economic activity in the provinces and localities, the Chinese economy had come out of recession and resumed its advance, prompting the *New York Times* to concede in December 1991, "It is one of the paradoxes of the 1990s: China, with a hard-line Communist leadership, is booming along at a 6 percent growth rate, with low inflation, foreign investment up, and exports and foreign exchange reserves at record highs."[71]

Yet by 1992 inflationary pressures were building, and in mid-1993 central authorities were again attempting to regain control of a "chaotic financial system, where rampant illegal lending and unsustainable credit expansion have helped overheat the world's fastest growing economy."[72] By the early 1990s, however, the capacity of Chinese central authorities to impose their policy preferences in the provinces was more limited than ever. As analysts noted, the central government "lost the power of the purse in the profound changes in government spending and revenue and wholesale overhaul of the tax system that marked the 1979–1989 decade of reform"; as the economy expanded in the 1980s, state revenue as a percentage of gross national product plummeted from levels in excess of 30 percent in the late 1970s to 18 percent and below in the early 1990s.[73] This fundamental change in the relationship between center and locality was the consequence of power-devolving and resource-appropriating processes set in motion during the Cultural Revolution decade and accelerated by post-Mao reform.

## The Expansion of Official Power and Privilege

In the late 1970s and throughout the 1980s, the power and privileges of Chinese Communist officials expanded massively. This process was the by-product of the full-scale restoration of veteran officialdom and the purge of the purgers launched at the Third Plenum. Yet even as Deng in the late 1970s proclaimed that "we have rehabilitated our veteran comrades one after another and reinstated nearly all of them in their original posts or equivalent ones," he was not insensible to the problems arising from the "emancipation" of veteran officials. Noting that "one of the chief subjects of conversation among the masses recently has been precisely the pursuit of personal privileges by cadres . . . mainly senior cadres," Deng warned against the abuse of official power. Whereas some rehabilitated senior officials displayed "an insatiable desire for a life of ease and comfort and are always making their homes bigger, better, and more beautiful," others "are in bad repute in their own units and elsewhere mostly because of their children's misdeeds."[74] Significantly, Deng linked these behavioral problems to the events of the Cultural Revolution decade and observed, "At what time in the past did a Party committee secretary—a secretary of a county or a commune Party committee, say—have as much power as today? Never!" "Some things that alienate us from the people, including preferential treatment, existed before the Cultural Revolution, though to a far less serious extent than today. At that time cadres had self-discipline and were concerned about the people."[75]

In the early 1980s, the central authorities attempted to counter mounting problems of official power abuse, privilege seeking, and organizational bloating by launching a campaign to reorganize and revitalize the party and state apparatus. Official corruption was explicitly targeted, and the details of a smuggling scandal involving "state cadres" *(guojia ganbu)* in the China Electronic Technology Import-Export Corporation were revealed in the central media in March 1982. Because the "smuggling and tax evasion" *(zouci taoshui)* and the "reaping of huge and sudden profits" *(mouqu baoli)* of these officials had cost the state hundreds of thousands of yuan in customs revenue and had harmed China's emerging consumer electronics industry as well, the Central Discipline Committee vowed to conduct a "thorough investigation, in which the more important the personage and agency, the more seriously and heavily they will be dealt with."[76] As Deng himself noted a month later, this was no isolated instance, but "an ill wind, and a strong one." Indeed, so many cadres had recently been caught up in "economic crime" that "unless we take it seriously and firmly stop it, the question of whether our Party will change its nature will arise."[77]

At the same time, an ambitious effort to reorganize and streamline the party and state apparatus at the central and provincial levels was undertaken. At the center occurred a far-reaching numerical reduction and functional concentration of agencies, committees, offices, and executive positions in the State Council. The number of vice premiers was reduced from an unwieldy thirteen to two; the number of sections and committees, and subordinate organizations, was reduced from ninety-eight to approximately fifty-two; and overall employment was reduced by some one-third. In Premier Zhao's words, the purpose of these carefully thought out and long overdue measures was to eliminate the "multi-headed leadership" *(lingdao duotou)* and "administrative fragmentation" *(guanli fensan)* that currently afflicted the central organs.[78]

At the provincial level, the reorganization and streamlining of the party and state apparatus appeared even more wide-ranging. According to the calculations of William deB. Mills, provincial leadership bodies—provincial party secretaries, members of provincial party standing committees, and governors and vice governors—had been reduced by "fully 50 percent" by mid-1983.[79] As "some 950 of China's 1,350 top provincial leaders retired and were replaced by about 160 new officials," this process "left China's provinces under the control of much smaller leading bodies composed of officials, who, presumably, would be both more efficient and more responsive to central policies." Despite stubborn official resistance in some provinces, in mid-1985, according to Mills, "the outwardly smooth and rapid transfer of provincial leadership was an impressive display of reformist power." He concluded, "The streamlining of provincial leadership in the spring of 1983 and the subsequent reforms at the provincial level and below have also demonstrated a move towards the establishment of a modern bureaucratic system in which the selection, promotion, and retirement of personnel is based on predictable, clearly-stated regulations."

The proposition that Chinese Communist officialdom became more modern in the course of post-Mao reform was most systematically put forward by Hong Yung Lee in his *From Revolutionary Cadres to Party Technocrats in Socialist China*. Explicitly invoking Weber's model of legal-rational bureaucracy, Lee asserted that "China's new leaders" were "bureaucratic technocrats" recruited, appointed, and promoted on the basis of education, merit, and professional expertise. In contrast to earlier generations of "revolutionary cadres," these new bureaucratic technocrats were pragmatic, nonideological problemsolvers and were more committed to "formal procedural rules" since they "do not enjoy the close and extensive informal ties that the revolutionary cadres developed during their prolonged careers."[80] Deploying the familiar modernization thesis, Lee suggested that this shift was both necessary and inevitable because the bureaucratic technocrats "have a better understanding of and better qualifications to deal with such prerequisites of industrialized society as functional specialization, the coordination of parts, rational decision making, and problem solving."[81]

But the notion that Chinese Communist officialdom became more modern and legal-rational in the course of post-Mao reform is sharply contradicted by the sociopolitical developments of the 1980s and early 1990s. In fact, the greatly expanded power of officials and their families in the post-Mao period was manifested in a steadily escalating binge of corruption, extortion, privilege seeking, influence peddling, and resource appropriation. Of course, Deng from the outset had cautioned against "people who abuse power and encroach upon the interests of the masses, pursue a privileged life-style for themselves and even act tyrannically and outrageously" and warned against the "appetites of their relatives and children."[82] In September 1985, however, party elder and long-standing market–material incentive proponent Chen Yun delivered a speech entitled "Combat Corrosive Ideology" in which he denounced the proliferation of "unhealthy tendencies" and "violations of law and discipline" in CCP ranks, and he spoke of "the in-

trusion of decadent capitalist ideology and workstyle." Thus, "many Party committees and cadres have let down their guard against this. . . . Whenever we talk
about the policy of opening up to the world and reinvigorating the domestic
economy, Party and administrative cadres and their children swarm forward to do
business." And "since the last quarter of 1984, some 20,000 various companies
have sprung up, a considerable number of which collaborate with law-breakers
and foreign businessmen. Taking advantage of reforms, these new companies have
been involved in all sorts of criminal activities, including speculating on the rise
and fall in prices, engaging in illegal trade, offering and taking bribes, and traffik-
ing in stolen goods."[83]

Foremost in Chen's mind, no doubt, was the Hainan smuggling and black market currency scandal of 1984–1985, the biggest case of official corruption to hit
China since the communists had come to power in 1949. Between January 1984
and March 1985, local officials on the island raised 4.2 billion yuan, which they
converted into hard currency on the black market and used to import huge
amounts of Japanese consumer goods (89,000 cars and light trucks, 2.7 million
color television sets, 250,000 VCRs, 122,000 motorcycles, etc.) for resale on the
mainland. Because consumers paid up to 300 percent of the original price, a "gold
rush" atmosphere developed, officials and employees in participating enterprises
were paid off handsomely, and resources intended for capital construction were
diverted and appropriated on an unprecedented scale. Yet by 1985, official corruption was already so widespread that top Chinese Communist leaders were complaining that "using one's position and powers to make a fortune from reform"
had infected "not only factories, mines, and other local institutions, but officials
all the way up to national ministries."[84] Three years later, as official power abuse
grew ever more prevalent, *People's Daily* commentators suggested that corruption
was an "inevitable accompaniment of social progress"; at the same time, polls revealed that 83.7 percent of urban residents listed the corrupt behavior of government officials as the thing they resented most.[85]

Popular outrage over official corruption was the second key contributing factor
in the sociopolitical ferment leading up to the June 4 crackdown. But official corruption was intrinsic to the post-Mao scene. Indeed, the prevalence and inexorable rise of official corruption provide the clearest illustration of my discussion
regarding power-devolving and resource-appropriating processes set in motion
during the Cultural Revolution decade and accelerated by post-Mao reform. We
have seen how resurgent officialdom waged a determined battle on behalf of its
theory and program in the late 1960s and 1970s; this victory was formalized at the
Third Plenum, and the power of officials at the regional, provincial, and local levels was expanded accordingly. Not surprisingly, most veteran officials were quick
to take personal advantage of this political victory as compensation for the attacks
they had suffered from 1966 to 1976.

Furthermore, official corruption was the logical consequence of the politics of
post-Mao reform. While demanding the purge of the purgers, Deng also spoke of
the need to select successors and noted the "many fine young people" who are

"professionally competent, have managerial ability, and really know how to do their work." Deng also stressed the importance of selecting "people who are politically and ideologically sound, strong in Party spirit . . . and have a good all-round record."[86] When the party and state apparatus was apparently reorganized and streamlined in the 1980s, however, the primary criteria for recruiting, appointing, and promoting new officials were not merit, education, professional competence, and managerial ability. Instead, political considerations and personal connections were paramount, and the beneficiaries of "bureaucratic reform" were overwhelmingly the children, relatives, and friends of veteran cadres. Lee, directly contradicting his own legal-rational bureaucratic technocrat argument, himself showed how veteran cadres were induced to "retire" in the early 1980s by being allowed to choose their own successors. Thus, "the groups that have most conspicuously benefited from the new policy are the children and the former secretaries of high-ranking cadres, as well as former leaders of the Communist Youth League." Furthermore, it was the children of veteran cadres who most readily met the political requirements since they, too, had suffered persecution during the Cultural Revolution and could be counted on not to betray their retired parents. In sum, post-Mao bureaucratic reform was nepotistic and particularistic from start to finish and bore scant resemblance to the "merit-based recruitment policy" that supposedly characterized the shift "from revolutionary cadres to party technocrats in socialist China."[87]

Of course, officials appointed on particularistic and nepotistic bases emulate and extend these practices, and throughout the 1980s and into the 1990s the children and relatives of high-ranking veteran officials *(gaogan zidi)* routinely profited from their high-level connections, regularly occupied senior positions in their elders' old institutional bailiwicks, and systematically used their favored position to secure lucative contracts, commissions, and fees. Just as such practices were established at the top in Republican China and were then extended throughout the structure of power, a similar pattern prevailed in post-Mao China. In late 1985, the minister in charge of the Commission on Science, Technology, and Industry was the son-in-law of Marshal Nie Rongzhen, a retired Politburo member who had run China's nuclear weapons program in the 1960s; the new minister of ordnance was the son-in-law of Marshal Ye Jianying, another retired Politburo member; and Chen Yun's daughter-in-law, employed by a U.S. computer firm and working toward a doctorate in engineering at the University of Michigan, was using her connections to secure a contract for the firm to market its software in China.[88] In November 1992, three and a half years after the June 4 crackdown, all of Deng's sons, daughters, and son-in-laws occupied prominent state positions, ranging from deputy director of the PLA Armaments Department, to vice chairman of the State Commission of Science and Technology, to assistant general manager of the China International Trust and Investment Company.[89]

It is evident that the configuration of power and privilege in post-Mao China, which hinges on the primacy of personal connections and the secondary importance of rules and regulations, more fully corresponds to Weber's model of patri-monial domination than to his model of legal-rational domination. Furthermore, the ascendancy of patrimonialism in contemporary China must be understood in light of the restructuring of power set in motion during the Cultural Revolution and accelerated by post-Mao reform.

## The Significance of the June 4 Crackdown

In April and May 1989, massive popular demonstrations in Peking's Tiananmen Square, and in other Chinese cities as well, directly confronted the Deng regime with protests against inflation and official corruption and demands for more democracy. As the world knows, these demonstrations were put down with brute force as hundreds and possibly thousands of civilian demonstrators and by-standers in Peking were killed by military and police units.[90]

Western analysts, from mainstream academics and journalists, to commenta-tors on the Left, reacted to the bloodletting with fury, despair, and more than a lit-tle hysteria. Thus, Brantly Womack expressed "profound shock and outrage at the massacre," called "the violence of the mass repression . . . unprecedented," and wondered "how long the regime might last" and "what might succeed it."[91] Simi-larly, Tsou spoke of "an immovable pyramid of power and a recompressed civil so-ciety" and a "polarization" of the party-state and society and pronounced, "The Beijing regime has achieved a victory only in the sense that it has been able to maintain itself in power, however poor its prospects for economic development, however uncertain its political future, however adverse its international circum-stances."[92] On the Left, Hinton denounced "the reactionary essence of China's current leading group," spoke of the "bloodstained" regime's "confrontation with the whole Chinese people," and termed June 4 "a stark watershed in China's mod-ern history."[93] Mainstream analysts also saw the crackdown as a critical turning point that signaled the end of the reform era. Fewsmith wrote, "The events of June 4, 1989, in a very real sense brought the Dengist period to a close"; David Bach-man went even further and spoke of the "failure" of the reforms of 1978–1989 and "their termination as symbolized by the Tiananmen massacre."[94] Nor were West-ern analysts alone in these dire assessments. As Wakeman reported in September 1989, "The most prevalent mood among urban intellectuals, it seems, is gloomy despair about China's future."[95]

In hindsight, it is evident that these analysts, and many others as well, were overcome by the bloody events of June 4. But in fact, the scale of Tiananmen re-pression was not unprecedented and was quite limited compared to the blood-shed of the Cultural Revolution decade and that of the preceding centuries. More-over, the repression signified neither the end of post-Mao reform nor the demise of the Deng regime. Rather, it is the continuity of the crackdown and its aftermath with the events of the Cultural Revolution decade and the post-Mao era that is striking.

First, the Chinese Communist regime under Mao, but even more consistently under Deng, had a well-established record of using military force to put down popular outbursts and upheavals. In Chapter 7, I emphasized the coercive and often violent behavior of the PLA throughout the Cultural Revolution decade and in the course of the "disciplinary" campaigns of 1968–1970 especially. But Mao was not alone in using the army to restore order, and it was Deng who sent troops into Hangzhou to crush the last outburst of Cultural Revolution mass radicalism in 1975.[96] Indeed, Deng from the outset premised post-Mao reform on the strict enforcing of law and order and "stability and unity" *(anding tuanjie)* and in January 1980 asserted, "We must continue to strike resolutely at various kinds of criminals, so as to ensure and consolidate a sound, secure public order. . . . Being soft on criminals only endangers the interests of the vast majority of people and the overall interests of the modernization drive."[97]

Throughout the 1980s, Chinese internal security forces were expanded and modernized for the express purpose of curbing popular outbursts and political dissent. In 1983, a new paramilitary force to counter internal riot and rebellion was established, the People's Armed Police (PAP) *(Renmin wuzhuang jingcha)*. "By 1989, there were over one million PAP troops garrisoned throughout China in newly constructed buildings like the multistoried headquarters bristling with radio antennae in the Western Beijing suburb of Haidian."[98] Just as the government arrested and imprisoned the leaders of the short-lived Democracy Wall movement in the late 1970s, it accused student prodemocracy demonstrators in December 1986 of trying to "disrupt stability and unity" *(pohuai anding tuanjie)* and to "derange production and social order" just as the Red Guards had twenty years earlier.[99] From the perspective of the Deng regime, the demonstrations leading up to the June 4 crackdown were only too reminiscent of the kind of "chaos" *(luan)* that had erupted during the opening phases of the Cultural Revolution; the demonstrations were dealt with accordingly. Just as CCP rulers had used the "pillar of the dictatorship of the proletariat" to repress mass radicalism in late 1967 and 1968, Deng acclaimed the army's actions in June 1989 as proof that "the People's Army is truly a great wall of iron and steel for the party and country."[100]

Second, the fears of the Deng regime were well founded. Just as the participants in the Democracy Wall movement of the late 1970s used tactics and aired demands stemming directly from the Cultural Revolution, many parallels linked the demonstrations of April and May 1989 to the popular upheavals of 1966–1967. To be sure, in contrast to the militant Red Guard rhetoric of class struggle and proletarian dictatorship in 1966, the demonstrations in 1989 called for the rule of law and democracy and espoused a philosophy of nonviolence. Nor were the events leading up to June 4 sanctioned from on high, and there was no authority figure to briefly protect the youthful demonstrators. Yet as in summer and fall 1966, a critique of the established Chinese political and social order keyed the mass demonstrations in April and May 1989. In rhetoric and imagery fully reminiscent of the

Cultural Revolution, a collection of 1989 writings and speeches contained a "large allegorical drawing at Peking University, in which a massive rock of feudalism is crushing the Chinese people while officials plunder the land's riches."[101] Just as traditional Chinese political culture was targeted in 1966–1967, a big-character poster in this collection was entitled "Unless the Net Is Torn, the Fish Will Die," condemned "huge networks of personal connections," and declared that "in the forty years since the founding of the People's Republic, the struggle against feudalism has never been interrupted, yet feudalism's ancient roots disappear only to reappear, tugging on people's souls."[102] Indeed, when demonstrators in 1989 called for democracy, their overriding grievances were the familiar ones of official power abuse and official corruption, and when they called for the rule of law, they articulated the familiar popular demand that officialdom be made more upright and more accountable. Hence, "the Democracy Movement was as much a protest against 'bureaucratism'—in Chinese eyes, the arbitrary exercise of power or the abuse of power by Party officials—as it was a demand for democracy."[103]

Finally, the June 4 crackdown did not signify the end of the post-Mao era or the termination of post-Mao reform. Instead, the processes of decentralization, regionalization, marketization, privatization, and commercial opening up to the outside world that had gained momentum in the 1980s were largely unaffected by the crackdown and in short order resumed their forward movement. Fewsmith, who had earlier proclaimed the "end of the Dengist era," conceded in 1994 that "economic reform in China has regained its momentum," yet he attributed this turn of events to Deng's ability to fight off "conservative" opponents with a different political and economic agenda and achieve a "tremendous personal victory."[104]

But the suggestion that Deng somehow personally salvaged the reform process from conservative forces in the wake of the crackdown is incredible. I have argued that post-Mao reform was a manifestation of the fundamental restructuring of power that the Chinese polity and economy had undergone in the course of the upheavals and conflicts of the Cultural Revolution decade. It therefore comes as no surprise that the events of June 4 had no lasting effect on processes of decentralization, privatization, and commercialization that were already well established at the regional, provincial, and local levels. I have also argued that Chinese Communist officialdom was the chief beneficiary of the restructuring of power set in motion during the Cultural Revolution and accelerated by post-Mao reform. Far from jeopardizing the power and legitimacy of the Deng regime, the ferocity of the June 4 crackdown underscored the determination of China's rulers to uphold their long-standing theory and program of economic liberalization and political authoritarianism.

## Conflict and Control in Contemporary China

The theory and program worked in the 1980s, and in the early 1990s the post-Mao upwelling of local initiatives, economic expansion, and entrepreneurial energies continued to accelerate. In 1993, new International Monetary Fund calculations revealed that the Chinese economy was four times larger than previously measured and in fact constituted the third largest in the world, producing $1.7 trillion in goods and services in 1992.[105] In 1992–1993, the Chinese economy expanded at the fastest rate in the world, prompting some Western analysts to warn of inflationary pressures, while others spoke glowingly of China as the "emerging economic powerhouse of the 21st century."[106] Ample evidence testified to China's burgeoning internal and international economic might. While foreign corporations made substantial long-term investments and signed multibillion-dollar trade and infrastructure development deals, firms such as Procter and Gamble, Unilever, Johnson and Johnson, and Colgate-Palmolive rushed to tap China's increasingly prosperous and potentially massive consumer market.[107] In 1992, China exported $25.68 billion worth of goods to the United States and imported $7.47 billion worth of U.S. goods in return; yet when this trade imbalance threatened the renewal of China's most-favored-nation status in 1993, Chinese officials were able to spend $1 billion on U.S. planes, cars, and oil equipment and induce firms such as Boeing, McDonnell Douglas, Motorola, General Electric, and Weyerhaeuser to lobby for renewal.[108] China was also able to use its growing economic might to enhance its geopolitical power by purchasing billions of dollars' worth of the most advanced Soviet military technology.[109]

Four years after the June 4 crackdown, while Western commentators acclaimed this economic boom, they continued to speak of the "riddle of China" and to contrast the political authoritarianism of the Deng regime with the mounting economic surge of the early 1990s.[110] The rampant official corruption and recurrent inflation plaguing post-Mao China were thus depicted as the inevitable consequences of a "half-reformed" system that still featured significant levels of central economic planning and state ownership and remained politically authoritarian.[111] As always, democracy and more market-oriented reform were held out as the only viable solutions to these problems. My perspective is different. I contend that conflict in post-Mao China stemmed from the mounting erosion of central power, whereby the same forces that propelled the post-Mao economic boom simultaneously gave rise to social, political, and economic conflicts both new and familiar.

We have seen that rising official corruption, recurrent inflationary pressures, and deteriorating central fiscal capacities both stemmed from and were accelerated by the decentralizing thrust of post-Mao reform. Other important sources of tension and potential conflict in contemporary China include widening developmental disparities, which separate the prosperous coastal areas from regions in the interior, increasingly affluent groups from the poor, and the booming and modernizing cities from the countryside.[112] As detailed in Chapters 2 and 6, the historical response of Chinese communism to the conflicts, crises, and dislocation of Republican China was the concentration of power and the centralization of authority. While the economy was being restructured in the 1950s with central planning and central resource allocation mechanisms, CCP "ideology and organization" were subjecting the society and polity to "a web of organization which covers all Chinese society and penetrates deep into its fabric."[113] During the Cultural Revolution, this powerful combination of macroeconomic controls and CCP ideology and organization experienced a massive sociopolitical battering from which it never fully recovered. As a result, official power holders in the post-Mao era increasingly relied on a different mix of policies to maintain control.

On the one hand, China's post-Mao rulers made economic development and the raising of mass living standards their key goal and the means by which they legitimated their power, and on the other, they backed up their hold on power with expanded and modernized coercive mechanisms. While triggering an economic boom of historic proportions, the decentralized, material incentive logic of post-Mao reform also resulted in pervasive official corruption, localism, inflation, an erosion of central fiscal capacities, and widening developmental and social disparities. During the June 4 crackdown, the Deng regime was able to use its power to forcibly curb popular outrage over corruption and inflation and induce an economic recession. Yet corruption and inflation soon resurfaced in even more widespread and formidable form, and in summer 1993 authorities at the top launched yet another effort to reassert central economic controls, reform the financial system, and curb official corruption. Thus, Vice Premier and Politburo member Zhu Rongji spoke of recalling speculative loans used in property and stock markets, scaling back infrastructure spending, reducing government operating expenses, raising interest rates, and bestowing new powers on central banking authorities.[114]

Similarly, CCP chief Jiang Zemin called official corruption a "virus" that threatened to undermine political stability and vowed to punish cases of "serious abuse of power for personal gains by leading government and party cadres." Meanwhile, party authorities issued new rules forbidding officials at the county level and above to engage in commercial or paid media activities; to give preferential treatment to spouses, children, relatives, or friends running businesses; to hold any post in an economic entity while in office; to trade in stocks; to accept gifts of money, negotiable securities, or credit cards; and so on.[115] But these by-now-well-worn pronouncements and prohibitions were more problematic than ever. Official corruption and inflation were rooted in the logic and structure of post-Mao reform, mirroring the Deng regime's inability and disinclination to fight decentralized processes of power and resource appropriation in the manner of assertive Chinese and Russian central rulers in imperial times and under communism.

By 1993, Chinese and Western observers were speaking of the resemblance between contemporary China and earlier periods of dynastic decay and political disarray and noting such similarities as rampant official corruption, repressive official policies, irrelevant official ideologies, regionalism, fragmentation, and incipient warlordism.[116] Yet some analysts were persuaded that the post-Mao economic boom made the crucial difference; that economic growth had created a more educated, technocratic, middle-class society; and that China in the future would increasingly resemble Taiwan and South Korea.[117]

But economic booms do not last forever and are typically followed by slow-downs, recessions, and busts. Significantly, whereas the post-Mao economic boom first got going in the countryside, rural areas in 1993 experienced serious political and social unrest as peasants squeezed by declining growth rates, falling incomes, inflation, and predatory local officials rose in protests.[118] In patterns of behavior paralleling those of local power holders in late-nineteenth- and early-twentieth-century China, rural officials were levying exorbitant taxes, paying peasants with worthless promissory notes, and pocketing the revenue themselves. As always, the central authorities vowed to crack down on official malfeasance. As Western commentators observed, however, "Efforts to mollify the peasants may not work. Power in China has decentralized to the point where Beijing has lost a great deal of control, particularly in the far-flung provinces. Theoretically, local officials face punishment if they tax peasants more than 5% of their income. But many local authorities simply ignore orders from the center and exact whatever fees they want."[119] The familiar processes of decentralized power and resource appropriation originating in the conflicts and upheavals of the Cultural Revolution decade and accelerated by post-Mao reform were exacting an increasingly heavy toll at all levels of Chinese society in the 1990s.

## The Transition from Socialism in China

An evolving synthesis of old patterns and new realities, the transition from socialism in China is variously driven by the power-restructuring events of the Cultural Revolution, the changes of the post-Mao period, and the resurfacing of political patterns reminiscent of nineteenth- and early-twentieth-century China. In China, and in other former socialist countries as well, the transition from socialism is characterized by four closely interrelated features: (1) economic and political decentralization, (2) marketization and privatization, (3) cultural liberalization and opening up to the outside world, and (4) political authoritarianism and nationalism.

In contrast to the centralization of political and economic decisionmaking power that prevailed in the 1950s and early 1960s, the transition from socialism in China is characterized by high levels of regional, provincial, and local fiscal and operational autonomy. Because these new centers of power themselves command considerable resources, they are independent-minded and often unamenable to central controls and policy preferences. We have seen that post-Mao reform formalized and accentuated the decentralization of power set in motion during the Cultural Revolution decade, a process that continued to accelerate in the 1980s and early 1990s.

In contrast to the unyielding hostility to markets, private enterprise, and private property holding that characterized Chinese and Soviet socialism in its classic form, the transition from socialism is driven by rapidly expanding processes of privatization and marketization. In the 1980s, Chinese agriculture was essentially decollectivized, retail trade was significantly privatized, and a vast export-oriented manufacturing sector was established, resulting in a fundamental transformation of China's socialist economy. In the early 1990s, processes of privatization and marketization were extended to the state-owned industrial sector, and the transformation of this bastion of socialism was begun. In the post-Mao period, both privileged and nonprivileged groups developed deep stakes in the privatization and marketization of the Chinese economy.

In a striking departure from the autarkic stance adopted by the communist nations historically, the transition from socialism in China hinges on significant cultural liberalization and a massive commercial opening up to the outside world. These are complementary processes that are manifested in myriad ways: direct foreign investment from Western and Japanese firms and from overseas Chinese, Hong Kong, and Taiwan; export-oriented joint manufacturing ventures, in southern China especially; the introduction and application of Western financial structures, management practices, and marketing techniques; and the importation of Western consumer culture in the form of movies, videos, television programs, consumer electronics, rock and roll, and blue jeans, among other things. At the same time, cultural liberalization and opening up to the outside world entail a loosening of social controls, which in the post-Mao period resulted in sharp increases in crime, prostitution, drug use, pornography, and a variety of corresponding social ills.

Political and economic decentralization, privatization and marketization, and cultural liberalization and opening up to the outside world represent historic departures from Chinese socialism in its historical form. But the political order in China remains authoritarian and closely linked to the socialist past. In contemporary China, power holders high and low resist legal and popular constraints, have scant tolerance for political dissent and organized political competition, and routinely practice personal rulership and autocracy. Property relations remain fluid and subject to political power, and personal relations, patron-client networks, and corruption supersede laws, regulations, and constitutions. Whereas revolution and communism were the ideals by which Chinese Communist rulers legitimated their power in the past, a modernized, prosperous, and powerful Chinese nation is now the end that sanctifies existing power arrangements. As we have seen, China's rulers aim to realize this purpose with a combination of economic liberalization and political authoritarianism, by which they seek to maintain the stability and unity on which economic modernization depends.

Viewed in historical perspective, China in the post-Mao era emerged as an economic giant and claimed its rightful place as one of the world's great political and military powers. This was the view of China's rulers, who affirmed China's new international status by building up a formidable geopolitical military presence and extending China's influence far and wide.[120] But a historical perspective also suggests a more pessimistic view. While triggering an economic boom, decentralized processes of power and resource appropriation in post-Mao China also resulted in conflicts and tensions that often paralleled the crisis conditions of late-nine-teenth- and early-twentieth-century China. As China enters the twenty-first century, the further acceleration of these processes raises the probability of political fragmentation, social crisis, and economic breakdown in the years to come.

## Notes

1. In 1992, China's GDP grew by 12 percent in real terms, exports surpassed those of either Taiwan or South Korea, $9 billion was invested from abroad, and foreign exchange reserves stood at $50 billion (Andrew Tanzer, "A Chinese Riddle for President Clinton," *Forbes,* January 18, 1993, 37).

2. For a colorful account of the proliferation of Western consumer culture in the 1980s, see Orville Schell, *Discos and Democracy—China in the Throes of Reform* (New York: Anchor, 1989).

3. In an account of the emergence of market-oriented rural reform in Anhui Province, Joseph Fewsmith noted the implementation of the "household responsibility system" in the early 1960s and then discussed its revival by Deng Xiaoping ally Wan Li in 1977, omitting entirely a consideration of the intervening decade and a half! See *Dilemmas of Reform in China: Political Conflict and Economic Debate* (Armonk, N.Y.: M. E. Sharpe, 1994), 20–27.

4. Harry Harding, *China's Second Revolution* (Washington, D.C.: Brookings Institution, 1987), 70, 2; Fewsmith, *Dilemmas of Reform in China,* 241. Fewsmith's analysis of the trajectory of post-Mao reform is focused almost exclusively on policy disputes, personal rivalries, and economic debates at the top.

5. Tang Tsou, "Political Change and Reform: The Middle Course," in *The Cultural Revolution and Post-Mao Reforms: A Historical Perspective* (Chicago: University of Chicago Press, 1986), 219.

6. Ibid., 219–221.

7. Victor Nee, "A Theory of Market Transition," *American Sociological Review* 54, 5 (October 1989):678. For Nee's subsequent qualification of his theory, see "Social Inequalities in Reforming State Socialism: Between Redistribution and Markets in China," *American Sociological Review* 56, 3 (June 1991):267–282.

8. R. Randle Edwards, "Civil and Social Rights: Theory and Practice in Chinese Law Today," in R. Randle Edwards, Louis Henkin, and Andrew Nathan, eds., *Human Rights in Contemporary China* (New York: Columbia University Press, 1986), 42.

9. Hong Yung Lee, *From Revolutionary Cadres to Party Technocrats in Socialist China* (Berkeley and Los Angeles: University of California Press, 1991) 387–388, 408.

10. Michael Buroway, "The End of Sovietology and the Renaissance of Modernization Theory," *Contemporary Sociology* 21, 6 (November 1992):774. Buroway provided a penetrating critique of the prevailing assumption among Western Soviet specialists on the inevitability of movement in the direction of a market economy and political democracy in the former Soviet Union.

11. Edwards, "Civil and Social Rights," 74–75.

12. Andrew J. Nathan, "Sources of Chinese Rights Thinking," in Edwards et al., eds., *Human Rights in Contemporary China,* 163.

13. Tsou, "Political Change and Reform," 257.

14. Lee, *From Revolutionary Cadres to Party Technocrats, in Socialist China,* 400.

15. Lynn T. White III, *Policies of Chaos: The Organizational Causes of Violence in China's Cultural Revolution* (Princeton: Princeton University Press, 1989), 335.

16. Harry Harding, "Political Development in Post-Mao China," in A. Doak Barnett and Ralph N. Clough, eds., *Modernizing China—Post-Mao Reform and Development* (Boulder: Westview Press, 1986), 17.

17. Jurgen Domes, "Introduction," in James T. Myers, Jurgen Domes, and Milton T. Yeh, eds., *Chinese Politics—Documents and Analysis,* vol. 2, *Ninth Party Congress (1969) to the Death of Mao (1976)* (Columbia: University of South Carolina Press, 1989), 8.

18. Carl Riskin, "Neither Plan nor Market: Mao's Political Economy," in William A. Joseph, Christine P.W. Wong, and David Zweig, eds., *New Perspectives on the Cultural Revolution* (Cambridge, Mass.: Harvard University Press, 1991), 133.

19. Carl Riskin, *China's Political Economy: The Quest for Development Since 1949* (New York: Oxford University Press, 1987), 282.

20. Barry Naughton, "The Decline of Central Control over Investment in Post-Mao China," in David M. Lampton, ed., *Policy Implementation in Post-Mao China* (Berkeley and Los Angeles: University of California Press, 1987), 54.

21. Christine Wong, "The Maoist 'Model' Reconsidered: Local Self-Reliance and the Financing of Rural Industrialization," in Joseph et al., eds., *New Perspectives on the Cultural Revolution,* 183–196.

22. David Zweig, *Agrarian Radicalism in China, 1968–1981* (Cambridge, Mass.: Harvard University Press, 1989), 11.

23. Wong, "The Maoist 'Model' Reconsidered," 195.

24. Zweig, *Agrarian Radicalism in China,* 167; see chap. 7 for a detailed discussion of decentralized power and resource appropriation during the Cultural Revolution decade.

25. Andrew G. Walder, "Some Ironies of the Maoist Legacy in Industry," in Mark Selden and Victor Lippit, eds., *The Transition to Socialism in China* (Armonk, N.Y.: M. E. Sharpe, 1982), 229.

26. For a classic account of official corruption, patron-client networks, and power and resource appropriation at the local level, in this instance involving a woman who rose to power during the Cultural Revolution, see Liu Binyan, *People or Monsters?* (Bloomington: Indiana University Press, 1983), 37, 48–49, 57.

27. For an account of a mother's attempt to get her daughter transferred back to Peking from the countryside by means of elaborate gift giving and subservience to the PLA officer in charge, see Yue Daiyun and Carolyn Wakeman, *To the Storm* (Berkeley and Los Angeles: University of California Press, 1985), 338–339. See also Andrew G. Walder, *Communist Neo-Traditionalism* (Berkeley and Los Angeles: University of California Press, 1986), 211.

28. *Renmin ribao,* January 14, 1977; cited in Nai-Ruenn Chen, "Economic Modernization in Post-Mao China: Policies, Problems, and Prospects," in *Chinese Economy Post-Mao* (Washington, D.C.: Joint Economic Committee, Congress of the United States, 1978), vol. 1, 182.

29. Hua Guofeng, "Political Report to the Eleventh National Congress of the CCP," in *Documents of the Eleventh National Congress of the CCP* (Peking: Foreign Languages Press, 1977), 35–37.

30. Ibid., 45, 83.

31. Ibid., 85–86.

32. While other leaders referred to "our wise leader Chairman Hua," Deng Xiaoping in his closing address contented himself with "Comrade Hua" and noted pointedly, "We must reject flashiness without substance and every sort of boasting," "there must be less empty talk and more hard work," and "we must face reality, for there are many problems to be tackled and many difficulties to be surmounted." ("Closing Address," in *Documents of the Eleventh National Congress of the CCP,* 191–195). We have seen that this is precisely the kind of language moderate leaders used to criticize Mao in the wake of the Great Leap disaster.

33. Lee, *From Revolutionary Cadres to Party Technocrats in Socialist China,* 147–148.

34. Ibid., 148–149.

35. Deng Xiaoping, "Jiefang cixiang, shishi qiushi, tuanjie yizhi, xiang qian kan" (Emancipate the mind, seek truth from facts, unite as one in looking to the future), December 13, 1978, in Deng Xiaoping, *Selected Works of Deng Xiaoping (1975–1982)* (Peking: Foreign Languages Press, 1984), 135.

36. Ibid., 136.

37. Ibid., 132.

38. Ibid., 134.

39. Ibid., 137.

40. Deng Xiaoping, "Zai zhongyang junwei quanti huiyi de jianghua" (Speech at the plenary meeting of the military commission of the central committee), December 28, 1977, in ibid., 70–71.

41. Deng, "Jiefang cixiang, shishi qiushi, tuanjie yizhi, xiang qian kan," 138.

42. Hence, "haven't we reversed many wrong verdicts pronounced during the period when Lin Biao and the Gang of Four were running rampant? If such persons are allowed to succeed us and hold power, they will certainly change those verdicts back again" (Deng Xiaoping, "Gaoji ganbu yao daitou fayang dang de youliang chuantong" [Senior cadres must take the lead in upholding the party's fine traditions], November 2, 1979, in Deng, *Selected Works of Deng Xiaoping,* 194).

43. "Xuexi 'Guanyu jianguo yilai dang de ruogan lishi wenti de jueyi'" (Study the "resolution on certain questions in the history of the party since 1949"), *Renmin ribao,* July 1, 1981, 1.

44. Ibid. In fact, "turning point" does not adequately convey the full meaning of the Chinese phrase *zhuan zhe,* the two words of which mean "turn" and "break," respectively. "Abrupt turn" and "sharp break" would be more accurate renderings.

45. Even when ideological campaigns were mounted during the 1980s, they encountered widespread popular resistance and cynicism, a legacy of the forced imposition of Maoist ideology during the Cultural Revolution. For an account of "skeptical youth" who by 1978 had "seen through" *(kan tou le)* Maoist dogma and believed in nothing, see Stanley Rosen, "Prosperity, Privatization, and China's Youth," *Problems of Communism* (March–April 1985):1–28.

46. Deng, "Jiefang cixiang, shishi qiushi, tuanjie yizhi, xiang qian kan," 142.

47. Louis Putterman, "The Restoration of the Peasant Household as Farm Production Unit in China: Some Incentive Theoretic Analysis," in Elizabeth J. Perry and Christine Wong, eds., *The Political Economy of Reform in Post-Mao China* (Cambridge, Mass.: Harvard University Press, 1985), 63–82.

48. Wang Ruipu, *Zhongguo nongcun shinian—1978–1988* (Ten years in China's villages—1978–1988) (Peking: PLA Press, 1989), 83.

49. Ibid., 84–85.

50. William Hinton, "Reform in Stride: Rural Change, 1984," in *The Great Reversal— The Privatization of China, 1978–1989* (New York: Monthly Review Press, 1990), 79.

51. Deng, "Jiefang cixiang, shishi qiushi, tuanjie yizhi, xiang qian kan," 141.

52. Barry Naughton, "False Starts and Second Winds: Financial Reforms in China's Industrial System," in Perry and Wong, eds., *The Political Economy of Reform in Post-Mao China*, 223–252.

53. Christine Wong, "Material Allocation and Decentralization: Impact of the Local Sector on Industrial Reform," in ibid., 253–278.

54. Ibid., 276.

55. Jim Rohwer, "When China Wakes," *The Economist*, November 28, 1992, 10.

56. Decentralization and inflation were mutually reinforcing in the 1980s. As Susan Shirk noted, "The increases in spending by local politicians and enterprise managers sparked by the recent reforms may not have led to improvements in enterprise efficiency or productivity, but they did lead to higher prices. . . . The most serious inflationary pressures came . . . from local politicians and factory managers who bid up prices of producers goods as they rushed to expand their local industrial bases" ("The Politics of Industrial Reform," in Perry and Wong, eds., *The Political Economy of Reform in Post-Mao China*, 203).

57. Robert F. Dernberger, "The Chinese Search for the Path of Self-Sustained Development in the 1980s: An Assessment," in *China Under the Four Modernizations*, Part 1 (Washington, D.C.: Joint Economic Committee, Congress of the United States, 1982), 45.

58. "Fahui youshi" (Give full play to advantages), *Renmin ribao*, June 30, 1980, 1.

59. "Jiji wenbu de tiaozheng nongye naibu de jiegou" (Actively and steadily readjust the internal structure of agriculture), *Renmin ribao*, May 9, 1980, 1.

60. "Jianchi sheme, fandui sheme" (What to persist in, what to oppose), *Renmin ribao*, June 26, 1980, 1.

61. "Dapo jingji fengsuo, tichang kaizhan jingsai" (Break economic blockades, promote open competition), *Renmin ribao*, March 3, 1982, 4.

62. "Shixing jingji zeren zhi, zhuyi jiejue xin wenti" (Implement the economic responsibility system, attentively resolve new problems), *Renmin ribao*, September 22, 1982, 1.

63. "Jianchi jihua jingji wei zhu he quanguo yi panqi" (Persist in the planned economy as the foundation and the entire nation as a single chessboard), *Renmin ribao*, March 5, 1982, 3.

64. "Qiye zhengdun yao yi tuixing jingji zeren zhi wei tupokou" (Enterprise readjustment must be carried out with the economic responsibility system as the breakthrough point), *Renmin ribao*, August 5, 1981, 1.

65. "Zhenxing nongye de xin keti" (New lessons for revitalizing agriculture), *Renmin ribao*, August 20, 1981, 1.

66. In 1983, Dorothy Solinger pointed to "the ways in which Marxism has struck deep roots in the trade sector, both in the state and in Chinese society. The result—a 'socialist' commerce that eschews the market—poses barriers to reform, promising though the proposals appear at first blush" ("Marxism and the Market in Socialist China: The Reforms of 1978–1979 in Context," in Victor Nee and David Mozingo, eds., *State and Society in Contemporary China* [Ithaca: Cornell University Press, 1983], 194).

67. Victor Fung, "China's Leaders Struggle to Apply Brakes, but Runaway Economic Growth Persists," *Wall Street Journal*, August 26, 1985, 20.

68. James P. Sterba, "Central Control Subdued Under Peking's Plan," *Wall Street Journal*, April 15, 1986, 39.

69. Dori Jones Yang, "China's Economy Is Careening Out of Control," *Business Week*, April 3, 1989, 54.

70. Dinah Lee, "Who's Minding the Store in China?" *Business Week*, August 14, 1989, 58–59.

71. Nicholas D. Kristof, "Hard Line in Beijing Fails to Kill Boom," *New York Times*, December 17, 1991, 1.

72. Lena H. Sun, "China Tries to Chill Boiling Economy," *Washington Post*, July 3, 1993, 1; Nicholas D. Kristof, "Beijing Restricts Land Speculation," *New York Times*, August 15, 1993, 7.

73. James McGregor, "China's Backward-Flowing Tax Leaves Beijing Up the Budgetary Creek," *Wall Street Journal*, November 12, 1990, 10. See also "China's Economy: Reform with a Life of Its Own," *Christian Science Monitor*, February 26, 1992, 10–11.

74. Deng, "Gaoji ganbu yao daitou fayang dang de youliang chuantong," 190.

75. Ibid., 191.

76. "Zhongjiwei zheng jixu diaocha chedi zhuijiu zerenzhe" (The central discipline committee continues to investigate and thoroughly affix blame on culpable persons), *Renmin ribao*, March 11, 1982, 1.

77. "Jianjue daji jingji fanzui huodong" (Resolutely attack criminal economic activities), April 10, 1982, in Deng, *Selected Works of Deng Xiaoping*, 357–358.

78. Zhao Ziyang, "Guanyu guowuyuan jigou gaige wenti de baogao" (Report on problems in the structural reform of the state council), *Renmin ribao*, March 8, 1982, 2.

79. William deB. Mills, "Leadership Change in China's Provinces," *Problems of Communism* (May–June 1985):24, 40. (All quotes in this paragraph are from this source.) For a different and more critical assessment of the 1983 reorganization, see Keith Forster, "Leaders of China's Provinces," *Problems of Communism* (November–December 1985): 80–90.

80. Lee, *From Revolutionary Cadres to Party Technocrats in Socialist China*, 402–405.

81. Ibid., 408.

82. Deng, "Gaoji ganbu yao daitou fayang dang de youliang chuantong," 191. Hence, "today some cadres' children have free access to classified documents and spread their contents at will. There have even been individual cases in which the sons and daughters of cadres have sold or given secret information to foreigners" (191).

83. Chen Yun, "Combat Corrosive Ideology," *Beijing Review*, October 14, 1985, 15–16.

84. Bo Yibo, quoted by John Burns, "'Proletarian Rectitude' Runs Amok Under China's New Economic Policy," *New York Times*, February 23, 1985, 5.

85. Edward A. Gargan, "As China's Economy Grows, So Grows Official Corruption," *New York Times*, July 10, 1988, 1. Significantly, "city dwellers were nearly as upset with what they saw as the tendency of retailers to keep raising prices unfairly" (1).

86. Deng Xiaoping, "Jianchi dang de luxian, gaijin gongzuo fangfa" (Adhere to the line of the party and improve work methods), in Deng, *Selected Works of Deng Xiaoping*, 245.

87. Lee, *From Revolutionary Cadres to Party Technocrats in Socialist China*, 281–285.

88. Barry Kramer, "Chinese Officials Still Give Preference to Kin, Despite Peking Policies," *Wall Street Journal*, October 29, 1985, 1.

89. Joyce Barnathan, "For Beijing's Brat Pack, There's Plenty of Room at the Top," *Business Week,* November 2, 1992, 48.

90. For a wide-ranging analysis of the social, political, and economic events leading up to June 4, see Cheng Chu-yuan, *Behind the Tiananmen Massacre* (Boulder: Westview Press, 1990).

91. Brantly Womack, "Introduction," in Brantly Womack, ed., *Contemporary Chinese Politics in Historical Perspective* (Cambridge: Cambridge University Press, 1991), 1.

92. Tang Tsou, "The Tiananmen Tragedy: The State-Society Relationship, Choices, and Mechanisms in Historical Perspective," in ibid., 267, 315–316.

93. Hinton, *The Great Reversal,* 7–9.

94. Joseph Fewsmith, "The Dengist Reforms in Historical Perspective," in Womack, ed., *Contemporary Chinese Politics in Historical Perspective,* 23; David Bachman, *Bureaucracy, Economy, and Leadership in China: The Institutional Origins of the Great Leap Forward* (Cambridge: Cambridge University Press, 1991), 8–9.

95. Frederic Wakeman Jr., "The June Fourth Movement in China," *Items* (Social Science Research Council) 43, 3 (September 1989):64.

96. Keith Forster, "Factional Politics in Zhejiang, 1973–1976," in Joseph et al., eds., *New Perspectives on the Cultural Revolution,* 105–130.

97. Deng Xiaoping, "Muqian de xingshi he renwu" (The present situation and tasks), in Deng, *Selected Works of Deng Xiaoping,* 217–218.

98. Frederic Wakeman Jr., "Models of Historical Change—the Chinese State and Society, 1839–1989," in Kenneth Lieberthal, Joyce Kallgren, Roderick MacFarquhar, and Frederick Wakeman Jr., eds., *Perspectives on Modern China* (Armonk, N.Y.: M. E. Sharpe, 1991), 91.

99. For the repression of the Democracy Wall Movement, see Andrew J. Nathan, *Chinese Democracy* (New York: Knopf, 1985), chap. 2. For December 1986, see Edward A. Gargan, "China Denounces Student Protests as 'Illegal Acts,'" *New York Times,* December 22, 1986, 1.

100. Cheng, *Behind the Tiananmen Massacre,* 228.

101. Han Minzhu, ed., *Cries for Democracy* (Princeton: Princeton University Press, 1990), 156.

102. Ibid., 36–38.

103. Ibid., 27.

104. Fewsmith, *Dilemmas of Reform in China,* 249. Thus, "the events of late 1989 and early 1990 make it clear that Deng's political opponents were willing to use the political momentum that they had gained in the wake of Tiananmen to push an economic and political agenda quite different from that of Deng's" (249).

105. Steve Greenhouse, "New Tally of World's Economies Catapults China into Third Place," *New York Times,* May 20, 1993, 1.

106. Lena H. Sun, "China's Output Growing at World's Fastest Rate," *Washington Post,* April 25, 1993, 25; Joyce Barnathan et al., "China—the Emerging Economic Powerhouse of the 21st Century," *Business Week,* May 17, 1993, 54–69.

107. Valerie Reitman, "Enticed by Visions of Enormous Numbers, More Western Marketers Move into China," *Wall Street Journal,* July 12, 1993, 1.

108. In one "buying spree" Chinese officials "spent $800 million for jetliners from Boeing in Seattle, $160 million for cars from Big Three automakers in Detroit, and $200 million for oil exploration equipment from firms in Texas and Louisiana" (Daniel Southerland,

"China Purchases $1 Billion in U.S. Goods," *Washington Post,* April 4, 1993, 23). See also Michael Weisskopf, "Backbone of the New China Lobby: U.S. Firms," *Washington Post,* June 14, 1993, 1.

109. Foreign Broadcast Information Service (FBIS) CHI-92-242, "Report: China's Military to Trade Weapons with CIS," *Tokyo Kyodo,* December 16, 1992.

110. Nicholas D. Kristof, "Riddle of China: Repression as Standard of Living Soars," *New York Times,* September 7, 1993, 1.

111. Paul Blustein, "Can 'Half-Reformed' China Last?" *Washington Post,* August 29, 1993, 1.

112. Per capita GNP in the booming cities of Shanghai, Peking, Tianjin, and Canton was four to five times the national average in 1991 and six to seven times the average in such interior provinces as Sichuan, Gansu, and Guangxi. See "Cut Along Dotted Lines," *The Economist,* June 26, 1993, 35.

113. Franz Schurmann, *Ideology and Organization in Communist China,* enl. ed. (Berkeley and Los Angeles: University of California Press, 1968), 17.

114. Joyce Barnathan et al., "Beijing Starts Pumping the Brakes," *Business Week,* July 19, 1993, 42–43.

115. Lena H. Sun, "Widespread Graft Prompts Chinese Anti-Corruption Drive," *Washington Post,* September 7, 1993, 10.

116. Nicholas D. Kristof, "China Sees 'Market-Leninism' as Way to Future," *New York Times,* September 6, 1993, 1.

117. Thomas B. Gold, quoted in ibid. For a serious discussion of the rise of civil society, democratization, and development along the lines of East Asian capitalist newly industrializing countries" in China, see Gordon White, *Riding the Tiger: The Politics of Economic Reform in Post-Mao China* (Stanford: Stanford University Press, 1993, chaps. 7, 8.

118. James McGregor, "Discontent Is Growing on China's Farms," *Wall Street Journal,* February 17, 1993, 8.

119. Joyce Barnathan, "Now, Even Peasants Hate Beijing," *Business Week,* July 5, 1993, 47.

120. In February 1995, the Chinese Navy occupied a reef in the South China Sea, territory claimed by the Philippines and only 130 miles offshore, a move that alarmed neighboring Asian countries and prompted U.S. analysts to call China "an emerging power seeking to write its own rules for international order rather than accepting existing norms" (Robert A. Manning and James J. Przystup, "China's Syndrome: Ambiguity," *Washington Post,* March 19, 1995, 1).

# 9

# Power Restructuring in the Period of Perestroika

In the late 1980s, the Soviet Union was engulfed in wide-ranging and apparently unprecedented power-restructuring processes. These momentous events, which by late 1991 had resulted in the breakup of the unitary Soviet state, have "no real analogs in the Western historical experience."[1] But power restructuring in the period of perestroika is not without comparative and historical parallel and should be understood in light of earlier power-restructuring episodes in Soviet and Chinese Communist history. In this chapter, I do not examine power restructuring under Gorbachev in the kind of detail accorded the Cultural Revolution and post-Mao reform. Instead, I advance a comparative and historical view of perestroika and assess the events of the late 1980s and early 1990s in light of the overall argument put forward in this book. In the present discussion, Gorbachev's effort to restructure and revitalize the Soviet system in the period of perestroika is framed in the broad context of post-Stalin power restructuring and compared to power restructuring under Khrushchev, Mao, and Mao's successors.

When Gorbachev launched his campaign to restructure and revitalize the Soviet system in the mid-1980s, he targeted key features of the Stalin system, especially the structures of central ministerial economic control and resource allocation and the processes of power concentration and political monopoly that continued to dominate Soviet life. These aspects of the Stalin system were reinforced under Brezhnev in the late 1960s and 1970s, even as other aspects of Stalinism were steadily modified to the advantage of Soviet political elites. At the same time, Gorbachev renewed Khrushchev's struggle to reenergize and make Soviet officialdom more accountable, a familiar aim greatly complicated in the 1980s by the accelerated processes of bureaucratic encrustation, organizational stability, and systemic stagnation that characterized the Brezhnev years.

Although Gorbachev followed in Khrushchev's footsteps, his power-restructuring methods became increasingly radical in the late 1980s and developed in directions that resembled, and often paralleled, power-restructuring methods deployed by Mao during the opening phases of the Cultural Revolution. Power decentralization and power deconcentration were essential ingredients in Gorbachev's evolving power-restructuring strategy, along with the deployment of top and bottom versus the middle tactics and attempts at personal rulership. As in China in 1966–1967, however, the decentralization and deconcentration of power resulted in massive social, political, and economic upheaval in the Soviet Union in the late 1980s and early 1990s, and the Gorbachev power-restructuring program was overwhelmed by the forces it unleashed. Like Mao, Gorbachev saw his effort to reform, revitalize, and salvage a socialist system transformed into an all-encompassing battle over power and resources. As in China during the Cultural Revolution decade, the major unintended consequences of power restructuring in the period of perestroika were a wholesale breakdown of established mechanisms of political and economic control, a systemic crisis, an acceleration of decentralized processes of power and resource appropriation, and a setting in motion of a historic transition from socialism. While probing these similarities, my discussion also identifies the crucial differences between the transition from socialism in Russia and in China.

## Conceptualizing Perestroika

In the period of perestroika, Western observers reacted to Gorbachev's reform and revitalization effort in very different ways. Western analyses of reform in the Soviet Union had long tended to be conservative, stressing the "durability and rigidity" of the Soviet system and "the improbability of fundamental change."[2] Accordingly, many commentators reacted cautiously at the start of perestroika and emphasized the limits of the measures Gorbachev was taking, the extent of his authoritarian and dictatorial powers, the continuity of his political methods with those of the past, and the strength of the system of power over which the general secretary presided. As Bialer argued in early 1986, "Reformism in the case of the new Soviet leaders has nothing in common with liberalism—a connection too often made erroneously in the West. . . . Mr. Gorbachev's reformism also stresses authoritarian rule, discipline, and predictable conformist behavior," and a year later Western analysts noted that "the Soviet leader is amassing virtually dictatorial powers."[3] Three years later, as the situation inside the Soviet Union grew increasingly volatile and chaotic, Bialer maintained that Gorbachev's "security in office" was unthreatened since "top Soviet power institutions are packed by personally loyal and disciplined Gorbachev supporters," while "the flow of power in the Party hierarchy is vertical—from the Secretary General and his loyalists down to the Politburo and the Secretariat, from the Politburo and Secretariat in turn to the Central Committee, and so on."[4] At the same time, Peter Hauslohner asserted, "Although there may now be serious and deeply felt grievances scattered throughout Soviet society, the extreme barriers to the organization and mobilization of opposition as well as the numerous resources and instruments at the leaders' disposal make it extremely unlikely that the government could lose control over events and could find its security threatened in the near future."[5]

These cautious views were countered by more optimistic and enthusiastic interpretations, which stressed the innovative and progressive dimensions, as well as the feasibility, of the Gorbachev reform and revitalization effort. Especially striking was the argument that perestroika was the logical manifestation of the changes and maturation that Soviet society had experienced in the two or three preceding decades. In 1988, Moshe Lewin argued that urbanization, scientific-technical development, and massive increases in the number of people with higher and specialized secondary education had transformed "the nation's overall social, professional, and cultural profile." In contrast to the backward, rural country that had produced Stalinism, Gorbachev's rise marked "the coalescence of a civil society capable of extracurricular action and opinion making, independent of the wishes of the state." Thus, "authoritarian coercion, once a favored tool, would no longer be of much use. Instead, internal politics is learning to use a new language: interplay and bargaining, yielding and conforming, pressuring and compromising, giving and taking."[6] Similarly, Blair Ruble asserted that, contrary to prevailing views in the West and the Soviet Union, "the Brezhnev period was not one of stagnation but of profound social transformation," when "the Soviet population increasingly came to resemble the industrialized world in terms of education attainment, employment patterns, cultural taste and, to a surprising degree, attitudes." As a result, "the combination of striking new policy initiatives from above and dramatic social change from below has created an environment in which the Soviet Union just might finally be able to step off the treadmill of failed reforms."[7]

Finally, Jerry F. Hough managed to combine elements of both the preceding perspectives in an idiosyncratic analysis of Gorbachev and perestroika. On the one hand, Hough stressed the familiar ways in which Gorbachev used the "General Secretary's machine" to steadily consolidate his power and build his personal authority in the 1980s. Hence, "the power to appoint cadres and to use the party political machine to secure and maintain power and authority remained a crucial one," further illustrating "the degree to which these forces continue to shape Soviet politics."[8] On the other hand, Hough underscored the transformative thrust of Gorbachev's policies and argued, "Gorbachev is today what he has always been—a modernizing, Westernizing czar such as Kemal Ataturk was in Turkey, Lee Kuan Yew was in Singapore, and many Third World rulers in countries like Taiwan and South Korea."[9] Indeed, Hough insisted that it was precisely Gorbachev's ability to concentrate power and thereby strengthen his own position at the expense of the opposition that would enable him to push his program forward and successfully control the "social forces" set in motion by perestroika.[10]

Viewed in hindsight, all these analyses turned out to be wrong, often spectacularly so. Whereas analyses stressing continuity were too cautious and failed to pinpoint the increasingly radical dimensions of Gorbachevian power restructuring on the late 1980s, more optimistic assessments failed to grasp the profoundly destabilizing implications and effects of Gorbachev's policies and reforms. And Hough ranks as the sovietologist whose predictions and prognostications of the

1980s and early 1990s were most consistently mistaken and most conclusively disproved.[11] For a more satisfactory understanding of the logic of perestroika and the failure of Gorbachevian power restructuring to achieve its purpose, the cataclysmic events of the late 1980s and early 1990s must be viewed in light of earlier power-restructuring efforts in the Soviet Union and in China especially.

## Brezhnevism and the Onset of Soviet Systemic Decline

In the late 1960s and early 1970s, the Soviet political economy became less dynamic and began to decelerate. This process first became apparent in the economic realm, as growth rates slowed throughout the 1970s and then plummeted in the early 1980s. It is now evident that this deceleration of economic growth was symptomatic of broader processes of systemic deterioration and decline, the full dimensions of which only became clear in the 1980s.

Even though some Western economic analysts linked the deceleration of economic growth in the 1970s to declining labor and capital productivity, they were unable to explain the origins of this process. As Ed A. Hewett concluded in 1988, "Western researchers have devoted considerable attention to the behavior of factor productivities in the Soviet economy. . . . But the results are mixed, and some important weaknesses in the Soviet data cannot be rectified. As a result, the precise causes of the growth slowdown remain unclear."[12] More recently, Soviet economist Grigorii Khanin analyzed declining factor productivity in light of long-term economic trends and specific political developments of the 1960s and 1970s. Whereas classic Soviet methods of extensive growth, based on huge increases in capital, labor, and land, produced impressive economic results in the 1930s, by the late 1950s and 1960s it had become more difficult to increase the volume of resources used.[13] By the 1960s and 1970s, moreover, the intensified superpower competition with the United States was retarding investment and growth in many sectors of the Soviet economy. As Michael Ellman and Vladimir Kontorovich noted in this regard, "One reason for the slower growth of fixed capital was the increasing diversion of resources to military spending, a result of a policy decision at the highest level. The achievement of strategic parity with the west and the macroeconomic stagnation, or decline, in the late 1970s to the early 1980s, are strongly related."[14] Khanin also observed, "Aside from the long-run trends, the economic decline of the early 1980s reflected the complete corruption of the Brezhnev administration by that time. Party and state organs were near paralysis, and transmitted this condition to the rest of society. Those at the top were enriching themselves, those at the bottom were stealing from the state and drinking. Despair and apathy reigned in society."[15]

To be sure, systemic decline under Brezhnev was in part the result of factors peculiar to the Soviet case, and the ruinous superpower competition with the United States and the West finds no direct parallel in China. But it is also evident that political decisions and power considerations, rather than economic forces, played the primary role in the deceleration of growth in the Brezhnev period. In Chapter 4, I delineated the logic of Brezhnevism and the CPSU power monopoly, official entrenchment and corruption, and the aversion to change Brezhnevism embodied. These tendencies, which Khrushchev energetically but unsuccessfully attacked, were accentuated with the passage of time. Even in the early and more vigorous years of the Brezhnev era, however, attempts to restructure and make the Soviet economic system more flexible and efficient were obstructed and distorted in ways that foreshadowed the subsequent stagnation and ossification of late Brezhnevism.

As I have discussed, Khrushchev's successors immediately moved to reverse his organizational changes of the late 1950s and early 1960s. In September 1965, major reforms of the system of macroeconomic organization and control were implemented. These measures, known as the 1965 reforms and put forward by Premier Alexei Kosygin, overturned Khrushchev's *sovnarkhozy* restructuring by reinstituting the ministerial system and "recentralizing power from the regional economic councils to twenty-three newly constituted (in some cases reconstituted) industrial ministries."[16] But the 1965 reforms sought more than a restoration of the status quo ante; they also attempted to increase enterprise autonomy by reducing the number of centrally mandated targets and indicators and to reform the pricing system. However, whereas "the administrative reform replacing the *sovnarkhozy* with a resurrected ministerial system was the most rapidly implemented portion of the 1965 reforms," the effort to improve enterprise incentives and flexibility soon became bogged down in red tape and fell by the wayside. Instead, Hewett concluded, the most important and lasting legacy of the 1965 reforms was "the ministerial system, reincarnated in 1965 and expanded since then. There were twenty-three industrial ministries in 1965; twenty years later there are more than twice that many."[17] Significantly, the second major economic reform of the Brezhnev period, the "1973 merger movement," also attempted to improve macroeconomic organizational efficiency by increasing, rather than decreasing, the centralization of economic controls.[18]

The logic of the 1965 and 1973 reforms was consistent with a principal feature of Brezhnevism—the reinforcing of political and administrative controls over the economy and society at large. Indeed, when in June 1988 Gorbachev pondered the fate of the 1965 reform and reminded his audience "that it dealt with almost the same things that we are projecting in our economic reform now," he queried, "So, where is the hitch? All those past efforts ran into the political system with its administrative methods of society management."[19] In hindsight, it is evident that the unchallenged primacy of political and managerial controls under Brezhnev inflicted catastrophic economic and technological damage. As Yegor Ligachev discussed, whereas the capitalist West underwent a technological and managerial revolution pivoting on computerization in the 1970s, the prevailing conventional wisdom in the Soviet Union was that "automated systems of management are a subordinate element with regard to the organizational mechanism of management."[20] Throughout the Brezhnev era, new layers of supervision continued to be added to an already ponderous administrative pyramid, and the debilitating governmentalization and bureaucratization that had become so widely evident by the late 1970s and early 1980s were thereby rooted in political decisions taken almost two decades earlier.

Yet pervasive governmentalization and bureaucratization did not result in political paralysis and organizational ossification in the 1930s, 1940s, and 1950s. Why not? In the view of Ellman and Kontorovich, "The history of the USSR from 1953–82 is one of almost continuous reduction of pressure from above. The magnitude of expected punishments was reduced drastically, and so was that of rewards."[21] But we have seen that, even though Khrushchev did reduce pressure from above during the first phase of his tenure as ruler, he subsequently attempted in various ways to increase pressures on the Soviet political elite and was finally overthrown as a result. With the advent of Brezhnev, however, Soviet central rulers abandoned the attempt to control officialdom with pressure from above and below. When former leader of the State Security Committee (KGB) Oleg Kalugin was asked in 1990 "whether there are zones in our country that are closed even to the KGB," he stated, "I am aware of only one such zone: the KGB is not permitted to collect and store any negative information on *nomenklatura* personnel. When I was working in Leningrad, I had a special list of these people: the secretaries of the *oblast* party committee, the chairman of the Leningrad city soviet and his deputies, and even the secretaries of the province Komsomol committee appeared to be included. In short, all the ruling elite."[22]

Even as political and administrative controls over the economy and society at large were strengthened, control of officialdom was loosened and eroded. This was both the deliberate intent of the Brezhnevian reduction of pressure on officialdom and the unintended consequence of Brezhnevian governmentalization and bureaucratization. Regarding the latter, Alexander J. Motyl observed, "Hypercentralization and bureaucratic extensiveness create ideal conditions—horizontal fragmentation and vertical segmentation—for regional officials to engage in localized empire building. . . . Decision-making becomes incoherent, resources are squandered, and the constraint to which the state aspires, and on the maintenance of which it is premised, cannot be effectively pursued. The state, in a word, 'decays.'"[23] Understood in light of my power-restructuring argument, even though the structures of party and state were multiplied in the 1960s and 1970s, decentralized processes of appropriation accelerated the flow of power and resources into the hands of political elites at the regional, provincial, and local levels.

## Andropov and the Campaign to Tighten Discipline

During Yuri Andropov's very brief tenure as general secretary, he attempted with some success to reverse Brezhnevian stagnation and decline by combining forceful methods reminiscent of earlier periods in Soviet history with a limited decentralization of economic decisionmaking power. In the spirit of the 1965 reforms, a series of decrees in 1983 and 1984 sought to improve performance at the enterprise level by expanding enterprise autonomy, on the one hand, and by more closely linking bonuses and performance, on the other.[24] While attempting to remedy the familiar defects of the Soviet system of central ministerial hegemony, economic centralization, and financial subsidies, however, Andropov's policies had as their cornerstone the restoration and tightening of political, organizational, and social discipline. The first part of 1983 witnessed the arrest and prosecution of large numbers of corrupt officials; the replacement of old and ineffective ministers with younger, more energetic ones; a tough police campaign against worker absenteeism; restrictions on worker mobility; and the strengthening of managers' disciplinary powers over workers.[25] In contrast to flaccid Brezhnevism, Andropov sought to effect systemic revitalization with classically Soviet methods of coercion, exhortation, and assertive central rulership.

The tightening of discipline under Andropov resulted in immediate, if modest, economic improvements in the mid-1980s. In an analysis of the Soviet railroad transport industry during this period, Kontorovich argued that the increased pressure on officialdom and application of sanctions keyed economic recovery and stabilization. Hence,

> Andropov contributed to the railroad recovery in three ways. In the very first days of his rule, he fired the old minister and installed a new one. He then initiated a discipline-tightening campaign in the economy, which was zealously followed by the new minister of railroads. Andropov also disregarded the advice of experts, who claimed that the railroads lacked capacity for adequate operation, and declared that the only thing lacking was discipline.[26]

To be sure, economic recovery and stabilization are not the same as economic growth and expansion. Yet "the recovery of the Soviet economy from its 1979–82 decline showed that the traditional economic system was viable. The system reacted favourably to policies appropriate to it (such as tightening discipline) given its specific characteristics."[27]

Yet Andropov departed from established Soviet practice by appealing to intellectuals for input, ideas, and solutions regarding the problem of economic growth. The result was the fateful "Novosibirsk Report," written by sociologist Tatyana Zaslavskaya and containing the radical criticism that "Soviet central planning had become obsolete—indeed a fetter on production—and that Soviet society, far from being the harmonious unity depicted in official propaganda, was riven by conflicts between rulers and ruled, and hobbled by alienation, apathy, and lack of motivation among the working class."[28]

On becoming general secretary in March 1985, Gorbachev continued Andropov's policies for the next year and a half. According to Thane Gustafson and Dawn Mann's mid-1986 analysis, Gorbachev's power-building and authority-building strategy consisted of two key elements. On the one hand, as Gorbachev vigorously wielded the "cadres weapon" and further accelerated the restructuring of party operations at the central, regional, and local levels, "not since the 1930s has there been so vast a turnover of the Soviet political and administrative elite in so short a time."[29] On the other hand, the new general secretary resumed his predecessor's effort to restore order and discipline at the societal level and in 1986 launched his ill-conceived antialcohol campaign, as well as a campaign against corruption and "unearned incomes." Coercion, exhortation, and increased political and organizational pressure from the top were thus the familiar and in no way revolutionary means by which Gorbachev initially sought to reinvigorate and restructure the Soviet system.

## The Logic of "Radical Renewal"

Yet by mid-1987, Gorbachev's power-restructuring strategy and rhetoric had changed and were moving in new, highly radical directions. Amending an earlier emphasis on the building of power through the cadres weapon, some analysts detected a populist shift in Gorbachev's political strategy and noted, "Unlike his predecessors, he is attempting to build support for a radical policy program *before* fully consolidating his power within the elite by conventional means, and he is looking for this support primarily at the local level."[30] Whereas "other general secretaries, notably Khrushchev, have played with populist approaches in the past, attempting to mobilize the masses against resistance to the party leader's policies at middle levels," "Gorbachev's gamble," Gustafson and Mann suggested, "could write very new rules to the game of Soviet politics."[31]

Understood in light of our discussion, Gorbachev's radical shift looks more familiar. While attempting to combat processes of corruption, bureaucratic entrenchment, and power and resource appropriation by bringing pressure to bear on Soviet officialdom from above *and* below, the Soviet leader now sought to effect systemic reform and revitalization with a radical decentralization and deconcentration of power. It was this decentralization and deconcentration of power that unleashed the forces that destroyed the Soviet system within a few short years. Moreover, it was the ideas of liberal Soviet intellectuals, especially those of Zaslavskaya, that were crucial in the shift to radical power restructuring.

Beginning with the "Novosibirsk Report" of 1983, and in a series of articles in the mid-1980s, Zaslavskaya first put forward in Marxian terms the argument that optimistic Western assessments of perestroika would repeat a few years later—that contemporary Soviet society and economy had matured and outgrown the political and administrative system erected in the 1930s. Hence, the "general reason" for the recent "deterioration of the economic indices" "consists in the lagging of the system of production relations, and hence of the mechanism of state management of the economy which is its reflection, behind the level of development of the productive forces. To put it in more concrete terms, it is expressed in the inability of this system to make provision for the full and sufficiently effective use of labor potential and intellectual resources of society."[32] Given that "the Soviet economy's productive forces have changed beyond recognition over the decades," and "the higher degree of scientific-technological and sociopolitical awareness of the workers, the increasing complexity of their needs and interests, and the development of their legal and personal consciousness," Zaslavskaya in 1985 asserted, "the self-evident conclusion is the need to alter the general strategy for managing the human factor of production: to put constraints on the administrative regulation of human activity and to concentrate attention on the regulation and stimulation of progressive modes of behavior."[33]

A crucial assumption of the Zaslavskaya argument was that the loosening of administrative controls would result in an "awakening of social energies" and that people would constructively and responsibly respond to their new freedoms. Thus, "the awakening of the social energy of the masses and their transformation into the real masters of the entire social economy, into the principal force in the management of society, presupposes certain changes in social thinking."[34] Rather than viewing people as labor resources to be administered and commanded, the state should focus its efforts on "activating the human factor," "unleashing . . . their [the people's] energy," and mobilizing "their creative energy, initiative, will, and self-discipline."[35] While stressing the economic merits and necessity of these changes, Zaslavskaya also spoke of "mass activity and social justice" and argued that "it is especially important to expand the possibility of work collectives and occupational and territorial groups to openly express, discuss, and defend their interests at various levels of management and to receive clear answers. . . . This is the most reliable means of accelerating social and economic progress."[36]

By early 1988, the notion that the Soviet system was both in need of and ready for radical change had been embraced at the top, and some Soviet commentators spoke openly of "revolutionary renewal," "a leap forward in social development," and the "transformation of fundamental structures in the economy, and the political and social areas, ensuring substantial changes in the people's intellectual life and ethics."[37] In the late 1980s, Gorbachev abandoned the cautious, top-down Andropov reform approach and shifted to a radical power-restructuring strategy geared along the lines of the Zaslavskaya thesis. In the mid-1980s, some Western analysts spoke of the "Khrushchevian echoes" of Gorbachev's policies and noted that both leaders pursued programs of internal innovation, economic decentralization, more rapid turnover of leading personnel, less secrecy in the conduct of public affairs, and anti-Stalinism.[38]

By 1988, however, Gorbachev's political strategy and tactics increasingly resembled those of the Maoists during the opening phases of the Cultural Revolution. Radical Gorbachevian power restructuring therefore sought to effect systemic revitalization by the decentralization and deconcentration of power and the unleashing of mass energies and enthusiasm. Further paralleling the Maoist pattern, the empowerment of nonprivileged groups was viewed as a way of tapping pent-up potential and of putting pressure on officialdom. As it turned out, the loosening of political controls set in motion a broad societal onslaught against the party and state officials who staffed the mechanisms of control.[39] As in China in 1966–1967, the Soviet political elite in the late 1980s was subjected to a sociopolitical battering from above and below.

## Gorbachevian Power Restructuring

In language suggestive of the opening phases of the Cultural Revolution, Gorbachev in the speech "Revolutionary Perestroika and the Ideology of Renewal" forcefully put forward the message of power deconcentration and popular empowerment at the Central Committee plenum in February 1988. While asserting that "half measures will not do," the general secretary stated that "it is time to stop issuing injunctions and commands."[40] He argued, "We must set forth as a task the overcoming in mass organizations of dominance of salaried functionaries, excessive organization, and red tape by way of handing over a part of the powers of central bodies to the grassroot level. The latter should be freed of any necessity to have every step they take okayed by the higher-standing executives."[41] Instead, "we should make Soviets at all levels agencies of state authority and administration that really work, demonstrating initiative, and enjoying full rights."[42] With striking populist imagery, Gorbachev insisted that "learning democracy" meant "relying on the masses," "fearlessly promoting criticism and self-criticism," and maintaining "a constant desire to be in the midst of the masses, in the midst of the most burning problems of life."[43]

By summer 1988, and during the Nineteenth All-Union Party Conference, Gorbachev's language and policies continued to move in increasingly radical directions. Most important, his insistence that "command-and-order methods be irrevocably abandoned" and that soviets be given "unlimited power in their districts, towns, regions, republics, and so on" was coupled with an attack on the power and authority of party and state officialdom and an attempt to make the Soviet political elite more accountable to the "masses."[44] Declaring that the "managerial apparatus remains unreasonably cumbersome," Gorbachev spoke of "an effective offensive against bureaucracy." Thus, "all delays, formalistic attitudes, and pettifogging in the managerial apparatus must be eliminated and situations where a person feels helpless before an indifferent and stubborn bureaucrat must be ruled out." Gorbachev put officialdom on notice, stating that "any attempt that infringes upon the legitimate rights of citizens by following departmental instructions and resorting to red tape must be nipped in the bud." He promised to "make full use of the cadre policy in the struggle against bureaucracy." Consequently, "any action taken by the apparatus to distort and erode the meaning of the laws and governmental decisions is unconstitutional," and errant "officials should be dismissed without delay, and attempts to shift them to other positions of authority must not be allowed." At the same time, Gorbachev subjected officialdom to scrutiny, criticism, and pressure from below. Hence, even though "accessibility and openness to control and verification by working people and the public is to be the rule in the work of the apparatus," "the performance of the apparatus should be discussed and assessed regularly at public assemblies, work collectives, and public organizations."

While Soviet power-restructuring advocates linked the loosening of administrative controls to the maturation of Soviet society, these same advocates also asserted that glasnost, the policy of "criticism and self-criticism and the assertion of openness and truthfulness in politics" "reflects the openness of society's political systems, and speaks of its strength, political viability, and moral health."[45] Hence, although "striving to inform the public of various faults, abuses, and cases of red tape and arrogance among Communists, as well as other negative phenomena, is encountering administrative resistance," "the Conference reaffirms that glasnost and open control and criticism by the masses is an essential condition for the effective functioning of the bodies of government."[46]

Finally, the loosening of administrative controls and glasnost was paralleled by a radical decentralization of political power. Thus,

> one of the central tasks is to create conditions for the greater independence of regions [through] the extending of the rights of the Union Republics and autonomous regions by delineating the jurisdiction of the USSR and that of the Soviet Republics, by decentralization and transfer of some government functions to local bodies, and by emphasizing their independence and responsibility in economic, social and cultural spheres, and in conservation of nature.[47]

Yet the resolutions of the Nineteenth All-Union Party Conference also affirmed that "the greater independence of the Union Republics and autonomous regions is seen by the Party in indissoluble connection with their responsibility for the strengthening and progress of our multinational state. The socialist ideal is not a detrimental unification, but a full-blooded and dynamic unity set in the context of national diversity."[48]

## Intended Versus Unintended Consequences

Gorbachev's power-restructuring initiatives released mass aspirations, unleashed pent-up tensions, and precipitated a genuine outpouring of popular energies throughout Soviet society. In the form of "popular fronts," a profusion of nonofficial organizations resulted, with agendas ranging from environmental protection, religious freedom, and charity work, to political reform, national independence, anti-Semitism, and the Great Russian tradition.[49] New and more assertive forms of mass political participation proliferated, most emphatically in the course of elections to the new Congress of People's Deputies in March 1989, when Soviet voters rejected numerous senior party figures and elected many candidates running in opposition to the party organization.[50] More closely paralleling the opening phases of the Cultural Revolution, Soviet officials by 1988–1989 were subjected for the first time in memory to direct popular scrutiny and pressure. Especially familiar was the spectacle of senior officials being grilled before citizens' meetings, where formerly high and mighty dignitaries were forced to respond to pointed questioning and to account for their past misdeeds.[51] The coal strike in Ukraine in summer 1989 was equally evocative of the Cultural Revolution, as miners angrily aired long-pent-up grievances against the prevailing structure of power and singled out official arrogance, the system of special privilege, and official corruption for public criticism.[52]

Encouraging pressure from below was a calculated component of Gorbachev's power-restructuring strategy. As Russell Bova noted, mass political pressure was the means by which Gorbachev sought from the start to better control Soviet officialdom and attack its rigidity, inertia, and resistance.[53] Hence, Gorbachev made use of the potentially disastrous coal strike by blaming it on the Ministry of Coal's authoritarian centralism and lack of attention to local problems; he also praised the miners for "putting the questions correctly" and "saying a great deal about how our Party and Soviet organs and çadres operate."[54] With the success of perestroika premised on the unleashing of pent-up energies, popular movements, mass upheaval, and the fomenting of political and social pressures from below were thus the intended consequences of Gorbachev's politics of radical renewal. As in the opening phases of the Cultural Revolution, however, the massive deconcentration and decentralization of power in the Soviet Union in the late 1980s proved impossible to control, and Gorbachevian power restructuring would soon be overwhelmed by the forces it had unleashed.

We have seen that Soviet power-restructuring advocates and many Western commentators saw Gorbachev's radical reforms as necessary and salutary measures for an economic system that Padma Desai termed "overplanned and overadministered."[55] Yet by the end of the 1980s and in the early 1990s, power-restructuring processes set in motion with the express purpose of remedying these defects had resulted in an economic breakdown of catastrophic proportions, an eruption of nationalism and localism, and an accelerating political fragmentation that would lead to the breakup of the unitary Soviet state erected in the 1920s. Why were Soviet power-restructuring advocates and most Western observers unable to foresee the devastating effects of radical power restructuring? How did power restructuring in the period of perestroika result in consequences Gorbachev neither anticipated nor intended?

In fact, Gorbachev was aware of the tensions and conflicts that the loosening of controls might release; yet he did not believe that reducing the power of the party and the Soviet state would undercut party leadership and the Soviet ideal. Like many Western analysts, moreover, Soviet power restructuring advocates were confident that the Soviet system could contain and would benefit from the added pressures of decontrol and glasnost. Therefore, even as he stepped up the pace of radical power restructuring in summer 1988, therefore, Gorbachev denounced "regional egoism" and "self-serving communalism." When speaking of decentralization, he stipulated "naturally, a decentralization that retains those functions of the central authorities without which one cannot assert the advantages of socialism or ensure the interests of the whole people."[56] Hence, the general secretary insisted,

> effecting a large-scale decentralization means to pump life-giving fresh blood into the capillaries of our political and economic system—but obviously, without in any way disrupting the blood intake of the brain and the heart of our body politic. . . . I think we'll all vote for more self-government, but against local high-handedness, for due consideration to be given to local interests, but always in harmony with the interests of all society. . . . Those who believe that the course directed at decentralization opens the door to self-serving communalism or regional egoism will be making a grave mistake.[57]

While recognizing that decontrol and glasnost might result in sociopolitical conflict, however, Soviet power-restructuring advocates argued that the venting of grievances and differences was natural, healthy, and beneficial. In Zaslavskaya's words, "Democracy, in the final analysis, is only the right of each social group to express, defend, and implement its own interests. It is not a confection which always has to be sweet and good tasting. . . . But is it so bad that such moods, enthusiasms, and groups declare themselves openly? Without openness and democracy all this would continue to exist, but it would be driven inside and concealed."[58] As it turned out, power deconcentration, power decentralization, and democracy in the period of perestroika precipitated an avalanche of unintended consequences that confirmed the worst fears of conservative opponents of reform, confounded Soviet power-restructuring advocates, and overturned the logic of radical renewal.

## The Assault on Systemic Building Blocks

While some leading Western commentators continued to sing Gorbachev's praises in the late 1980s and early 1990s and applaud the successes of his leadership and political strategy, other analysts, both Soviet and Western, were less sanguine. We have seen that Hough remained supremely confident of Gorbachev's ability to contain the social forces unleashed by perestroika. Similarly, Breslauer hailed Gorbachev's "transformative leadership" and his strategy of "destroying the old system, and the public consciousness which had permitted it to survive, while constructing new channels of genuine political participation."[59] But other analysts were sounding the alarm. In 1990, Motyl warned, "The current Soviet leadership is treading on especially thin ice because Gorbachev's program of perestroika combined all the necessary ingredients for an acceleration of national Communism and contextually nationalist behavior"; he further noted, "The visible growth in 1987–1990 of aggressively national and nationalist sentiments in all the republics was the first sign of the immense dangers that lie ahead."[60] At the same time, Galina V. Starovoitova spoke of the "further breakdown of the center" and observed, "A fundamental shift has taken place, as important political conflicts and power struggles no longer take place in the center, but in the republics."[61] In Andranik Migranyan's assessment, the "collapse of governmental authority throughout the country" by 1990 was the result of "some fundamental mistakes and misconceptions built into [Gorbachev's] strategy of transition."[62] Gorbachev's emphasis on the primacy of political reform and "mass democratization" therefore "had the consequence of releasing all centrifugal forces that, in response to their liberation from a suffocating regime, would seek alternative identities, both individual and collective, but without institutionalized forms of conflict resolution into which to channel their demands."[63]

As the destabilizing consequences of radical renewal multiplied, the political and economic situation in the Soviet Union grew increasingly chaotic in the early 1990s, and the unitary Soviet state finally broke up in late 1991, Gorbachev's power-restructuring strategy failed massively and disastrously. The origins of this failure were neither complex nor mysterious. Simply put, "Gorbachev was quite successful in dismantling the old system, but failed to create a viable new one." As Ellman and Kontorovich further noted, "The leadership itself made a major contribution to the collapse by weakening, or removing altogether, three crucial, load-bearing 'bricks' from the building it was trying to rebuild: the central bureaucratic apparatus; the official ideology; and the active role of the party in the economy."[64] On the premise that the concentration and control system erected in the 1930s needed, and could take, radical reform, vital building blocks that held the rickety and idiosyncratic Soviet system together in the 1980s were subjected to a deliberate battering from above and below in the period of perestroika.

But the radicalism of this attack on the power of the Soviet party-state was profoundly unsettling and destabilizing. In seeking to loosen the political and economic stranglehold of the apparatus, Gorbachev desacralized the leading role of the party in Soviet society, unleashed and sanctioned an assault from below, and as general secretary prohibited officialdom from retaliating. Yet, in Theodore Draper's words, "it is a truism that the system was held together by the total control of the Communist Party. . . . Whatever ups and downs the Party had from Lenin to Stalin to Khrushchev to Brezhnev, it alone kept the centrifugal forces of this immense, mosaic country from breaking apart."[65] By 1988–1989, the assault on the CPSU power monopoly had resulted in a "party apparatus in revolt and disarray," with many party leaders blaming the "chaos and confusion in the party and government, the economy, and society in general on Gorbachev's leadership, in particular his impatience, impulsiveness, and misconceived policies."[66]

Another major component of Gorbachevian power restructuring—glasnost and the decentralization of the power of the Soviet state—was equally unsettling and destabilizing. As Gail Lapidus noted, "In the national republics as in Moscow, the extension of glasnost to the national question opened the door to an ever-widening public discussion of highly sensitive issues, a virtual outpouring of long-repressed resentments, and growing demands for fundamental policy changes." Although Gorbachev viewed glasnost as a manifestation of the strength and maturity of the Soviet system, its effect was to erode the "core values and institutions which had long served as the integrating forces in the Soviet multinational system," to bring into question "the entire definition of the Soviet political community," and to compel "a reassessment of the nature and future of the Soviet federation itself."[67]

In seeking to put constraints on the administrative regulation of human activity, and to jettison command and order methods, Soviet power-restructuring advocates failed to appreciate the structural centrality of these mechanisms and the fact that the unity of the Soviet system was premised on precisely such features. By subjecting the power monopoly of the party and the principle of the unitary Soviet state to a sociopolitical battering, Gorbachev undercut the vital building blocks that held the Soviet system together and thereby precipitated a systemwide crisis and breakdown.

## The Battle for Power and Resources

Prior to the disintegration of the unitary Soviet state, Western analysts conventionally credited Gorbachev with having initiated the democratization, decentralization, and marketization of the Soviet system.[68] In the wake of the Soviet breakup, other commentators claimed that resurgent nationalism in the former Soviet republics was a manifestation of democratization and marketization.[69] Our power-restructuring analysis suggests an entirely different view of the effects of Gorbachevian power restructuring. As in China during the Cultural Revolution, the major consequence of the deconcentration and decentralization of power in the period of perestroika was the eruption of an all-out battle for power and resources. This battle was conducted under many different guises, but the fundamental goal was the same—the appropriation and redistribution of power and resources previously monopolized, controlled, or claimed by the Soviet party-state.

We have seen that decentralized processes of power and resource appropriation were already well advanced in the Brezhnev period. Prior to the onset of perestroika, however, processes of appropriation were contained within the CPSU power monopoly. The effect of Gorbachevian power restructuring was to enlarge the arena of the battle for power and resources, whose participants now included previously suppressed and nonprivileged groups, as well as members of local political elites seeking to protect and advance their interests. As in China during the Cultural Revolution decade, the primary long-term consequence of Gorbachevian power restructuring was to massively accelerate decentralized processes of power and resource appropriation. In the former Soviet republics and in Russia itself, nationalism was the means by which participants in the battle for power and resources sought to advance their claims.[70] These processes underlay the breakup of the unitary Soviet state and in the early 1990s continued to gain momentum.

The eruption of assertive nationalism in the late 1980s confounded Soviet power-restructuring advocates. Even though nationalist popular movements articulated genuine popular sentiment, put pressure on Soviet officialdom, and demanded real political and social change, their aims and those of Gorbachev differed fundamentally. Whereas Gorbachev saw mass movements as a way of revitalizing the Soviet system, nationalists viewed the onslaught on CPSU bureaucratism as the first step in dismantling the Soviet system altogether. Even more vexing, and historically familiar, was the ability of local elites to manipulate social and ethnic cleavages and deflect political pressure by championing local interests. As in China in the late 1960s, embattled elites in the period of perestroika did not passively submit to the assault from above and below. Rather, nationalism, localism, factionalism, and chaos became weapons in the hands of local power holders and were effective means of resisting Gorbachevian power restructuring or turning the process to their own advantage.

The first important manifestations of these phenomena occurred in Nagorno-Karabakh in 1988, prompting Gorbachev to complain that "nationalist passions benefit all anti-perestroika forces. By stoking up inter-ethnic conflicts, they are out to distract public opinion and evade reponsibility for what they have done over the years of stagnation."[71] Yet Gorbachev was also forced to concede, "We can see that democratic rights and the new conditions opened up and created by perestroika are clearly being used for anti-democratic purposes."[72]

In the late 1980s, embattled elites throughout the non-Russian republics were able to entangle local populations in ethnic conflicts by inflaming latent tensions and cleavages. In Uzbekistan, thousands of Meshkhetians were suddenly killed, wounded, and driven from their homes by Uzbek gangs in June 1989. Subsequent polling of the local population revealed that economic resentments against this small minority had been fanned "by people who needed to divert attention from themselves. . . . 72% of the people believe events were planned in advance."[73] One month later, similar patterns were evident in interethnic feuding in Georgia. According to one local observer, "Things will not change for the better as long as certain leading personnel continue to occupy their posts. . . . What have things come to when Communists, people called upon in the line of duty to maintain order and be internationalists, promote confrontation and implacable enmity?"[74] Nor were tactics of instigating masses to struggle against masses confined to the non-Russian republics. By 1989–1990, anti-Semitic organizations were flourishing in the Russian Republic, and anti-Semitic propaganda was finding an outlet in prominent publications, with the sympathy and support of top officials.[75] As in China in late 1960s, leaders of the embattled Soviet apparatus promoted conflict by deploying well-honed political skills and considerable organizational resources in their own defense.[76]

While some embattled elites fanned ethnic tensions, other local party officials sought cover by associating themselves with national interests. Gorbachev's directives and denunciations notwithstanding, the Lithuanian Communist Party formally declared itself committed to the creation of a free and independent nation in December 1989.[77] In the manner of CCP officials who had rebuilt their power and popular support during the Cultural Revolution by advocating local interests, Lithuanian party leaders rebuilt their power and popular legitimacy by similar means. In the late 1980s, political elites successfully employed tactics of this type throughout the Soviet Union, and by 1990 the tendency for newly elected regional and municipal executive committees to "become the repository of power for those officials driven out of Communist Party agencies" was widely evident.[78]

## Authoritarian Drift and the Failure of the Kremlin Coup

By the end of the 1980s, Gorbachevian power restructuring had been swamped by an unanticipated eruption of national independence movements and ethnic conflicts, strikes and economic breakdown, localism, factionalism, and increasingly sophisticated political opposition. Like Mao in 1967–1968, Gorbachev attempted to grapple with an out-of-control situation by reasserting central authority. Thus, when the Supreme Soviet legalized the right to strike in October 1989, it also prohibited strikes in enterprises in permanent production, strikes endangering life or public health, strikes seeking to overthrow or change the Soviet system by force, and strikes by nationalist groups.[79] With the formal disbanding of the CPSU power monopoly and the introduction of multiparty elections in March 1990, Gorbachev also had himself appointed to a five-year term as Soviet president.[80] In 1990, Gorbachev made forceful use of his executive powers by issuing emergency economic decrees and using central military power to put down nationalist outbreaks in Armenia and Azerbaijan.[81] In mid-January 1991, Interior Ministry troops attacked nationalist forces in Lithuania and Latvia, killing and wounding dozens of people; at the same time, presidential decrees gave the police extensive powers over the properties, stocks, cash, and records of domestic and foreign businesses and authorized reinforced police and army patrols in Soviet cities.[82]

Authoritarian drift at the top culminated in the historic events of August 19–21, 1991, when leaders of the Soviet police, military, and military-industrial establishments declared a state of emergency; imposed martial law in Moscow, Leningrad, and the Baltic states; and attempted to reconcentrate power. Under the rubric of imposing law and order and ending bloody interethnic conflicts, the State Committee for the State of Emergency in the USSR sought to rein in accelerating processes of chaos, fragmentation, and breakdown with the traditional instruments of Soviet central authority.[83] But it was too late. In retrospect, it is evident that three sociopolitical developments underlay the failure of the Kremlin coup.

First, and most important by far, the instruments of coercion were politically split and never fully deployed. Within hours of the coup attempt, key military units and top commanders in Moscow defected to the opposition, while KGB and Interior Ministry forces either kept a low profile or actively disobeyed orders.[84] Hence, whereas the coup leaders planned a ferocious campaign of repression and were able to deploy hundreds of armored vehicles in the streets of Moscow, the KBG general in command of fifteen thousand elite troops refused to arrest Boris Yeltsin or to crush mass demonstrations, while other police and military units actually supported the opposition.[85] There was consequently little bloodshed, a curious outcome given the violence of Soviet history and subsequent events in Russia and the massive bloodlettings of the Cultural Revolution and the June 4 crackdown in China.

Second, processes of decentralization in the period of perestroika had already undercut beyond repair the power of the centralized Soviet state. Even though the leaders of the State Committee for the State of Emergency demanded that "all political and administrative organs of the Union of Soviet Socialist Republics and of union and autonomous republics, territories, regions, cities, districts, towns, and villages must follow without deviation the regime of the state of emergency," the days when such pronouncements could be effectively issued from Moscow were past.[86] Within twenty-four hours of the coup attempt, leaders in the large and politically potent republics of Ukraine and Kazakhstan had expressed opposition and declared the orders of the State Committee null and void on their territory; meanwhile coal miners in Ukraine and the Russian Republic went on strike.[87]

Third, spontaneous outbreaks of popular opposition to the coup erupted in Leningrad and in Moscow especially. At the time, the spectacle of tens of thousands of people flocking to the Russian Federation White House in defense of Yeltsin and "democracy" was deemed a watershed in the political history of Russia, prompting some commentators to assert, "The August Revolution provided a major test of popular allegiance in Russia: would the people, including the officers and soldiers of the armed forces, side with Russia against the central authorities of the Soviet party-state?"[88] But these hopes, problematic in any case, were not to be realized.[89] Little more than two years after the Kremlin coup and the putative triumph of the Russian people, the White House was gutted by tank fire on the orders of President Yeltsin, and a few months later the leaders of the coup were freed from prison and cleared of all charges at the behest of rising authoritarian-nationalist political forces.

As the Kremlin coup succumbed to this broad coalescence of opposition, its defeat both confirmed and accelerated power-restructuring processes set in motion in the late 1980s. Within days of the failed coup attempt, all activities of the CPSU were formally suspended, its offices closed, and its vast properties and funds turned over to individual republics. Meanwhile, one republic after another declared its independence from the Soviet Union, thereby fatally undercutting the unitary Soviet state.[90] These cataclysmic events, never envisioned or anticipated by Soviet power-restructuring advocates in the late 1980s, were the consequences of the power-deconcentrating and power-decentralizing processes set in motion in the period of perestroika.

## A Transition to Democracy and a Market Economy?

When Ukraine seceded from the USSR, Gorbachev resigned his post as Soviet president, and the Union was formally dissolved in December 1991, Boris Yeltsin's aides declared that "the first popularly elected president in Russia's history is irrevocably committed to the consolidation of Russia's fledgling democracy and the construction of a free-market economy."[91] These sentiments were widely echoed in the West, and commentators hailed the collapse of communism and the end of the Soviet empire and spoke of a historic transition to democracy and the market in Russia and the former Soviet republics. Once again, I suggest entirely different conclusions.

I have argued that key aspects of power restructuring in the period of perestroika paralleled the restructuring of power in China during the Cultural Revolution decade—important similarities include the deliberate deconcentration of power and suspension of control mechanisms, the eruption of pent-up tensions and repressed grievances, three-way battles for power and resources, official survival strategies, the rise of new power centers at the regional and local levels, and the acceleration of decentralized processes of power and resource appropriation. Accordingly, I suggest that the transition from socialism in the former Soviet Union will unfold in a manner resembling transitional processes manifested in China in the 1980s. As in China, the key features of this emerging transitional synthesis are political and economic decentralization, privatization and marketization, cultural liberalization and opening up to the outside world, and political authoritarianism and nationalism. Within this broadly comparable transitional framework, however, crucial historical and structural differences distinguish the transition from socialism in Russia from the Chinese pattern.

Most important, the spectacular economic growth in China in the 1980s is manifestly dissimilar to the precipitous economic collapse throughout the former Soviet Union in the late 1980s and early 1990s. As Daniel Yergin and Thane Gustafson noted, "The Chinese economic miracle was initiated and sustained in its first decade by local agriculture," and "its second decade was sparked by capital and entrepreneurship supplied by the overseas Chinese, and was concentrated primarily in coastal 'free economic zones,' characterized by a rebirth of a strong commercial tradition. These vital engines of growth are missing in Russia."[92] Instead, the assault on systemic building blocks resulted in economic breakdown and a precipitous decline in mass living standards, processes subsequently intensified by the rapid implementation of price decontrol, privatization, and "shock therapy" in 1992–1993.

It may be premature to contrast the post-Mao economic boom to the economic breakdown of the late 1980s and early 1990s in the Soviet Union and its successor states. After all, the Chinese economic expansion of the 1980s was more than a decade removed from the most intense and widespread upheavals of the Cultural Revolution. Perhaps economic performance in Russia can be compared to post-Mao economic performance when the polity and economy are stabilized. As Yergin and Gustafson argued, Russia is an industrial giant and possesses many advantages on which a "Russian economic miracle" might be built—excess capacity of many raw and semiprocessed materials; abundant and low-wage scientific and engineering personnel, trained and literate industrial labor power; excess capacity in many industrial plants, pipelines, and railroads; unexploited managerial energy and talent; and enormous pent-up demand for consumer goods and services.[93]

But my discussion in the preceding chapters may suggest a less fortunate outcome. When the historical trajectory of Soviet and Chinese socialism are compared, the essential structural stability of the Soviet system from the 1940s until the onset of perestroika stands in striking contrast to the repeated sociopolitical, economic, and structural upheavals experienced in China until the 1980s, when yet another revolution occurred. Whereas the Stalin system of centralization, statization, and heavy industrialization was victorious during Stalin's lifetime, successfully withstood Khrushchev's reform efforts, and was strongly reinforced in the Brezhnev era, the upheavals of the Great Leap Forward and the Cultural Revolution undercut Soviet-style centralization, eroded Maoist ideas, and opened up the way for competing processes of decentralization, marketization, and privatization in China. It is probable that these differences in the trajectory of socialism in the Soviet Union and China explain the different economic outcomes in the transition from socialism thus far. Whether a Russian economic miracle takes place or not, however, the future configuration of political and economic power in the former Soviet Union will resemble post-Mao China more than the capitalist West.

The major consequences of Gorbachevian power restructuring were a massive decentralization of political and economic power and a fundamental shift in the relationship between center and locality. Whereas regional power centers became increasingly important in post-Mao China, the multiethnic Soviet Union broke up into separate nations in the period of perestroika. As in post-Mao China, however, Russian central rulers in the wake of the breakup confront increasingly assertive and well-endowed centers of power at the regional, provincial, and local levels. Just as Chinese central authorities must constantly battle regional and provincial centers of power for control of revenues and resources, Russian deputy prime minister Boris Fedorov on June 2, 1993, denounced the "unacceptable demands" of the republics of Tatarstan, Sakha, Chechnya, and Karelia for the "exclusive right to levy taxes and to launch new currencies" and warned that such developments would lead to the breakup of the Russian state.[94] One month later, the provinces of St. Petersburg, Amur, Vologda, Kaliningrad, and Khabarovsk declared themselves independent of the central government and central authorities.[95]

At the same time, the crisis and collapse of the CPSU power monopoly precipitated an all-out scramble, with former communist officials in the lead, to appropriate power and resources at the local level. Whereas Western commentators and Soviet power-restructuring advocates viewed privatization and marketization as a remedy to the myriad defects of the Soviet economic system, in the former Soviet Union these processes pivoted on the appropriation of state assets and resources by the politically well connected and the financially well heeled and were rife with corruption. Party functionaries were already buying up shares in the enterprises under their management before the failed August coup, and in October 1991 KGB chief Vadim Bakatin observed, "You get the impression that the new authorities, having taken property away from the center, are in no hurry to give it up."[96] A few months later, processes of "spontaneous privatization" were sweeping Russia, with "workers and managers taking control as though they already own the assets."[97] In 1992, a surge of corruption, smuggling, and capital flight swept Russia as former party and state officials used their political connections and clout to acquire and illegally export huge quantities of raw materials, amass fortunes, and divert billions of dollars to offshore companies and Western bank accounts.[98] This pattern is familiar, and we have seen how Chinese Communist officials routinely used their personal connections and political power to take advantage of and reap handsome profits from processes of privatization and marketization. With the collapse of the old system of centralization and control, however, the appropriation of assets and resources by official power holders and their allies in the former Soviet Union lacks any constraint whatsoever.

## The Emerging Post-Soviet Political Order

The rise of new centers of power at the regional and local levels and the further extension of processes of decentralized power and resource appropriation in the wake of the Soviet breakup underscore the historical continuity of these events with power-restructuring patterns in Chinese and Russian history in imperial times, under communism, and today. Patterns of continuity are also evident in the political realm, where the most striking characteristic of the emerging post-Soviet order is pervasive political authoritarianism.

Despite the disbanding of the CPSU, power remained overwhelmingly concentrated in the hands of former communist officials in the wake of the Soviet breakup. Former CPSU leaders shelved Marxist-Leninist ideology and CPSU affiliation in favor of nationalist, social democratic, and free-market platforms in

Russia. Presidents Nursultan Nazarbayev and Leonid Kravchuk in Kazakhstan and Ukraine, respectively, former republican first party secretaries turned champions of national self-determination, exemplified the pattern of continuity of leading personnel in the Soviet successor states. Not surprisingly, these former communist rulers continued to wield power in familiar ways. In Uzbekistan, the instruments of Soviet police and military power were simply renamed and subordinated to the new, decentralized center of power in the wake of the failed coup attempt, with no change in structure and personnel.[99] In Russia, commentators as early as fall 1991 noted the "new authoritarianism" of local leaders and their penchant for issuing decrees; executives in administrative districts, it was observed, continued to wield power in a manner indistinguishable from that of former district Soviet executive committees.[100]

In 1992–1993, Western commentators repeatedly claimed that the forces of democracy and reform led by President Yeltsin were engaged in a life and death struggle with various "hard-line" forces and that the fate of democracy and reform in Russia hung in the balance. When Yeltsin won a majority in the April 1993 referendum, Jeffrey D. Sachs hailed the "overwhelming mandate for his leadership" and proclaimed, "Democracy and market reforms triumphed spectacularly in Russia's referendum."[101] But Sachs was badly mistaken and about to be conclusively disproved by events. In fact, Yeltsin blended political authoritarianism with economic reformism in his style of rule and as early as October 1992 had used decrees to ban his opponents, ostensibly to protect Russia's nascent democracy.[102] Contrary to proponents of the "Yeltsin, democracy, and reform" thesis, however, Yeltsin's deportment in the period leading up to the April 1993 referendum was not that of a democrat but that of a Russian central ruler seeking to assert his power, to isolate and delegitimate his political opponents in parliament and in the provinces, and to appeal to the masses. In March 1993, again invoking the threat to reform and decrying the "attack of the former party *nomenklatura*," Yeltsin attempted to assume emergency powers and to rule by presidential decree, until "the crisis of power is concluded."[103] As parliament immediately challenged the legality of Yeltsin's special powers and the leaders of autonomous regions and republics denounced the move as "unconstitutional" and "an attempt to impose an authoritarian regime," the struggle for power in Russia intensified.[104]

The struggle between Yeltsin and parliament apparently culminated in late September and early October 1993, especially in the events of October 3–4. While Western governments and commentators continued to embrace the proposition that Yeltsin's attempt to implement economic and political reforms was being stymied by a reactionary legislative body elected under old Soviet rules and composed of communist holdouts and hard-liners, this notion was being squarely contradicted by the political deportment of the Russian government. When tensions finally came to a head, the struggle with parliament was "resolved" by military force. Yet the shelling of the Russian White House on October 4, 1993, only underscored the authoritarian deportment of the central authorities. Lending substance to accusations that "so-called presidential rule will in fact be a dictatorship," the Yeltsin government in the days leading up to the crisis of October 3–4 and in its aftermath unilaterally dissolved the political opposition, banned noncompliant newspapers and political parties, assumed control of all media outlets, suspended the courts, launched a police crackdown on undesirable migrant groups in Moscow, and issued a torrent of presidential decrees.[105]

Assessed in light of these events, notions of Yeltsin, democracy, and reform are obviously untenable. Instead, it is more accurate to speak of power contests and a battle between central authority and competing centers of power, both in parliament and at the regional and local levels. Indeed, Yeltsin's effort to concentrate power and implement central policy objectives by waging a war on competing centers of power parallels power-restructuring patterns I have charted throughout this book.

By late 1993 and 1994, the pressing question was not whether the "democratization" of Russia would occur but rather what kind of political authoritarianism would succeed the classic Soviet variant. Would it be the decentralized authoritarianism of the many independent kingdoms that had arisen in the wake of the Soviet breakup, where local bosses held sway in decentralized systems of concentrated power and local autonomy and "self-determination" were the means by which local elites and the former nomenklatura defended and preserved their power?[106] Or would it be Yeltsin's authoritarian reformism, with its emphasis on strong, powerful government; law and order; increased presidential powers; and gradual reform?[107] Indeed, in the wake of the December 12, 1993, elections, many shell-shocked liberal commentators were ready to jettison democracy altogether and pinned their hopes for reform on a strong Russian presidency.[108]

## An Authoritarian-Nationalist Reconfiguration

But these were not the only possibilities. The great irony of the December 12, 1993, elections was that democracy and increased political pluralism actually reinforced the pattern of authoritarianism and nationalism that characterizes the transition from socialism in China and Russia. The two major outcomes of the election were thus the dramatic rise of the militant nationalist-authoritarian Liberal Democratic Party and the approval of a new Russian constitution that concentrated vast new powers in the hands of the Russian president. While conclusively overturning the Yeltsin, democracy, and reform thesis, these developments continued to defy Western analyses.

In the aftermath of the Soviet breakup, some Western observers argued that nationalism and separatism were the most important and enduring results of perestroika. According to Lapidus, "The entire map of Eurasia has been irrevocably altered by the events of the last few years," as "the former republics of the Soviet Union are now transforming themselves into increasingly sovereign states with a growing capacity, as well as desire, to manage their own political, economic, social, and military affairs autonomously."[109] Victor Zaslavsky argued that the "traditional imperial nationalism" of the Soviet and czarist past had been "for the foreseeable future" displaced by "separatist and isolationist" nationalism, which rejected the high cost of maintaining the empire, and by "liberal-democratic nationalism," which "is predicated on continued close cooperation with the West combined with consistent attempts to gain popular acceptance of marketization reforms."[110] Yet throughout 1993, and in the wake of the December 12 elections more than ever, the evidence of an authoritarian-nationalist reconfiguration in Russia and other parts of the former Soviet Union grew increasingly apparent.

On the peripheries of Russia and beyond, Russian military forces regularly played the deciding role in conflicts in Tajikistan, Georgia, Moldova and Trans-Dniester, Armenia, and Azerbaijan throughout 1993.[111] But the results of the December 12 elections accelerated the movement in the direction of an authoritarian-nationalist reconfiguration in Russia, and even as foreign governments denounced the statements of ultranationalist Vladimir Zhirinovsky, the Yeltsin government assumed a traditional imperial stance. In mid-January 1994, Yeltsin called Russia a "great power" and "first among equals" in the Commonwealth and stated, "Our countries are growing closer together. Each understands more and more clearly that alone it cannot cope with the difficult problems it faces."[112] By fall 1994, Russian and Western commentators were speaking of Yeltsin's imperial political deportment, noting his increasing isolation and reliance on a few "palace favorites" and comparing him to Brezhnev.[113]

But the movement in the direction of an authoritarian-nationalist reconfiguration was fully manifested with the outbreak of the Chechnya war in December 1994. As Western observers and Russian liberals recoiled in horror and incomprehension, and journalists compiled myriad reports of Russian ineptitude, incompetent leadership, low morale, shoddy weaponry, corruption, desertion, and insubordination, the military onslaught against the Chechen rebels ponderously and relentlessly moved forward.[114] By February, Chechen resistance in Grozny had been broken, the city itself destroyed, thousands of soldiers on both sides killed, tens of thousands of civilians slaughtered or driven from their homes, and the rebels forced into the surrounding countryside and villages, where they were subjected to intensifying Russian attacks.[115] Although most commentators decried the catastrophic effects of the war on "reform" and "democracy" in Russia, other conclusions can be drawn. Understood in light of my discussion, with the wholesale destruction and slaughter in Chechnya, Russia's authoritarian nationalist rulers smashed a strategically situated regional power center and unambiguously served notice that the breakup of Russia itself would not be tolerated.

Even as the post-Soviet Russian state's war on a competing center of power unfolded, however, there was no reversing the fundamental restructuring of power set in motion in the period of perestroika. As in post-Mao China, along with mounting authoritarianism and nationalism, processes of decentralization, privatization, cultural liberalization, and opening up to the outside world proceeded apace in Russia in the early 1990s. As in China, this potent combination of old patterns and new realities will continue to drive the transition from socialism in the former Soviet Union in the 1990s and beyond. Yet Russia must also contend with economic decline, deteriorating mass living standards, technological backwardness, and the complex legacy of Brezhnevian stagnation and former superpower status.

## Notes

1. Gail W. Lapidus, "From Democratization to Disintegration: The Impact of Perestroika on the National Question," in Gail W. Lapidus, Victor Zaslavsky, and Philip Goldman, eds., *From Union to Commonwealth—Nationalism and Separatism in the Soviet Republics* (Cambridge: Cambridge University Press, 1992), 66.

2. Timothy J. Colton, *The Dilemma of Reform in the Soviet Union* (New York: Council on Foreign Relations, 1984), 58–59. Hence, "revolutionary cataclysm is prohibitively unlikely because the essential prerequisite for it—an overall crisis of the political system—does not exist" (58).

3. Seweryn Bialer and Joan Afferica, "Gorbachev's Preference for Technocrats," *New York Times*, February 11, 1986, 31; Mark D'Anastasio, "Kremlin-Watchers Suspect Gorbachev Is Crying Wolf on Domestic Opposition," *Wall Street Journal*, March 17, 1987, 33. For another analysis stressing Gorbachev's limited aims, see William E. Odom, "How Far Can Soviet Reform Go?" *Problems of Communism* (November–December 1987):18–33.

4. Seweryn Bialer, "The Yeltsin Affair: The Dilemma of the Left in Gorbachev's Revolution," in Seweryn Bialer, ed., *Politics, Society, and Nationality—Inside Gorbachev's Russia* (Boulder: Westview Press, 1989), 114–115.

5. Peter Hauslohner, "Politics Before Gorbachev: De-Stalinization and the Roots of Reform," in ibid., 79.

6. Moshe Lewin, *The Gorbachev Phenomenon* (Berkeley and Los Angeles: University of California Press, 1988), 46–47, 147, 152. Although Lewin was careful to qualify his formulations with the caveat "à la russe," it is apparent that he believed Soviet society had become more "modern" in the Western sense.

7. Blair A. Ruble, "Stepping Off the Treadmill of Failed Reforms," in Harley D. Balzer, ed., *Five Years That Shook the World—Gorbachev's Unfinished Revolution* (Boulder: Westview Press, 1991), 14, 24, 27.

8. Jerry F. Hough, "Gorbachev Consolidating Power," *Problems of Communism* (July–August 1987):28.

9. Jerry F. Hough, "Understanding Gorbachev: The Importance of Politics," in Ed A. Hewett and Victor H. Winston, eds., *Milestones in Glasnost and Perestroyka—Politics and People* (Washington, D.C.: Brookings Institution, 1991), 477.

10. "If, however, we are asking whether Gorbachev can control Soviet social forces and remain in power until the end of the century, that is a very different question, and so is the probable answer, as long as the General Secretary remains healthy. It is too soon to forget the old lessons we once learned about the power of a general secretary in the Soviet political system" (Hough, "Gorbachev Consolidating Power," 43).

11. For a devastating critique of Hough and a compilation of his many erroneous assertions and predictions, see Theodore Draper, "Who Killed Soviet Communism?" *New York Review of Books,* June 11, 1992, 7–14. Thus, "Sovietology à la Hough is in need of thorough self-examination. He was wrong about Brezhnev's progressiveness; the conclusive defeat of the 'conservative opposition' as early as 1988; the underestimation of all 'varieties of nationalism'; the immoderate glorification of Gorbachev" (9).

12. Ed A. Hewett, *Reforming the Soviet Economy—Equality Versus Efficiency* (Washington, D.C.: Brookings Institution, 1988), 72–73.

13. Grigorii Khanin, "Economic Growth in the 1980s," in Michael Ellman and Vladimir Kontorovich, eds., *The Disintegration of the Soviet Economic System* (London: Routledge, 1992), 75–79.

14. Michael Ellman and Vladimir Kontorovich, "Overview," in ibid., 9. While low-priority economic sectors were starved and neglected, the Soviet military-industrial sector engaged in overproduction and overkill. In the mid-1980s, "Moscow's nuclear arsenal peaked at 45,000 warheads—12,000 more than generally believed, twice the number held by the United States at the time, and exceeding all estimates save those of the most hawkish analysts" (William J. Broad, "At the End, Soviet Atomic Overkill," *International Herald Tribune,* September 27, 1993, 1).

15. Khanin, "Economic Growth in the 1980s," 79.

16. Hewett, *Reforming the Soviet Economy,* 230.

17. Ibid., 237–238.

18. Hence, "the industrial reorganization begun in 1973 was an attempt to concentrate power in the center of the decision-making hierarchy, simultaneously drawing power away from the ministries to the VPOs (All-Union Industrial Associations) and away from the enterprises to the production and scientific-production associations" (ibid., 245–249).

19. "Mikhail Gorbachev's Speech at the 19th All-Union Party Conference, June 30, 1988," *Pravda,* July 1, 1988, in *Reprints from the Soviet Press* 47, 2 (July 31, 1988):7.

20. Yegor Ligachev, *Inside Gorbachev's Kremlin* (New York: Pantheon, 1993), 46. Thus, "I would like to reinsert in history a Central Committee plenum that never took place, one that was supposed to be devoted to the scientific and technological revolution. Planning for this plenum had begun back in Brezhnev's day. Many people in the Party understood that we were on the threshhold of a new scientific and technological revolution that would revitalize our concept of productive forces and relations. The developed countries of the West were just beginning to reorganize their industry and agriculture; with our enormous scientific, technological, and intellectual potential, we could have managed to get on the train of the revolution racing toward the third millennium. But year after year passed, and the plenum was continually postponed" (45).

21. Ellman and Kontorovich, "Overview," 10. "The end of terror after 1953, the winding down of forced labor, the abolition of restrictions on labor mobility dating from 1940, and other measures of Khrushchev's de-Stalinization package represented the first round of this process. Brezhnev's policy of 'stability in cadres' and the spread of corruption in this period represented the second round" (10).

22. Cited in "The KGB Has Not Changed Its Principles . . . Yet," *Komsomolskaya Pravda,* June 20, 1990, in Isaac J. Tarasulo, ed., *Perils of Perestroika: Viewpoints from the Soviet Press* (Wilmington, Del.: Scholarly Resources, 1992), 109–110. Moreover, "the only organization that can give any instructions to the KGB is the party Central Committee. . . . The document said that it was forbidden to conduct any operations . . . and there

followed a list of officials. In the event of receiving adverse materials concerning these people, these materials were to be destroyed immediately on the spot" (109).

23. Alexander J. Motyl, *Sovietology, Rationality, Nationality* (New York: Columbia University Press, 1990), 65.

24. Hewett, *Reforming the Soviet Economy,* 260–273.

25. Ellman and Kontorovich, "Overview," 14.

26. Vladimir Kontorovich, "Discipline and Growth in the Soviet Economy," *Problems of Communism* (November–December 1985):27.

27. Ellman and Kontorovich, "Overview," 15.

28. Martin Malia, *The Soviet Tragedy: A History of Socialism in Russia, 1917–1991* (New York: Free Press, 1994), 408.

29. Thane Gustafson and Dawn Mann, "Gorbachev's First Year: Building Power and Authority," *Problems of Communism* (May–June 1986):2.

30. Thane Gustafson and Dawn Mann, "Gorbachev's Next Gamble," *Problems of Communism* (July–August 1987):20.

31. Ibid.

32. "The Novosibirsk Report," in Tatyana Zaslavskaya and Murray Yanowitch, eds., *A Voice of Reform* (Armonk, N.Y.: M. E. Sharpe, 1989), 159.

33. Tatyana Zaslavskaya, "Economics Through the Prism of Sociology," in ibid., 47–48.

34. Tatyana Zaslavskaya, "Creative Activity of the Masses—Social Reserves of Growth," in ibid., 72.

35. Ibid., 77.

36. Ibid., 80.

37. Vadim Semyonov, "Dialectics of Restructuring—a Leap Forward in Social Development," *Socialism: Theory and Practice* 4 (April 1988), in *Reprints from the Soviet Press* 46, 9–10 (May 1988):20.

38. Sidney I. Ploss, "A New Soviet Era?" *Foreign Policy* 62 (Spring 1986):50.

39. For a discussion of Gorbachev's suspension of the CPSU power monopoly in the fall 1988 elections and the political free-for-all that ensued, see Ligachev, *Inside Gorbachev's Kremlin,* chap. 2. From Ligachev's perspective, the consequences were catastrophic: "The Central Committee sent out one directive after another to local Party offices: Don't interfere. Keep your distance. Confusion reigned in a number of Party Committees. They saw that many unworthy people had announced their candidacies, even former convicts who had committed serious crimes. As for loudmouths and demagogues who built their platform only on anti-Soviet and anti-Communist planks, their number was legion. You would think that under these conditions, Party propaganda would be increased, providing more support for its candidates and exposing groundless and unrealistic populist promises. But the Central Committee offered no political orientation, and the local Party offices were helpless" (91–92).

40. Mikhail Gorbachev, "Revolutionary Perestroika and the Ideology of Renewal," *Pravda,* February, 19, 1988, in *Reprints from the Soviet Press* 47, 3 (August 15, 1988):5.

41. Ibid., 9.

42. Ibid., 10.

43. Ibid., 20.

44. "On Combating Bureaucracy" (Resolutions of the 19th All-Union Party Conference), *Pravda,* July 9, 1988, in *Reprints from the Soviet Press* 47, 3 (August 15, 1988):5–10. (All quotes in this paragraph are from this source.)

45. "On Glasnost," in ibid., 18.

46. Ibid., 18, 19.

47. "On Relations Between Soviet Nationalities" in ibid., 12.

48. Ibid.

49. Bill Keller, "Moscow Bubbles in Ferment over Party Meeting," *New York Times,* June 26, 1988, 6.

50. Bill Keller, "Soviet Voters Deal a Mortifying Blow to Party Officials," *New York Times,* March 28, 1989, 1.

51. Bill Keller, "In the Gauntlet of Democracy, a Soviet Editor Takes Knocks," *New York Times,* June 18, 1988, 1.

52. FBIS-SOV-89-141, "Ryzhkov Meets Donbass Miners," *Vremya,* June 24, 1989, 51.

53. Russell Bova, "On Perestroika: The Role of Workplace Participation," *Problems of Communism* (July–August 1987):76–86.

54. FBIS-SOV-89-140, "Gorbachev Addresses Supreme Soviet on Miners' Strike," *Moscow Television,* July 24, 1989, 39.

55. Padma Desai, *Perestroika in Perspective—the Design and Dilemmas of Soviet Reform* (Princeton: Princeton University Press, 1989), 8.

56. "Report by Mikhail Gorbachev to the 19th All-Union Party Conference of the CPSU," *Novosti Press Agency,* June 28, 1988, in *Reprints from the Soviet Press* 47, 1 (July 15, 1988), 55.

57. Ibid., 55, 56.

58. "Interview: Restructuring Corresponds to the Strategic Interests of the Majority," in Zaslavskaya and Yanowitch, eds., *A Voice of Reform,* 147–148.

59. George W. Breslauer, "Gorbachev: Diverse Perspectives," in Hewett and Winston, eds., *Milestones in Glasnost and Perestroyka,* 485. In this piece, which was "selectively updated in July 1991," Breslauer further stated, "I too, if forced to bet, would wager on Gorbachev's political longevity.... I do not share ... the perception that the center has collapsed in Soviet politics. I still view Gorbachev as an indispensable liaison and mediator, whose political power and radical centrism offset backlash tendencies, force compromises on extremists to the left, and create bandwagoning incentives for many fence-sitters" (490). One month later, Gorbachev's power was shattered in the failed Kremlin coup, with the breakup of the Soviet Union following in a few months.

60. Motyl, *Sovietology, Rationality, Nationality,* 98.

61. Galina V. Starovoitova, "The Soviet Union in 1990," in Balzer, ed., *Five Years That Shook the World,* 202–203.

62. Andranik Migranyan, "Gorbachev's Leadership: A Soviet View," in Hewett and Winston, eds., *Milestones in Glasnost and Perestroyka,* 460, 461.

63. Ibid., 460–461.

64. Ellman and Kontorovich, "Overview," 31.

65. Draper, "Who Killed Soviet Communism?" 12.

66. Rolf H.W. Theen, "Party-State Relations Under Gorbachev: From Partocracy to 'Party' State?" in Mel Gurtov, ed., *The Transformation of Socialism—Perestroika and Reform in the Soviet Union and China* (Boulder: Westview Press, 1990), 77.

67. Lapidus, "From Democratization to Disintegration," 47, 59.

68. In Breslauer's words, "Legitimation in principle of movement in the direction of a market-driven economic order, a multi-party system, and the right to secede from the

Union" ("Evaluating Gorbachev as Leader," in Hewett and Winston, eds., *Milestones in Glasnost and Perestroyka*, 392).

69. Hence, "the Soviet experience should serve as a reminder that the nexus between nationalism, marketization, and a liberal-democratic world order is much stronger than liberal and Marxist critics of nationalism will admit" (Philip Goldman, Gail W. Lapidus, and Victor Zaslavsky, "Introduction: Soviet Federalism—its Origins, Evolution, and Demise," in Lapidus et al., eds., *From Union to Commonwealth*, 19).

70. As a Lithuanian nationalist leader observed in January 1991, "In our country, the real perestroika is so late in coming not just because of the Stalinists and those who did so well under Brezhnev are constantly obstructing progress. The trouble is that, together with all those who are honestly trying to push through the reforms, there exists an assortment of chameleons, who want to be seen as leaders of the process, though they are the ones who in the past stifled any new ideas. It is a bitter thing to have to admit, but in Lithuania such people are having a field day" (Piatras Keidoshus and Vitautas Petkiavicius, "Confessions of a 'Renegade,'" *Literaturnaya Gazeta* 1 [January 1991], in Tarasulo, *Perils of Perestroika*, 45).

71. "On Practical Work to Implement the Decisions of the 19th All-Union Party Conference," *Pravda*, July 30, 1988, in *Reprints from the Soviet Press* 47, 5 (September 15, 1988):18.

72. "Mikhail Gorbachev's Speech at the USSR Supreme Soviet Presidium," *Pravda*, July 20, 1988, in *Reprints from the Soviet Press* 47, 4 (August 31, 1988):11.

73. FBIS-SOV-89-144, "Sociologists View Reasons for Uzbek Strife," *Pravda*, July 2, 1989, 70.

74. FBIS-SOV-89-142, "Local Officials Implicated in Abkhaz Violence," *Izvestiya*, July 26, 1989, 74.

75. Vitalli I. Goldanskii, "Anti-Semitism: The Return of a Russian Nightmare," *Washington Post*, February 18, 1990, 1.

76. As the liberal Gavrill Popov, then mayor of Moscow, noted in August 1990, the apparatus "is adopting the tactics we radicals used in previous stages of the struggle during the last few years" (Gavrill Popov, "Dangers of Democracy," *New York Review of Books*, August 19, 1990, 27).

77. David Remnick, "Moscow Assails Lithuanian Party," *Washington Post*, December 27, 1989, 8.

78. Ruble, "Stepping Off the Treadmill of Failed Reforms," 22–23.

79. Michael Dobbs, "Soviets Limit Right to Strike," *Washington Post*, January 25, 1990, 23.

80. Bill Keller, "Democracy, Gorbachev's Way," *New York Times*, March 18, 1990, 1.

81. Michael Dobbs, "Soviets Shell Blockading Baku Ships," *Washington Post*, January 25, 1990, 1.

82. Michael Dobbs, "Curfew Imposed on Lithuania, Other Baltics Fear Soviet Attack," *Washington Post*, January 14, 1991, 1; David Remnick, "KGB Police Given Power over Firms," *Washington Post*, January 27, 1991, 14; David Remnick, "Police-Army Teams Start Patrols," *Washington Post*, February 2, 1991, 11.

83. State Committee for the State of Emergency in the USSR, "A Mortal Danger Has Come," *TASS*, August 19, 1991, carried in *New York Times*, August 20, 1991, 13.

84. Defections included elite army divisions deployed in the capital, KGB antiterrorist units, officers of the General Staff, and rapid deployment airborne forces commanders. See

"The Failed Coup," *Soviet/East European Report* (Radio Free Europe/Radio Liberty Research Institute) 8, 43 (September 10, 1991):2–3.

85. Victoria E. Bonnell and Gregory Freidin, "Introduction," in Victoria E. Bonnell, Ann Cooper, and Gregory Freidin, eds., *Russia at the Barricades: Eyewitness Accounts of the August 1991 Coup* (Armonk, N.Y.: M. E. Sharpe, 1994), 18–19.

86. "Document 3: Resolution No. 1 of the USSR State Committee for the State of Emergency," in ibid., 38.

87. Fred Hiatt, "Soviet Coup Opposition Reported Widening," *Washington Post,* August 21, 1991, 23–25.

88. Bonnell and Freidin, "Introduction," 20.

89. As one Western commentator observed in March 1995, "The greatest victory of August 1991—when Russians beat back the attempted coup against Mikhail Gorbachev, and Boris Yeltsin emerged at the head of the democrats and modernizers—was the sense that ordinary people had finally seized some control over their destiny. . . . Such feelings persist and grow, especially in the young, but for those much past 45, the confidence has been short-lived. First, it was built on a myth—in fact most Russians did nothing to stop the coup, which nearly succeeded. Second, and more important, political and economic mismanagement of reform have made Russia's path away from 70 years of repression more tortuous than it might have been" (Steven Erlanger, "In Russia, Success Isn't Such a Popular Idea," *New York Times,* March 12, 1995, 4).

90. Serge Schmemann, "Soviets Bar Communist Party; Republics Press Search for New Order," *New York Times,* August 30, 1991, 1; James Rupert, "2 Central Asian Republics Quit USSR," *Washington Post,* September 1, 1991, 1.

91. Michael Dobbs, "Up from Humilation," *Washington Post,* December 27, 1991, 16.

92. Daniel Yergin and Thane Gustafson, *Russia 2010* (New York: Random House, 1993), 165.

93. Ibid., 169.

94. Radio Free Europe/Radio Liberty, "Deputy Prime Minister Fedorov on Demand of Republics," *Daily Report* 105 (June 4, 1993):1.

95. Radio Free Europe/Radio Liberty, "Amur Oblast Declares Itself Independent," *Daily Report,* 138 (July 22, 1993):1.

96. "Privatization in the Soviet Union: Fanning the Spark of Capitalism," *The Economist,* May 18, 1991, 82; FBIS-SOV-91-209, "Vadim Bakatin on Principles of Security Reforms," *Izvestiya,* October 26, 1991, 26.

97. "Privatizing Russia," *The Economist,* February 15, 1992, 20.

98. See *Washington Post* series "The Profits of Chaos," Michael Dobbs and Steve Coll, January 31–February 2, 1993, for a detailed account of this process. Thus, "the key to understanding how *biznes* is conducted in the new Russia frequently lies in knowing who were pals with whom in the now defunct party and KGB. The Soviet era 'old comrade network' lives on in an intricate web of personal relationships that stretches from the resource-rich fiefdoms of Siberia and the Urals to the Moscow ministries that issue export licenses to the Westerners who buy raw materials and send them abroad" (February 1, 1993, 14).

99. Thus, "a National Security Service, subordinated to the republican president, has replaced the KGB in Uzbekistan, by the presidential decree of Islam Karimov" (FBIS-SOV-91-189, "New 'National Security Service,'" *TASS,* September 27, 1991):98.

100. FBIS-SOV-91-188, "'Local Authorities' New Powers Assessed," *Pravda*, September 13, 1991, 18.

101. Jeffrey D. Sachs, "Hey, Pundits, What About Yeltsin?" *New York Times*, April 30, 1993, 31.

102. Elisabeth Rubinfein, "Yeltsin Using Special Edicts to Quell Rivals," *Wall Street Journal*, October 29, 1992, 10.

103. "Boris N. Yeltsin's Address," *New York Times*, March 21, 1993, 12.

104. Margaret Shapiro and Fred Hiatt, "Russia's Legislature Moves to Oust Yeltsin," *Washington Post*, March 22, 1993, 1. See also Michael Dobbs, "Russian Republics Split with Yeltsin," *Washington Post*, March 23, 1993, 1.

105. David Filipov, "Rutskoi Accuses President of 'Dictatorship'," *Moscow Daily News*, September 18, 1993, 1; Margaret Shapiro, "Yeltsin's 'Essential' Crackdown Provokes Charges of Expediency," *Washington Post*, October 16, 1993, 14; Margaret Shapiro, "Moscow Uses Crisis to Expel Migrants," *Washington Post*, October 12, 1993, 23.

106. For an account of local officials using the disintegration of Russia to preserve the power of the nomenklatura, see Radio Free Europe/Radio Liberty, "Shakhrai on Power Struggle," *Daily Report* 132 (July 14, 1993):1.

107. Radio Free Europe/Radio Liberty, "Yeltsin's Press Conference," *Daily Report* 245 (December 23, 1993):1.

108. Hence, "what is striking is how many of Russia's elite, expressing shame and disgust, are in some ways blaming Russians themselves, concluding that the masses are not, after all, ready for democracy" (Fred Hiatt, "Russian Elite Sees Vote as Betrayal," *Washington Post*, December 21, 1993, 17).

109. Lapidus, "From Democratization to Disintegration," 66.

110. Victor Zaslavsky, "The Evolution of Separatism in Soviet Society Under Gorbachev," in Lapidus et al., eds., *From Union to Commonwealth*, 88.

111. In January 1993, former CPSU rulers in Tajikistan, with the active assistance of Russian military forces, gained the upper hand in a civil war that had resulted in an estimated twenty thousand to forty thousand dead and hundreds of thousands of refugees. See Steve LeVine, "Brutal Tajik War Shakes All Central Asia," *Washington Post*, February 5, 1993, 1.

112. Radio Free Europe/Radio Liberty, "Yeltsin: Russia 'First Among Equals' in Commonwealth," *Daily Report* 7 (January 12, 1994):1.

113. Alan Cooperman, "President Boris Brezhnev," *U.S. News and World Report*, November 7, 1994, 52.

114. For a typical journalistic account detailing the sorry performance of the Russian Army and enumerating the many defeats inflicted on it by the Chechen rebels, see Michael Specter, "For Russia's Troops, Humbling Days," *New York Times*, January 1, 1995, 1.

115. Russian leaflets dropped on other Chechen cities read, "Resisting Federal troops will lead to powerful retaliatory strikes, the total destruction of the city, and the death not only of members of armed formations but also of the peaceful population" (Lee Hockstader, "We're Not Even People Anymore," *Washington Post*, March 19, 1995, 1).

# 10

# Power Restructuring in Historical and Comparative Perspective

As rulers, various elite configurations, and nonprivileged groups engage in political interaction, power is regularly restructured in all sociopolitical settings. My discussion has examined the manifestations of this universal phenomenon in two great world-historical settings. Yet the restructuring and redistribution of power are manifested in myriad ways. In this book, I have charted the political macrosociology of China and Russia with an exploration of power restructuring in imperial times, under communism, and today. The analysis has been guided by two complementary objectives—to spell out the overarching logic of power restructuring in China and Russia and to delineate the sociopolitical contours of specific power-restructuring events. Guenther Roth once wrote that the purpose of comparative study is the explanation of a given historical problem.[1] I have chosen to view the phenomenon of power restructuring in China and Russia from a historical and a comparative perspective.

Throughout the discussion, I have attempted to advance a historical and comparative view of power relations and political process in two civilizations that have experienced closely related forms of imperial rule, old regime crisis, communist revolution, communist state building, and power-decentralizing, power-deconcentrating, and transitional processes. At the same time, I have used the evidence arising from a broad array of specific power-restructuring episodes to inform my overall argument. I have used the Chinese power-restructuring experience to illuminate comparable processes in Russia and the Soviet Union and the Russian and Soviet experience to elucidate the Chinese case. Numerous power-restructuring phenomena have been identified—power concentration, wars on competing centers of power, battles for power and resources, decentralized power and resource appropriation, top and bottom versus the middle power contests, power decentralization, and power deconcentration. All these phenomena have been compared and contrasted. The unifying purpose of this exercise has been the identification of similarities and differences in a large number of comparable cases.

I have focused attention on three broad patterns—continuity, interaction, and synthesis. Power restructuring in China and Russia has repeatedly pivoted on the concentration and deconcentration of political power and on the ebb and flow of central power. Power restructuring is driven by sociopolitical interactions, in the course of which central rulers, political and economic elites, and nonprivileged groups in myriad combinations engage in contests to control, appropriate, and redistribute power and resources. Dramatic restructurings of power have ensued, often in the form of unanticipated outcomes and new political and cultural syntheses.

## The Analytic Utility of Weberian Patrimonialism

Throughout the discussion, analytic approaches to power and politics in China and Russia based either explicitly or implicitly on the historical and developmental experience of Western Europe and the United States have been singled out for critical assessment. I have argued that power restructuring in China and Russia cannot be understood in terms of modernization, rationalization, a transition to democracy and market economy, the rise of a liberal-democratic world order, institutional pluralism, and the like. Instead, I have relied on a conceptual construct that more satisfactorily encompasses the historical and contemporary realities of power relations and political process in China and Russia—Weberian patrimonialism.

As deployed in these pages, the Weberian view of patrimonial society and patrimonial politics yields vital insights into power dynamics in China and Russia, historically and presently. I have argued that the key features of patrimonial society and patrimonial politics are personalism, patron-client networks, fluid property relations, the secondary significance of the rule of law, and processes of power and resource appropriation. It has been suggested that corruption, stagnation, and backwardness are the most important consequences of patrimonial power arrangements. But we have seen that the defining characteristics of power dynamics in patrimonial sociopolitical settings are the interaction among central rulers, political and economic elites, and nonprivileged groups and the more or less open or hidden battle to control, appropriate, and redistribute power and resources.

These interactions and power contests have determined the ebb and flow of central power in China and Russia and have periodically resulted in dramatic restructurings of power. We have seen that central rulers in imperial times and under communism waged fierce and often unremitting struggles against processes of decentralized power and resource appropriation. Notable examples in this discussion include the Ming and Qing autocracies, Ivan the Terrible and the Petrine autocracy, and Stalin and Mao. Yet an equally important part of the story has been the enduring capacity of nominally subordinate political and economic elites to contest the authority of central rulers; to resist, circumvent, and distort power-restructuring processes set in motion from the top; and to advance their interests at the expense of state power and nonprivileged groups. My discussion has underscored the far-reaching consequences of such elite victories in Catherinian Russia, post–Taiping Rebellion China, the Revolution of 1905, the Brezhnev era, and the Cultural Revolution and the post-Mao period.

Finally, I have focused special attention on the massive involvement of nonprivileged groups in the great power-restructuring events of the twentieth century—the Russian and Chinese Revolutions, the Stalin revolution, the Cultural Revolution, and perestroika. It was the unprecedented engagement of the Russian and Chinese masses in these events that produced sociopolitical upheavals of such scale and intensity. While pivoting on the recurrent significance of three-way power contests, my discussion has examined these interactions in four distinct, yet often overlapping stages in the political history of China and Russia—imperial power restructuring, revolutionary power restructuring, post-Stalin power restructuring, and the transitional power restructuring of the 1980s and 1990s.

## Imperial Power Restructuring

Following Weber, I have located the three-way contest among ruler, staff, and subjects at the center of my analysis of power relations and political process in late imperial China and czarist Russia. The many recurrent manifestations of this contest have included the building of state-controlled avenues of political and economic mobility, the enhancing of centralized resource mobilization capacities, the concentration of political and economic power, and systematic wars against competing centers of power. We have seen that the emergence and consolidation of centralized autocracies in Ming and Qing China and in Muscovite Russia were undergirded by processes of political and cultural synthesis. Yet even as the Russian and Chinese elites in imperial times mouthed "unconditional support for the autocracy" and "limitless reverence for the emperor," they regularly and often effectively resisted the concentration of power in the hands of central rulers. Although rulers and elites had a shared interest in controlling the mass population and appropriating its production, the distribution of these proceeds was regularly contested.

Even though some central rulers waged violent or uncompromising wars on competing centers of power, not all Chinese and Russian rulers were concerned solely with the forceful curbing of the power- and resource-appropriating impulses of the privileged orders. Rather, the war on competing centers of power was fused with the building of new elites and and the establishing of new state-elite alliances. It was the achievement of the most accomplished of these central rulers, such as the early Qing emperors and Peter I, to develop and impose power arrangements that simultaneously reinforced central power, elicited the support and cooperation of the political elite, and held the three-way battle for power and resources in check. By the same token, the systemic crises of the late nineteenth century and the preconditions of the Russian and Chinese Revolutions originated in the erosion of long-standing state-elite alliances and the ensuing breakdown of imperial power arrangements.

The crisis of the old regime in China and Russia stemmed from the confluence of three historical processes—intensified three-way contests to control, appropriate, and redistribute power and resources; military and technological pressures from the outside world; and the rise of revolutionary sociopolitical forces. Whereas imperial power arrangements had in the past successfully confronted and overcome individual challenges of this type, their simultaneous advent marked the end of the old order and the onset of a revolutionary restructuring of power.

## Revolutionary Power Restructuring

The revolutionary upheavals of the twentieth century massively accelerated the restructuring of power in China and Russia. The Soviet and Chinese Communist systems were revitalized versions of the Russian and Chinese empires, in which numerous features of successful imperial rule, such as power concentration, systems of centralized political and social control, state-sponsored developmental projects, and state-controlled avenues of mobility, were reconstituted and extended to new heights. The continuity of power dynamics in Communist China with the imperial past was emphasized by analysts who spoke of "politics at Mao's court," "where the final power was in the hands of one man and other leaders sought to divine his intent."[2] But revolutionary power restructuring differed qualitatively from its imperial predecessor. In the Soviet Union and Communist China, Marxist-Leninist ideology and organization broadened the scope and intensity of the struggle for power and resources, and revolutionary power restructuring in China and Russia pivoted on the wholesale destruction and reconstruction of entire social, economic, and political structures. Under conditions of revolutionary power restructuring, wars on competing centers of political and economic power and systematic elite building were coupled with processes of mass mobilization, the unprecedented involvement of the masses in sociopolitical interactions, and the wide-ranging incorporation of formerly nonprivileged social strata into new ruling groups.

In the Soviet 1920s, state building, industrialization, and elite building were infused with a distinctively Marxist-Leninist tone, which emphasized class warfare and the systematic recruitment, training, and promotion of lower-class groups. My discussion has emphasized the continuity of the Stalin system with these power-restructuring processes, which were already in motion in the 1920s and early 1930s. In China, comparable processes of revolutionary power restructuring underlay the rise of Chinese communism, the establishing of new power arrangements in the base areas prior to 1949, and the historic creation of a new political, economic, and social order throughout China in the 1950s. Revolutionary power restructuring culminated in the erecting of mighty communist state structures in the Soviet Union and Communist China, which, like their imperial predecessors, deployed power-concentrating and power-centralizing mechanisms in maintaining political and social control and holding the three-way struggle for power and resources in check. Unlike imperial predecessors, the communist state penetrated society more deeply, established its authority on an unprecedented scale, and effected the structural transformation of China and Russia.

Yet these power-building achievements were complicated by familiar processes of decentralized power and resource appropriation. Soviet and Chinese Communist central rulers, even at the height of their coercive and mobilizational powers, were confronted with and continued to wage wars on competing centers of power. Although old regime elites and peasants were successfully subjected to the power of the communist state, there soon appeared a more formidable challenge in the form of a "new class" of communist officials. Themselves the creation and beneficiaries of revolutionary power restructuring, this new elite group's members were eager to garner the material benefits of their political power for themselves and their families. Whereas the Stalin system relied on terror and unremitting pressure from above to curb the power- and resource-appropriating impulses of communist officialdom, post-Stalin power restructuring in China and the Soviet Union pivoted on the deconcentration and decentralization of political and economic power.

## Post-Stalin Power Restructuring

Post-Stalin power restructuring in the Soviet Union and China constitutes the analytic core of this book. While attending to important differences, my discussion has highlighted the many similarities of power restructuring under Khrushchev, Gorbachev, and Mao. The most important sociopolitical consequences of revolutionary power restructuring and the erecting of the Stalin system were the centralization and concentration of political and economic power and the monopolistic power of a self-aggrandizing new ruling class of communist officials. Post-Stalin power restructuring in China and the Soviet Union sought to redress this complex and burdensome legacy by increasing mass political participation and decentralizing and deconcentrating power.

Yet post-Stalin power restructuring was first launched by leaders who were themselves the products and adherents of the Stalin system. By fusing elements of the Marxist-Leninist-Stalinist tradition with power-decentralizing and power-deconcentrating processes, post-Stalin power-restructuring proponents sought to revitalize and perfect Soviet and Chinese socialism. But we have seen that post-Stalin power restructuring repeatedly failed to achieve its stated aims and instead precipitated varying degrees of political conflict, sociopolitical turmoil, and systemic breakdown. In China and in the Soviet Union, efforts to restructure power encountered the determined resistance of the communist political elite and opened up the way for new appropriations of power and resources by this elite at the regional, provincial, and local levels. At the same time, the major unintended consequence of power restructuring during the Cultural Revolution decade and in the period of perestroika was the setting in motion of a historic transition from socialism.

As the initiator of post-Stalin power restructuring, Khrushchev's first efforts to loosen the controls of the Stalin system were limited and were welcomed by the political elite. De-Stalinization and the *sovnarkhozy* reforms directly benefited Soviet power holders, but Khrushchev's subsequent efforts to deconcentrate the communist power monopoly were too threatening and finally resulted in the overthrow of the ruler by his subordinates. Under Brezhnev, communist officialdom mounted a successful counteroffensive in defense of its power and position; while preserving key aspects of the Stalin system of power centralization and power concentration, the Brezhnev system guaranteed and extended the monopolistic power and privileges of the Soviet political elite.

In China, Maoist power restructuring during the opening phases of the Cultural Revolution also targeted the power and privileges of communist officialdom. My discussion of the Cultural Revolution highlighted the social conflicts and power contests that erupted and showed how the Chinese Communist political elite was able to resist, countermobilize, and finally defeat Maoist power restructuring and the social forces marshaled on its behalf. Although the effort to curb the power and privileges of communist officialdom failed, the effects of Maoist power deconcentration were so disruptive that systemic changes were set in motion, albeit in directions that Mao neither anticipated nor desired. Most important, Maoist power restructuring resulted in a fundamental devolution and fragmentation of political and economic power and in an acceleration of decentralized processes of power and resource appropriation. I have argued that these events, rooted in the upheavals of the late 1960s, established the structural and political preconditions for the momentous post-Mao transformations of the 1980s.

Finally, my discussion has framed power restructuring in the period of perestroika in the context of post-Stalin power restructuring and highlighted its analogs in the Khrushchev period and the Cultural Revolution. As in China, Gorbachevian power restructuring pivoted on the decentralization and deconcentration of power, the loosening of controls, the unleashing of nonprivileged groups, and the uncoupling of the power monopoly of the CPSU. The unintended and unforeseen consequences of radical renewal in the Soviet Union were the eruption of social conflicts and power contests, the devolution and fragmentation of power, and systemic breakdown. Even though the CPSU lost its power monopoly, the battle to curb the power and privileges of officialdom failed nonetheless. As in China during the Cultural Revolution, power restructuring in the period of perestroika opened up the way for decentralized appropriations of power and resources by political elites at the regional, provincial, and local levels. These events established the structural and political preconditions for a transition from socialism in Russia and the former Soviet Union.

## The Transition from Socialism in China and Russia

In the 1980s and 1990s, a historic transition from socialism unfolded in China and the former Soviet Union. Rather than attempting to depict this process as a transition to democracy and a market economy, I have argued that the transition from socialism was inadvertently set in motion by the political decisions of Chinese Communist and Soviet leaders seeking to revitalize socialism and was driven by the tumultuous sociopolitical interactions and power contests that erupted when controls normally enforced by the state were suspended and delegitimated. Viewed in this light, the future trajectory of the transition from socialism in China and Russia will continue to be driven by internal developments, the internal correlation of forces, and the sociopolitical interactions and power contests delineated in these pages.

The transition from socialism in China and Russia represents an emerging synthesis of political and economic decentralization, privatization and marketization, cultural liberalization and opening up to the outside world, and authoritarianism and nationalism. Even though these transitional processes represent a fundamental departure from Soviet and Chinese socialism in its classic form, they neither imply nor replicate the Western historical, institutional, and developmental experience. Rather, the transition from socialism in China and Russia is an emerging synthesis of old patterns and new realities—closely linked with the recent communist past, on the one hand, and directly engaging the new global realities of the late twentieth century, on the other. In China, these transitional processes resulted in an economic transformation of historic proportions, thereby establishing the possibility of market-driven development and reform in a political and social setting that does not conform with the Western experience. Although the economics of the transition from socialism in Russia and the former Soviet Union are different, I have argued that many of the transitional processes evident in Russia in the 1990s parallel the Chinese pattern.

## The Implications of the Analysis

The central task of this book has been the identification and comparative discussion of an array of momentous power-restructuring episodes and processes in China and Russia in imperial times, under communism, and today. The central analytic device has been the concept of three-way contests to control, appropriate, and redistribute power and resources. We have seen that this contest comes to the fore during power-restructuring initiatives, when attempts are made to reshape the distribution of power and resources. My discussion has shown that individual rulers and leaders matter. Personal rulership has been recurrent in imperial times, under communism, and over the course of post-Stalin power restructuring. Time and again, the political decisions of individual rulers and leaders have keyed far-reaching power-restructuring initiatives. But it is one thing to set events in motion and quite another to determine their outcome. My discussion has documented the many instances when the power-restructuring ambitions of apparently all-powerful autocrats were frustrated, resisted, distorted, and defeated. The limits of personal rulership have been revealed with special clarity in my discussion of post-Stalin power restructuring.

When systems of centralized power and concentrated power are decentralized and deconcentrated, previously suppressed tensions, grievances, and aspirations erupt. This eruption takes many different forms—national independence, regionalism, localism, agricultural decollectivization, marketization, entrepreneurism, elections, ethnic conflict, and civil war. But the force that drives these processes is more basic. All these processes are manifestations of sociopolitical struggles to control, appropriate, and redistribute power and resources in a setting where the rules of the game have been abruptly changed. These power contests, rather than systemic revitalization or democratization, are the most important consequence of the power-decentralizing and power-deconcentrating processes delineated in these pages.

Although my discussion has centered on power restructuring in China and Russia in the twentieth century, this analytic perspective can be extended to other settings, and the results are sobering. In the early 1990s, the former Yugoslavia was torn apart by the bloodiest conflict in Europe since World War II. This conflict, variously attributed to nationalism, ethnic hatred, and religious tensions, was first and foremost a battle to control, appropriate, and redistribute the power and resources that suddenly came up for grabs with the breakup of the unitary Yugoslav state in the late 1980s. Comparable processes unfolded in South Africa in the 1990s when the monopolistic controls enforced by the white state were modified and partially abandoned. Perhaps the demise of apartheid will result in a transition to democracy. Yet as formerly disenfranchised groups sought to seize power and resources they believed were rightfully theirs, privileged groups mobilized in defense of their power and position, and the urban population organized autonomous "self-defense units" and militias, South Africa in the mid-1990s was confronted with mounting political conflict, widespread processes of local militarization and incipient warlordism, and the possibility of a bloody civil war and free-for-all.[3] Like the initiators of post-Stalin power restructuring in China and the Soviet Union, the dismantlers of apartheid may be overwhelmed by the forces they set in motion. In Algeria, in the wake of processes of political liberalization in the early 1990s and the unanticipated electoral consequences thereof, a bloody civil war pitting nonprivileged groups against more advantageously situated strata was already under way.[4]

As a consequence of the transition from socialism, both China and Russia have become less governable internally. We have seen that restructuring a system of concentrated power entails the suspension of wars on competing centers of power and thereby a systemic opening up to decentralized processes of power and resource appropriation. Hence, the power-restructuring dilemmas facing China and Russia in the 1990s and beyond will not be the familiar ones of excessive centralization and concentration of power. Rather, the new challenges are those of regionalism, localism, chaos, and anarchy. After the forceful centralizing processes of the Soviet and Chinese Communist empires, and in the wake of Maoist and Gorbachevian power restructuring, the vast Eurasian expanse of China and Russia has entered a period of decentralization and fragmentation. Will these processes continue to accelerate, or are the Chinese and Russian states still capable of rebuilding central power and successfully enforcing central policies? Much will depend on the outcome of power restructuring in China and Russia in the twenty-first century.

### Notes

1. Guenther Roth, "Introduction," in Max Weber, *Economy and Society* (Berkeley and Los Angeles: University of California Press, 1978), vol. 1, xxxvii.

2. Frederick C. Teiwes, *Politics at Mao's Court: Gao Gang and Party Factionalism in the Early 1950s* (Armonk, N.Y.: M. E. Sharpe, 1990), 153. For the most recent account of Mao as emperor, replete with twentieth-century versions of the imperial harem, eunuchs, and courtiers, see Li Zhisui, with Anne F. Thurston, *The Private Life of Chairman Mao* (New York: Random House, 1994).

3. Bill Keller, "Zulu and Afrikaner Leaders Rally the Wrathful," *New York Times,* January 30, 1994, 10; Bill Keller, "Townships' Guardians a Law unto Themselves," *New York Times,* February 1, 1994, 4.

4. Nora Boustany, "Journalism: Algeria's Fatal Profession," *Washington Post,* March 23, 1995, 20.

# Selected Bibliography

## Theory, History, and Comparisons

Alexander, Jeffrey C. *Theoretical Logic in Sociology.* Vol. 3: *The Classical Attempt at Theoretical Synthesis: Max Weber.* Berkeley and Los Angeles: University of California Press, 1983.

Allsen, Thomas T. *Mongol Imperialism.* Berkeley and Los Angeles: University of California Press, 1987.

Brzezinski, Zbigniew. *The Grand Failure: The Birth and Death of Communism in the Twentieth Century.* New York: Collier, 1989.

Friedrich, Carl J., and Zbigniew Brzezinski. *Totalitarian Dictatorship and Autocracy.* Cambridge, Mass.: Harvard University Press, 1965.

Goldstone, Jack A. *Revolution and Rebellion in the Early Modern World.* Berkeley and Los Angeles: University of California Press, 1991.

Gurtov, Mel, ed. *The Transformation of Socialism—Perestroika and Reform in the Soviet Union and China.* Boulder: Westview Press, 1990.

Huntington, Samuel P. *Political Order in Changing Societies.* New Haven: Yale University Press, 1968.

Jowitt, Kenneth. *Revolutionary Breakthroughs and National Development.* Berkeley and Los Angeles: University of California Press, 1971.

Lindblom, Charles E. *Politics and Markets.* New York: Basic Books, 1977.

Lowenthal, Richard. "Development Versus Utopia in Communist Policy." In Chalmers Johnson, ed., *Change in Communist Systems.* Stanford: Stanford University Press, 1970.

Lupher, Mark. "Power Restructuring in China and the Soviet Union." *Theory and Society* 21, 5 (October 1992).

Mann, Michael. *The Sources of Social Power.* Cambridge: Cambridge University Press, 1986.

Marx, Karl, and Friedrich Engels. *The Communist Manifesto.* New York: International Publishers, 1948.

Moore, Barrington Jr. *Social Origins of Dictatorship and Democracy.* Boston: Beacon Press, 1966.

Mousnier, Roland E. *The Institutions of France Under the Absolute Monarchy.* Vol. 2: *The Organs of State and Society.* Chicago: University of Chicago Press, 1984.

Murvar, Vatro, ed. *Theory of Liberty, Legitimacy, and Power: New Directions in the Intellectual and Scientific Legacy of Max Weber.* London: Routledge and Kegan Paul, 1985.

Rosenberg, Hans. *Bureaucracy, Aristocracy, and Autocracy.* Cambridge, Mass.: Harvard University Press, 1958.

Selznick, Philip. *The Organizational Weapon.* New York: McGraw-Hill, 1952.

Skocpol, Theda. *States and Social Revolutions.* Cambridge: Cambridge University Press, 1979.

Tilly, Charles. *Coercion, Capital, and the European States, AD 990–1990.* Cambridge, Mass.: Basil Blackwell, 1990.

Unger, Roberto Mangabeira. *Plasticity into Power.* Cambridge: Cambridge University Press, 1987.

Weber, Max. *Economy and Society.* Vols. 1, 2. Ed. Guenther Roth and Claus Wittich. Berkeley and Los Angeles: University of California Press, 1978.

Westoby, Adam. *The Evolution of Communism.* New York: Free Press, 1989.

Wittfogel, Karl A. *Oriental Despotism.* New Haven: Yale University Press, 1957.

## Russia and the Soviet Union

Alexander, John T. *Autocratic Politics in a National Crisis.* Bloomington: Indiana University Press, 1969.

Ascher, Abraham. *The Revolution of 1905: Authority Restored.* Stanford: Stanford University Press, 1992.

———. *The Revolution of 1905: Russia in Disarray.* Stanford: Stanford University Press, 1988.

Atkinson, Dorothy. *The End of the Russian Land Commune.* Stanford: Stanford University Press, 1983.

Bailes, Kendall E. *Technology and Society Under Lenin and Stalin.* Princeton: Princeton University Press, 1978.

Ball, Alan M. *Russia's Last Capitalists: The Nepmen, 1921–1929.* Berkeley and Los Angeles: University of California Press, 1987.

Balzer, Harley D., ed. *Five Years That Shook the World—Gorbachev's Unfinished Revolution.* Boulder: Westview Press, 1991.

Beck, F., and W. Godin. *Russian Purge and the Extraction of Confession.* New York: Viking, 1951.

Bialer, Seweryn. *Stalin's Successors.* Cambridge: Cambridge University Press, 1980.

———, ed. *Politics, Society, and Nationality—Inside Gorbachev's Russia.* Boulder: Westview Press, 1989.

———. *Stalin and His Generals: Soviet Military Memoirs of World War II.* New York: Pegasus, 1969.

Blum, Jerome. *Lord and Peasant in Russia.* Princeton: Princeton University Press, 1961.

Boffa, Guiseppe. *The Stalin Phenomenon.* Ithaca: Cornell University Press, 1990.

Bonnell, Victoria, E. *Roots of Rebellion: Workers' Politics and Organizations in St. Petersburg and Moscow, 1900–1914.* Berkeley and Los Angeles: University of California Press, 1983.

Bonnell, Victoria E., Ann Cooper, and Gregory Freidin, eds. *Russia at the Barricades: Eyewitness Accounts of the August 1991 Coup.* Armonk, N.Y.: M. E. Sharpe, 1994.

Breslauer, George W. *Khrushchev and Brezhnev as Leaders: Building Authority in Soviet Politics.* London: George Allen and Unwin, 1982.

Brown, Edward. *Russian Literature Since the Revolution.* Cambridge, Mass.: Harvard University Press, 1982.

Brumberg, Abraham, ed. *Russia Under Khrushchev.* New York: Praeger, 1962.

Bunyan, James. *The Origins of Forced Labor in the Soviet Union, 1917–1921.* Baltimore: Johns Hopkins University Press, 1967.

Burlatsky, Fedor. *Khrushchev and the First Russian Spring.* Trans. Daphne Skillen. London: Weidenfeld and Nicolson, 1991.

Carr, E. H. *The Bolshevik Revolution, 1917–1923.* Vol. 2. Harmondsworth: Penguin, 1972.

———. *Foundations of a Planned Economy, 1926–1929.* Vol. 2. New York: Macmillan, 1971.

Carr, E. H., and R. W. Davies. *Foundations of a Planned Economy, 1926–1929.* Vol. 1. New York: Macmillan, 1969.

Chase, William J. *Workers, Society, and the Soviet State: Labor and Life in Moscow, 1918–1929.* Urbana: University of Illinois Press, 1990.

Cohen, Stephen F. *Bukharin and the Bolshevik Revolution.* New York: Oxford University Press, 1980.

———. *Rethinking the Soviet Experience: Politics & History Since 1917.* New York: Oxford University Press, 1985.

Cohen, Stephen F., Alexander Rabinowitch, and Robert Sharlet, eds. *The Soviet Union Since Stalin.* Bloomington: Indiana University Press, 1980.

Colton, Timothy J. *The Dilemma of Reform in the Soviet Union.* New York: Council on Foreign Relations, 1984.

Conquest, Robert. *The Great Terror: Stalin's Purge of the Thirties.* Toronto: Macmillan, 1969.

———. *The Harvest of Sorrow.* New York: Oxford University Press, 1986.

———. *Kolyma.* New York: Viking, 1978.

———. *Power and Policy in the USSR.* New York: Harper, 1961.

Crankshaw, Edward. *Khrushchev: A Career.* New York: Viking, 1966.

———. *Khrushchev's Russia.* Baltimore: Penguin, 1959.

Crummey, Robert O. *Aristocrats and Servitors: The Boyar Elite in Russia, 1613–1689.* Princeton: Princeton University Press, 1983.

———. *The Formation of Muscovy, 1304–1613.* London: Longman, 1987.

———, ed. *Reform in Russia and the USSR.* Urbana: University of Illinois Press, 1989.

Custine, Marquis de. *Empire of the Czar: A Journey Through Eternal Russia.* New York: Doubleday, 1989.

Dallin, David J., and Boris I. Nicolaevsky. *Forced Labor in Soviet Russia.* New Haven: Yale University Press, 1947.

Dan, Theodore. *The Origins of Bolshevism.* New York: Harper and Row, 1964.

Daniels, Robert V. *The Conscience of the Revolution: Communist Opposition in Soviet Russia.* Cambridge, Mass.: Harvard University Press, 1960.

Deutscher, Issac. *Stalin: A Political Biography.* New York: Oxford University Press, 1966.

Djilas, Milovan. *Conversations with Stalin.* New York: Harcourt, Brace and World, 1962.

———. *The New Class.* New York: Praeger, 1957.

Dunham, Vera S. *In Stalin's Time: Middle-Class Values in Soviet Fiction.* Cambridge: Cambridge University Press, 1976.

Eklof, Ben, John Bushnell, and Larissa Zakharova, eds. *Russia's Great Reforms, 1855–1881.* Bloomington: Indiana University Press, 1994.

Ellman, Michael, and Vladimir Kontorovich. *The Disintegration of the Soviet Economic System.* New York: Routledge, 1992.

Emmons, Terence, and Wayne S. Vucinich, eds. *The Zemstvo in Russia: An Experiment in Self-Government.* Cambridge: Cambridge University Press, 1982.

Fainsod, Merle. *How Russia Is Ruled.* Rev. ed. enl. Cambridge, Mass.: Harvard University Press, 1965.

————. *Smolensk Under Soviet Rule.* New York: Vintage, 1958.

Fennell, John. *The Emergence of Moscow, 1304–1359.* Berkeley and Los Angeles: University of California Press, 1968.

Field, Daniel. *Rebels in the Name of the Tsar.* Boston: Unwin Hyman, 1989.

Fitzpatrick, Sheila. *The Russian Revolution, 1917–1932.* New York: Oxford University Press, 1984.

————. "Stalin and the Making of a New Elite." *Slavic Review* 38, 3 (1979).

————, ed. *Cultural Revolution in Russia.* Bloomington: Indiana University Press, 1978.

————. *Education and Social Mobility in the Soviet Union, 1921–1934.* Cambridge: Cambridge University Press, 1979.

Fuller, William C. *Power and Strategy in Russia, 1600–1914.* New York: Free Press, 1992.

Gerschenkron, Alexander. *Continuity in History and Other Essays.* Cambridge, Mass.: Harvard University Press, 1968.

Getty, J. Arch. *Origins of the Great Purges: The Soviet Communist Party Reconsidered, 1933–1938.* Cambridge: Cambridge University Press, 1985.

Getty, J. Arch, and Roberta Thompson Manning, eds. *Stalinist Terror: New Perspectives.* Cambridge: Cambridge University Press, 1993.

Ginzburg, Evgenia. *Journey into the Whirlwind.* New York: Harcourt, Brace and World, 1967.

Hahn, Werner G. *Postwar Soviet Politics: The Fall of Zhdanov and the Defeat of Moderation, 1946–1953.* Ithaca: Cornell University Press, 1982.

Haxthausen, August von. *Studies on the Interior of Russia.* Ed. S. Frederick Starr. Chicago: University of Chicago Press, 1972.

Hellie, Richard. *Enserfment and Military Change in Muscovy.* Chicago: University of Chicago Press, 1971.

————, trans. and ed. *The Muscovite Law Code (Ulozhenie) of 1649.* Irvine, Calif.: Charles Schlacks Jr., 1988.

Hewett, Ed A. *Reforming the Soviet Economy—Equality versus Efficiency.* Washington, D.C.: Brookings Institution, 1988.

Hewett, Ed A., and Victor H. Winston, eds. *Milestones in Glasnost and Perestroyka—Politics and People.* Washington, D.C.: Brookings Institution, 1991.

Hoch, Steven L. *Serfdom and Social Control in Russia.* Chicago: University of Chicago Press, 1986.

Hosking, Geoffrey. *The First Socialist Society: A History of the Soviet Union from Within.* Cambridge, Mass.: Harvard University Press, 1985.

Hough, Jerry F. "A Harebrained Scheme in Retrospect." *Problems of Communism* 14 (July–August 1965).

————. *The Soviet Prefects: The Local Party Organs in Industrial Decision-Making.* Cambridge, Mass.: Harvard University Press, 1969.

————. *The Soviet Union and Social Science Theory.* Cambridge, Mass.: Harvard University Press, 1977.

Hough, Jerry F., and Merle Fainsod. *How the Soviet Union Is Governed.* Cambridge, Mass.: Harvard University Press, 1979.

Jowitt, Ken. "Soviet Neotraditionalism: The Political Corruption of a Leninist Regime." *Soviet Studies* 35, 3 (July 1983).

Kahan, Arcadius. *The Plow, the Hammer, and the Knout: An Economic History of Eighteenth-Century Russia.* Chicago: University of Chicago Press, 1985.

Keenan, Edward L. *The Kurbskii-Groznyi Apocrypha.* Cambridge, Mass.: Harvard University Press, 1971.

Keep, John L.H. *The Russian Revolution: A Study in Mass Mobilization.* New York: Norton, 1976.

Khrushchev, Nikita S. *Khrushchev Remembers.* Boston: Little, Brown, 1970.

———. *Khrushchev Remembers: The Last Testament.* Boston: Little, Brown, 1974.

Khrushchev, Sergei. *Khrushchev on Khrushchev: An Inside Account of the Man and the Era.* Trans. and ed. William Taubman. Boston: Little, Brown, 1990.

Kliuchevsky, V. O. *A History Of Russia.* Vols. 1, 2, 5. New York: Russell and Russell, 1955.

———. *Peter the Great.* Trans. Liliana Archibald. New York: St. Martin's Press, 1958.

Koenker, Diane P., William G. Rosenberg, and Ronald Grigor Suny, eds. *Party, State, and Society in the Russian Civil War.* Bloomington: Indiana University Press, 1989.

Kolkowicz, Roman. *The Soviet Military and the Communist Party.* Princeton: Princeton University Press, 1967.

Kollmann, Nancy Shields. *Kinship and Politics: The Making of the Muscovite Political System, 1345–1547.* Stanford: Stanford University Press, 1987.

Kravchenko, Victor. *I Chose Freedom.* New York: Charles Scribner, 1946.

Kuromiya, Hiroaki. *Stalin's Industrial Revolution: Politics and Workers, 1928–1932.* Cambridge: Cambridge University Press, 1988.

Laird, Roy D., ed. *Soviet Agricultural and Peasant Affairs.* Lawrence: University of Kansas Press, 1963.

Lapidus, Gail W., Victor Zaslavsky, and Philip Goldman, eds. *From Union to Commonwealth—Nationalism and Separatism in the Soviet Republics.* Cambridge: Cambridge University Press, 1992.

Ledonne, John P. *Absolutism and Ruling Class: The Formation of the Russian Political Order, 1700–1825.* New York: Oxford University Press, 1991.

———. *Ruling Russia: Politics and Administration in the Age of Absolutism.* Princeton: Princeton University Press, 1984.

Lewin, Moshe. *The Gorbachev Phenomenon.* Berkeley and Los Angeles: University of California Press, 1988.

———. *Lenin's Last Struggle.* New York: Monthly Review Press, 1968.

———. *The Making of the Soviet System.* New York: Pantheon, 1985.

———. *Political Undercurrents in the Soviet Economic Debates.* Princeton: Princeton University Press, 1974.

———. *Russian Peasants and Soviet Power.* Evanston, Ill.: Northwestern University Press, 1968.

Ligachev, Yegor. *Inside Gorbachev's Kremlin.* New York: Pantheon, 1993.

Linden, Carl A. *Khrushchev and the Soviet Leadership, 1957–1964.* Baltimore: Johns Hopkins University Press, 1966.

Madariaga, Isabel de. *Russia in the Age of Catherine the Great.* New Haven: Yale University Press, 1981.

Malia, Martin. *The Soviet Tragedy: A History of Socialism in Russia, 1917–1991.* New York: Free Press, 1994.

Manning, Roberta Thompson. *The Crisis of the Old Order in Russia.* Princeton: Princeton University Press, 1982.

McCauley, Martin, ed. *Khrushchev and Khrushchevism.* Bloomington: Indiana University Press, 1987.

McDaniel, Tim. *Autocracy, Capitalism, and Revolution in Russia.* Berkeley and Los Angeles: University of California Press, 1988.

Medvedev, Roy A. *Let History Judge.* New York: Knopf, 1972.

Medvedev, Roy A., and Zhores Medvedev. *Khrushchev: The Years in Power.* New York: Norton, 1978.

Meehan-Waters, Brenda. *Autocracy and Aristocracy: The Russian Service Elite of 1730.* New Brunswick: Rutgers University Press, 1982.

Mendelsohn, Ezra, and Marshall S. Shatz, eds. *Imperial Russia, 1700–1917: State-Society Opposition.* DeKalb: Northern Illinois University Press, 1988.

Motyl, Alexander J. *Sovietology, Rationality, Nationality.* New York: Columbia University Press, 1990.

Nicolaevsky, Boris I. *Power and the Soviet Elite.* Ann Arbor: University of Michigan Press, 1975.

Nove, Alec. *An Economic History of the USSR.* Baltimore: Penguin, 1969.

Pintner, Walter M., and Don K. Rowney, eds. *Russian Officialdom: The Bureaucratization of Russian Society from the Seventeenth to the Twentieth Century.* London: Macmillan/University of North Carolina Press, 1980.

Pipes, Richard. *Russia Under the Bolshevik Regime.* New York: Knopf, 1993.

———. *Russia Under the Old Regime.* New York: Scribner's, 1974.

Platonov, S. F. *Ivan the Terrible.* Ed. and trans. Joseph L. Wieczynski. Gulf Breeze, Fla.: Academic International Press, 1974.

Preobrazhensky, E. A. *The Crisis of Soviet Industrialization: Selected Essays.* Ed. Donald A. Filtzer. White Plains, N.Y.: M. E. Sharpe, 1979.

Raeff, Marc. *The Origins of the Russian Intelligentsia.* New York: Harcourt Brace Jovanovich, 1966.

———. *Plans for Political Reform in Imperial Russia, 1730–1905.* Englewood Cliffs, N.J.: Prentice-Hall, 1966.

———. *Understanding Imperial Russia.* New York: Columbia University Press, 1984.

Ransel, David L. *The Politics of Catherinian Russia: The Panin Party.* New Haven: Yale University Press, 1975.

Riasanovsky, Nicholas V. *A History of Russia.* New York: Oxford University Press, 1963.

———. *The Image of Peter the Great in Russian History and Thought.* New York: Oxford University Press, 1985.

Rieber, Alfred J. *The Politics of Autocracy: Letters of Alexander II to Prince A. I. Bariatinskii, 1857–1894.* Paris: Mouton, 1966.

Robbins, Richard G. Jr. *Famine in Russia, 1891–1892.* New York: Columbia University Press, 1975.

Robinson, Geroid T. *Rural Russia Under the Old Regime.* New York: Macmillan, 1949.

Sablinsky, Walter. *The Road to Bloody Sunday: Father Gapon and the St. Petersburg Massacre of 1905.* Princeton: Princeton University Press, 1976.

Schapiro, Leonard. *The Communist Party of the Soviet Union.* 2d ed. New York: Vintage, 1971.

Schwartz, Harry. *Russia's Soviet Economy.* Englewood Cliffs, N.J.: Prentice-Hall, 1958.

Scott, John. *Behind the Urals.* Cambridge, Mass.: Riverside Press, 1942.

Shanin, Teodor. *Russia, 1905–1907: Revolution as a Moment of Truth.* New Haven: Yale University Press, 1986.

Shlapentokh, Vladimir. *Soviet Intellectuals and Political Power: The Post-Stalin Era.* Princeton: Princeton University Press, 1990.

Simis, Konstantin. *USSR: The Corrupt Society.* New York: Simon and Schuster, 1982.

Sinyavsky, Andrei. *Soviet Civilization: A Cultural History.* New York: Arcade, 1990.

Skrynnikov, Ruslan G. *Ivan the Terrible.* Trans. and ed. Hugh F. Graham. Gulf Breeze, Fla.: Academic International Press, 1981.

Solzhenitsyn, Alexander. *The Gulag Archipelago.* New York: Harper and Row, 1973.

Starr, S. Frederick. *Decentralization and Self-Government in Russia, 1830–1870.* Princeton: Princeton University Press, 1972.

Stites, Richard. *Revolutionary Dreams.* New York: Oxford University Press, 1989.

Tatu, Michel. *Power in the Kremlin.* New York: Viking, 1970.

Trotsky, Leon. *The Revolution Betrayed.* New York: Pathfinder, 1972.

Tucker, Robert C., ed. *Stalin in Power: The Revolution from Above, 1928–1941.* New York: Norton, 1990.

———. *Stalinism.* New York: Norton, 1977.

Tumarkin, Nina. *Lenin Lives! The Lenin Cult in Soviet Russia.* Cambridge, Mass.: Harvard University Press, 1983.

Vernadsky, George. *The Mongols and Russia.* New Haven: Yale University Press, 1953.

———. *The Tsardom of Moscow, 1547–1682.* Parts 1, 2. New Haven: Yale University Press, 1969.

Viola, Lynne. *The Best Sons of the Fatherland: Workers in the Vanguard of Soviet Collectivization.* New York: Oxford University Press, 1987.

Volkogonov, Dimitri. *Stalin: Triumph and Tragedy.* New York: Grove Press, 1991.

Voslensky, Michael. *Nomenklatura.* Garden City, N.Y.: Doubleday, 1984.

Wadekin, Karl-Eugen. *The Private Sector in Soviet Agriculture.* Berkeley and Los Angeles: University of California Press, 1973.

Wat, Aleksar.der. *My Century: The Odyssey of a Polish Intellectual.* Berkeley and Los Angeles: University of California Press, 1988.

Wcislo, Francis William. *Reforming Rural Russia: State, Local Society, and National Politics, 1855–1914.* Princeton: Princeton University Press, 1990.

Werth, Alexander. *Russia: The Post-War Years.* New York: Taplinger, 1971.

———. *Russia at War, 1941–1945.* New York: Dutton, 1964.

Wortman, Richard S. *The Development of a Russian Legal Consciousness* Chicago: University of Chicago Press, 1976.

Yanov, Alex. *The Drama of the Soviet 1960s.* Berkeley: Institute of International Studies, University of California at Berkeley, 1984.

———. *The Origins of Autocracy.* Berkeley and Los Angeles: University of California Press, 1981.

Yergin, Daniel, and Thane Gustafson. *Russia 2010.* New York: Random House, 1993.

Zaslavskaya, Tatyana. *A Voice of Reform.* Ed. Murray Yanowitch. Armonk, N.Y.: M. E. Sharpe, 1989.

# China

Bachman, David. *Bureaucracy, Economy, and Leadership in China: The Institutional Origins of the Great Leap Forward.* Cambridge: Cambridge University Press, 1991.

Bartlett, Beatrice S. *Monarchs and Ministers: The Grand Council in Mid-Ch'ing China, 1723–1820.* Berkeley and Los Angeles: University of California Press, 1991.

Baum, Richard. *Prelude to Revolution.* New York: Columbia University Press, 1975.

Bianco, Lucien. *Origins of the Chinese Revolution, 1915–1949.* Stanford: Stanford University Press, 1971.

Chan, Albert. *The Glory and Fall of the Ming Dynasty.* Norman: University of Oklahoma Press, 1982.

Chan, Anita. *Children of Mao: Personality Development and Political Activism in the Red Guard Generation.* London: Macmillan, 1985.

Chan, Anita, Richard Madsen, and Jonathan Unger. *Chen Village.* Berkeley and Los Angeles: University of California Press, 1984.

Chang, Parris H. *Power and Policy in China.* 2d ed. University Park: Pennsylvania State University Press, 1981.

————. "Provincial Party Leaders' Strategies for Survival During the Cultural Revolution." In Robert Scalapino, ed., *Elites in the People's Republic of China.* Seattle: University of Washington Press, 1972.

Chen, Yung-fa. *Making Revolution—the Communist Movement in Eastern and Central China, 1937–1945.* Berkeley and Los Angeles: University of California Press, 1987.

Cheng, Chu-yuan. *Behind The Tiananmen Massacre.* Boulder: Westview Press, 1990.

Cheng, Tiejun, and Mark Selden. "The Origins and Social Consequences of China's *Hukou* System." *China Quarterly* 139 (September 1994).

Chesneaux, Jean, ed. *Popular Movements and Secret Societies in China, 1840–1950.* Stanford: Stanford University Press, 1976.

Ch'u T'ung-tsu. *Local Government in China Under the Ch'ing.* Cambridge, Mass.: Harvard University Press, 1962.

Coble, Parks M. Jr. *The Shanghai Capitalists and the Nationalist Government, 1927–1937.* Cambridge, Mass.: Harvard University Press, 1980.

Crook, Isabel, and David Crook. *Ten Mile Inn: Mass Movement in a Chinese Village.* New York: Pantheon, 1979.

Dardess, John W. *Confucianism and Autocracy: Professional Elites in the Founding of the Ming Dynasty.* Berkeley and Los Angeles: University of California Press, 1983.

————. *Conquerors and Confucians: Aspects of Political Change in Late Yuan China.* New York: Columbia University Press, 1973.

Deng Xiaoping. *Selected Works of Deng Xiaoping (1975–1982).* Peking: Foreign Languages Press, 1984.

Dittmer, Lowell. *Liu Shao-ch'i and the Chinese Cultural Revolution.* Berkeley and Los Angeles: University of California Press, 1974.

Domes, Jurgen. *China After the Cultural Revolution: Politics Between the Two Party Congresses.* Berkeley and Los Angeles: University of California Press, 1977.

————. *The Internal Politics of China, 1949–1972.* New York: Praeger, 1973.

————. "Introduction." In James T. Myers, Jurgen Domes, and Milton D. Yeh, eds., *Chinese Politics—Documents and Analysis.* Vol. 2. Columbia: University of South Carolina Press, 1989.

Dreyer, Edward L. *Early Ming China: A Political History, 1355–1435.* Stanford: Stanford University Press, 1982.

Duara, Prasenjit. *Culture, Power, and the State—Rural North China, 1900–1942.* Stanford: Stanford University Press, 1988.

Edwards, R. Randle, Louis Henkin, and Andrew J. Nathan, eds. *Human Rights in Contemporary China.* New York: Columbia University Press, 1986.

Esherick, Joseph W. *Reform and Revolution in China: The 1911 Revolution in Hunan and Hubei.* Berkeley and Los Angeles: University of California Press, 1976.

Esherick, Joseph W., and Mary Backus Rankin, eds. *Chinese Local Elites and Patterns of Dominance.* Berkeley and Los Angeles: University of California Press, 1990.

Feuerwerker, Albert. *State and Society in Eighteenth-Century China: The Ch'ing Empire in Its Glory.* Ann Arbor: Center for Chinese Studies, University of Michigan, 1976.

Fewsmith, Joseph. *Dilemmas of Reform in China: Political Conflict and Economic Debate.* Armonk, N.Y.: M. E. Sharpe, 1994.

Folsom, Kenneth. *Friends, Guests, and Colleagues.* Berkeley and Los Angeles: University of California Press, 1968.

Friedman, Edward, Paul G. Pickowicz, and Mark Selden. *Chinese Village, Socialist State.* New Haven: Yale University Press, 1991.

Gernet, Jacques. *Daily Life in China on the Eve of the Mongol Invasion, 1250–1276.* Stanford: Stanford University Press, 1962.

Goldstein, Avery. *From Bandwagon to Balance-of-Power Politics.* Stanford: Stanford University Press, 1991.

Han, Minzhu. *Cries for Democracy.* Princeton: Princeton University Press, 1990.

Harding, Harry. *China's Second Revolution.* Washington, D.C.: Brookings Institution, 1987.

———. *Organizing China: The Problem of Bureaucracy, 1949–1976.* Stanford: Stanford University Press, 1981.

Hinton, William. *The Great Reversal—the Privatization of China, 1978–1989.* New York: Monthly Review Press, 1990.

———. *Shenfan.* New York: Random House, 1983.

Ho, Ping-ti. *The Ladder of Success in Imperial China.* New York: Columbia University Press, 1962.

Hsiao, Kung-chuan. *Rural China: Imperial Control in the Nineteenth Century.* Seattle: University of Washington Press, 1960.

Hsiao, Tso-liang. *The Land Revolution in China.* Seattle: University of Washington Press, 1969.

Huang, Pei. *Autocracy at Work: A Study of the Yongzheng Period, 1723–1735.* Bloomington: Indiana University Press, 1974.

Huang, Philip C.C. *The Peasant Economy and Social Change in North China.* Stanford: Stanford University Press, 1985.

Huang, Ray. *China: A Macro History.* Armonk, N.Y.: M. E. Sharpe, 1988.

———. *1587: A Year of No Significance.* New Haven: Yale University Press, 1981.

Hucker, Charles O. *The Censorial System of Ming China.* Stanford: Stanford University Press, 1966.

———. *The Ming Dynasty: Its Origins and Evolving Institutions.* Ann Arbor: Center for Chinese Studies, University of Michigan, 1976.

———. *The Traditional Chinese State in Ming Times (1368–1644).* Tucson: University of Arizona Press, 1961.

Johnson, Chalmers. *Peasant Nationalism and Communist Power.* Stanford: Stanford University Press, 1962.

Joseph, William A., Christine P.W. Wong, and David Zweig, eds. *New Perspectives on the Cultural Revolution.* Cambridge, Mass.: Harvard University Press, 1991.

Kuhn, Philip A. *Rebellion and Its Enemies in Late Imperial China.* Cambridge, Mass.: Harvard University Press, 1980.

Lampton, David M., ed. *Policy Implementation in Post-Mao China.* Berkeley and Los Angeles: University of California Press, 1987.

Langlois, John D. Jr., ed. *China Under Mongol Rule.* Princeton: Princeton University Press, 1981.

Lardy, Nicholas R. *Agriculture in China's Modern Development.* Cambridge: Cambridge University Press, 1983.

Lee, Hong Yung. *From Revolutionary Cadres to Party Technocrats in Socialist China.* Berkeley and Los Angeles: University of California Press, 1991.

———. *The Politics of the Chinese Cultural Revolution.* Berkeley and Los Angeles: University of California Press, 1978.

Levine, Steven I. *Anvil of Victory: The Communist Revolution in Manchuria.* New York: Columbia University Press, 1987.

Lewis, John Wilson, and Xue Litai. *China Builds the Bomb.* Stanford: Stanford University Press, 1988.

Li, Zhisui, with Anne F. Thurston. *The Private Life of Chairman Mao.* New York: Random House, 1994.

Liang, Heng, and Judith Shapiro. *Son of the Revolution.* New York: Vintage, 1983.

Lieberthal, Kenneth, Joyce Kallgren, Roderick MacFarquhar, and Frederic Wakeman Jr., eds. *Perspectives on Modern China.* Armonk, N.Y.: M. E. Sharpe, 1991.

Liu, Binyan. *People or Monsters?* Bloomington: Indiana University Press, 1983.

Lupher, Mark. "Revolutionary Little Red Devils: The Social Psychology of Rebel Youth, 1966–1967." In Anne Behnke Kinney, ed., *Chinese Views of Childhood.* Manoa: University of Hawaii Press, 1995.

MacFarquhar, Roderick. *The Origins of the Cultural Revolution 1: Contradictions Among the People.* New York: Columbia University Press, 1974.

———. *The Origins of the Cultural Revolution 2: The Great Leap Forward, 1958–1960.* New York: Columbia University Press, 1983.

MacFarquhar, Roderick, Timothy Cheek, and Eugene Wu, eds. *The Secret Speeches of Chairman Mao: From the Hundred Flowers to the Great Leap Forward.* Cambridge, Mass.: Harvard University Press, 1989.

Mao Zedong. *On the Correct Handling of Contradictions Among the People.* Peking: People's Publishing, 1957.

McCormick, Barrett L. *Political Reform in Post-Mao China.* Berkeley and Los Angeles: University of California Press, 1990.

Meisner, Maurice. *Li Dazhao and the Origins of Chinese Marxism.* Cambridge, Mass.: Harvard University Press, 1967.

Milton, David, and Nancy Dall. *The Wind Will Not Subside.* New York: Pantheon, 1976.

Naquin, Susan. *Millenarian Rebellion in China.* New Haven: Yale University Press, 1976.

Naquin, Susan, and Evelyn S. Rawski. *Chinese Society in the Eighteenth Century.* New Haven: Yale University Press, 1987.

Nathan, Andrew J. *Chinese Democracy.* New York: Knopf, 1985.

Nee, Victor. *The Cultural Revolution at Peking University.* New York: Monthly Review Press, 1969.

Nee, Victor, and David Mozingo, eds. *State and Society in Contemporary China.* Ithaca: Cornell University Press, 1983.

Oi, Jean C. *State and Peasant in Contemporary China.* Berkeley and Los Angeles: University of California Press, 1989.

Oxman, Robert B. *Ruling from Horseback: Manchu Politics in the Oboi Regency, 1661–1669*. Chicago: University of Chicago Press, 1975.

Pepper, Suzanne. *Civil War in China: The Political Struggle, 1945–1949*. Berkeley and Los Angeles: University of California Press, 1978.

Perry, Elizabeth J. *Rebels and Revolutionaries in North China, 1845–1945*. Stanford: Stanford University Press, 1980.

———. "Shanghai's Strike Wave of 1957." *China Quarterly* 137 (March 1994).

———. "State and Society in Contemporary China." *World Politics* 41, 4 (July 1989).

Perry, Elizabeth J., and Christine Wong, eds. *The Political Economy of Reform in Post-Mao China*. Cambridge, Mass.: Harvard University Press, 1985.

Rawski, Thomas G. *Economic Growth in Prewar China*. Berkeley and Los Angeles: University of California Press, 1989.

Riskin, Carl. *China's Political Economy: The Quest for Development Since 1949*. New York: Oxford University Press, 1987.

Rosen, Stanley. *Red Guard Factionalism and the Cultural Revolution in Guangzhou (Canton)*. Boulder: Westview Press, 1982.

Schurmann, Franz. "China's 'New Economic Policy'—Transition or Beginning?" In Roderick MacFarquhar, ed., *China Under Mao: Politics Takes Command*. Cambridge, Mass.: MIT Press, 1966.

———. *Ideology and Organization in Communist China*. Enl. ed. Berkeley and Los Angeles: University of California Press, 1968.

Selden, Mark. *The Political Economy of Chinese Socialism*. Armonk, N.Y.: M. E. Sharpe, 1988.

———. *The Yenan Way in Revolutionary China*. Cambridge, Mass.: Harvard University Press, 1971.

Selden, Mark, and Victor Lippits, eds. *The Transition to Socialism in China*. Armonk, N.Y.: M. E. Sharpe, 1982.

Spence, Jona.han D. *Emperor of China*. New York: Vintage, 1975.

———. *The Search for Modern China*. New York: Norton, 1990.

———. *Ts'ao Yin and the K'ang-hsi Emperor*. New Haven: Yale University Press, 1966.

Spence, Jonathan D., and John E. Wills, eds. *From Ming to Ch'ing*. New Haven: Yale University Press, 1979.

Teiwes, Frederick C. *Politics and Purges in China*. 2d ed. Armonk, N.Y.: M. E. Sharpe, 1993.

———. *Politics at Mao's Court: Gao Gang and Party Factionalism in the Early 1950s*. Armonk, N.Y.: M. E. Sharpe, 1990.

Thaxton, Ralph. *China Turned Rightside Up*. New Haven: Yale University Press, 1983.

Thurston, Anne F. *Enemies of the People*. New York: Knopf, 1987.

Tsou, Tang. *The Cultural Revolution and Post-Mao Reform: A Historical Perspective*. Chicago: University of Chicago Press, 1986.

Vogel, Ezra. *Canton Under Communism: Programs and Politics in a Provincial Capital, 1949–1968*. Cambridge, Mass.: Harvard University Press, 1969.

Wakeman, Frederic Jr. *The Fall of Imperial China*. New York: Free Press, 1975.

———. *The Great Enterprise: The Manchu Reconstruction of Imperial Order in Seventeenth-Century China*. Vols. 1, 2. Berkeley and Los Angeles: University of California Press, 1985.

Wakeman, Frederic Jr., and Carolyn Grant, eds. *Conflict and Control in Late Imperial China*. Berkeley and Los Angeles: University of California Press, 1975.

Walder, Andrew G. *Communist Neo-Traditionalism*. Berkeley and Los Angeles: University of California Press, 1986.

Walker, Richard L. *China Under Communism: The First Five Years*. New Haven: Yale University Press, 1955.

Wang, Yeh-chien. *Land Taxation in Imperial China, 1750–1911*. Cambridge, Mass.: Harvard University Press, 1973.

Watt, John R. *The District Magistrate in Late Imperial China*. New York: Columbia University Press, 1972.

White, Gordon. *Riding the Tiger: The Politics of Economic Reform in Post-Mao China*. Stanford: Stanford University Press, 1993.

White, Lynn T. III. *Policies of Chaos: The Organizational Causes of Violence in China's Cultural Revolution*. Princeton: Princeton University Press, 1989.

Will, Pierre-Etienne. *Bureaucracy and Famine in China*. Stanford: Stanford University Press, 1990.

Womack, Brantly. "Transfigured Community: Neo-Traditionalism and Work Unit Socialism in China." *China Quarterly* 126 (June 1991).

———, ed. *Contemporary Chinese Politics in Historical Perspective*. Cambridge: Cambridge University Press, 1991.

Wong, R. Bin. "China and World History." *Imperial China* 6, 2 (December 1985).

Wu, Silas H.L. *Communication and Imperial Control in China*. Cambridge, Mass.: Harvard University Press, 1970.

Yue, Daiyun, and Carolyn Wakeman. *To the Storm: The Odyssey of a Revolutionary Chinese Woman*. Berkeley and Los Angeles: University of California Press, 1985.

Zelin, Madeleine. *The Magistrate's Tael: Rationalizing Fiscal Reform in Eighteenth-Century Ch'ing China*. Berkeley and Los Angeles: University of California Press, 1984.

Zweig, David. *Agrarian Radicalism in China, 1968–1981*. Cambridge, Mass.: Harvard University Press, 1989.

## Scholarly Journals

*American Sociological Review*
*China Quarterly*
*Contemporary Sociology*
*Foreign Policy*
*Imperial China*
*Issues and Studies*
*Problems of Communism*
*Slavic Review*
*Soviet Studies*
*Theory and Society*
*World Politics*

## Periodicals

*Business Week*
*Christian Science Monitor*
*Economist*

*Forbes*
*Hongqi* (Red Flag)
*International Herald Tribune*
*Jiefangjun bao* (Liberation army newspaper)
*Moscow Daily News*
*New York Review of Books*
*New York Times*
*New York Times Book Review*
*Peking Review*
*Renmin ribao* (People's daily)
*U.S. News and World Report*
*Wall Street Journal*
*Washington Post*
*Wenhui bao* (Literary digest)

## News Services

*Communist China Digest*
*Foreign Broadcast Information Service*
*Joint Publications Research Service*
*Radio Free Europe/Radio Liberty Daily Report*
*Reprints from the Soviet Press*
*Soviet/East European Report*
*Survey of China Mainland Press*

## Document Collections

*Chinese Politics—Documents and Analysis—Ninth Party Congress (1969) to the Death of Mao (1976)*. Ed. James T. Myers, Jurgen Domes, and Milton D. Yeh. Columbia: University of South Carolina Press, 1989.

*Documents of the Eleventh National Congress of the CCP*. Peking: Foreign Languages Press, 1977.

*Resolutions and Decisions of the Communist Party of the Soviet Union, 1898–1981*. Vol. 4: *The Khrushchev Years*. Ed. Grey Hodnett. Toronto: University of Toronto Press, 1974.

*Resolutions and Decisions of the Communist Party of the Soviet Union, 1898–1981*, Vol. 5: *The Brezhnev Years*. Ed. Donald V. Schwartz. Toronto: University of Toronto Press, 1982.

*Selected Big Character Posters of the Great Proletarian Cultural Revolution*. Peking: People's Press, 1966.

*The Tenth National Congress of the CCP (Documents)*. Peking: Foreign Languages Press, 1973.

# About the Book and Author

The massive economic transformations and political upheavals that have been sweeping China and the Soviet Union in the final decades of the twentieth century are among the great dramas of our time. Yet the origins of these revolutionary changes are murky and their outcomes unclear. Have we witnessed the demise of an archaic authoritarian order and the rise of pluralism and democracy, or are the tumultuous events of the post-Mao era and the period of perestroika more usefully viewed in light of broader patterns of power and politics in Chinese and Russian history?

Considering these questions with a new interpretation of power relations and political processes in China and Russia, Mark Lupher explores the imperial era, the communist period, and the current situation in both countries. Rather than speaking of "reform," which too often is understood as liberalization along Western lines, his discussion is focused on power restructuring—the ebb and flow of state power; the centralization and decentralization of political and economic power; and the three-way struggles between central rulers, various elites, and nonprivileged groups that drive these processes.

Lupher's power-restructuring analysis is noteworthy in combining broad comparative-historical analysis and conceptualization with a closely focused discussion and reinterpretation of the Chinese Cultural Revolution—the core of his book. By comparing and bringing new light to bear on a series of pivotal episodes in Chinese and Russian history, he furthers our understanding and assessment of processes that will continue to unfold in China, Russia, and the former Soviet republics.

Mark Lupher is assistant professor of sociology at the University of Virginia.

# Index

Administration for Checking Party Organs, 141
Alexander I, reforms by, 71–72
Alexander II, Great Reforms of, 73
Alexis, Secret Chancery and, 86(n67)
Anastasia, Czarina, 84(n36)
Andropov, Yuri, 275
    discipline campaign of, 272–274
    economic recovery and, 273
Antialcohol campaign, 274
Anti-Confucius campaign, 224
Anti-Party Group, 152, 161(n58), 163(n90),
    164(n110)
    outmaneuvering, 146, 155
Anti-Semitic organizations, 282–283
Appropriation, 5
    processes of, 12, 13
    resource, 19, 26, 117–118, 238, 243, 244, 245,
    247, 258, 261(n26)
*Aristocrats and Servitors* (Crummey), 55
Armenia, conflict in, 283, 290
Auditing Commission, 151
August Revolution. See Kremlin coup
Authoritarianism, 283–285, 288, 289, 290
    official, 179
    post-Soviet, 287
Authority-social mobilization approach, 102,
    103, 106, 204, 219–222, 240, 243
    in China, 172, 173, 178, 180, 181–182
    opposition to, 119
    Stalin and, 110
Azerbaijan, conflict in, 283, 290

Bachman, David, 172, 174
    on Tiananmen massacre, 253
    Great Leap Forward and, 195(n54)
    on Khrushchev/Mao, 193(n25)
Bailes, Kendall E., 6, 95, 101, 120
    on technical intelligentsia, 116
Bakatin, Vadim, 287
Ball, Alan M.: on NEP, 99
"Bandwagon" thesis, 177
Bannermen, 30, 48(n62)
Bartlett, Beatrice S., 34
    on Yongzheng, 31
Baum, Richard: on rural cadres, 184
Beck, F.: on NKVD, 122
Beria, Lavrentii, 160(nn34, 41)
Bialer, Seweryn, 124, 142, 149

on Khrushchev/Brezhnev, 157
on Soviet reformism, 268
Big-character posters (*dazibao*), 185, 186, 189,
    190, 197(n87), 255
    banning, 187
Bloody Sunday (1905), 78–79
Blum, Jerome, 60
Bolsheviks, 54
    bureaucracy and, 102
    centralization by, 98
    military/administrative structures of, 93
    power/leadership and, 104
    power restructuring by, 81
    transformation of, 100–101, 103
    War Communism and, 95–96
Boltnikov rebellion, 82(n10)
Bond servants, 30, 48(n62)
Bonnell, Victoria E.: on Bloody Sunday, 78–79
Bourgeois specialists, 95, 97
    rehabilitation of, 131(n131)
    role of, 101–102
Boyars, 61, 64
Breslauer, George W., 143, 158(n13), 279,
    294(n68)
    on Gorbachev, 294(n59)
    on Khrushchev/Brezhnev, 137, 155, 158(n7)
    on Khrushchev/bureaucrats, 148
Brezhnev, Leonid, 14, 155, 267, 290, 292(n11),
    295(n70)
    consensus building by, 156
    counterrevolution by, 156–157
    economic reform by, 271–272
    interventionist powers and, 157
    officialdom and, 157, 165(n117)
    political pluralism and, 7
    power restructuring by, 136, 300, 303
    stability in cadres and, 292(n21)
Brezhnevism, 273
    systemic decline and, 156–157, 270–272
Brown, Edward J.: on purges, 122–123
Brzezinski, Zbigniew
    on Stalinism, 94
    terminal crisis and, 4
Bukharin, Nikolay, 94
    economic gradualism and, 103
    market-material incentive approach and,
    102–103
    on proletarian coercion, 96